Servants of All

Servants of All

Professional Management of City Government

Brigham Young University Press

Edited by
LeRoy F. Harlow

Library of Congress Cataloging in Publication Data
Main entry under title:

Servants of all.

   Includes indexes.
   1. Municipal government by city manager—United
States—Addresses, essays, lectures. I. Harlow,
Leroy F.
JS344.C5S47   352'.0084'0973   80-39899
ISBN 0-8425-1892-4

Brigham Young University Press, Provo, Utah 84602
Printed in the United States of America
5   4   3   2

Local assemblies of the people constitute the strength of free nations. Municipal institutions are to liberty what primary schools are to science: they bring it within the people's reach, and teach them how to use and enjoy it. A nation may establish a system of free government, but without the spirit of municipal institutions it cannot have the spirit of liberty.

—Alexis De Tocqueville

Contents

Preface

In 1977 Brigham Young University Press published my book, *Without Fear or Favor: Odyssey of a City Manager.* Richard S. Childs, "father" of the council-manager plan of local government, wrote me about the book, "In the literature of the manager plan your testimony is a case study in depth." Mark E. Keane, executive director of the International City Management Association, wrote,

> You have done what so many others have promised, but practically no one else has ever done before. Your book will boost the morale of all the rest of us who have shared that kind of experience and will be an inspiration to those who are coming into the profession.
>
> I . . . applaud your concluding with suggestions to citizens as to how they can improve their local government.

City managers, former city managers, elected officials, public administration students, and private citizens wrote or called about the book from various parts of the country, all appreciative or complimentary. However, Professor David A. Booth of the University of Massachusetts, in a review for *Public Management* (August 1977), the journal of the International City Management Association, wrote,

> My greatest regret is that you waited so long to write it (the book). Over twenty years have passed since you completed your last manager stint, and some readers may feel that the book is dated for that reason. . . . In contrast to what you had to do, today's managers must oversee racial integration, mastermind the distribution of federal revenue-sharing funds, cope with heightened racial and ethnic consciousness and identity, work with neighborhood councils, participate in regional or metropolitan COGs, bargain with militant municipal

employee unions, and contend with spiraling budgets in the face of decreasing, or at best level, property tax revenues.

   . . . I also regret that you made no effort to utilize or comment on the standard research literature and its principal themes and findings. Because it neither confirms nor contradicts any research findings of the last twenty years, your book does nothing to bridge the widening gap between the profession and academia.

Professor Booth closed with this plea.

   I hope you will encourage other city managers to share their experiences with us, not only because they are instructive, interesting and helpful, but because the case study literature is still very thin, and we still do not really know very much about what demographic, social, economic, cultural, legal, and institutional variables are most frequently associated with administrative leadership, effectiveness, and innovation. We live in a much more disturbed world than we did yesterday; cities may not be as governable as they were; managers face harder times ahead. They deserve all the help that they can get.

   I followed Professor Booth's suggestion. Early in 1978 I wrote to a representative list of city managers and ex-city managers—of large, medium-size, small, central, satellite, and independent cities; minorities; and in every section of the country. I asked if they would be interested in the publication of some of the highlights of their professional city manager experience. This would be a sequel to *Without Fear or Favor* that would enlarge the list of topics I wrote about, and bring the situations up to today. I invited those who were interested to send me a synopsis of each "incident, event, episode, topic, principle, issue, etc." that they considered the "most significant, dramatic, interesting, educational, amusing, etc." of their professional experiences. The response was gratifying.

   Thus, the bulk of this book consists of more than one hundred episodes selected to provide a broad and balanced picture of the real world of professional city* management. They were written by some two dozen men and women career managers who have served nearly one hundred cities and counties in half the fifty states and the District of Columbia. They describe difficult, significant—sometimes amusing—situations these managers encountered, and how they felt, what they saw and did, their

---

*I use *city* to mean all kinds of municipal government: boroughs, towns, villages—even urban counties that perform city-type functions. Also, for our purposes, *city, municipality,* and *municipal government* are interchangeable terms.

   Similarly, the title "city manager" has a special definition in the local-government field. However, titles such as "village manager," "county manager," "town administrator," "city administrator," and "chief administrative officer" also are in common use. For our purposes here, I intend the term *city manager* to include these other titles.

interpretations of others' motives and actions, their own reactions, their frustrations, and even their sorrows, satisfactions, and philosophies.

The episodes were written by the persons whose abbreviated local government biographies are listed in the Who's Who section. The episodes were then edited and approved by their authors. I hope these efforts will aid Professor Booth and other students of local government in their search for information about the variables "associated with administrative leadership, effectiveness, and innovation." Even more important, though, is the possibility that the experiences of these career public servants will point the way to less misgovernment in our country and will help more people get the improved government they deserve.

The book is intended for the general reader who wants a better understanding of city government and how it works, so he* can deal effectively with City Hall when necessary and can feel comfortable about the decisions he makes that help determine the kind and quality of local government he will have in his community. This could include almost every young person and adult in his capacity as a purely private citizen as well as men and women who are active in civic organizations and public office. In addition, both the men and women just entering public service and those of longer service may learn and take courage from the city managers who have given these first-hand accounts of their professional experience. Professors and students of political science and public administration may find the book useful as a supplement to their regular texts and casebooks on local government.

As to the latter, I am indebted to Professor Booth for suggesting that I encourage other city managers to share their experiences. Therefore, I hope this book will partially overcome the shortcomings of my previous book but, more especially, that it will help bridge the gap Professor Booth sees between the city manager profession and academia.

I lay no claim for this as a scholarly work. Because of the differences in available time, writing skills, interests, and circumstances among the contributors, there is bound to be a diversity of focus and depth among the episodes. I am reminded of the criticisms leveled against the cases in the Inter-University Case Program (ICP) as far back as 1952, 1955, and 1958 by three well-known political scientists. The critics complained that

> Unlike scientific data the cases do not provide students with an opportunity to develop or test some well-defined hypotheses. [Wengert]

> They [the forty-six cases to mid-1954] have no designed relationship to one another, methodological or substantive, and the totality of the series is rather formless. . . .

*We recognize that the reader may be either a female or a male, but until we have in our language one pronoun denominating both genders, we will use the masculine. —Editor.

Yet it seems doubtful that much progress will be made toward these [ICP] goals without some attempt at ordering the content of the cases as a basis for comparative analysis and increasing the opportunity for generalization. [Somers]

On these propositions and questions, many of which antedate the case program, the cases shed little light. Instead of helping us to validate the former and answer the latter (which *only* the case method can do!) they enlarge the number of untested declarations and unresolved questions with which our discipline already abounds. [Kaufman]*

My reading and use of individual cases and casebooks since then discloses little improvement along the lines suggested by these scholars, and this book is hardly an exception to my observations.

Certainly it would be helpful if professors and students could have books about local government that are designed to facilitate their teaching/learning and research activities. But perhaps there is an even more urgent need for books that will help the general reader who votes and pays the tax bills to understand local government. Professor Booth indicates that the case study literature is thin, whether prepared by observers of the local-government scene or by those actually in it. The latter deficiency is especially unfortunate because there is considerable difference between, on the one hand, what an observer sees or hears, and thinks he understands and tries to report, and, on the other hand, the actual thoughts, feelings, reactions, and interpretations of those who personally carry the burdens of administrative responsibility on the front lines of career governmental service.

Perhaps the reason local-government case studies, and this book, do not fit all the specifications outlined by Professors Wengert, Somers, and Kaufman is the complexity of virtually every local-government issue. Each involves many facets, factors, actors, attitudes, postures, opinions, and interests. This makes it extremely difficult to dissect any issue, sort out the parts, and then put the whole on paper in some logical order so that the reader can get a handhold on the matter and follow through to his own evaluations, conclusions, and possible actions.

Neither the contributors nor the editor have succeeded totally in disentangling the myriad parts involved in many of the episodes reported here. But I have tried to present these real-life experiences in such a way that the reader can discover his own meaning in what happened, relate to and internalize the situations, and act on his discoveries.

Also, I have identified thirty themes dealt with in these episodes that occurred from Maine to California and North Dakota to Florida, I have grouped the episodes according to what in my best judgment are their

---

*Frederick C. Mosher, *Governmental Reorganizations: Cases and Commentary* (New York: Bobbs-Merrill Co., 1967), p. xi.

dominant themes, and have followed this by identifying their subsidiary themes. For example, an episode may describe action in a crisis situation that required important decisions involving race relations. The episode will be listed by page number in the "Theme Index" under three headings: Prejudice and Race Relations, Crisis Management, and Decision-Making. If the dominant theme of the episode is crisis management, the page number under the heading Crisis Management will be in italics. The page number of the episode will also be listed under the headings Prejudice and Race Relations, and Decision-Making, but the page number will not be in italics. If your interest is crisis management, by looking up that heading and finding all the italic page numbers you can identify all the episodes in which crisis management is the dominant theme. If you wish to locate the episodes that deal with a particular theme in only a subsidiary way, those episodes will be noted by a page number in regular type. The Theme Index is located at the back of the book, just ahead of the general index.

Although most of the episodes describe one or more experiences of a city manager, and he is the principal actor, there are many other actors—mayors, councilpersons, department heads, municipal employees, other officials, consultants, merchants, family members, and other private citizens. Whether the reader is a concerned citizen, another public administrator, or a student of local government—or all three—he will enjoy an exciting and rewarding learning experience if, as he reads each situation, he asks himself, "If *I* were [any one of the several actors] what would *I* do?"

LeRoy F. Harlow
Provo, Utah

Who's Who
of Contributors

John Biery. City Engineer, Director of Public Works, Assistant City Manager, Acting City Manager, Jackson, Michigan; City Manager, Midland, Michigan; City Manager, Colorado Springs, Colorado.

Harriette W. Cookingham. Wife of L. Perry Cookingham.

L. Perry Cookingham. Village Manager, Clawson, Michigan; City Manager, Plymouth, Michigan; City Manager, Saginaw, Michigan; City Manager, Kansas City, Missouri; City Manager, Fort Worth, Texas; President, International City Management Association.

Joseph R. Coupal, Jr. Town Manager, Bethlehem, New Hampshire; Assistant City Manager, Concord, New Hampshire; Town Manager, Ipswich, Maine; City Manager, Bangor, Maine; Director of Highways, State of Iowa,; Deputy Federal Highway Administrator, U.S. Government; President, International City Management Association.

John C. Crowley. City Manager, Monterey Park, California; City Director (Councilman), Pasadena, California.

Richard H. Custer. Assistant to City Manager, Acting City Manager, Two Rivers, Wisconsin; Town Manager, Fort Fairfield, Maine; Town Manager, Windsor, Connecticut; City Manager, Kenosha, Wisconsin; City Manager, Zanesville, Ohio; Town Manager, West Hartford, Connecticut; President, International City Management Association.

Thomas W. Fletcher. Assistant to City Manager, San Leandro, California; City Administrator, Davis, California; Assistant to City Manager, San Diego, California; City Manager, San Diego, California; Deputy Assistant Secretary, U.S. Department of Housing and Urban Development, U.S. Government; Deputy Mayor, District of Columbia; City Manager, San Jose, California.

Agda G. Harlow. Wife of LeRoy F. Harlow.

LeRoy F. Harlow. City Manager, Sweet Home, Oregon; City Manager, Alberta Lea, Minnesota; City Manager, Fargo, North Dakota; Village Manager, Richfield, Minnesota; City Manager, Daytona Beach, Florida; Executive Secretary, Cuyahoga County (Cleveland, Ohio) Mayors and City Managers Association.

Dale F. Helsel. Assistant City Manager, Bedford, Ohio; Borough Manager, Bellefonte, Pennsylvania; City Manager, Painesville, Ohio; City Manager, Middletown, Ohio.

Charles T. Henry. City Manager, Shorewood, Wisconsin; City Manager, University City, Missouri; City Manager, Eugene, Oregon.

Bert W. Johnson. Finance Director, Winnetka, Illinois; City Manager, Lebanon, Missouri; City Manager, Boulder, Colorado; City Manager, Evanston, Illinois; County Manager, Arlington, Virginia; President, International City Management Association.

Adolph J. Koenig. City Manager, Plymouth, Michigan; City Manager, Fort Atkinson, Wisconsin; City Manager, Wilmette, Illinois; City Manager, Jackson, Michigan; City Manager, Anchorage, Alaska; City Manager, Milford, Connecticut; City Manager, St. Clair Shores, Michigan; City Manager, San Clemente, California; City Manager, Walled Lake, Michigan; Vice-president, International City Management Association.

Peter F. Lydens. Assistant to City Manager, Winston-Salem, North Carolina; City Manager, Mount Airy, North Carolina; City Manager, Thomasville, North Carolina; City Manager, Gastonia, North Carolina; City Manager, Suffolk, Virginia.

Cecil E. Massey. City Manager, Hereford, Texas; City Manager, Haltom City, Texas; City Manager, Weatherford, Texas; City Manager, Weslaco, Texas; City Manager, Lockhart, Texas.

John N. Matzer, Jr. Administrative Analyst, Philadelphia, Pennsylvania; Assistant Business Administrator, Trenton, New Jersey; Director of Finance, Trenton, New Jersey; City Administrator, Trenton, New Jersey; Village Manager, Skokie, Illinois; City Manager, Beverly Hills, California.

Thomas F. Maxwell. Assistant to City Manager, Kansas City, Missouri; City Manager, University City, Missouri; City Manager, Columbia, South Carolina; City Manager, Norfolk, Virginia; Vice-president, International City Management Association.

Mildred P. McDonald. Assistant Town Manager, Acting Town Manager, Town Manager, Southern Pines, North Carolina.

Oliver S. Merriam. Assistant to City Manager, Salem, Oregon; Assistant City Manager, Saginaw, Michigan; City Manager, North Miami Beach, Florida; Assistant to County Manager, Arlington, Virginia; City Manager,

Oak Park, Michigan.

James J. Mott. Assistant to City Manager, Coral Gables, Florida; Planning Analyst, Richmond, Virginia; Town Manager, Big Stone Gap, Virginia; City Manager West Palm Beach, Florida.

William H. Parness. Assistant to City Manager, Santa Cruz, California; City Manager, Claremont, California; City Manager, San Rafael, California; City Manager, Livermore, California; City Manager, Bellevue, Washington.

C. Eugene Perkins. City Manager, Winston-Salem, North Carolina; City Manager, Columbia, Missouri; City Manager, Glendale, California.

Elaine W. Roberts. Inspector, Town Hall Manager, Town Clerk, Town Administrator, Town Treasurer, Town Manager, Highland Beach, Florida.

David D. Rowlands. Town Manager, Mount Lebanon, Pennsylvania; City Manager, Eau Claire, Wisconsin; City Manager, Tacoma, Washington; City Administrator, Huntington Beach, California; President, International City Management Association.

Sally H. Rowlands. Wife of David D. Rowlands.

Kennedy Shaw. Assistant to City Manager, Westerville, Ohio; City Administrator, East Ann Arbor, Michigan; Township Manager, Cedar Grove, New Jersey; Township Administrator, East Brunswick, New Jersey; City Administrator, Plainfield, New Jersey; Executive Director, Massachusetts League of Cities and Towns.

Richard G. Simmons. Assistant to City Manager, Kissimmee, Florida; Assistant City Manager, Melbourne, Florida; Administrative Intern, Phoenix, Arizona; Administrative Officer, Eau Gallie, Florida; City Manager, Melbourne, Florida; City Manager, Haines City, Florida; City Manager, Winter Park, Florida; City Manager, West Palm Beach, Florida.

Robert M. Tinstman. Assistant City Manager, Kansas City, Missouri; City Manager, Abilene, Texas; City Manager, Oklahoma City, Oklahoma; City Manager, Austin, Texas.

Buford M. Watson, Jr. Assistant to City Manager, San Angelo, Texas; City Manager, Henryetta, Oklahoma; City Manager, Muskogee, Oklahoma; City Manager, Sioux City, Iowa; City Manager, Lawrence, Kansas; Vice-President, International City Management Association.

Introduction

At any given moment, 100 million Americans are being protected and served by one or more local governments whose organization is designed along the lines of the council-manager plan, a product of the first major attempt in this country to apply professional management to local government affairs. Perhaps you are one of that number. If not—but even if so—you may wonder who originated the plan, and when, and why.

A Slice of Twentieth-Century American Political History

Richard S. Childs, an enthusiastic advocate of more representative, democratic, and economical local government, was the principal designer of the council-manager plan. Originally distressed by city ballots that were so long that he must vote for candidates he knew nothing about, he conceived of electing a small policy-making board of directors (council) that would have overall and ultimate responsibility for the local government. In turn that board would name a trained and experienced specialist in municipal-government administration to assist the board in its work, to be its chief adviser, and to manage the day-to-day administration of its policies. This was 1910.

In 1912 Sumter, South Carolina, became the first city to officially adopt the council-manager plan. Today about three thousand villages, boroughs, towns, cities, counties, and legally constituted councils of local governments use the plan or some modification of it. Over the years, adoptions of the plan have averaged close to four a month. Few communities have abandoned the plan, and some of those have returned to it. Today, council-manager government is the most popular form for American cities of 10,000 population and larger.

What Other Options Do Americans Have?

In some European countries, the council-manager plan or other forms of professional local government management are mandated by the national government. Not so in our country. Because in the United States the national government has only those powers granted to it in our federal Constitution—and creation and control of local government is not given to our national government in that fundamental document—the powers and structure of our local governments are determined at the state level. In several states, the legislature has power to create, design, and control the local governments. Hence the expression, "Local governments are creatures of the State." Other state constitutions reserve to the people of the communities the right to design and determine the structure and powers of their local governments (so long as what the people choose does not conflict with the state constitution or state laws). This right in the local people is called "home rule."

In the United States, city governments operate under one of three basic forms—mayor-council, commission, or council-manager—modified to fit local circumstances. Because our nation is so vast and diverse, with fifty states and 80,000 local governments, this freedom of choice about forms of local government has produced innumerable variations of the basic forms. There is room here, and in the appendix, to mention only the major modifications.

Cities using the mayor-council form are said to have either a "strong mayor" or a "weak mayor" form. In the first form the mayor is empowered to make most or all appointments of the city's officers and employees without council confirmation, and to direct the work of all the departments. He may also have power to appoint council committees and their chairmen, and to veto council actions. In this form the council is limited strictly to the drafting and passing of local laws.

In a "weak mayor" form, the mayor may have few or no appointing powers, or his appointments may be subject to council approval. Municipal departments may be controlled and directed by council committees. And the mayor has no veto power over council legislation or administrative actions.

In the commission form, the original plan called for the voters to elect members of the multimember commission, and for the commission members to distribute departmental control among themselves. Des Moines, Iowa, modified this plan to provide that the voters would decide which commission member would head which department. Thus, under the "Des Moines Plan," voters elected a public-safety commissioner, a public-works commissioner, a finance commissioner, and so on.

Since 1915 the National Municipal League, a citizens' organization for better government founded in 1894 (47 East 68th Street, New York, N.Y. 10021), has recommended and promulgated adoption of the council-manager plan as a basic feature of its Model City Charter. The "model" council-manager plan provides that all council members be elected at large (by voters of the whole community) and that the council members then choose a "mayor" (chairman of the council) from among their number, and appoint a city manager. These arrangements have been modified in some places to have council members elected from districts, and for the mayor to be elected directly by the people of the whole community.

Briefly, the manager's responsibilities are to appoint and if necessary discipline or remove city employees, direct and supervise the administration of all departments, offices, and agencies of the city, attend all council meetings with the right to take part in discussions but not to vote, see that the laws and ordinances of the city are enforced, prepare and recommend the annual budget, keep the council and the public informed of the city's financial and administrative status and activities, and plan and recommend actions to meet the city's present and future needs. These responsibilities, too, vary from place to place, depending on the provisions of state law or of the locally adopted city charter or ordinances.

Two major modifications of the plan as originally conceived by Richard S. Childs provide for a chief administrative officer (CAO) in lieu of a manager. Ordinarily, this is a position with fewer powers than that of a manager. In one modification, the CAO is responsible to the mayor or other chief executive; in the other modification, the CAO reports to the governing body.

The basic mayor-council form, the basic commission form, and the basic council-manager form and its two major modifications are shown on organization charts in the Appendix. Common arguments for and against each option accompany the charts.

How Professionally Managed Municipalities Are "Recognized"

Neither the mayor-council nor the commission form is considered a professionally managed form of local government, because in either form any citizen who meets minimum qualifications of citizenship, residence, and age may run for office, be elected, and serve as the manager of the government.

By contrast, municipalities that require their managers to be professionally qualified must meet detailed and rigid requirements in order to be "recognized" as professionally managed governments. For a decade or more the International City Management Association* has used formal criteria in judging whether or not a given local government that operates under a bona fide council-manager plan or a modified council-manager

---

*On 1 July 1969 the name of the International City Managers Association was changed to the International City Management Association. This association will be referred to as the ICMA throughout the book.

plan is providing professional management of the municipality's overall administrative affairs.

To be recognized as a council-manager government, the municipality must meet these criteria:

- The manager should be appointed by a majority of the council for an indefinite term and should be removable only by a majority of the council.
- The position should have direct responsibility for policy formulation on overall problems.
- The manager should be designated by legislation as having responsibility for preparation of the budget, presentation to the council, and direct responsibility for the administration of the council-approved budget.
- The manager should be delegated by legislation the full authority for the appointment and removal of at least most heads of principal departments and functions.
- Those department heads whom the manager appoints should be designated by legislation as administratively responsible to the manager.
- Responsibilities of the position should include extensive external relationships with other governments and organizations, involving the overall problems of city operations.
- Applicants for the position should be judged on the basis of their educational and administrative background.

The criteria for recognition as a "general management" government are less rigid with respect to the administrator's appointment and control of department heads, and his budget responsibilities.

A municipality is recognized by ICMA and is listed in the association's annual directory of recognized local governments only after an application supported by required documentation has been submitted to the ICMA, reviewed, and formally approved. Despite some arguments against the council-manager plan and its modifications (see Appendix), the number of local governments using appointed professional administrators under one title or another continues to grow. At the start of 1980, 3,433 governments had official ICMA recognition, 2,614 in the council-manager category and 819 in the general-management category.

The Real World of Professional Management of Local Government

Some two dozen men and women with almost five hundred years of professional city-government manager responsibility have consented to share with us the highlights of that experience. Their professional lives are diverse and complex; they are also demanding, challenging, exciting, and rewarding examples of public service.

To bring some order to this large array of diverse experience, the work of these city managers is viewed from five broad perspectives, as follows:

Part One focuses on the involvement in the political system of the community. Part Two relates to interfaces with the economic system. Part Three shows how the manager's work meshes with the local social system. The episodes in Part Four present close-up pictures of what it is like to be the general manager of a political, economic, and social complex that any one of us might call "our town," "our city," or "our county." In Part Five these city managers make their concluding contribution to our understanding of democracy effectively at work, offering some personal and professional philosophy distilled from years of being the "servants of all."

Each part includes a brief introduction that is intended to provide background on a major facet of this multifaceted profession; however, by no means are all aspects of city management covered here. This is a start. Perhaps others who follow will fill the gaps.

Carved in the portico of the National Archives in Washington, D.C., are the words, "The Past Is Prologue." Perhaps the experiences of these men and women who have served and are now serving in city halls and county courthouses, where so often the forces within our society intersect, are prologues for our future. We would be derelict not to use their contributions as a basis for making the future better than the past. Part Six, the closing commentary, is an effort in that direction.

Part One

The City Manager and the Political System

The offices of mayor and city manager are sometimes confused in the public mind. The difference is that the city manager is not a politician. Unlike the mayor, the city manager does not run against other candidates in an election for the office; he is chosen by the people's elected representatives sitting as the city council; he works for all the people, not for any special constituency; he may only recommend, not decide, policy issues; and his term of office is controlled by the city council. In the council-manager plan, the mayor is chairman of what is really the city's board of directors (usually called the city council, although in Pasadena, California, the city council is officially the city "board of directors"), and the city manager is general manager of the city government.

Although the city manager's position is nonpolitical in the above sense, he must keep in mind that his every official act has possible or actual implications for the three principal elements of the democratic community he serves: the public, with its infinite variety of interests, opinions, and wants; the people's elected representatives (the city council), whose selection and accomplishment of city goals must satisfy the electorate; and the total governmental machinery within the community—both that part for which he is administratively responsible, and the several overlapping governments with which he must coordinate his programs and activities.

In this first part of the book, twelve city managers describe their experiences with the political system. Two of them tell about the steps in adopting and installing professional management in a city; some describe how aroused citizens changed a situation they didn't like; another explains why he helped, through an annexation process, to abolish his city—and his job along with it; one discusses the details of merging two cities; and several tell of their interaction with city councils and individual members.

They give examples of legal constraints on city government. One manager introduces us to the political machine system under "Boss" Tom Pendergast in Kansas City, and a couple of the others add details on how politics works. Other city managers comment on terminations of city managers.

What will an understanding of Part One teach us? That good-government supporters need vigilance and persistence; that bookkeeping machines don't vote; that state government and the courts have more power over local affairs than have local officials; and that some politicians seem to have effectively contradicted Lincoln's dictum that you can fool some of the people all the time, and all the people some of the time, but not all the people all the time.

Adopting and Installing Professional Management

A Winston-Salem Saga
C. Eugene Perkins*

After fifteen years of managing private water and electric utilities, three years of World War II service in the Army Corps of Engineers, and three years directing route development for a transcontinental airline, I decided to become a city manager. My first appointment was as first city manager for Winston-Salem, North Carolina, in 1948.

Sponsored by a cross-section "Committee of 100" of interested and influential citizens, a council-manager charter had been narrowly approved by the Winston-Salem voters. It retained the ward system of eight aldermen and a mayor, all elected on a partisan basis. The committee had drafted a slate of business executives and civic leaders, who were elected on a platform to provide more efficient and effective city government. My arrival created much local interest, and that thrilled me. I liked and respected the courteous and helpful mayor and aldermen and most of the citizens I met. The two daily newspapers, under one ownership, were staffed with capable, friendly reporters and writers.

The board of aldermen arranged for me to have a small cubicle and desk and a big Buick, and for the mayor, the board of aldermen, and me to share one secretary. I requested a larger office and a smaller car. Although it was obvious that the mayor and board members had little understanding of a city manager's duties and requirements, they were

---

*The Checkerboard Corridor, a 1968 novel, was written by a Winston-Salem reporter. Its hero was a city manager, and the book is based on events while C. Eugene Perkins was serving as city manager.

most cooperative, telling me repeatedly, "Go ahead with the things that need to be done. Just keep us informed, so that we will understand." In short, Winston-Salem appeared to be an almost ideal community for a first-time city manager.

On the other hand, the city government was considerably less than ideal, organizationally and operationally. In addition to the usual city operating departments—fire, police, public works, recreation, and so on— the city government was responsible for the maintenance and operation of school buildings, two general hospitals, two cemeteries, a Farmers' Market and a municipal stadium. Responsibility for all the city's activities was spread among sixteen standing committees of aldermen. Each alderman was chairman of two committees and member of four others. The committees made policy decisions, and the chairmen exercised considerable supervision over administrative matters.

There was no merit system for employees, no job description or classification, no personnel officer, no formal training program. To a large extent, employees progressed upward through seniority.

Budget procedures common in well-managed cities were almost unknown. Work programs and pay scales were dependent on the ability of department heads to sell their recommendations to their committees, and on the committees' ability to persuade the full board of aldermen. Department heads who were effective with the finance committee might end up with better pay scales for their employees than did the less influential department heads.

Each activity did its own purchasing, usually at retail prices. For example, the city bought its recreational supplies from neighborhood retail outlets. School cafeterias and hospitals bought food on the same basis, with tremendous variance in costs. Opportunities to make wholesale purchases at substantial discounts were largely ignored.

We soon recognized that we needed to relieve the council committees of the burden of administrative decisions they were not qualified to make. One example may help to illustrate that need. An alderman committee approved a proposal to purchase $80,000 of equipment to expand the fire-alarm system. The money was in the budget. Fortunately, the board decided to defer execution of the contract until I arrived and had time to review the contract. I found that another $370,000 would be needed for installation and extension before the $80,000 of equipment could be used. That money was not available.

We cancelled the proposed alarm-system improvement. However, as I had anticipated, and advised the board, the cancellation precipitated a National Board of Fire Underwriters survey of the community's fire-protection capability and the community rating for fire-insurance premiums.

In those days, at least in that area, the details about deficiency points charged against the city by the underwriters were not available to the city government. After I made numerous requests to the regional and finally the national office of the Board of Fire Underwriters, they gave us the information. It showed that establishment of a training program and a fire-prevention activity would be worth several times as much toward removing the deficiency points as would the expansion of the alarm system.

Getting Organized

One of my first organizational actions was to create a buildings and grounds division to centralize the maintenance of 165 buildings, school grounds, and public parks. The second was to create a central purchasing activity.

Black employees constituted a considerable percentage of the city employee group. They were used for the lower-paying jobs, and almost none of them had supervisory positions. (I was told that black employees would not take directions from other blacks.) Two examples I found in the water department illustrate the inequities which existed in the utilization of whites and blacks.

During the depression of the thirties, when black workers were paid twenty-five cents an hour, the position of "lid-lifter" was created. Upon inquiry I learned that a white water-meter reader was accompanied by a black "lid-lifter" to remove the lid of the meter box while the white reader entered the reading in the meter book. Theoretically this might result in more meters being read in a given period, but actually it didn't.

Another custom was for meters to be installed and removed by a two-man crew using a pickup truck. A white man drove the truck and kept the records. A black man did the mechanical work of installation or removal, but at a considerably lower pay scale. The number of water meters tested annually was so low it was obvious that only meters which had stopped entirely were being removed and repaired.

I eliminated the positions of "lid-lifter" and meter-repair truck driver and arranged for blacks to drive trucks and keep records. I appointed some blacks to supervisory positions. The change created no problems. Elimination of the positions did not necessarily result in a work-force reduction because we needed their services in other activities; but productivity increased greatly. We purchased new meter-testing equipment and sent the meter repairmen to meter factories for training in testing and repair methods. As a result, water revenues increased substantially.

On my recommendation, the board of aldermen engaged Public Administration Service, a Chicago-based consulting organization, to help us establish a personnel department and design and install a modern position-classification and pay plan that would assure equal pay for equal work and greater equity among the various city activities.

Other Improvements

At about the same time, we experienced the beginning of a water-supply problem. A summer drought brought Winston-Salem close to a water shortage. This prompted some civic leaders to propose a $4 million bond issue to bring additional water from nearby Yadkin River. Opponents of the bond issue forced a promise that if the bonds were approved the project would not be started until after a careful needs study. The bonds were approved and the board of aldermen gave me the assignment to study the water problem and recommend if and when the project should proceed.

The evidence was clear. Winston-Salem would continue to grow and so would its water needs. Furthermore, costs were going up. At a public hearing I presented charts and data and recommended that we proceed immediately. An industry executive and others urged the board to wait, maintaining that construction costs would likely decrease within two or three years. The board voted to proceed.

Four years later we had another drought. A consulting engineer reported that without the augmented supply, the city would have had to ration water and close down water-consuming industries for thirty to sixty days.

For years Winston-Salem had been plagued by a major air-pollution problem. The burning of soft coal for heating and industry created heavy smoke emissions. In addition, wide areas of the city received a daily film of dust from tobacco factory emissions, and the incineration of furniture-factory wastes kept a constant pall over the town.

At that time Pittsburgh, St. Louis, Dayton, and a few other cities had made marked improvements in air quality. The board of aldermen suggested we undertake an air-pollution control program. We secured other cities' regulations, recruited an experienced engineer from Dayton, established an advisory committee, adopted a good ordinance, and were in business. Local industry and commercial interests cooperated fully, and within one year we had a noticeable improvement in air quality.

Perhaps the project of greatest importance to the community arose from the Junior Chamber of Commerce's interest in getting better housing and more sanitary living conditions in the black section of town.

We created a special task force consisting of the building superintendent, a health-department sanitary engineer, and a public-works department engineer. Their job was to survey and report on the existing conditions, map the areas needing attention, and make recommendations. The survey disclosed that there were 6,000 substandard shack-homes in the area studied. Most of them had no inside plumbing, and many had windows without glass, leaky roofs, and walls with cracks you could see through. Also, most of them were built on stilts, in groups, and were supposed to have access to a common water faucet and toilet. However, the toilets were usually plugged and inoperative, leaving residents with no sanitary disposal facilities. The grounds in these areas were indescribably filthy.

The board of aldermen enacted a minimum-standards housing ordinance, one of the early ones. The ordinance required that every dwelling have hot water, bathing facilities, and an inside toilet. If the cost of these improvements exceeded half the estimated value of the building, the building had to be demolished rather than improved.

Many landlords objected vociferously, coming up with the time-worn objection, "If you put in a bathtub, the blacks will just put coal in it." But the board of aldermen stood firm, requiring compliance with the new standards within a reasonable period. Because a large number of dwellings would be demolished, the board and the city-county planning board set up the mechanics for urban redevelopment and a housing authority to provide housing to replace the demolished units.

We followed through to make certain there was no delay in making needed repairs to leaky roofs, broken windows, and inoperative plumbing. Also, we developed a plan for low-cost street paving in those areas, thus changing muddy roads to paved roads.

The improvements provided better health and greater comfort—and not only for people in the slum areas. The entire community was improved, because thousands of the black residents worked in white homes, caring for the children and cooking for the families.

Most of the programs outlined above were instituted during the first year of council-manager government. It was the second year for the incumbent aldermen, which meant an election was at hand. One incumbent moved outside the city, another retired from his firm and civic work, and a third retired because of poor health.

Still smarting from the loss of the charter election and encouraged by the narrow margin of favorable votes at the time of adoption, opponents of the new charter quietly and effectively supported candidates where there were vacancies and elected two aldermen. While neither new alderman had openly expressed opposition to the form of government, they shortly became an opposition faction in the board.

The incumbent mayor had been elected president of a national organization which required his frequent absence from the city. As a result, his reelection efforts were minimal. His opponent, who had unsuccessfully sought public office seven times previously, became mayor. A few months after the election, the *Twin-City Sentinel* described the situation editorially, as follows:

> It is now clear that the Mayor did not give up last June, after he backed down in his fight with the City Manager. Immediately after he became Mayor, he created a row at City Hall to see 'who's going to be boss' of the City of Winston-Salem. His bid for personal power resulted in such an uproar of public opinion that he was forced to withdraw. He

declared that all of the furor at City Hall was so much 'newspaper talk'.
Although the Mayor gave the appearance of cooperating with the City
Manager, two of the members of the Board of Aldermen engaged in a
continued sniping campaign against the city manager form of
government.

Had I been more experienced in the political arena, I might have recognized the potential hazards and made some efforts to give the public
more information about the new programs, the reorganization activities,
the need for bringing in several highly qualified out-of-town professionals
to supervise the hospitals, the water department, the city engineer's office,
and others. However, the local press had done an excellent public information job in both their news columns and editorials. For instance, in one
lengthy editorial they listed the above accomplishments plus several more,
then closed with, "In short, the people of Winston-Salem have been given
more and better services and with such financial efficiency that there has
been no necessity to raise the tax rate, even in a time of inflation."

At the next election for aldermen, more of the original incumbents
were unavailable for one reason or another. But there was no evidence of
unusual political activity. With one or two exceptions, and these candidates received few votes, there were no open attacks on either the form of
government or me. Thus, the fourth year of government under the new
charter began with quiet and calm. From all appearances, we were off to
another year of progress and improvement. Then, suddenly, the blow fell.

The Beginning of the End

A few hours before a regular board meeting, the mayor came to my office.
He advised me that a majority of the board of aldermen wanted my resignation, effective immediately, and that if given, they would provide thirty
days terminal pay and say that I had resigned voluntarily.

The ordinances provided that the city manager could be removed only
by resolution and that one negative vote would postpone adoption for
two weeks. Recognizing that the mayor was trying to take advantage of
the absence that day of some of the original aldermen, and knowing that I
would have strong support from civic leaders and organizations when they
learned the status of affairs, I refused to resign.

Just before the end of the meeting that night, one of the new aldermen, a former policeman, arose and said, "I have a mandate from my constituents to fire the city manager, and I so move." The city attorney
quickly stated, "The city manager can be removed only by resolution, so
your motion is out of order," then read aloud the pertinent sections of the
law. The mayor replied, "I have it from eminent legal authority that such
a motion is legal, and I will accept it and call for the vote."

Although the motion to fire me was definitely illegal, I did not challenge it. I said to the press, "If a majority of the board of aldermen do not want to retain me as city manager, then I no longer wish to be associated with them. I expect to continue in city government elsewhere and will be a city manager long after the Winston-Salem voters have removed from office those responsible for firing me."

I conclude my Winston-Salem saga with the following editorial from the *Twin-City Sentinel* (2 July 1951):

He Put Principles Above Politics—

City Manager Gene Perkins Was Sacrificed
In Cause of Good Municipal Government

C. E. Perkins can be called correctly a "martyr to the cause" of good City Manager government.

Here is a real man who refused to bow to the politicians, the special interests, the pressure groups.

Leaders in our American cities who believe in the City Manager form of government may be proud of City Manager Gene Perkins. He defended the principles of honest and efficient municipal administration. He is competent. He is a man of character, integrity, high standards and exceptional ability. He is an example of what is good in the City Manager-Council system of municipal government.

Victory in Defeat

Sometimes a defeat is not a defeat. Often it is really a victory.

So the firing of City Manager Perkins, illegally and with dictator-like haste, by a majority of the newly-elected Board of Aldermen last Friday night, was actually a signal victory for Mr. Perkins and for the City Manager system of government. His firing was not a disgrace. Instead, it was the reflection of a glorious achievement that will receive nationwide acclaim among the advocates of merit, competence and efficiency in government. The method and the background of the discharge were a fine testimonial to a capable administrator.

Iron Curtain Technique

They found no fault with him. No one made an accusation.

As in a kangaroo court of an Iron Curtain country, a man arose and read a motion and sat down. Apparently fearful of public opinion, the majority faction in the Board of Aldermen would not wait for the legal two-weeks' postponement of action. The Mayor of Winston-Salem still tried to maintain the illusion that he supported the City Manager. He spoke in praise of Gene Perkins, but at the same time he accepted a motion which had been termed unlawful by the City Attorney.

Who Fights Good Government?

Students of municipal government could advantageously study Winston-Salem's present crisis as an excellent case history of the opposing forces of good city management versus political influence and favoritism in local government.

This is not the first time a clique has deposed a City Manager. It has happened in a number of places. Who are the enemies and what are the conditions inimicable to the manager system of government in any city? Easily recognizable and subject to being categorized, these forces roughly are:

1. *Political machines, intent on running city governments.*

2. *Private groups and individuals who would ride gravy-trains financed by city contracts.*

3. *Special interests who object to city regulations and municipal restrictions designed for the general public interest, such as building inspections, zoning ordinances, health and sanitation requirements.*

4. *Groups intent on controlling city jobs and establishing loose personnel procedures based on who knows whom, who's kin to whom, and who supported whom, in the elections.*

Perkins' Achievements

City Manager Gene Perkins has vigorously opposed insidious political attempts to infiltrate the administration of Winston-Salem. Here are some of the accomplishments for which he can take much of the credit:

1. Establishment of a classification and merit system and a scientifically-proved plan for salary and wage scales for city employees.

2. Generally increased efficiency in all departments of the city government.

3. Decrease in unit costs of services rendered the public. (Savings in garbage collection have been estimated at $50,000, while increasing garbage services.)

4. Expansion of Winston-Salem's water works—laying a pipe line to the Yadkin River, to eliminate the annual threat of drought.

5. The City has moved against unhealthful conditions, such as stream pollution, slum housing, inadequate drainage, and unsanitary conditions in residential neighborhoods and in public eating places.

6. There has been an unprecedented program of paving city streets and other streets improvements. More streets were paved in 1949–50, for example, than in the previous eight years together.

7. In public works there have been tremendous increases in building inspections, sewage treatment and refuse collections.

8. Centralized purchasing to save money and greater care to require bidding for city contracts, based on clear specifications, has meant savings to taxpayers.

9. There has been increased efficiency in the fire and police departments.

10. The City's Finance Department has been re-organized to assure better fiscal accounting.

11. Bonded indebtedness of the city built up during many years, has been systematically reduced.

In short, the people of Winston-Salem have been given more and better servic_s and with such financial efficiency there has been no necessity to raise the tax rate, even in a time of national inflation.

What Kind of Man?

What kind of administrator is Gene Perkins, and what is his philosophy which has resulted in these improvements in our city's services?

Perkins is an engineer and a keen executive. He believes that city government is big business and should be run like a business—with the city manager corresponding to the chief administrator of a company or a corporation, and the city aldermen (or board of directors) determining policy. He believes in strict demarcation of powers between the policy makers and the administration, and he contends that policy makers should not try to mix in administration, nor should administrators intrude into policy-making. He holds that a basic requirement of good city administration is organization of capable and satisfied city employees in the several departments. A recent survey among city employees showed a feeling of increased security and pleasure among the employees since the new classification and pay plan installed by Mr. Perkins. He is personable and exceptionally fluent in his analyses of city problems and explanations of technical details to various municipal boards and commissions and he is scrupulously strict and articulate about any condition or program entering into the conduct of good government. If he thinks a measure is right, he will say so, fully and completely, presenting well-documented facts to substantiate his position. If he hasn't gathered enough facts to state an opinion yet, he will so indicate. If he thinks a measure is wrong, he will mince no words and pull no punches in saying so. Everybody knows where Gene Perkins stands on any administrative matter. There is no equivocation. An exceptionally hard worker himself, he expects a full day's work of others. However, he believes Winston-Salem's more than 1,200 city employees can do better work on a 5-day-week plan, and he established that procedure for employees as a part of the merit and pay formula. Winston-Salem employees now do better work in less time and there is less lost motion, more efficiency and economy.

Why Was He Fired?

That is the picture of a competent City Manager. What influences entered into his discharge? Several of the factors which are inimicable to the City Manager-Aldermanic system of local government contributed to his discharge.

During the past two years, City Manager Perkins has been the victim of politically-inspired needling, rumors, pussy-footing. Attempts to "get something on him" have been traced to alleged sources by competent investigators. Each time the rumors have been exploded, the charges refuted. But the smear campaign continued.

Finally, with no indictment against him, with none able to stand and call him guilty of anything, and without regard to law, they voted City Manager Perkins out of his job.

In true perspective, it will be regarded as a triumph for Gene Perkins and for the tradition of honest city government. It was a dismal day for the people of Winston-Salem.

To whom it may concern: Here is a capable city manager who has sacrificed himself for good government.

An Unhappy Inheritance
L. Perry Cookingham

When I became city manager of Kansas City, I knew the city had problems, but I did not know the details and the extent of the financial and operational difficulties I had inherited.

As to the financial problems, state law restricted city revenue almost exclusively to the property tax. No municipal sales tax or income or earnings taxes were permitted. The city's real estate tax limit was $1.50 per hundred dollars of assessed valuation. The amounts of property assessments were controlled by the county, at absurdly low percentages of the full and true value of the real property. Moreover, I soon found a current deficit of about $22 million (this in addition to long-term debt of $60 to $70 million). Since the yearly budget was about $12.5 million, the current deficit was equal to almost two years of operating needs. One of our first jobs was to liquidate that deficit.

The deficit consisted of several parts: an $8-$10 million shortage in the water sinking fund,* another $8-$10 million of back-pay claims filed by city employees, numerous personal injury claims, $500,000 of unpaid vendors' bills, and miscellaneous items.

Previous councils had authorized transfers from the water sinking fund to the general debt and interest fund, to redeem general-obligation serial bonds when they came due. Because the water-bond sinking fund

---

*Cities often issued *term* bonds, all of which matured—came due—on the same future date. The city was obligated to make periodic deposits into a fund so that on the maturity date there would be enough money in the fund to redeem—pay off—the matured bonds. The fund into which the deposits were to be made is called a "sinking fund." Today most cities issue *serial* bonds; that is, bonds are issued with a series of staggered maturity dates so that the issue is paid off bit by bit, in installments as the bonds come due.

was virtually empty, we had to refund (reissue) the water bonds to raise money to redeem the bonds that were due. This cost the taxpayers double the amount of interest it would have cost had the transfers not been made.

It had been the practice to cut the employees' pay at midyear or a little later if the city found it was running short of funds and could not balance the budget. The cuts were made without amending the compensation ordinance. The firemen sued the city, claiming the deductions were illegal and that they were entitled to back pay. They won. We felt that all city employees whose salaries had been cut were entitled to the same treatment, so we settled the claims by making back-pay payments to all those persons who could prove that they had performed services for the city.

Apparently the city simply ignored the personal injury claims, which had accumulated over several years. We negotiated settlements with the claimants.

Some of the vendors' claims were denied because the vendors had no contracts with the city. Where we could determine that supplies and services had been provided and were used and useful, we settled by paying cash.

As I recall, we did not have to borrow any money to pay off these claims because we had been able to effect economies by good administrative practices. For example, when an employee terminated, we analyzed the position and did not appoint a replacement unless it was clearly needed. We stopped the use of city cars, equipment, and supplies for private use, as well as use of city manpower and equipment on private property. We established competitive bidding for supplies and construction work. And, where existing contracts were not in the best interest of the city, we renegotiated them.

Change and improvement did not always come easily, however. For instance, on my first day on the job I saw so many people converging on the city treasurer's office I thought it must be a tax revolt or a riot. But I learned from the finance director that it was only citizens lining up to get their tax statements and pay their taxes. The city didn't prebill the taxes. Instead the taxpayers had to come to the city hall, wait in line while a clerk looked up their property description and prepared their tax bill, then wait in another line to pay the tax.

I discussed with the council the desirability of installing a tax-accounting system, using tax-billing machines and printing the tax bill as a by-product of preparing the tax roll. It took time to sell the council on the idea; in fact, I had to install tax-accounting equipment and sample tax bills to show them how the operation would work. Finally they agreed that if I could find the money—about $60,000 at the time—they would approve the installation. We found the necessary money and made the installation.

The next year we were able to prebill the taxes. The collections increased immediately, and materially over any previous year. Later I inquired why the city had not installed machine bookkeeping many years before. One of the councilmen gave me a succinct and significant answer: "Bookkeeping machines don't vote!"

The old government employed a lot of extra clerks during tax time so that the political machine could count on more votes at the next election. However, I felt that it was more important to give convenient public service to all the taxpayers than it was to give a few weeks work to some precinct workers. Besides, I felt it was the city's obligation to create an environment which would give people work in private enterprise rather than trying to provide jobs for them in city government, at taxpayer expense.

Citizen
Participation

Toward an All-America City*

Thomas F. Maxwell

In August 1950 I went to Columbia, South Carolina, as the city's first city manager. Before going I had investigated and found that the former mayor had been a czar for twenty years and that there had been considerable corruption in the police and other departments. There had been protected gambling and prostitution and a huge payoff for purchase of parking meters. One attorney had a monopoly on zoning changes, and there were other similar conditions usually found in a city controlled by a political faction. Consequently, I obtained prior agreement of the newly elected council-manager city council that I would have a free hand to eliminate all political favoritism and corruption, specifically, that I could order the police department and the municipal judge to stop fixing tickets for city commissioners (standard practice under the former government),

---

*For more than thirty years the National Municipal League has sponsored an annual All-America Cities Awards competition. The program recognizes communities of all sizes, kinds, and localities that have achieved marked improvement through effective citizen action. Winners are chosen from a group of finalists selected by a screening committee. Finalists' representatives present their stories to a jury composed of leaders of major businesses, and labor, civic and philanthropic organizations, which makes the final selection of winners. The jury hears the finalists' presentations during the National Municipal League's annual National Conference on Government. Individual citizens, citizen groups, and public officials are invited to submit entries for their communities. Entry blanks and instructions are available from: National Municipal League, 47 East 68th Street, New York, N.Y. 10021

and that I could end the commissioners' privilege of canceling taxpayers' tax delinquent penalties.

Despite the agreement, I went to Columbia with some trepidation, not knowing how a Yankee would be received in the hotbed of politics that I assumed characterized the capital city of a southern state. My fears proved to be unwarranted, however; the people of Columbia were the most friendly, gracious, and hospitable I have found anywhere. It was not long before I heard rumors that tickets were still being fixed. When I was able to pinpoint the councilman who was allegedly involved, I visited him at his office. There I told him that I was receiving these complaints and rumors that were causing me considerable embarrassment, and I flat out asked him if there was any truth to them. Sheepishly he admitted that for certain of his clients he had been fixing tickets for many years, but that now, although he continued to take the tickets, he was paying for them out of his own pocket, leaving the impression that he had fixed the tickets. He agreed that it was the wrong thing to do and that he would no longer do it, and I heard no more rumors about anyone ever being able to fix tickets in the city of Columbia.

However, this solved only the ticket-fixing problem. The general clean-up brought retaliation from the politicians formerly in control, and after only eighteen months they forced a vote to abandon the council-manager form of government and revert to the old commission form. The original vote to adopt the council-manager plan had been rather close, with a very small turnout of voters. In the election to abandon the council-manager plan, the vote was five times as large and was eight to one in favor of retaining the council-manager plan. My constant position was that citizen participation was the key to good government. We held town meetings in all areas of the city, explaining the new form of government and urging citizen participation.

That expression of citizen support, together with the reorganization of the government, installation for the first time of budgetary control and sound accounting procedures, elimination of graft, establishment of the first planning commission and other actions, brought the city an All-America City Award.

Right Action for the Wrong Reason
Joseph R. Coupal, Jr.

Ipswich, Massachusetts, has more occupied seventeenth-century houses than any other community in the country. Beautiful in its coastal setting and famed for its clams, the town was and still is fragmented in terms of religion, ethnicity, economics, and social groups. The split reflects differences among Yankee textile millowners and operators, Polish textile workers, a Greek fishing community, new, young residents escaping the Boston metropolitan area, and old settlers whose families go back two centuries.

For years prior to 1951, the chairman of the board of selectmen had also held (probably illegally) the position of town accountant. Holding the two positions, he was able to control welfare, purchasing, and several other town functions. Consequently, in a 1951 town meeting, the voters adopted a manager plan for the town government and provided that the issue could not be voted on again for three years.

Unfortunately, the promoters of the new government focused on the wrong reason for its approval. Rather than emphasize effectiveness and efficiency, they emphasized the need to "clean up" the town government.

At the same town meeting, the voters elected a slate of five selectmen who had run on a town-manager platform and were pledged to recruit a trained professional manager. I went to work for them in April 1951. We had three years to prove the value of council-manager government.

First, we cleaned out the town offices, physically. From the file cabinet and under the counters, we carried out two wastebaskets full of empty liquor bottles. We reorganized the government structure, establishing central departments of purchasing, personnel, accounting, public health, recreation, and public works. For three consecutive years the tax rates were reduced, the outstanding indebtedness was reduced, the town surplus was increased, and services were increased dramatically.

With that much progress, the proponents of the manager plan were confident there was no possibility of its being rejected at the 1954 town meeting. They made little effort to get a positive vote.

But the opponents of the plan had been working diligently in the background to overthrow the manager form of government. They had kept a low profile, but then, three days before the town meeting, they put on a blitz campaign against the plan. When the votes were counted, election officials ruled that the plan had lost by some forty-seven votes. Proponents of the plan were prevented from getting a recount when some of the ballots were "lost," and I shall always believe there was chicanery at the polls in that election.

The victors mounted a "march" on my home, and planted flares on the front lawn. Eventually the state police came and restored some order.

The event upset a majority of the people. The next day, they started a petition for a special town meeting, and within six months the special meeting had been held and the town manager plan had been reinstated. By that time, however, I had been hired by the City of Bangor, Maine, where they were seeking a manager who would resist such political actions. It was a better job at a higher salary, and I served as city manager of Bangor for thirteen years.

Let George Do It

LeRoy F. Harlow

Despite urging by chambers of commerce and others, few businessmen take a continuing, front-line part in local government. Occasionally they will involve themselves in issues that affect the interests of their companies, but generally they are reluctant to serve in a political capacity. Among those who are willing, the demands on their time and energy, and the need to make unpopular decisions, sometimes result in early resignations. Sometimes, too, the owners of the business, their partners, or important customers force them to resign. Finally, those who take on substantial governmental responsibility at local, state, or national levels often get "a belly full" in a hurry and beat a hasty retreat to the relative stability and security of their private businesses, where they have fewer bosses, can make their own decisions, need not compromise so often, and can remain cleanly aloof from "dirty politics." As a consequence, public offices go by default to attorneys (who benefit from the free advertising and some status), retired businessmen who have nothing to lose, people in such minor business positions that they are not identified with a particular firm, and the full-time office seekers.

Even as civic-minded a community as Albert Lea, Minnesota, had difficulty retaining able businessmen for more than very short-term local-government assignments. On one occasion the council tried to get volunteers for an appraisal advisory board. The board was to help the city assessor set values on local property for tax purposes. We needed only three men, but we got so many turn-downs that to get three we had to invite a dozen.

One of the first three to accept was an active realtor with extensive experience in property appraisals. We asked him to serve because of his professional qualifications, and because he was known to complain on more than one occasion that "the politicians" were making all the decisions, leaving businessmen no opportunity.

When I called to ask if he thought he could find time to serve on this important part-time committee, he readily accepted. But before the group had its first meeting, he came to my office. Sheepishly, he said he could not serve after all. His reason: His landlord owned considerable property in town, and our man "couldn't afford to offend" his landlord by being a party to determining property values for local tax purposes.

This forced us to seek another qualified businessman—one who would be willing to apply a bit of his abilities in the public interest, rather than saying in effect, "Let George do it."

Talk Is Not Always Cheap

L. Perry Cookingham

I was appointed city manager of Kansas City, Missouri, in 1940 by a reform coalition city council that was led by Citizens Association candidates who had won a majority of council seats after the fall of the Pendergast machine. During my nineteen-year tenure there, the most constant and troublesome problem I had was finding the funds to provide the improvements the city needed, and the services the citizens wanted.

Near the end of my Kansas City service, large central cities all over the country were feeling the effects of the flight of residents, businesses, and industries to the suburbs. Many of these cities, especially in Pennsylvania and Ohio, had adopted state-legislature-authorized earnings taxes to meet the problem. Consequently, I recommended to the city council that they submit the proposal to the voters. I suggested that they propose a one percent tax rate because the city needed the revenue that rate would produce, and also because I thought it would be as easy to get approval of a one percent rate as it would be to obtain approval of a one-half percent tax or a lesser amount.

On the day the citizens were voting for the first time on the proposal, I received a telephone call from a man I did not know by name because he refused to identify himself. However, I did recognize by the voice that he was a person who called me frequently about city government situations he did not like, and who was long-winded.

This time the conversation lasted about thirty-five minutes. He told me in no uncertain terms that the proposition was going to fail by a four-to-one vote. He said he had walked from the Missouri River (on the north) to 85th Street (the southern city limit), and from the Kansas state line to the eastern city limit, and everyone he talked to was against the earnings tax.

He said, "After the election, you'd better pick up your papers and leave town, because you are through in Kansas City."

After he had consumed about thirty minutes of my time, and I had listened patiently, a lady came on the line. She asked, "Why don't you get off this line and give somebody else a chance to use it?"

I replied to the lady, "Who is this man I am talking to? He won't tell me his name?"

She said, "Don't you know?"

I said, "No."

She said, "Give me your number and I'll call you back and tell you who he is."

I gave her the number and my secretary's name, and told her to tell the secretary that I had asked her to call me.

A few minutes later I was able to terminate the conversation with the gentleman, and shortly thereafter the lady called back.

"He wouldn't tell you his name?"

"No. All I know is that he doesn't like Kansas City."

"Well, why don't he get out; why don't he move someplace else?"

"I don't know. Who is he?"

"We call him 'Crazy Louis.' He's against everything, and you'd know he would be against the earnings tax. But, I'm for it, because I think the city needs the money."

This was an interesting experience for several reasons. For one, it illustrates how widely the views of citizens can differ over the same important issue.

Also, it shows that the current (1979) taxpayer "revolt" is not a new phenomenon. The gentleman's prognostication was 100 percent right. The earnings tax did fail that time by a four-to-one vote. (Later the tax was voted in at one-half percent, and still later it was raised to one percent. Today it is the principal source of revenue for the Kansas City general fund.) At the next election the Citizens Association candidates were defeated, probably in part because of the constant urging of the administration for more funds.

Finally, it shows how the same people who complain the loudest and longest about spending money for needed purposes can indirectly waste money and think nothing of it. This kind of inconsistency is one of the problems a manager must tolerate. I had a policy of never hanging up until a citizen-caller had run out of steam. Yet, it cost the taxpayers quite a sum of money to pay me for listening to this and other chronic complainers who offered nothing constructive but only vented their feelings and opinions.

Annexation
and Merger

Municipal Euthanasia
Kennedy Shaw

It was the summer of 1955 when I arrived in East Ann Arbor, Michigan, as its first (and, as it turned out, last) city administrator. Many people wonder how an administrator could recommend the elimination of his own position. There is no question in my mind that the citizens, the community, and the administrator all benefited.

I was a year out of graduate school in public administration at the University of Michigan, and I had spent the intervening year as the assistant to Ralph Snyder in Westerville, Ohio, a city of 5,000 in the central part of the state near Columbus. Under Ralph's gentle despotism I had begun to learn a little about being a city manager.

When I heard about the opening in East Ann Arbor through a friend at the University of Michigan, I immediately applied. When I arrived for my interview by the mayor and the seven-member council, I put on my rose-colored glasses and looked around. I saw a two-square-mile community on the southeastern edge of Ann Arbor, bordering on the main route connecting Ann Arbor and Ypsilanti. The nucleus of the town was a housing unit that had been built during World War II to house students and their families who were going to school under various government programs. Following the war a rash of small, mostly wooden homes had been built under the Veterans Administration program. For the most part, these were the first homes of young couples starting to raise their families. There were about 2500 people in the area and only a sprinkling of retail and industrial firms. What little tax base there was consisted essentially of residential or open-space properties.

The community had been built without sewers, and most of the houses were on small lots, which created difficult septic-tank problems. This necessitated the community's negotiating a contract with the City of Ann Arbor. Just before my arrival sewer lines had been installed in the gravel streets and the sewage had begun being treated by Ann Arbor at a fairly expensive rate. There were no water lines. Consequently, the people depended on wells for water. The lack of water and the expensive sewage treatment made it difficult to attract industrial firms.

The town had been incorporated just a few years before (largely to take advantage of the state funds for road maintenance that were available to cities). The mayor and the seven-member council represented the diversity of the community. The mayor was an American Airlines pilot, and the council included the assistant director of the Survey Research Center at the University of Michigan, a couple of housewives, a businessman or two, and one retiree who was very active in the volunteer fire department. The volunteer fire group was the best organized unit in the community, having some forty members and owning its own building and two fire engines.

I enthusiastically accepted the job offer and began my duties in August 1955. There were three other full-time employees—a book-keeper/clerk and two men in the public-works operation. The police chief worked part-time, as did the four patrolmen (whose regular jobs were with the sheriff's department).

My duties involved acting as clerk to the city council, inspecting buildings, purchasing, assessing buildings, supervising the public-works crew, handling relationships with the volunteer fire department, and over-seeing the police department.

After the first flush of enthusiasm had worn off and as I began to look at the long-term ability of the community to support itself financially, I began to realize that East Ann Arbor would not be just another growing community. The lack of a water supply, the expensive sewer arrangements with Ann Arbor, and the lack of paved roads made the long-term prospects bleak.

The community did have a contractual relationship with a professional planner who taught at the University of Michigan and with whom I worked on subdivision approval and analysis of zoning questions in the community. After I had been there about six months, he and I agreed at one of our regular monthly meetings that we should take a long-range look at the economics of the community.

We gathered a good deal of data from the county planning board and the City of Ann Arbor as well as from the state government. We took a long, hard look at the capital needs, including road, water, and sewage improvements, and at the potential tax base. Our data confirmed our suspicions: East Ann Arbor was in financial trouble. As a result we jointly recommended to the city council that we seek annexation to Ann Arbor.

Based on their reading and analysis of the report that we generated, five of the city councilmen agreed that we should initiate talks with Ann Arbor. The retired councilman who was active with the volunteer fire department, had some concerns, particularly about the future of the volunteer fire department.

I then went to the newly appointed administrator for the City of Ann Arbor and presented our material. Ann Arbor then had a population of about 50,000 people but was beginning to experience some real growth both in area and in population. Although there was no real enthusiasm for the merger, the city administration and the Ann Arbor city planners felt that it would be better for both cities if Ann Arbor were to annex East Ann Arbor, utilizing Ann Arbor's financial and other resources to improve East Ann Arbor, rather than have to contend with a blighted situation in the future. The Ann Arbor city council agreed with the position, and the stage was then set for presenting the issue to the public. It was necessary that the question appear on the ballot in both communities and that it pass in both. If the vote was favorable, it would become the first annexation of one city by another in the history of the state.

The vote, which was to be held at the general election on the first Tuesday in November 1956, was preceded by a vigorous educational program in both communities. The mayor and I appeared on television and radio, and material explaining the reasons for the merger was mailed to the citizenry.

Inasmuch as the volunteer fire department had expressed some concern about being able to continue in existence, I met with the administrator and the fire chief of Ann Arbor. The fire chief did not want a volunteer group as part of his department, but finally he agreed (in writing) that if the merger passed, he would continue the volunteer fire company on an evaluation basis for the foreseeable future. He also agreed to place new equipment in the East Ann Arbor fire house. This blunted the major arguments of some of the East Ann Arbor volunteer fire-department personnel but their unrest continued to simmer.

About two weeks before the election, the East Ann Arbor League of Women Voters put out a very complete position paper on the annexation question. In their paper they provided a list of reasons for and against the pro position and for and against the anti position. On the Friday before the election, all East Ann Arbor homes received flyers that were unsigned but that everyone knew had originated with the volunteer firemen. The flyers contained the reasons against the pro position and the reasons for the anti position as they had appeared in the League of Women Voters material. This thoroughly upset the League of Women Voters officers. The mayor and I met with them on Saturday morning, and, as a result of that meeting, we prepared a flyer from the mayor and city council pointing out the dishonesty of the volunteer firemen's flyer, indicating the fair treatment that the volunteer firemen had received from the City of Ann

Arbor, and strongly supporting the annexation question.

The final result was that the question passed by 70 percent in both communities, and on 1 January 1957 East Ann Arbor passed out of existence and became part of Ann Arbor. As a result of the publicity, and after having served for three months as the assistant to the city administrator in Ann Arbor (helping to effect the transition), I went on to a better-paying position as assistant to the dean of Statewide Education at the University of Michigan.

I have since been back to East Ann Arbor. The streets were paved following installation of waterlines, and the surrounding area has been pleasantly developed with a mixture of homes, retail businesses, and industry. It was, as the administrator of Ann Arbor put it, the first annexation that he knew of that was at the same time an urban-renewal project.

One tiny postscript is that Ann Arbor City council members were so upset by the dishonest tactics and open objections of the volunteer firemen that they canceled their agreement, disbanded the volunteer fire agency, and put in full-time firemen at the East Ann Arbor station immediately following the annexation.

How Two Cities Were Merged
Peter F. Lydens

The increasing need to work together and stretch incomes seems likely to produce more local-government mergers in the years ahead. I hope my experience in the merger of two Virginia cities will help others who become involved in a similar process.

In March 1973 a charter was adopted providing for the merger of the City of Nansemond (population 37,000, area 428 square miles), which until July 1972 had been a county, and the City of Suffolk (population 9,000, area 2.2 square miles). On 1 August 1973 I was appointed manager of both cities; the merger was to become effective five months later.

Here are some of the problems we faced and the steps we took to deal with them. I will conclude with general comments.

Organization Problems

1. *Span of Control.* In mergers there is a tendency to establish a great number of departments with directors reporting to the city manager. This organization alleviates the problem of appointing former department heads to division-head positions, one step removed from the city manager,

but it creates too broad a span of control with little or no coordination and control.

Our Action. We combined several former departments in new major departments. We considered appointing two assistant city managers so that all department heads could report to one of the two to assure smoother operation of related departments.

2. *Duplicate Offices/Lack of Coordination.* Previously property assessment had been the responsibility of the two commissioners of the revenue. The new charter called for a city assessor appointed by the city council.

In Virginia two constitutional officers are responsible for city billings and collections—the commissioner of the revenue and the city treasurer. These elected officials had different sets of administrative policies.

In Nansemond accounting was performed by the city manager's office and the city treasurer's office; in Suffolk, by the comptroller's office and the city treasurer's office.

Purchasing was informal and decentralized. In Nansemond department heads (and the sheriff on automotive equipment) had primary responsibility; in Suffolk, each responsible departmental employee had coupons that he or she filled out and signed, authorizing a vendor to fill the order and bill the city.

Neither city had a finance director.

Our Action. We established a finance department, headed by a finance director appointed by the city manager. The council-appointed assessor reported to the finance director on administrative matters. Accounting, except for accounts-receivable records, was assigned to the accounting division established within the new finance department. Initially the finance director acted as purchasing agent; later a purchasing agent was appointed, under the finance director.

3. *Combining Like Departments.* What, if anything, should be done before the formal merger date about combining like departments, such as the police departments? Each city had a fully developed department. Should they operate independently until the date of formal merger, or should steps be taken beforehand to assure smooth operations on the first day of merger?

Our Action. A new organization was determined, and personnel were chosen for each position. New insignia, uniforms, and police-car coloration were designed. We obtained permission from both city councils for their police officers to work in the other's jurisdiction prior to formal merger, for the purposes of geographical and operational orientation. Having this permission, we decided to establish the new department several months prior to the actual merger in order to debug any problems that might arise. This move was successful, and the same procedure was followed with the fire department and the recreation department.

Management Systems Problems

1. *Loose Financial Management.* Before the merger, the finance committees of the two city councils prepared budget proposals. There were no budget calendars, no standard worksheets, no instructions to department heads on what to include in their written justifications for budget requests, and no uniform account codes or definitions of activities and objects of expenditure.

As I mentioned above, purchasing was informal and decentralized. One could not track purchases.

The councils, the city managers, and the department heads lacked financial information on which to base important decisions.

Nansemond's vehicles were serviced at the school bus garage, Suffolk's at the limited-service city garage. Much of the repair work, especially on police cars, was done in private shops and garages, with the result that vehicle maintenance and operating costs varied widely. In both cities, many employees received car or mileage allowances in lieu of using city vehicles.

Finally, there were no written rules and procedures on travel, property control and responsibility, safety, accident reporting, and so on.

Our Action. We established a uniform code of expenditure accounts for budgeting and accounting purposes. We set up a calendar of dates when departmental estimates were due in the city manager's office, when departmental requests would be reviewed by the city manager, when his consolidated budget would go to the city council, and when the council would hold its budget hearings. The budget calendar was sent to department heads along with detailed instructions on preparation of estimates. The city manager's budget recommendation to the council included a budget message and explanations of outstanding features of each budget activity.

We formalized the purchasing procedure. Thereafter, department heads requisitioned budget-approved items on a form that went to the finance department to determine if funds were available in the department's budget accounts. Then the purchasing agent sought competitive bids for both goods and services. Purchase orders were issued to successful vendors, with a copy sent to the receiving department. Departments reported the quantity and condition of goods received, and these reports were compared with vendors' bills before payment was made. Procedures were established to eliminate erroneous duplicate billings and payments, which had been a problem.

Accounting, payroll, and budget-control data were put on a computer, from which current and complete reports were regularly prepared for use by the council, the city manager, department heads, and the public.

The garage operation was assigned to the public works and utilities director's office. With additional space and equipment at the city garage and three qualified mechanics and three auto servicemen, most of the repair work and all preventive maintenance was performed by city personnel. Also, additional city-owned vehicles were acquired, identified by a city decal, and assigned to employees needing transportation on their city jobs. Vehicle replacement standards were prepared and implemented. A quasi motor pool was created for offices and departments having occasional transportation needs. Car allowances were replaced by a mileage allowance tied to the state's allowance rate.

Rules and procedures were incorporated into an administrative regulations manual for guidance of the eleven departments in the new city.

2. *Informal Personnel Procedures.* The charter and the related merger agreement stipulated that all 350 employees of the two cities should be retained on the payroll. This provided an abundance of personnel, but not necessarily with the qualifications needed in the new departments. Furthermore, except for the recent inadequate classification and pay plans put together by the state personnel department, neither city had any formal personnel-management system. Their de facto systems were based on a few outdated ordinances related to personnel.
Our Action. Two months after the new city became a legal entity, we completed and submitted to the new city council a comprehensive personnel ordinance. We reworked the state's classification and pay plans and tied them into the first merged-cities budget. The council adopted the personnel ordinance and position-classification and pay plans with little change.

3. *Inadequate Communications.* Both before and after the merger, we had problems with inadequate and ineffective communications internally and externally. Internally, excessive reliance was placed on council committees, with the result that not all council members were kept well-informed on many city matters. Also, the city managers' offices had not kept the councils adequately informed. For instance, there was little advance consideration of matters that would be on the council meeting agendas; in fact, there were virtually no agendas. Further, there were no regular monthly reports to the council of departmental activities.

Externally there was need to clear up misconceptions about the merger and to keep the public informed of programs, projects, and progress.
Our Action. We started a number of communications practices. There were twice-a-month council meetings (as a committee of the whole) to consider proposed agenda items. A comprehensive agenda was sent to council members five days before the meetings. Besides a listing of items, the agenda had explanatory memoranda, concise backup information, the appropriate resolution or ordinance in draft form if required, and the city manager's recommendation. We provided the council with monthly departmental activity and expenditure reports. We even began periodic

rap sessions between the manager, with some of his staff, and the city council.

Externally we considered weekly coffee hours with the chamber of commerce executive director, the city manager, and two or three citizens in an effort to answer questions and get feedback from the community's informal power structure. We designated my administrative assistant as public information officer, working with department heads on public information. Of course we worked closely with the newspapers, radio stations, and television stations, giving them information they wanted and suggesting ideas for feature-type coverage. And we accepted every opportunity for city representatives to address civic clubs.

Some Conclusions

From my experience, I offer the following suggestions and comments to anyone who may be involved in merging two or more local governments.
1. Where possible, informally test and refine any proposed new organizational structure and management system before the actual merger.
2. Again where possible, resolve policy differences and conflicts before merger, or as soon as possible thereafter. The new city code and major administrative manuals should be ready for adoption immediately after merger.
3. Make sure that each new program to be initiated has been debugged before it is presented to the public.
4. If there are no comprehensive long-range plans, especially for capital improvements and financing, move promptly to develop such a plan.
5. Don't count on the merger to save money. More effective service and lower unit costs can be achieved. But because the public will expect additional services, total expenditures may not go down, especially during inflationary periods.
6. Not all the hard work is done when the new charter has been adopted and a date set for merger. The merged city will inherit ten to twenty years of needs and problems and will find itself with opportunities to solve these needs and problems and to offer new programs to provide greater services to the new city. Taking advantage of the opportunities requires laying a firm foundation of planning, organization, management systems, communications systems, and policies so that the new government is established and operated on a solid footing and with direction. Solving the problems and establishing new programs takes time, money, and manpower.

Council-Manager Relations

Setting the Course
L. Perry Cookingham

When I was selected in 1940 to be city manager of Kansas City, Missouri, I was not too anxious to undertake the job. Although thirteen years of machine-dominated rule of the city by the infamous Pendergast machine had been ended by a coalition of so-called "good" Democrats, the Republican organization, and many active women, I did not feel that the people of Kansas City were ready for the kind of government that I knew about. Yet, when the job was offered to me, I felt obligated to accept. I wanted to prove that council-manager government would work, even in Kansas City.

The clean-up group had won control of the city council on the campaign slogan "Sweep the City Hall Clean." Many of the winners and their supporters took their victory as a mandate to terminate all city employees and start over with an entirely new staff. This created a perplexing problem for me. Consequently, before I was appointed I told the council that I would not fire anybody until I found them unqualified to do the job. Besides, I said, I could fire only department heads; the department heads would have to terminate their unqualified subordinates.

The council indicated that they *knew* the department heads were not qualified and insisted that they be fired. I said, "You'll have to appoint someone to do the firing before I take over the job, but I want to make the appointments to replace the persons terminated." The council responded by hiring me as a consultant and appointing as city manager a young lawyer who had been active in the clean-up. The young city manager began the task of terminating the department heads, firing at least two a week.

For the next six weeks I flew down to Kansas City from Saginaw, Michigan (where I was city manager), each Thursday afternoon. I interviewed candidates for the department head vacancies on Fridays, Saturdays, and sometimes Sunday mornings, then flew back to my job in Saginaw. When I had a staff of department heads of my own choosing, I left Saginaw and assumed the city manager duties in Kansas City.

Then the department heads began the task of terminating employees they felt were unqualified or had been engaged in questionable activities. This went on for almost six months. About two thousand employees were terminated. Fortunately, what otherwise would have been a heartless thing to do, took place in the few months prior to the start of World War II, when defense industry jobs were plentiful. Most of the terminated employees went to work immediately, in jobs that paid more than the city was able to pay. (Today the strength of the unions probably would prohibit such action following a political turnover such as occurred in Kansas City in 1940.)

By this time I felt we had terminated about all we could without injuring the municipal service, but the pressure to continue the terminations did not let up. I advised the council that not all the former employees were unqualified, that if they were the city government would have fallen many years before it actually did. But the pressure persisted. Finally I insisted that we had gone as far as we could and suggested that I analyze each of the remaining positions occupied by "holdover" employees.

The acting personnel director (a professional borrowed from Public Administration Service, the Chicago consulting organization), Dr. Lyman Moore (my assistant), and I worked for a week analyzing the two thousand or more holdover employees still on the payroll. The following week I decided not only to report our findings to the city council, but, if they could not see the situation as I viewed it, to resign and give somebody else a chance to undertake the task.

On the day of the council meeting I wrote out my resignation, put it in my pocket, and went into an informal meeting of the council with the analysis of the holdover employees, the positions they held, and their importance to the operations of the city government. I think the session lasted more than three hours. I read the report, gave them our analysis, and added other significant information.

At the conclusion of my report, the council member who had been most insistent upon more rapid terminations slammed his fist on the desk. As he did so, I reached for my resignation, not knowing what he was about to say. What he did say was this: "This is a most commendable report. I did not realize the city manager had such a tremendous responsibility in operating the facilities and the institutions of this city government. From now on I am not going to say anything more about termination of employees. I think the job of running this city is in the hands of the city manager and from now on he should have all the say about who is to remain on the payroll and who is not."

This was a turning point in my relationship with the city council, after which I had fifteen years of fine relationships and enjoyed my work immensely.

Excellence-Proud Evanston
Challenges Its Manager

Bert W. Johnson

Evanston, Illinois (80,000 population), north of Chicago on Lake Michigan, had much to be proud of: famous churches, hospitals, and schools (including Northwestern University and two seminaries), beautiful homes on wide streets with parklike tree lawns. Evanston's leadership agreed that the community was blessed in every respect, from traffic safety to community participation. For long-time residents, the letter *E* not only means Evanston, but Excellence and Earned Encomiums. Consequently, it is understandable that when the council-manager plan first became available under 1951 Illinois legislation, Evanston promptly adopted it to assure continued good government.

The eighteen-member city council had learned well the tricks of "divide and conquer" to dominate any mayor so did not look kindly on bringing in a trained chief executive. Most members expressed their opposition to the new idea of local government as unnecessary and costly. But Evanston's do-gooder instinct prevailed, the plan was adopted, and I went to work as the first city manager—in December 1953, eight months after voter approval of the plan. Among 157 candidates for the appointment, my most formidable competitor was Joseph L. Rose, the soft-spoken director of public works who, with the retiring mayor, had a twelve-year history of subservience and service to the many city council committees.

Efforts to appoint Mr. Rose, a "don't rock our boat" candidate, were thwarted by council member Paul F. Gorby. Gorby played out his role as a do-gooder, committed to excellence, by using the recruitment standards of Marshall Field & Company, where he was director of personnel. His persistence was strengthened by the first mayor elected under the council-manager plan, John R. Kimbark, a highly regarded establishment-oriented former member of the council. To assuage the city council and city bureaucracy, I agreed to appoint Mr. Rose my executive assistant.

The "true blue" do-gooders were suspicious of the council's foot dragging in appointing a manager, suspecting something self-protecting in
their actions. Adding to their concern was the fact that a new police chief
had been appointed hastily to replace the fatally stricken incumbent chief.
O. D. Buckles, the corporation counsel and acting city manager, had told
the council that because no acting chief could be legally appointed and
because the police department could not function without a chief until
my arrival a few weeks away, the candidate must be appointed now. I
shared others' misgivings about this precipitous action.

And, as might be expected, in March 1954—just three months after
my appointment—police corruption was alleged. The new state attorney,
Benjamin Adamowski, was following up on rumors of permitted gambling "in sacrosanct Evanston." Television commentator Len O'Connor
was in hot pursuit of what he termed a "pay-off scandal." "Would now
the highly heralded city manager," O'Connor shouted, "be equal to the
mess he was facing?" The proud citizens of Evanston were sure they had
in me the answer to these problems.

In an executive session of the city council, I sought and received
approval to employ two ex-FBI agents to follow up on the allegations.
These investigators filed a highly critical report concerning our chief in
his former role as captain in charge of detectives. The do-gooders seemed
on target, and action was mine to take. I sensed a career crisis on my
hands. Somehow, I thought I needed advice as to alternative actions I
should take. To refuse to act was out of the question. So I wrote to O.
W. Wilson, famed author on police administration and dean of the
School of Criminology at the University of California at Berkeley, listing
four alternative actions I was considering. His long-awaited response said
in part,

> In my opinion the confidential report merely indicates gambling exists
> in Evanston.... It consists of substantially nothing more than allega-
> tions.... Accordingly, I recommend that you do not follow any of the
> four alternatives that you have listed in your letter.

His advice helped me avoid a serious mistake. The firing or demotion
of the new chief would have been well received by many who believed
that I was bringing a "new breath of fresh air" to the high conscience
level of Evanston. But the "oldtimers" would have held me accountable
for unnecessarily tarnishing their beloved Evanston.

In reporting to the City Council concerning our investigation, I told
them, "The events to date, in my opinion, do not give any reason at all [I
chose my words carefully] to believe a climate of corruption exists in the
Evanston Police Department." General applause followed.

This responsible action won for me a respect that continued as long as
I remained city manager in Evanston. And when, after nine years, I

accepted a position in Arlington, Virginia, the mayor of Evanston, Otto R. Hills, said, "This man's devotion to excellence is not just talk. He lives there."

Paralysis by Analysis
Bert W. Johnson

Until my appointment as the fourth manager of Arlington County, Virginia, my challenge as a city manager had been to provide leadership. In Arlington there is so much so-called leadership that in June 1973 it required a confrontation.

On arrival in Arlington I was quoted in the *Washington Post* as saying that there are two main facets of a manager's job: (1) to be the chief hired hand responsible for quietly, effectively, and efficiently carrying out the policies of the governing body and (2) to prepare and present alternative courses of action from which the governing body can choose and decide on policy. But in Arlington citizen committees, given charters as commissions, proliferated—all in the name of citizen participation and what Arlington politicians call "negative patronage." The results were a growing paralysis and creakiness that not only burdened staffing requirements but, more important, overburdened the members of our governing body.

Arlington was the first county to vote council-manager, in 1932. An ideal situation obtains: only five prime office holders are elected, on an at-large basis for staggered four-year terms. The county board elects its own chairman, who is in fact the mayor, as the county manager is in fact the city manager. The school board is appointed by the county board, whose members also determine funding levels for the schools.

By 1973 the county board earnestly pursued a multiplication of its citizen advisory groups. A planning commission was legally required. But beyond that the board established commissions for transportation, the environment, criminal justice, parks and recreation, neighborhood conservation, fiscal affairs, and human resources. The pitch: to utilize the wealth of talent among the many dedicated people who have come to Arlington from every part of the country. The actual result: paralysis, especially for the members of the county board sifting sometimes conflicting recommendations.

All board members yearned for a solution to a growing malaise, including three-term winner Joseph L. Fisher, now a congressman from Virginia's Tenth District, and two-term winner Ellen Bozman, who set up her own committee to ascertain if there were in fact too many political

actors or prima donnas with whom to deal. No significant cutback was
accomplished, particularly since charters were in effect for many of the
groups and virtually all had been set up on a staggering term of appointment. In fact, some board members argued that if county board members
were given a personal staff they would be able to cope with the mass of
paperwork and reports coming from the manager and from advisory committees and commissions. At one point it was even suggested that reduc-
tions of administrative staff could offset the new positions under the
direct control of each board member.

The principal protagonist for separate staffing was two-term winner
Joseph Wholey, a Ph.D. in mathematics and former Pentagon "whiz kid"
and the hardest-working member I ever knew. Very serious, never much
for small talk, Joe Wholey drove all of us to tears at times in his relentless
search for truth, as he deemed truth to be. Several notebooks are now in
storage, in which staff response to "Wholeygrams" are testimony that
every question, every request for information and for legal definition were
given prompt and professional attention. Wholey is said to have toiled
eighty hours per week, forty as member of the county board and forty as a
research-writer for a "think tank" agency, the Urban Institute.

It was during the development of the budget for fiscal 1974 that the
drive for personal staffing became acute. There were comparisons made to
the staffs provided members of local governing boards in nearby Maryland
counties operating under the elective executive plan. Then there was the
example of the Congress, which does not rely on the existing bureaucracy
but provides an ever-growing congressional staff for guidance. Both examples were, I thought, costly ways of conducting public business. Furthermore, I pointed out that council-manager government is a responsive
unification of power and that my nontenured position and the board's full
power to inquire into conduct and performance were ample safeguards.

There seemed to be no let up, particularly on Joe Wholey's part. The
fiscal 1974 budget was adopted, providing funding for personally
appointed analysts for the Arlington county board, a significant and awe-
some first, if ever I detected one.

When Joe Wholey requested that I have a position specification set
up for these positions my opportunity for confrontation arose. I should
have known Joe Wholey would go through a sequence of excellence by
requesting that position specifications be established. So it was what I was
to include in these specifications that gave me an opportunity for an
appropriate response.

Accordingly, I wrote this memo to the county board:

> This proposal (budgeting for staff assistants) may be a healthy devel-
> opment in the public process—the taste of mustard, the whiff of cordite,
> so to speak. I foresee, however, a likely tension in the relationship
> between the new political appointee and our career people: To whom is

the appointee to be accountable? What will be his/her access to departments for information and analysis? What will be his/her clerical support? His/her staffing interface? The line between policy and administration is never clear cut. There is no substitute for effective communication of purpose and objective. How could this be achieved? I respectfully invite a further delineation of the problems I have identified before further proceeding with Joe Wholey's request that I prepare the job description.

No one responded. No one again talked about separate staffing for members of the Arlington County Board while I continued in office. At this juncture, at least, I successfully halted a plan that would aid and abet the local-government malaise of paralysis by analysis.

Legalisms

Tactical Solutions

L. Perry Cookingham

Following my selection as city manager of Kansas City, Missouri, I attended the council meeting where the appointment was to be made official. I expected that someone would make a motion to appoint me city manager, but the council adjourned without taking that action.

Of course I asked the mayor why my appointment had not come up. He replied that a lawsuit had been filed which, if successful, would prevent my taking office, and the council wanted one more week to consider how to handle the situation. He said the suit, by a group of opposition politicians, cited a provision in the state constitution which required that a person holding public office be a Missouri resident at least one year.

I was already on the job and was being paid an hourly rate as a consultant, and the mayor told me not to be concerned because the council had agreed that if the suit prevailed they would continue my employment as a consultant until I had met the residence requirement.

In addition to filing the suit, the opposition group had organized what they called the "Can Cookingham Club," with the subtitle "Missouri for Missourians. Uphold the Constitution." The club had memberships for one dollar, two dollars, or five dollars. Later, I got one of the membership applications and bought a one-dollar membership. In the meantime the council appointed me to the city-manager position, and the city's attorneys were able to get a delay of court action on the suit until I had been a resident of the state for a year. The council then reappointed me, which made my appointment fully legal.

CAN COOKINGHAM CLUB
KANSAS CITY FOR KANSAS CITIANS

MEMBER

$1.00
CONTRIBUTION

UPHOLD THE CONSTITUTION
MISSOURI FOR MISSOURIANS

CAN COOKINGHAM CLUB
KANSAS CITY FOR KANSAS CITIANS

MEMBER

$2.00
CONTRIBUTION

UPHOLD THE CONSTITUTION
MISSOURI FOR MISSOURIANS

CAN COOKINGHAM CLUB
KANSAS CITY FOR KANSAS CITIANS

MEMBER

$5.00
CONTRIBUTION

UPHOLD THE CONSTITUTION
MISSOURI FOR MISSOURIANS

Membership cards of organization opposed to appointment of Cookingham in Kansas City.

Creatures of the State
Thomas F. Maxwell

Many citizens seem unaware of the limitations placed on local governments, including cities, by our state governments. People don't realize that except for the powers that may have been granted to the cities by the state, through the state constitution or otherwise, so far as cities are concerned the state is sovereign. The state grants, and the state takes away. In other words, cities are truly creatures of the state government and subject to its will. A frustrating incident that occurred in University City, Missouri, illustrates the limitations that may be imposed by state law on a city government.

One of our policemen, in pursuit of a burglar, fired a warning shot. The shot happened to go through the window of a fifth-floor apartment belonging to a lady who had been one of the most ardent League of Women Voters supporters of the council-manager form of government. After passing through her window, the shot hit a mirror and destroyed it.

Fortunately, she was not in the apartment at the time. Quite naturally, though, she was upset over the incident (as was I) and quite reasonably thought that the least the city should do was to reimburse her for having her window repaired and for the value of the mirror that had been destroyed. Of course, I was extremely apologetic about the incident when she called. And when I found it was undoubtedly the act of our policeman, I assured her that the city would take care of the damages.

But when I requested an appropriation to reimburse her, the city attorney ruled that the city was not responsible for property damage caused by a police officer in the lawful pursuit of his duty and that the city council could not legally make the requested appropriation. Members of the council and I offered to personally reimburse the lovely lady, which she refused. But because the incident was discussed in open council meeting, it made the newspapers and was an all-around embarrassment.

This is only one of several occasions when the needs and requests of citizens have seemed reasonably to be within the authority of the city but were in fact outside its jurisdiction. This incident taught me that the city lacks power to do many things. And I learned never to promise anybody the city would do anything that I was not certain we had the legal right to do.

It's the Little Things . . .
Mildred P. McDonald

I empathize with elected officials and private citizens who are anxious to get things done but are hampered by the seemingly unreasonable slowness of government "bureaucrats" and their "nit-picking" and "red tape." From another perspective, this kind of deliberateness is actually a kind of stitch-in-time-saves-nine efficiency. Let me cite two examples from my experience where a little more time taken to check details could have prevented a lot of trouble. Both were the by-products of a controversial annexation program.

I had served a year as acting manager of Southern Pines, North Carolina, when the council appointed a town manager in March 1974 and I resumed my former position as assistant town manager and town clerk responsible for all town records.

The new manager quickly initiated some large-scale annexations. The first addition to the town went through with no protest and no problem. But a 1976 effort to annex four areas, including a large old residential area, two smaller residential areas, and two large industries did not go so smoothly. In fact there were protests on every hand. Nevertheless, the town effected the annexation and began to provide services to the annexed areas.

The annexation was not all that angered the people. Preceding the annexation, we had held a bond referendum for the sewer system for these areas and had just agreed to become part of a regional sewer system administered by the county. The affected people felt the town had added insult to injury by forcing them not only to accept a sewer system they didn't want but were also forcing them to pay for it.

Shortly after the transition, when fire-protection payments had been refunded and the town had begun collecting garbage and providing other services, a group of property owners in the annexed area filed suit against the town. Services had to be stopped, but billing for garbage collection, fire protection, and so on continued. Such confusion you never saw.

Naturally, the plaintiffs' attorney was in the town hall searching records, getting copies of this, that, and the other. He asked me for the Resolution of Intent adopted by the council in connection with the annexation. I searched the council meeting minutes but in vain. The council had acted on a simple motion, with no mention of a resolution. This was only the second time the town had been in an annexation proceeding, other than small areas brought in by petition, and our planner as well as the rest of us had slipped up on the matter of a required resolution. We simply were not on top of things, and of course the lawyers made a great thing of this.

At the first court hearing, the judge ruled in favor of the town, declaring the council's intent was clear even though it had failed to follow the strict letter of the law. The plaintiffs appealed the decision, and after many months the court of appeals ruled in favor of the town but made the annexation effective on the day the case was concluded. This meant a year's delay in receipt of town revenue from the annexed area.

We carefully computed the number of days for which taxes were collectible, and sent out the bills. This also stirred up a hornets' nest of questions and complaints.

At about this time, the town manager resigned, and once again I was designated acting manager. This was just before contracts were to be awarded for sewer construction in the affected areas. The day that work started in the largest residential area, my troubles multiplied. Still angry at having been annexed, and even angrier at having the sewer lines forced on them, residents telephoned me day and night with complaints about the contractor and the way he was laying the lines. They fussed about everything imaginable. They failed to acknowledge that you cannot lay pipe without disturbing the earth, and they were so impatient about clean-up that our public works director was spending his entire working hours and then some trying to keep people happy. We wound up digging up pipe and also having to employ a firm to test the fill and compaction in the areas where pipelines were laid.

The mayor during this turmoil was an architect and life-long town resident. He had been elected by a large majority vote, but his popularity hit rock bottom with the folks in the annexed areas. At the municipal election that occurred during the sewer-construction period, he lost his bid for reelection.

My second example in support of taking time to check details is also in connection with the infamous sewer program. The engineers' plans for the sewage collector system called for some of the lines to cross private property. This made it necessary to obtain a number of easements from the owners, that is, written permission to lay the sewer lines on their property. I personally spent many hours calling on people in their homes, attempting to explain what we were doing and why. But because of resentment over annexation and the sewer assessment, the people were not easily persuaded. They simply did not want to give the town anything.

The public works director and I tried hard to overcome that past bitterness and were generally successful. One notable exception, a good friend of ours, came out of his home carrying a shotgun and ordered the surveyors off his property. He would not budge from his stand, and we had to lay the line along a different route.

We received excellent cooperation from the state highway department in obtaining encroachment agreements for any installations which had to be on state right-of-way. Finally, we had all the necessary signatures on the dotted line, at no cost to the town. This enabled us to lay the lines, build pumping stations, and install all the other facilities. We were elated.

Then one day an out-of-town couple called at my office. The wife and I recognized each other as childhood friends, though we had hardly seen each other since she had married and moved to a town two counties away. After a friendly chat about old times, I was taken by surprise when they suddenly demanded to know why we had installed an unsightly pumping station on their property. I was startled by their question but tried to remain calm and assure them that I would certainly look into the matter and determine what had happened. I felt that since she and I had known each other since childhood we could perhaps work the thing out on a friendly basis.

Subsequent checking of the state right-of-way with highway department officials revealed that on this particular stretch of road the state had no right-of-way beyond the ditch line. This was almost unheard of, but sure enough, our big new sewage pumping station was right on my friend's property. Moreover, because these were absentee owners, we had even overlooked contacting them about the annexation, and they were not aware until they came to town that their property had been brought into the town limits, let alone that a portion of it had been taken over by a lift station.

We had a number of friendly chats about the problem, but friendship and childhood ties did not change their attitude one bit about the pumping station. Their first demand was that it be immediately removed. Our engineers advised us that this was impossible, because the ditch was the only location in which the pump station could adequately handle flows from the area it was intended to serve. Also, the cost of moving it would be astounding, even if we had a place to put it. Nor could we utilize any other point nearby because the same folks owned the whole stretch along that particular road and they were as adamant about one part of their property as another.

We discussed with our legal counsel the possibility of condemnation, but he advised us that in addition to the cost of such an action the amount the court would probably award the property owners would be prohibitive, since this was in a high property-valuation area.

After many conferences and discussions among engineers, attorneys, and the owners, we were able to reach an agreement. The town agreed to screen the pump station totally with landscaping, remove the electric service pole to some distance, bringing in the wiring underground, and pay an agreed sum of money. The dollar amount was much less than it would have been to go through condemnation proceedings, and was in the best interest of the town. Handling the negotiations this way prevented the ill feeling that goes with court suits. We actually came out pretty well under the circumstances, especially considering that we'd been over a barrel.

We have now completed the sewer project. Unfortunately, the testing did prove that some of the work was not done according to specifications.

As a result, we required an extended guarantee period on the work, a bond ensuring this, and a large cash payment both for materials not put in according to specifications and for the full cost of liquidated damages for overrun, allowing only the days we could really justify for weather conditions. We thought this might end up in litigation, but although it might have been easier to allow the number of days the contractor claimed, I could not in good conscience do it. So I just had to take my licks. Perhaps our engineers or our own personnel could have done a better job of inspecting the work as the project progressed, but it was still my position that the contractor should have constructed the lines in accordance with the contract specifications, regardless of our short-comings. After all our assurances to the complaining citizens that the work was being done properly, it was really difficult for me to report publicly that there were discrepancies—that the specifications had not been followed completely. However, I did not want this thing to come back to haunt me at a later date. I would rather put all the cards on the table in the beginning with no surprises later.

These two experiences taught me clearly that it's the little things that trip you up, slow you down, and cost time, money, and peace of mind.

The Separation of Powers Principle
LeRoy F. Harlow

The Sweet Home, Oregon, city charter provided that the city council appoint the city manager (who also served as city recorder) and the municipal judge. The city manager made the other appointments to city offices.

On a couple of occasions when the judge informed the council that he would have to be out of town, the council started to appoint me to serve temporarily as municipal judge. Both times I objected, saying I thought it improper, under the principle of separation of governmental powers, to have the same person who had jurisdiction over the police department also be the judge. In my opinion the judicial branch of the city government should be independent of the legislative and executive branches.

Because I objected, the council appointed someone else, but they didn't like it. It was a bother to them to find someone who could take the time to serve as municipal judge, and they had to pay him extra. They thought I was splitting hairs.

I had heard that some mayors and city managers served also as city judges, contrary to what I thought was proper if people arrested by the

police were to have impartial justice, so I wrote to the then executive
director of the city managers' professional association for advice. I sent
him a copy of our charter and asked (1) whether under its terms the
appointment of the same person to both offices would be in order and,
more important, (2) whether such a dual appointment would be contrary
to the principles of council-manager government.

He replied that he interpreted our charter as requiring the council to
appoint two different persons. He said he doubted there were more than
two or three places where the manager served as police judge or municipal
judge, but he would say it is definitely contrary to the principle of
council-manager government that the manager also serve as municipal
judge. He said further that he believed that even if it were legally possible,
neither the council nor the manager would want the manager to be placed
in the embarrassing positions that are bound to arise when the manager
also serves as municipal judge.

Although some of the councilmen didn't agree, they didn't press me
further on the matter.

Paying with a Dead Horse
James Joshua Mott

The ability to dispose of dead horses is probably not included in many city
manager job descriptions. The ability to bury many things, including
memories—yes, many times. But dead horses, no. So I had to learn the
hard way.

One day in Big Stone Gap, Virginia, I received two telephone calls
from town residents who lived in a section of the coal hills. "A dead
horse," they said, "is beginning to smell. The town ought to do something about it."

"Thank you. I'll look into the matter right away." As taxpayers, they
had a perfect right to raise a stink about it. (Such things, I said to myself,
happen all the time to the savoir faire professional manager.)

It seemed in this instance that a lady who sold groceries from her
home had complained and complained to a man about his unpaid grocery
bill. One day he told her he would give her his horse, which he had tied
to her front porch, if she would be quiet.

Figuring she would not get any money or anything else for the groceries, she agreed.

Next day the horse keeled over and died—without tearing down the
porch, fortunately.

"Unfair contract," she thought. (Remember, this was long before the TV series *Paper Chase,* about contracts.) "Tilt," she said to herself and got in touch with the man.

"Take him or her back. The deal's off. It's gift horses, not payment horses, you don't look in the mouth." To no avail.

There was no humane society or other arrangement for disposal of dead animals in Big Stone Gap. The public works department had (using some initiative, I thought) covered the carcass with coal and tried to burn it. But it did not burn very well. Pulling it away did not work either. It came apart. Result: the telephone calls I had received.

A new mobilization of the works crew finally resulted in the removal of the horse remains. Someone told the lady that next spring the flower bed beside her porch would grow prettier flowers.

Politics

How the "Boss" System Works

Thomas F. Maxwell*

Although he never held a public office, Thomas Joseph Pendergast, the political boss of Kansas City and much of the state, was a master politician–the equal of Boss Tweed of New York and Mayor Daley of Chicago. Vice and corruption were rampant in the city, with full protection of drug-store slot machines, houses of prostitution, night spots with naked waitresses, and almost anything else you can imagine. But Pendergast never permitted any of that to extend beyond 25th Street. Consequently, the middle and upper classes, all of whom lived south of 25th Street, were never confronted with illegal activities in their neighborhoods.

Pendergast was something of a benevolent despot. He had his precinct captains give turkeys to the poor at Christmas and, in the bitter winters, provide coal for those unable to pay. Of course this largess went only to the Pendergast faithfuls.

I was well aware that if you needed an ambulance you didn't call the hospital because they would refer you to the precinct captain, so you called the precinct captain. If somebody who wanted the water turned on his new residence called the water department, he was referred to the precinct captain, who had it turned on–and dropped around to tell the new resident who had performed that service. If you wanted a ticket fixed, you went to the precinct captain. As a matter of fact, if you wanted any city

---

*Tom Maxwell's first municipal job was as assistant to City Manager Cookingham following the Kansas City reform movement that ousted the Pendergast machine.

service, you obtained it through the precinct captain, who usually was carried on the city payroll as a sidewalk inspector. Before the reform government took over, there were sixty-two sidewalk inspectors on the city payroll. We were never able to find a record of a single report from any of the sixty-two sidewalk inspectors that they had found a defect in any sidewalk.

The people of Kansas City adopted a council-manager charter in 1926, but the city manager was under the complete domination of Pendergast until Pendergast's downfall in 1939. In 1940 the reform council brought in Mr. L. Perry Cookingham, a professional city manager who was then city manager of Saginaw, Michigan. Mr. Cookingham served Kansas City for nineteen years. He achieved a dramatic change in city government, which I as a native of Kansas City was able to appreciate fully.

Politics!
Robert M. Tinstman

Oklahoma City, Oklahoma, was without doubt my toughest challenge as a city manager. In 1963 I was recruited and appointed by unanimous vote following a reform election spearheaded by the ARG (Association for Responsible Government). It was quickly apparent that the mayor (a Methodist minister and president of Oklahoma City University) and four others elected on the ARG slate comprised a slim (but solid) majority, the old guard "black hats" remaining entrenched as the other half of the city council. And it will suffice to say that the manager of the local chamber of commerce and the newspaper publisher were not accustomed to dealing with the reform group and a new, "professional" city manager.

Then the mayor resigned to go elsewhere.

During the subsequent months of deadlocked maneuvering to select a new mayor, two of the old guards were considerate enough to tell me a few days in advance that they had nothing personal against me but intended to vote for my termination at the next council meeting. One of the "reform" council members (F. C. Love, who later became president of Kerr-McGee) would then be in South America on business. But the solution to this problem was simple: when the issue of my termination was raised, the three other reform council members left the council chambers, breaking the necessary quorum and the motion of the considerate but determined old guard failed.

My beginnings at Oklahoma City reminded me frequently of Mr. Cookingham's early days in Kansas City. Patronage activities were rampant among council members.

The evidence was clear. The files contained numerous old guard council members' name cards with notes to the personnel director recommending a particular individual for employment. Needless to say, a new personnel director was appointed soon after my taking office.

Rackets were being run in the garbage-collection department. Supervisors were lending money to employees and were requiring that employees buy their large metal trash-carrying containers from the supervisors, and at an inflated price. These activities were stopped, but not before our new superintendent had received threats against himself and his family. For my own part, I had to endure a cussing out from the "lady" terminated as office manager in the garbage department.

At the council meeting following my termination of the finance director (my predecessor as city manager), a large group appeared before the city council. Their spokesman, the finance director's minister, described the former employee's character in glowing terms and demanded to know the cause for the "precipitous" termination. Reluctantly and only upon the minister's insistence, I spent some fifteen or twenty minutes reviewing documents that revealed months of concerted efforts to obtain the director's improved cooperation and performance and which revealed that he had been given an opportunity to resign and avoid the public embarrassment. At the conclusion of my response, the minister conceded that obviously I had certain facts not known to him—and sat down.

Woman Power
Richard G. Simmons

One of my special appointments while serving as city manager of Winter Park, Florida, was that of chairman of the Resource Recovery Council of Florida. We were working under a state legislative act introduced by a legislator from a county that was the home of many beer bottlers. The statute was generally good, except that buried in the contents of the law was a provision that cities and counties could not pass packaging legislation. It was my opinion that the thrust of this provision was to require cities to get into expensive resource recovery programs, which would prevent the buildup of pressure for passage of a bottle bill. If recycling procedures were made a part of the refuse systems, no bottling bill would be passed.

As the result of public hearings around the state, we had a great number of requests that we support a proposed bottling bill. After an all-day hearing on the bottling legislation, the Resource Recovery Council recommended to the Legislature that they support the bill. This prompted the legislator who originally had introduced the Resource Recovery Act to threaten to wipe out our council or cut off all its appropriations. He declared that the council did not have authority to hold hearings on the bottling bill, to which I responded by pointing out our specific legislative authority to make recommendations to the legislature. But he was on an important appropriations committee, so it looked as though we were in trouble.

The week before the legislature was to vote on the bottling bill, I received a letter from the president of the Garden Clubs of Florida. In her letter, she indicated that their organization was supporting the proposed bottling legislation. I happened to notice that the lady was from the legislator's home town. I assumed that she wielded considerable influence, so I called her. I emphasized that I was sure this legislator was a good man and wanted to support the legislation, but said that I felt he had not done his best in supporting the bill and wondered if she could help us with him. She said that she certainly thought she could, that his wife was a member of her garden club, and that when he came home that weekend she would set up an appointment through his wife and see if she could gain his support.

I don't know what happened in that meeting, but I do know that on Monday morning his attitude was noticeably changed and that the Resource Recovery Council survived another year.

Handling the Small-Town Demagogue
Richard G. Simmons

In Melbourne, Florida, the first city in which I served as city manager, the charter required that all five commissioners run at one time and that the five highest vote-getters be installed. This election arrangement produced some unusual results. In particular, there was one woman who had served two or three terms with breaks in between. If ten or more people were running for the five seats, she was elected because she could count on a few regular votes from women, and if enough candidates were running, this small vote would assure her of election. If fewer than ten were running, she lost.

The commissioner was an excellent actress and liked to play the part of the misunderstood widow taken advantage of by the male members of the commission. She had the vocabulary of a drunken sailor, had extensive holdings of apartments and other real estate, and drove a Lincoln, but that didn't inhibit her show at each commission meeting.

She always called anyone who disagreed with her thoughts a louse. Each time before election, she would propose to pave all the streets in the minority area of town without assessment. The fact that we had no money to pave the streets and the policy that we always paved by assessment made no difference. The other commissioners would, of course, have to vote four to one against paving the streets, but at election time she could always say, "I voted to pave your streets, and the louses disagreed."

To say that these performances disturbed the other commissioners is an understatement, and they set out to stop her play-acting before the packed houses looking for the only adult entertainment in town. One of the commissioners found a good solution and became the director of the play which unfolded twice a month on Tuesday evenings. It seems that the woman and her former husband had operated a bar during World War II and were once arrested for selling alcohol on Sunday to underage sailors. This commissioner obtained photostatic copies of a newspaper clipping about the arrest, and when the lady would start her big scene at each commission meeting, he would simply take the photostat out of his brief-case, pass it to her, and tell her that this would be the next item on the agenda if her scene continued. It was amazing to see the abrupt change in her presentation.

Wild suggestions made by the commission minority were reduced drastically.

They Made Their Point
David D. Rowlands

An overflow crowd once attended a Tacoma, Washington, city council meeting at which a dog leash law was to be considered. Just after some opponents of the leash law had spoken, nine people suddenly entered the council chamber, handed each council member a long-handled shovel, and told them to come out to their neighborhood and remove the "debris" from their lawns if the council did not see fit to pass the ordinance. The ordinance passed!

Homestead Exemption and Political Turmoil
LeRoy F. Harlow

Daytona Beach, Florida, had a long history of political turmoil and division within the community, and especially within the city commission. At the root of this difficulty, it seemed to me, was the issue of homestead exemption, which issue caused the commission to split frequently three to two.

The issue arose this way. The Florida state constitution provided that the first $5,000 of assessed valuation of owner-occupied residential property was exempt from general property taxes. In setting the assessed valuation of residential property, the assessor applied a 30 percent assessment ratio to the full value. Thus, thousands of residences whose real market value ranged up to $16,000 and more were assessed at less than $5,000 and thus escaped taxation. The motels, and commercial properties, and the homes worth more than $16,000, carried the tax load.

Few if any black families lived in homes costing more than $16,000, and many white families also lived in modest homes. Most of these homes were concentrated in the two election zones on the mainland side of the city. The motels, beach rental homes, higher-priced homes, and much of the commercial property were in the two election zones on the beach side. The fifth zone, which straddled the inland waterway, was partly on the mainland side and partly on the beach side. It was a mixture, with considerable commercial property.

Candidates for the city commission from the two mainland zones could make almost unlimited promises to voters in their zones, knowing their constituents would not have to pay the bills. The opposite was true on the beach side. Any constituent complaining about taxes was most likely from the beach side, and the chief objection was probably that equipment purchased with tax money would be used much of the time in other areas of the city.

In short, the power to vote for improvements was divided equally among the five election zones, but the burden of payment was distributed unequally. The result: ongoing conflict between the two sides of town, and a two-to-two struggle within the city commission to win the fifth member—even to the point of offering bribes for that tie-breaking vote.

Political Cricket

Thomas F. Maxwell

The long-time mayor of a large Mississippi city was in Columbia, South Carolina, for a meeting just when the local press was reporting our tax decrease. When I happened to meet him at the conference he was attending, he commented that he figured it must be an election year in our city. I asked why he thought that, since it didn't happen to be so.

"Well," he replied incredulously, "why in the world did you reduce the tax rate? We always reduce the tax rate right before elections and then increase it the following year to make up for the loss we suffered from the decrease for the election."

As courteously and gently as I could, I told him that city managers didn't feel that that procedure was exactly cricket.

His response: "Cricket or not, it sure works. I've been mayor for twenty-five years doing just that."

Terminations

Closing a Career
L. Perry Cookingham

I became city manager of Kansas City, Missouri, in 1940, and for fifteen years enjoyed most cordial relations with the city's several mayors and council members as we worked together to make and keep Kansas City a fine place to live. In 1955, two of the members elected to the council made my job more difficult but not impossible. But in 1959 five council members were elected whose campaigns included termination of the city manager.

At the first meeting of the new council nothing was said about my termination, nor was anything said afterward. However, one of the councilmen—a former "Pendergast councilman" but also a good friend of mine—sat in with the newly elected council members at several of their informal sessions. After each meeting he came by my office to tell me what had transpired. Finally he told me that the new council was not going to fire me because they did not want to injure my professional career. "But," he said, "they are going to make it so tough for you that you will wish you had never seen Kansas City."

With this information I felt that after almost nineteen years I had done about all I could do for Kansas City and so announced my resignation, to be effective 30 June 1959, when I would have completed nineteen years. At the same time I decided to get out of the city manager profession. However, I found it impossible to leave without saying "no" to three or four cities that had called me the day I offered my resignation at Kansas City.

One of these cities was Fort Worth, Texas. They would not take "no" for an answer, so I accepted their offer. But I told the council that I would remain only two or three years, during which time I would try to improve the city government and also train a person to take my place. After four years in Forth Worth, I was succeeded by Jerry Brownlee, who had been my budget director in Kansas City and whom I had taken with me to Fort Worth as my assistant.

I would like to add here that I couldn't have had a better wife for the business I was in than Harriette Cookingham. She always encouraged me to do the best job that I could and "let the chips fall where they may," and she was always willing to move on for new challenges. For my part, I never worried about losing our job as long as we did the right thing, because I always felt that if I lost my job in one city we would get another one and it would be a better one than in the city we left. From Clawson, Michigan, to Fort Worth, Texas, that certainly was true of my thirty-six-year career as a city manager.

You Are Welcome to Leave
Richard G. Simmons

In Melbourne, Florida, the first city I served as city manager, I inherited a budget problem. The previous manager having been sick at budget time, the commission had balanced the budget. To avoid cutting services, the commission had overestimated revenues. When I arrived, about five months into the budget period, we were running at a deficit. This required a lot of cutback.

During the same period, the volunteer fire department decided that they needed a new assembly room with pool tables and other recreational facilities—for which there was no money. To win their point, they threatened to go on strike and leave us with no fire department to serve the community.

Without the knowledge of the volunteer firemen, I immediately selected people from the streets department and the refuse department and gave them accelerated training. They were all residents of the city, many had two-way radios in their vehicles, and some had served as volunteer firemen. Then I contacted the National Board of Fire Underwriters and told them our problems and plans. They indicated that they would continue our same fire rating as long as we had an adequate number of trained people.

When the volunteer firefighters came before the commission and threatened to walk out if they did not get their pool table and recreation room, the commission responded that they were welcome to do so, that we had other trained people to take their place. We won the battle.

Three years later we were able to give them the recreation room and pool table.

More than a decade later, after some service in the military and in other cities, I again became city manager in Melbourne. The council was split three to two and was in a bad mood. The previous manager had left after six months because the majority of the commission would not approve some of his requests. And he had persuaded the city engineer to resign.

Before I applied for the job, the former manager told me that the finance director was also going to resign, to show the Melbourne City Council how necessary he was to the community. So when I arrived, I asked the finance director if he was going to stay or, as I had heard, resign. He replied that he would think about it and let me know.

At the time, a controversy was raging over the airport authority's issuing of bonds for airport improvements and pledging that airport revenues would pay the bonds. The controversy was the result of a surprise audit by the U.S. General Accounting Office following a tip that funds were being manipulated at the airport. The GAO was demanding all sorts of information and making life miserable for the commission.

During this time someone from the Federal Aviation Administration showed the mayor and me a photocopy of a letter on official city stationery from the finance director to the GAO. The letter said that funds were being manipulated. The person who showed us the copy of the letter pointed out that he was not supposed to have the letter and that we could not reveal the contents of the letter or its source. It was simply for our information.

The mayor was visibly upset by the charges, which were not true. And although I had been in town only six weeks, the mayor—who was on the majority side of the split commission—felt that I should do something.

The finance-director position was combined with the city-clerk position, and the salary for the combined positions was set as one salary in the budget. The appointment, too, was a combination: the city manager appointed the finance director, and the city commission appointed the city clerk. I called the finance director/city clerk to my office, pointed out that his work was not satisfactory, and told him if he wished to resign he was welcome to; otherwise, I said, I was dismissing him as finance director. He responded with some static, after which I pointed out that the manager was responsible for preparing the budget and setting salaries, and that I considered the finance director's position worth approximately $12,000 a year and the city clerk's $2,000. He resigned.

Without telling the commission why he had resigned, I reported having accepted his resignation as finance director and recommended that they accept it as city clerk. On a three-to-two vote, the commission accepted that resignation.

Part Two

The City Manager
and the Economic System

Why do two out of three Americans live in cities? Why are more than 90 percent of all the jobs in this country in cities? Is it reasonable to assume that there is a correlation between the two figures—that people want to live in or near the source of employment (as well as cultural, educational, and entertainment) opportunities?

Would the employment opportunities exist in the municipalities if there were no formalized local government machinery to provide such essentials as water, sewage-disposal service, and public transit; fire, police, structural, sanitation, health, planning, and zoning services; surfaced and lighted streets and sidewalks, drainage facilities, and traffic control; and, parks, playgrounds, libraries and cultural facilities and programs—not to mention public schools?

The private sector could not function properly without city services. On the other hand, the residents and the municipal governments need the goods and services that the private sector provides. Moreover, the residents need private-sector jobs, and the municipalities need the tax base that only the private sector can provide. Occasionally, a single service cuts both ways. For example, the local government's taxing policies may be good for the municipality but adversely affect the net income of the business. In fact, a single city activity may both help and hinder a private enterprise at one and the same time. For example, the private firm may want planning and zoning requirements to protect its property values but will incur higher costs in complying with those requirements. Of course, the people benefit most when the private and public sectors can devise and carry out policies advantageous to both parties.

In the episodes that follow, one city manager describes in detail how city government and the private sector in two cities reversed critical economic downtrends by joining forces. A couple of managers add a light touch by describing the activities of two ambitious community promoters. Three managers tell how they tackled specific utility problems in their cities.

Accounts of successful cooperation between the private and public sectors show that the two can work together for the general good. We have here also a demonstration that one man making his voice heard often can be decisive in resolving sensitive and controversial public issues. On the other hand, some episodes show how mixing local politics with such life-and-death questions as water for domestic, business, and fire-protection purposes can adversely affect the entire community.

Economic
Development

What Do You Do When
Your City Goes Bust?
Thomas W. Fletcher

One spring day in 1960, when I was assistant to the city manager of San
Diego, an employee of Convair came to my office to warn me that the
giant company was in serious financial trouble because of cost overruns in
their new line of commercial planes, the 880s and 990s. As a citizen, he
was concerned that if they made the choice to go out of business rather
than sell at a loss, the results would be disastrous for the economy of San
Diego.

It was hard for me to accept this warning. Convair was the largest
employer in the San Diego area and one of the major airplane manufacturers in the country. They employed more than 50,000. They had test-
flown their new 880 just the year before and had been making periodic
announcements about substantial sales to major national and international
airlines.

During the next several weeks I made some discreet inquiries but
found absolutely no information to confirm his warning.

One year later, in the spring of 1961, San Diego was in deep economic trouble. Convair had stopped manufacturing airplanes and in the
process had laid off almost 30,000 industrial workers, tripling San Diego's
unemployment rate. Almost all other businesses and construction employees were being laid off. We were in a depression. To compound our economic problems *Time* magazine wrote a feature article titled "Boom City,
Bust City" comparing San Diego with Atlanta. This article had the effect
of heading off additional capital investment in San Diego.

After a series of meetings between government and business leaders, we launched a two-pronged attack to restore our economy. First we organized the business community into action groups. The area's economy was divided into a number of sectors: agriculture, food processing, fishing, shipbuilding, manufacturing, electronics, banking, construction, retailing, tourism, and government. Each sector created its own study commission under the general direction of the chamber of commerce. And each commission was asked to deal with three questions: What is the status of our industry at the present time? What are our opportunities and limitations? What do we have to do to improve our opportunities and reduce our limitations?

These studies were done without federal funding or control. As a matter of fact, a federal economist was quoted as saying that our efforts were doomed to failure because they were *not* under governmental control. But we felt that the only way to get the job done was to involve those who had most to gain or lose. The coordination was provided by a committee of representatives from each economic sector under the joint chairmanship of the mayor and the president of the chamber of commerce.

This unusual government/business partnership was a direct result of our recognition of the political realities in San Diego. First, government and business had never been close. Neither side had seen a compelling need for much collaboration. Because our economy had been stable for years, our contacts had been on an as-needed basis. Second, business leaders generally lived in La Jolla and never really thought of themselves as San Diegans. Third, San Diego was politically very conservative. We were at the peak of the Birch Society influence. Any effort to use federal funds would have been counterproductive.

It seemed that the best approach was to be collaborative, with the city government maintaining a low profile.

At the conclusion of our studies, we adopted an action plan that entailed the continued involvement of each sector. Some of the actions involved the city:

- Recognizing that our geography made rail and truck transportation expensive, the city secured more favorable shipping rates for San Diego industries.
- To encourage tourism, the city implemented a 5 percent room tax, the income to be used in advertising the San Diego area nationwide.
- To encourage industrial development, a large tract of city-owned land was transferred to an industrial-development commission. This land was made available only to outside industries, and the price was based on the number of employees hired. Hiring more employees each year also reduced the yearly payment.
- The city acquired an abandoned navy airfield and converted the buildings for use by "incubator" industries who wanted to get

started. They were given rent-free space for one year and then were
helped to find other locations.

- A HOST (Hospitality Oriented Services and Trades) commission
  was created under the direction of the mayor to provide training to
  employees of businesses with high public contact so that they
  could improve the image of the city.

The other major thrust to restore San Diego's economy was to revi-
talize the downtown business area. Downtown San Diego had suffered
the same decline plaguing major central cities, and the Convair bust was
increasing that decline. A private business organization, San Diegans, Inc.,
had been formed several years earlier to help solve the downtown problem. Members realized that we could not and should not try to return the
downtown to its former retail economy but could and should become a
business and financial center. City studies indicated that we had the smallest square footage of office space in the nation for cities of more than
500,000. Not one high-rise building had been built downtown since the
El Cortez Hotel in 1923.

The members of San Diegans, Inc., came to the city council in the
summer of 1961 and insisted that the only way was for the city to build
its convention center/theater/city hall complex downtown. They claimed
that construction of this facility would stimulate the building of office
buildings.

When I became city manager in September 1961, I was given the
mandate to build that complex, but the city council insisted that the
funding come from a general-obligation bond issue.

And there lay the insurmountable problem. These facilities had been
planned for at least ten years, and a bond issue had been on the ballot six
times during those years. Each election had received a majority vote, but
not the two-thirds required under state law for passage of a general-obligation bond issue. The closest vote had been near 65 percent early in 1960.
The city council thought that by putting it back on the ballot six months
later they would be able to get the necessary few additional votes. But
apparently the citizens were fed up: we got only 52 percent—the lowest of
the six elections.

My judgment was that we had to find a way to build these facilities
without a general-obligation bond election. But how? Finding the money
was no real problem. We already had $3 million in our capital-outlay
funds to buy the three square blocks of downtown property. The $21 mil-
lion for construction could be secured from our own employee pension
fund. Several years earlier, municipal officials had been able to change the
state law to permit the investment of public-employee pension funds in
real estate. Up to this time not one cent of our pension funds had been
invested in San Diego, and our retirement board was ready to begin. The
city government had an additional reason for increasing the earnings of
this fund: we were required to make substantial annual payments to keep

the fund actuarially sound. So we were able to negotiate a mortgage loan from the board at 5 percent interest. Even though this rate was very low, it was still not as low as the current market for general-obligation bonds. If we did not keep the interest rate as low as the bond issue rate, we would have serious political problems.

During this period I was reading the result of a citizen-attitude survey taken to determine why people had voted "no" on our last bond issue. One recurring comment was that because the complex was for the benefit of the downtown interests, they, not the homeowner, should pay for it. There was my answer! Not only for the effective interest rate but for the political acceptance. What we needed was a substantial contribution from the business sector as an outright gift. But we had to hurry. The city council had already set the date when they would have to pass the resolution to put the issue on the ballot. And if it was put on the ballot, it would be defeated and we certainly could not build our complex.

That week I appeared before the board of San Diegans, Inc., and made my proposal. There was a stunned and shocked silence. Then: "A million and a half? You're out of your mind. We can't do it." After they had returned to silence for about five minutes (it seemed like an hour), Mr. Morley Golden, a retired contractor and opera lover got to his feet and said, "I want to see *Aida* in our new theater before I die, and I am already seventy-five. I pledge $200,000." Two other members of the board left to make phone calls. When they returned, we had an additional $300,000. We were one third of the way there.

The chairman of the board appeared before the city council the next day and made the proposal that if they could raise the $1.5 million, the city should go ahead with the construction without a bond election. He pointed out that the voters had always given a majority approval, that they just didn't want it on their tax bills. We had already determined that we could pay the amortization of the retirement loan out of income from the complex, sales tax, and room tax. The council agreed to wait for six weeks. At the end of that time, San Diegans, Inc., had raised $1.6 million, and we were on our way.

Two years later the facilities were opened. Five new high-rise buildings were completed or going up, and Morley saw his *Aida*. The coordinating committee representing all the economic sectors of the community continued to meet for several years, until San Diego's economy was once more moving forward.

Stop Growth!
Thomas W. Fletcher

Between 1950 and 1970, San Jose, California, experienced the most rapid growth of any major city in the United States. Its population grew from 130,000 to almost 500,000, and its area from 40 to more than 130 square miles. Until the late 1960s, with full support of the business community, it had been official city policy to encourage this growth.

Then began a growing unrest in the community. The environmentalists were pointing out the negative consequences of uncontrolled growth and urban sprawl. And they were heard: in June 1969 a new majority was elected to the city council with a clear mandate to stop growth.

The current city manager had been with the city nineteen years. He felt the time had come for him to retire. I accepted the appointment as city manager effective December 1969.

I was aware that it was the council's intent to put the brakes on growth. Consequently, during my employment interview with the council, I indicated that if appointed I would make that my number one priority, but that I could not assure them what I felt should be done until I had had time to study the situation.

In the two months between my appointment and starting work in San Jose, I tried to find what was in the public-administration and public-policy literature dealing with urban-growth control. I found substantial information on growth problems, but practically nothing (besides moratoria) for controlling growth. I visited the Rand Corporation to find out what they knew, only to discover their knowledge was likewise limited. Consequently, when I arrived in San Jose, I found myself caught between a mandate and a vacuum.

My first efforts were to determine the problems that rapid growth had produced. They were many, and serious. For example, because developers wanted to use the cheaper land away from the city center, most growth had been leapfrog type, with long, narrow extensions of streets and utilities. Although our incorporation encompassed 130 square miles, a line around our external limits would have included almost 300 square miles. A map of San Jose looked like a crazy quilt. The city had facilitated this type of growth by making major extensions of street and utility services without the property taxes or service fees to pay for them. The result was a physical arrangement that was costly to the city and confusing both to citizens and to public employees.

During my first month on the job I had a good example of the confusion created by the patchwork development. A citizen came in to tell me of a problem he had. Driving through an intersection, he was hit by another car. He called the San Jose Police Department to report the accident. They asked what part of the intersection he was in when hit. When he told them, they said that that was the county's side of the intersection and that he should call the county sheriff's office. He did. When the sheriffs arrived, they told him that although his car had been hit while in the county, it had landed on the City of Campbell side of the intersection, and that he would have to call the Campbell Police Department! Of course, this kind of confusion contributes to inefficient local-government service, and adds to the costs of police enforcement, fire protection, street maintenance, and the like.

The proper location of public facilities for new residents, and how to pay for them were two additional problems. Parks, libraries, fire stations, and other facilities are located on a radius principle, so that the facilities are in close proximity to those who use or need them. The spotty development meant that there were people living in the area who needed services, but a new facility would not serve enough people to justify the costs of its construction. On the other hand, San Jose voters had stopped approving bond issues. They were tired of paying for facilities for newcomers. The first year I was there we had a multimillion dollar series of general-obligation bond issues on the ballot. Most issues received less than 50 percent of the vote, let alone the 66.7 percent required.

At the same time I was reviewing the consequences of growth, I also started a study to determine the economic impact of a reduction or cessation of growth. Not surprisingly, my economic study indicated that the single largest industry in San Jose was its growth. At least $150 million a year was directly related to growth. This was a bigger economic force than either of our two largest industry plants, International Business Machines or the Food Machinery Corporation. Any serious curtailment of growth would spell disaster. So now I found myself between a mandate and a hard place. I had the basic information I needed, but how did I use it? What I needed was a plan that would eliminate the negative effects of growth, but at the same time would keep our economic life healthy.

First I had the planning department prepare a set of plans that would indicate the service areas of all our existing facilities—streets, utilities, fire stations, schools, libraries, and parks. All these facilities and their areas of coverage were shown on transparent maps. The transparent overlays were laid on our basic land-use maps. We then determined the amount of vacant undeveloped land that lay within the service areas of these facilities—land that could be developed without requiring any major service extensions.

Although there were some obvious facility gaps, we could draw a line around the city, yet still continue to grow at our same rate for the next fifteen years before any extension beyond the developed limits would be required.

From these facts, we drafted a plan that called for the division of the city into two zones: (1) development zone and (2) urban reserves. Development would be permitted in the development zone. No development would be permitted in the reserve area unless the developer would pay 100 percent of all extension costs, and even then only after an economic-impact study had satisfied the city government. (This was several years before the advent of the environmental-impact study requirements we now have across the country.)

Dividing lines between the two zones were called "transition lines." A transition line could be expanded into an urban-reserve area only when growth had moved to the boundary. Our purpose was to assure that expansion would be orderly and cost-effective.

In January 1971 we presented our plan to the city council and the building industry. Both groups approved the plan immediately. But a major hurdle still remained. Most undeveloped land in the development zone was still in the county, and the county supervisors could permit development in these areas if they wished. Fortunately, we were able to convince the supervisors to adopt a policy of not authorizing development within our city's area of influence (about 400 square miles).

The final problem was critical—financing. As growth took place in the development zone, a number of public facilities would be needed. We knew the taxpayers were not going to vote more general bonded indebtedness, so how could we pay for these capital improvements?

I had started having a monthly luncheon meeting with representatives of the home-building industry, and a similar meeting with representatives of the real-estate community. In the first year's meetings we tried to eliminate some of their problems with city government. By the end of that year, we had developed a close working relationship, and when I discussed with them the problem of growth control, they were willing to approve our growth plan.

After we had completed our growth policy, I started talking to them about our capital-outlay problems. I pointed out that we might still have to curtail growth if we couldn't get the necessary funds—about $2.5 million per year at our current growth rate. They also realized that without these facilities they would have difficulty selling their developments. Together the city, the home-building industry, and the real-estate board hammered out an agreement that called for a building permit fee that would raise $1.5 million per year, and a tax on all property sales that would also raise $1.5 million per year, a total of $3 million a year. The additional $0.5 million would be used to rehabilitate public facilities in existing developed areas. This provision was necessary to get the support of the real-estate board because some of their sales were in older parts of the city. The fee rates would rise and fall with growth rates and inflation, which would also match the capital-outlay needs and costs.

When this financing plan was presented to the city council, it was adopted that same night, with the full support of the affected industries. In the next few months other cities attempted to adopt a similar plan, but all went down to defeat because those cities had not prepared the industries nor given them anything in return.

The growth-control plan and the financing plan are still in effect in San Jose, and recently San Jose was selected in a national poll as one of the ten best city environments in the United States.

The Most Interesting Mayor
I Never Met
Charles T. Henry

A city manager's life is not always politics and pressures. Managers sometimes have fascinating, challenging, satisfying episodes. I for one had a unique opportunity to promote community legends when I became acquainted with—but never met, of course—the founder and first mayor of University City, Missouri, Edward Gardner ("E.G.") Lewis. Unlike other mayors I have known, whose incomes were more psychic than monetary, E.G. worked diligently at building cities for personal profit. There is room for only the briefest sketch of this incredible character.

The son of a Kentucky preacher, E.G. arrived in St. Louis near the turn of the century with almost no material resources, but with boundless energy, a pleasing personality, and an adventuresome, creative, superior mind. He started as a door-to-door salesman, then married a woman who bore him no children but fortunately for them gave birth to a feminist movement that flourished for newly two decades.

Foreseeing speculative opportunities in creating a community just beyond the western edge of St. Louis—at the end of the trolley line, adjacent to the soon-to-open Louisiana Purchase Exposition and the proposed location for Washington University—E.G. designed a city for 25,000 people.

He also plunged into the magazine-publishing business, establishing the *Woman's Magazine,* the highly successful and earliest woman's magazine in the country. He and his wife organized the Women's League, also known as the Women's National Republic, which eventually had more than 150 chapters throughout the country. Their magazine promoted women's rights, and the thousands of subscribers supported the magazine.

At this point E.G.'s pet project was to create a women's university. He had eminent architects design an impressive campus of some half-dozen buildings patterned after Greek, Egyptian, and Byzantine temples and covering several blocks. About half the buildings were constructed, including an octagonal tower, the Magazine Building, which was embellished with lions and cherubs on roofs, cornices, and entrances. (This is the present city hall.)

Aware of the economic potential of the St. Louis World's Fair in promoting his new University Heights Subdivision, E.G. erected a summer tent-city with a large dining tent and elaborately furnished smoking-salon tent. He acquired a handsome horse-drawn carriage to transport fairgoers to and from his tent city. To attract the attention of the fairgoers, he installed a gigantic searchlight atop the Magazine Building, the first such in the United States, and sponsored a hot-air balloon cross-country race with attendant advertising.

To finance his many ventures, E.G. developed and promoted through his magazine the first postal savings plan in the United States, complete with elaborately engraved certificates and promises of fat returns to investors. He built his own banking facility opposite the Magazine Building.

In 1906 E.G. incorporated University City and was elected mayor. The city prospered for a few years, but about 1910 he was hauled into court on mail-fraud charges. In his effort to win the court battle he published a book titled *The Siege of University City,* exonerating himself and condemning his enemies. But he lost his university buildings, his postal-banking service, homes, and about everything else. In 1912 he and his wife moved to Atascadero, California, where she purchased the 23,000-acre Rancho Atascadero.

Having a vision of a year-round resort of fashionable hotels for the gentle folk, they built sixty miles of road and laid twenty miles of water mains in a professionally designed subdivision intermingled with orchards. Affairs prospered. An administration building with appropriate statuary was erected, as was the handsome Atascadero Inn, the "Printery," a community building and pool complex, two golf courses, a Cloister Inn resort with the major buildings and cottages at the beach near Morro Bay, and a cannery (by way of commercial enterprise). The colony grew slowly but surely, and in 1917 the community held a grand E.G. Lewis Day to celebrate the accomplishments of their benefactor and leader.

By the middle twenties E.G. had extended himself into additional enterprises, including oil exploration and silver mining. Again he was drawn to creating, planning, and investing other people's monies in a tremendous real-estate development on the Palos Verdes Peninsula in southern California.

Then lightning struck. In its fifteenth attempt, the U.S. Post Office hauled E.G. into court on mail-fraud charges. This time, the Court experience produced more than levy fines and costs. E.G., the beloved leader of thousands of women, friends, and citizens of Atascadero, if not of University City, was dispatched to the federal penitentiary at McNeil Island. Being a model prisoner, however, he was released on probation in the early thirties, only to land back in the slammer for parole violations, as he couldn't keep himself from trying to restore some of his Atascadero fortunes and property dealings—in violation of his parole. Again E.G. was

down but not totally out. He was a popular inmate and was able to promote and create a penitentiary newspaper and library. He became the
warden's private secretary and indeed probably enjoyed himself in the
penitentiary. Upon his release, well into his sixties, he finally decided to
live in quiet retirement in Atascadero until leaving this world with good
conscience at the age of eighty-one.

Epilogue: The Second Siege of University City

What conceivable impact could this improbable and charismatic character
have upon the city manager of University City and the affairs of University City after fifty years? From my point of view, E.G.'s influence sometimes was personal and pleasurable. At other times he and his influence
became a significant community force. On the personal level, he provided
me with a very agreeable working environment in the Magazine Building
with its Florentine carved-marble spiral stairways, its magnificent gilded
copings, its heavily carved oak panelings, its statues of Greek goddesses
and lions, its painted ceiling murals of angelic-looking women holding
cog wheels, electric light bulbs, and other symbols of scientific and industrial progress. It was a pleasure to lean back in my chair on a sunny working afternoon and bask in the colorful shade of beautiful stained-glass
windows while viewing the lightly clad women, perfect in feature and
form, painted on the ceiling of my office. Thank you, E.G.

But E.G. actually made the city manager's life at University City far
more interesting than relaxing. In fact, the pursuit and restoration of
"Lewisiana" memorabilia became both an integral part of the manager's
job and a necessary service to the community of University City. A kind
of historic-preservation fever began to permeate the community.

Unlike Atascadero, where the Atascadero Inn burned, the packing
plant burned, and the Cloisters were destroyed while the town more-or-
less stagnated as a small, sleepy village, University City blossomed into a
truly beautiful residential community of more than 50,000 population by
1960. Most of Lewis's monumental works remain, except the Egyptian
temple, which, after serving as another printing building, and then a
movie-producing studio, was replaced by a magnificent Jewish Reformed
temple. It is now a music institute. Other parts of his university have
become schools and school-administration buildings. The powerhouse was
razed for playground space and city public-safety buildings.

The prosperity and tranquility of University City did not continue
unabated. During the 1960s, racial changes throughout the community
caused considerable insecurity among many residents. Some real-estate
practitioners worked hard at blockbusting, and even the Federal Home
Loan Bank Board headquarters in Des Moines, Iowa, effectively redlined
the entire city by discouraging savings and loan associations lending in

University City. Thus, University City was again under siege by the banking and real-estate community.

Fortunately, all this negative action has been overcome. Today the racial balance is stabilized, housing values in University City have skyrocketed, and private investment in new housing and properties is flowing into whatever vacant land is available.

The numerous techniques used to achieve this result included stricter housing-code enforcement, sustaining high levels of municipal service in all neighborhoods, undertaking major rehabilitation renewal in both private housing and commercial facilities, cultivating strong neighborhood organizations, establishing volunteer house-showing services (to combat real-estate steering), conducting periodic house and garden tours, shaking up the Federal Home Loan Bank Board via Senator Eagleton, and above all, pride in the city and its heritage. Old E.G. and his strange and wonderful works proved to be the focus of much of that latter effort.

The restoration of the 84-inch searchlight is a good example of unique and productive assignments. A very creative member of the city engineering department became so fascinated with Lewis's exploits, the searchlight in particular, that he spent almost all his spare time (and perhaps a lot of job time) running down spare parts and skills necessary to activate this giant searchlight. He succeeded, despite an occasional personal bout with John Barleycorn. Once illuminated, the searchlight attracted people from miles around. (Consequently, on a typical bond-election day, we painted a huge YES on the backside of the searchlight, a gesture good for an extra five hundred supportive votes.) Of course, my job included finding the money and resources to pursue this bizarre project.

However, the greatest demonstration of E.G. as a living force in community morale was our annual spring weekend street festival, a series of events, held around the Magazine Building, demonstrating to the world what a livewire community University City really was, contrary to the ugly mouthings of real-estate agents. The first such celebration started on a Friday night in April with a full-dress, champagne ball held in the city council chambers on the fifth floor of the Magazine Building, where in years gone by E.G. had held balls for his employees. All seats of the council chamber were removed, and huge 1920 Aubrey Beardsley sketches of graceful women were pasted on the walls. Potted palms, champagne by the case, bartenders, and dance bands were brought in. In line with E.G.'s approach to such affairs, a magnificent and fully restored 1937 Cadillac delivered the manager and his family to the entrance, where we were greeted by the city council and a baroque music quartet on the Florentine staircase landing. The ballroom was packed, money flowed freely, and the event was a tremendous financial success as we danced and wined through the night. The next two days included tours through the city hall, reviews and presentation of Lewis memorabilia, and displays. All around the civic center were dozens of ethnic food and beverage stands, games of chance,

City Hall, University City, Missouri. Originally intended as centerpiece for a proposed women's university.

arts-and-crafts stands, and the like. Fifty thousand people flocked to this event from all over the metropolitan area. It was the first one of several such successful annual affairs now held in University City. As with E.G.'s searchlight and tent city of sixty-five years earlier, I am sure many prospective real-estate purchasers have been attracted and impressed. Thank you, E.G., for this fun and for your help. We did well by you.

Although some may remember Mayor Edward Gardner Lewis as simply a cheat and a scoundrel, always too free with other people's money, I and many others think he was a fabulous, thoroughly delightful, charismatic producer, a gifted planner and entrepreneur, even if a rogue. His career as a magnificent manipulator of the American free-enterprise system outshines anything Hollywood has produced, and so I say, "May your blithe spirit live on, E.G."

Where's *Your* Proof?
Thomas F. Maxwell

In Norfolk, Virginia, one of our citizens was an extremely active, vigorous gentleman in his late seventies, a true Virginian whose family went back in the city's history for several generations. I will call him Harry.

As I understand it, at one time Harry was president of a savings and loan company in the city. During the Great Depression, when banks and savings institutions went broke throughout the nation and millions of depositors lost their money, Harry's institution also failed. This was through no fault of his, and no one ever attached any blame to him. Nevertheless, he had a nervous breakdown, and years before I met him he had spent time in a mental institution, where he had recovered fully.

Harry was constantly promoting some type of real-estate complex, usually of enormous size and often involving the city and city-owned or -controlled land. He called on me frequently to discuss his elaborate proposals, none of which ever worked out, and although most of his projects seemed to me to be entirely impractical and visionary, I always listened to him with great respect and real affection.

One day he came to me all fired up about building a parking garage over some existing low buildings and a city street and alley. His plan necessitated acquiring the air rights over the proposed area. He had talked to the private property owners and thought he could acquire the rights over their properties. He wanted the city to provide air rights over the street and alley, and because he could find no one to finance the project, he wanted the city to build the garage and operate it. He backed his proposal with figures purporting to show the demand for parking in the area and costs projections prepared by a traffic engineer he had engaged.

His idea had all kinds of complications that I knew would make the council unwilling to even consider it. However, he insisted on seeing the council. Of course they all knew him, and when I explained the situation, they agreed to meet with him.

At the meeting, Harry outlined his project. Finally the mayor, an abrupt man, said to him, "Harry, you're crazy." With that, Harry reached into his coat pocket, whipped out a piece of paper, shook it at the mayor, and said, "I'm not crazy. Here's my certificate from such-and-such hospital that proves I'm not crazy. Now, where's *your* certificate?"

The shock on the mayor's face was unbelievable. The remark and the reaction had everybody rolling on the floor. The project never materialized, but with the razing of about 40 percent of our downtown district in a redevelopment project, Norfolk became probably the largest parking-lot operator in the whole country—a claim we will relinquish only when the rebuilding is completed.

Public Transit

What Kind of Town?

Dale F. Helsel

For months public transportation had been the focus of much public discussion in our city, Middletown, Ohio. Tom Ortman, manager of the privately owned Ortman-Stewart Bus Company, indicated that his company could no longer provide bus service without a city subsidy. He summarized his viewpoint to the city commission: "Society spends a lot of money for the convenience of the automobile; why not for buses?" The commission responded to Mr. Ortman in writing: While bus service "is essential and should be available, it is the consensus of the City Commission that the City should not use public tax revenues to subsidize public bus transportation in the present form at this time."

In 1972 a June newspaper headline read "Bus Service Here Will Halt January 1 Without Subsidy." This gave me six months to find a solution to the problem. Consequently, I was surprised the following September when, on returning from the ICMA conference, I read "City Buses End Tuesday." Without having had a chance to solve the first transportation-service crisis, I was in another. Only this time, instead of having six months to deal with it, I had five days.

That was a busy September. Besides the bus crisis, we were in the midst of converting refuse collection from a city operation to a private contractor and were preparing to take over ambulance service from private operators. But I simply could not let the bus service cease. A town without public transportation was not my image of what Middletown should be. It was not the kind of town I had been working to build, and it was not the kind of town the elected officials had told me they wanted to see.

Yet the commission did not favor a city subsidy. Only Commissioner Saunders had spoken in favor of subsidizing the private bus company. Commissioner Mary Alice Mack wanted bus service but questioned where the money for the subsidy could be found. Commissioner Sorrell was against subsidizing a private bus company. The fifth commissioner, Tom Blake, wondered if new ways could be found to help the existing service, a position Chairman Inwood favored. Blake asked if supplemental bus service for school children had been explored as a means of increasing ridership. Chairman Inwood noted that bus lines were having trouble throughout the country and wondered, "Are there innovations that could help? So far all I have seen are cutbacks of service and increases of fares." Further, I had told the commissioners that if the city began subsidizing bus service in addition to taking care of present bus riders, bus service to all areas of town on an equal basis might have to be provided. In that case, the subsidy could outgrow the city's ability to pay.

Also, I was remembering my discussion with the Middletown Chamber of Commerce's transportation committee, composed of representatives of our major industries, various businessmen, and our state legislator. We were seated in a large circle in the chamber office, and the chairman started asking each person's opinion, beginning immediately to my left. Member after member said, "Keep the City out of the bus business." One member said, "I don't know why you want to subsidize Ortman-Stewart. You won't subsidize my business." Around the room each one echoed the earlier verdicts: "Public transportation is strictly a private matter. The city has no business in it. If the Ortman-Stewart Company cannot operate without a loss, it should go out of business."

However, the last person to speak was Wilbur Cohen, head of a metal-resource recovery operation and president of the chamber of commerce. He said, "We need buses in Middletown. What kind of town would this be without bus transportation?" In two short sentences, Wilbur had not only raised the issue but also provided me with an answer.

Although I was aware of the commissioners' reluctance to subsidize the private bus company, I didn't want to let the buses stop running without giving the commissioners a chance to change their minds. Filled with excitement provoked by the headline—and the Tuesday deadline—I telephoned Chairman Inwood and requested a special city commission meeting. I wanted the commission to take a positive stand on the question of public transportation. The chairman reminded me that the regularly scheduled meeting was only a few days away. "We can talk about it then," he said.

But next Tuesday was too late. Failing to get the chairman to call a special meeting, I began calling the other four members. One was out of town. One was going out of town and could not attend a meeting anyway. Mary Alice was alarmed that the buses were going to stop.

"What are we going to do?" she asked. "We can't just let them quit running. We have to do something."

I told Mary Alice my problems in setting up a meeting. She replied, "What good would a meeting do anyway?" I suggested giving the bus company a one-month subsidy. That would keep the buses going while we tried to work out a long-range plan of action. I told her the position each of the commissioners was taking on the issue. A few moments later I received a call from Commissioner Choppy Saunders. Choppy said to me, "We don't need a meeting. Go ahead and keep the buses going for another month, as you suggested to Mary Alice." Apparently he had done some telephoning himself and knew there would be support for a short extension.

My next step was to negotiate a month's extension. I asked Mary Alice to go with me because she is an accountant and I thought her knowledge of business accounting would be useful in helping find a proper subsidy. Saturday she and I went to the Ortman-Stewart office located in their main garage, originally a livery stable. We found several old buses there, used for spare parts for the newer models. Mr. Ortman told us he had purchased only two new buses since 1961, and the average bus age was thirteen years. We examined the buses, new and old, perused Mr. Ortman's financial statements, and offered him a subsidy that he agreed to.

The following Tuesday the City Commission ratified a contract for one month at $2,000. Support was unanimous, a five-to-zero vote. Next day the newspaper carried the headline, "City Buses Get Reprieve." Not only did the buses get a reprieve, I got one too—a month. I knew that if one month wasn't enough time to formulate a program, I could get further extensions, which I later did. Of the four necessary ingredients in any public project, I now had an important one—time. The other three—information, public support, and money—would come later.

Richard Clark, my administrative assistant, began gathering information on the hardware side of the bus business. Previously he had worked on a "dial-a-ride" report for the city, so he understood the principles of public transportation. In his words, "It's hard to believe how many little details there are to running a bus company, and how hard it is to find suppliers. For example, the transfer dispenser—you know, the little thing that never wears out. No one makes them anymore." Perhaps that was an exaggeration, but certainly many bus items were not readily available to someone unfamiliar with public-transportation operations.

Richard prepared a budget and a fare schedule. He checked delivery dates on buses, signs, coin boxes, uniforms, and transfer dispensers. He drove his own car along proposed routes. On his drives he stopped occasionally to simulate getting into or out of a bus. In this way he tested the routes and the time tables.

We had a new department of human resources created with Emergency Employment Act funds—a federal project to decrease general unemployment by increasing public employment. I requested the department to conduct a public opinion survey, asking such questions as,

- Have you ever used public transportation?
- Would you ever use buses if they were within two blocks of your home?
- Do any members of your family use the public transportation?
- Do you think the City has any fiscal responsibility for maintaining public transportation in the City?

From this survey we learned that although large numbers of people did not use the system and had no intention of using it, many believed that there ought to be public transportation in Middletown. Some had elderly parents who needed to use the buses. Some felt that in five to ten years they would not be able to drive their own cars and would themselves be dependent on public transportation. Some knew people in the city who were dependent upon the buses and felt that we should supply these people bus service.

Middletown's major employer is Armco, Inc., with its corporate headquarters and largest steel-making operations here. Since its founding in 1900 by George M. Verity, Armco has responded to requests for help in the community. I asked for and received the loan of a systems analyst to help chart the origins and destinations of bus riders, to design a routing system that would meet our needs at the lowest cost, and to determine just who uses public transportation. Using an Armco computer, we established a random-sampling route. From information fed into the computer, a report was prepared showing the age distribution of the riders, purpose of the trips, and suggested route and time changes.

Because of the arguments against subsidizing a private business, and because of the perceived inability of the private bus company to respond to public needs, I concluded that the only way to keep public transportation in Middletown was for the city to assume the responsibility.

At just this time a federal revenue-sharing program was announced that would make federal money available to cities for new projects. It was to be a three-year program. I thought that within that three-year period, public transportation would become important enough in our city to be supported by our own resources.

I went to the city commission armed with the public-opinion survey, the Armco profile on bus riders, and a budget that included a suggestion to spend a portion of our first year's allocation of general revenue-sharing funds to purchase buses. My proposal to the commission allowed the private bus company to cease operations at the first of the year and the city to begin operations immediately thereafter, with new buses. Included in the proposal was a new routing system that took in the shopping centers, the hospital, the branch university, and the high school. The proposal was accepted, and on 2 January 1973 the city's brand-new buses began operating.

The buses were painted purple and white, our high school colors. They were small, carrying only nineteen passengers. They operated on fixed, half-hour routes from a central point. Whenever necessary, we have made changes in transfer points, routes, and schedules. The ridership increased steadily in the first year and has more than doubled in the six years we have been operating.

Public transportation and the city's operation of it have been accepted. The issue of private versus public ownership is no longer debated in Middletown. Although the price of gas has more than doubled and the price of labor has increased by two-thirds, the bus system has managed to maintain the same fare structure these six years. Federal and state subsidies have enabled us to keep the city's share of the program fairly constant over the years even though we have continued to buy modern buses and add routes.

To update the question Wilbur Cohen asked at that chamber of commerce meeting, one might ask, "What kind of city is Middletown today?" I can answer: It is a city that cares for the citizens who do not have automobiles to transport them. It is a city that makes low-cost transportation available to its citizens so that they can visit banks, doctors' offices, grocery stores, the hospital, government offices, schools, friends, and places of employment. Finally, it is a city where even a pleasant bus ride around town is possible.

Water
Problems

Muddy Waters
Oliver S. Merriam

At age thirty I was ready for my first city manager position, I thought. I had prepared for eight years: a carefully selected graduate school, an internship, two assistant city manager jobs under known and respected professionals, and a deep personal commitment to the cause of effective local government.

I was concerned that the average tenure for city managers in North Miami Beach, Florida, was only a little over eighteen months, but in my interviews with the city council they assured me that the majority wanted a professional city manager like me. Perhaps the invocation at the council meeting in which I was sworn in should have warned me. The Reverend Hazel Gaines, a middle-aged black gentleman who worked as a city refuse collector prayed, "Bless this poor lamb, our new city manager." But in 1974 the citizens of North Miami Beach needed the progressive style of government I was prepared to bring.

The public hearing on allocation of taxicab licenses, which preceded my second employment interview on that day's council agenda (an indication of the importance the council placed on the selection of a city manager), turned into hours of haranguing between the mayor and opposing council members. But it took me some time to understand that issues were seldom put to rest in North Miami Beach; rather, they were dug up and dragged into the foray again and again, year after year.

The conduct of city business provided a sort of intermission between the marathon arguments. Soon I perceived that the city council's civic duties included providing free entertainment to the many listless old folks in their audiences. I observed day-dreaming senior citizens perk up as the volume of councilmanic debate increased. The steady drone of gossip in the back of the room would hush, then the old gents who had been exchanging anecdotes and shaking hands with elected officials in the out-side hallway would shuffle back in. An especially excited citizen would arise, take the open mike in the front of the room, break into the debate, and accuse one councilman or another of stupidity (or maybe all the council members—or even all the citizens—were stupid), and the audience would roar and stamp their feet to show their approval. Then a member of the council would reply with a caustic remark, and there might be grumbles or laughter from the audience, depending upon the council member's wit.

It was a special kind of game without any written rules. The council members knew and understood that points were awarded for verbal abuse heaped upon the opposition and for shot-from-the-hip remarks that drew laughter and catcalls from the audience. The attention of the local news-papers, and particularly the appearance of one's name in print, was a real prize. Better yet was a quotation or (wonderful best of all forms of hap-piness!) a newspaper picture of the council member. Eventually I came to concur with the Miami Beach newspaper's description of our council meetings: a circus complete with animals and clowns, the mayor the ringmaster.

The convoluted interrelationships of personal rivalries and animosities, value systems, local politics, and whatnot reflected in our city council, compounded by the intergovernmental politics of other units in the met-ropolitan area, are beyond the scope of this account. There is space enough to highlight in outline form only one of the city's problems, the issue of municipal water supply.

The city's water system had been acquired and developed in a piece-meal fashion. Salt water had infiltrated into the oldest municipal well fields because, as fresh water had been pumped up from the porous, water-filled rock below, salt-laden groundwater from the eastern coastal areas flowed in. The city had been forced to develop new wells to the west, away from the ocean's intruding salt water. The city had purchased two small systems that provided a better water supply, but the terms of pur-chase provided that the city would provide continuing water service to customers in the unincorporated area, beyond the city limits, and that the city would permit water connections to new customers as the land was developed.

During April, May, and June (the dry season in South Florida), resi-dents who live on the ocean side of the salt-water intrusion line can't use their own brackish well water and pumps to irrigate their lawns. And in the subtropical sun, lawns that aren't irrigated turn brown quickly. Thus, in the dry season, the demand for city water increases.

Because the water-plant expansion program had been delayed by litigation, and because the development boom along the coastal area had increased the demand for city water, the water plants weren't able to meet the additional dry-season demand. But if the water-distribution mains weren't filled with water pumped from the plants, the pressure in the mains could fall below the critical lower limit of twenty pounds per square inch. Below this pressure the untreated groundwater surrounding the buried pipes could seep into the mains and contaminate the potable water supply. That would be a public health disaster.

Our water system was part of the utilities department, whose director was John Marchaise. John was a large man, overweight. When we first met, he was visibly nervous, his palms wet with perspiration when we shook hands. He spoke rapidly in clipped phrases and incomplete sentences. Before he had finished telling me about one problem, or before he had completed an idea, he would run on to the next problem, not allowing time for a reply, nor wanting one.

He tried to tell me he was getting along all right with most of his employees but that the greatest problems of the utilities department had been created by a political club called the Property Owners Association. This group had put council members Taylor, Helfand, and McDonald into office. In turn, these council members had appointed a club leader, Joe Moffat, to a vacancy on the utilities commission. Joe Moffat was a persistent, vocal obstacle to the conduct of utilities business. Moreover, the same political club had been blocking utility improvements for years, first by opposing utility revenue-bond issues in local elections and then by introducing obstructive legal proceedings.

When the flow of visitors to my office had subsided sufficiently to permit me to begin to organize my own work schedule, I asked John to take me on a tour of the plant facilities. John chose instead to take me out to lunch in the company of Bert Lobel, the former city attorney, who, in the face of objections from the utility commissioner, Joe Moffat, was clinging tenaciously to his $9000-a-year post as the legal advisor to the utilities commission. On the way to the restaurant, John and Bert proudly pointed to a number of large condominiums along the coast that were outside the city limits but connected to the city system. It was good business, they said, to encourage these connections: the new customers would eventually pay for the plant expansion and system improvements through their water bills, while the city residents would, in effect, become the owners of a more valuable utility-plant system.

Councilman Taylor also visited me in my office, where he willingly explained his point of view. First he pointed out the tall condominiums that could be seen in the distance from every window of the city hall. These buildings marked the city limits, he said. Metropolitan Dade County government officials had permitted the city to be surrounded by huge populations of new condominium residents, and while those huge new structures contributed nothing to the city's tax base, the great influx of population had destroyed the city's quiet suburban atmosphere. The streets were now crowded with traffic, and the city's water and sewer systems were hard pressed to keep up with new service demands. These high-rise buildings cast their shadows everywhere, blocking out the treasured Florida sunshine and the precious sea breeze.

Taylor explained that he and his newly elected friends on the council had ordered John Marchaise to stop expanding the utilities service district into the unincorporated area of Metropolitan Dade County. Specifically, he had directed Marchaise not to allow any new water connections to major new developments. Marchaise, he said, had deliberately violated this directive when he permitted a connection to a new condominium development many miles to the west of the city on the northwestern edge of the utility's established service district.

One nice spring day, after ten hours of budgeting, signing checks, shaking hands, and answering telephone complaints at city hall, I came home to find that our water wasn't running. As a matter of fact, in the upper floors of the building *nobody's* water was running, and a crowd of angry residents was milling around the elevator entrance. Although the building superintendent was nowhere to be found, he had posted a notice on the mailbox wall, inside the lobby doors. The superintendent's notice said that mud in the city water had caused the building's water pumps to break down.

Our building-inspection department head, Bill Corcoran, was soon on the scene. Bill found the building superintendent. He also found that the building's water pump had developed electrical problems many weeks before. The electrical repairman had switched on the auxiliary pump, but he didn't complete repairs on the primary pump because of a dispute with the building superintendent over an unpaid service bill. Then the auxiliary pump failed and the water quit running. In the face of the residents' wrath the dispute was quickly settled and the water service was restored by sunset. I wished that all our city water problems could be so easily resolved.

I was upset with our building superintendent for placing the blame for his own laxity upon the city water supply, but he was only one of hundreds who were doing likewise. The managers of many down-at-the-heels, twenty-year-old motels along the ocean front were demanding that the city repaint their swimming pools and replace their aging plumbing and air-conditioning equipment. They claimed that the city's dirty water had stained their pool paint and damaged their plumbing facilities. Angry housewives were complaining about their splotchy laundry, and a local dentist was demanding that the city replace his chair and expensive dental equipment that he said had been damaged by the mud in the city water.

Of course our water customers were neither aware nor concerned about some of the technical problems at the water plant, which I was rapidly learning about from our operators and a federal inspector from the

Occupational Safety and Health Administration. Our customers were disturbed about the mud that splashed on their toothbrushes, settled in their drinking glasses, in the laundry water, and in water heaters, toilet bowls, and elsewhere. Angry citizens brought jugs and tumblers filled with dirty water to the city council meeting. And then Dr. Stasslaw, the public health director for Metropolitan Dade County, released a prime-time evening news announcement advising North Miami Beach water customers to boil their water before drinking it. That was when things really got hot!

The city council was behind the proverbial eight ball. This precipitated an angry debate about who was to blame for the dirty water. The mayor blamed the utility commissioner, Joe Moffat, and his friends in the property-owners association who had tied up the water-plant improvement program in litigation over the wording of a 1973 bond-referendum ballot question. The litigants had complained that the wording of the ballot question had "promised" the voters $1 million in federal aid to improve the utility, and Uncle Sam had made no such commitment.

Councilwoman Margery McDonald came to the defense of her friend Joe by presenting a demand, addressed to the Army Corps of Engineers, that the army promptly provide the city with water from Lake Okeechobee (more than a hundred miles to the north). Councilman Tony DeLeonardis replied sardonically that our city really had no water problem. Lots of fresh water was available in the ground, he said. All we needed were more wells to pump it out. The mayor ended the debate at about midnight by proposing that the city clerk forward all the dirty-water complaints to the city manager. The city manager, said the mayor, would, of course, be responsible for finding a prompt solution to the water complaints.

The next morning's *Miami Herald* quoted Councilman DeLeonardis's statement that we really didn't have a problem. When Dr. Stasslaw read this, he responded immediately with a moratorium prohibiting connections to the North Miami Beach water system. The Dade County Department of Environmental Protection followed with a similar moratorium.

It is important to note that these two Metropolitan Dade County government departments—public health and environmental protection—were rivals for the power to regulate water and sewer utilities in their jurisdiction. And then yet another county agency made its presence known: the Dade County Utilities Commission. This commission, which regulated the rates of privately owned utilities, announced it would immediately schedule public hearings in the North Miami Beach City Hall to provide our customers further opportunity to air their complaints.

This outraged our city council members. They urged the city attorney to swat back at these pesky county officials, but the attorney demurred. Instead, he announced his own plan: residents with even-numbered addresses would water lawns only on even-numbered dates, odd-numbered houses on odd-numbered dates. In the resultant publicity surrounding this announcement, he was the man of the hour.

At about this time, Utilities Director John Marchaise suffered a heart attack. Unable to return to his job, he arranged to retire, and I became the acting director of public utilities.

The mayor proposed that North Miami Beach sell its utility system to Metropolitan Dade County, as the City of Miami had done several years before. But my explorations with the county authorities were unproductive. The mayor also proposed that the city appeal to the federal government for assistance. Although my pursuit of federal aid to bail out the city's ailing water utility was not fruitful, the continuing publicity about our water problems did bring us some notable visitors from Washington. On one Friday evening in June, the mayor's secretary called to tell me to be at a certain water plant the next morning, following a previously scheduled bikeway dedication ceremony. Late Saturday morning I met the mayor at the water plant, and Congressman Lehman appeared with several of his staff aides. The congressman advised us to stay put until his colleague Mo Udall (then an unofficial candidate for president) arrived. Upon Udall's arrival, Congressman Lehman trouped across the street, cameramen and reporters in his wake. He asked a neighbor lady if she would provide him with a sample of her water. Shyly the lady obliged, and the cameras clicked and whirred. Holding the glass of water up where everyone could see it, Lehman led the parade back across the street to the city's water plant, where he triumphantly presented the glass to our laboratory technician for "swift testing." The technician also obliged and in a few minutes reported, almost apologetically, that the water sample was clean. Water samples, he continued, had been passing the laboratory's tests for color, pH, turbidity, and chlorine content for most of that week. Now Mo Udall turned his head slightly toward me, showing the photographers his handsome profile, his blue eyes fixed on the distant western horizon. "We also have water problems back in my home state, Arizona," he said to me in an understanding tone. "We have to dig our wells hundreds of feet down."

Later, Congressman Lehman was to respond to our appeals for help when he announced that the EPA would test our water for carcinogens. Still later the congressman angrily announced that the EPA had tested the "wrong" water supply. They had looked for carcinogens in the Metropolitan Dade County Water Sewer Authority system. That was about the extent of federal aid to the city water utility.

Dade County's regulatory utility commission soon began their series of hearings at our city hall. The chairman of the commission announced that the purpose of the hearings was to determine whether or not the utility's municipal owners (our city's residents) ought to be fined for providing themselves and the other residents of the county with poor-quality water. The inspectors from the Dade County Department of Environmental Affairs announced that they had tested hundreds of samples of poor-quality city water. The city attorney defended by cross-examining the inspectors, demanding proof, demanding to see the samples, and demanding that each of the water samples be linked by an unbroken chain of evidence to the city's water-supply system.

The county health department officials were more helpful. In addition to the suggestion they had repeatedly made before, that I fire the utilities director in exchange for their lifting the moratorium, they suggested I seek the technical expertise of Florida's foremost expert on water-treatment chemistry, Dr. James Singley of the University of Florida. I followed the latter suggestion.

Dr. Singley's first report to me, which he delivered orally in the privacy of my office, was that the condition of our water-treatment plants was indeed the most deplorable he had ever seen, anywhere, in his many years of consulting.

It wasn't for lack of effort on my part that I elicited little more than sympathy and free advice from my fellow managers in the area. Although steadfastly congenial and sympathetic, the Metropolitan Dade County Manager and his staff representative steered clear of our water issue. The manager of neighboring North Miami, on our southern border, was also most sympathetic. I think he truly perceived a number of mutually advantageous possibilities for a productive work relationship between us. However, when our city council proposed to their city council that the water-distribution systems of our two cities be interconnected in the interests of cooperation, goodwill, and fellowship among the elected officials, the North Miami city manager and his utility staff were less than enthusiastic. After reflecting on the problem for a month or two, their utilities director suggested that fire hoses might be utilized to provide a temporary interconnection between the two systems in the event of an emergency on either side. But, of course, these 6-inch canvas hoses could come nowhere near supplying the 35 million gallons consumed in a peak day by the North Miami Beach water customers.

Dr. Singley had agreed to provide our plant operators with on-the-job training while he was developing his written recommendations. When he presented his report to me, it contained two sections. The first dealt with a number of recommended technical modifications to the plant controls and processing systems. I gave these recommendations to the consulting engineer with directions to review and implement them with all possible speed and keep me informed on the schedule of implementation. The second section dealt with the reorganization of the utility department and the institutionalization of the training program Dr. Singley had started.

I assumed personal responsibility for implementing the reorganization. I got the reluctant civil-service commission to approve some necessary job-class specifications, persuaded John Marchaise to accept a disability retirement, and recruited and hired a new utility director.

Our utility's consulting engineers proposed that a short term, two-year, plant-facilities improvement program be financed with an $8.5 million revenue-bond issue. A majority of the utilities commission agreed that their fiscal advisor, Stanley Cohen, should prepare a water-rate schedule that would provide income sufficient to support the debt-service requirements of the proposed revenue-bond issue, plus the senior debt outstanding. But Commissioner Joe Moffat was openly suspicious of the consulting engineers, and he, alone among the utility commission members, was unwilling to proceed.

Shortly after the master plan was presented, Joe's friend, Benjamin Kurtzman, a fellow director of the Property Owners Association, called me and offered to set up a meeting with Joe in my office so that we might reconcile our differences about the consulting-engineers' report. When the three of us met around my conference table, Joe explained that he was concerned lest the city provide water to those new high-rise developments closing in on our town. Joe proposed that the city build plant facilities large enough to meet the needs of city residents, and that none of the new plant production capacity be made available to those odious condominiums outside the city.

Bringing out a map of the water-distribution system and pointing to the grid of water mains, I explained to Joe that the system was interconnected in such a way that it would be impossible to isolate our customers in the unincorporated area. Further, I explained, it would not be legally permissible to discriminate against customers in the unincorporated area. All the customers were paying equally for their water, and for their new water connections, too, and they were legally entitled to potable water. But Joe wouldn't listen. He was sure we could find a way to separate our facilities and provide the best water to city customers. No amount of reasoning would change his mind.

The three council members supported by the Property Owners Association, McDonald, Helfand, and Taylor, all echoed Joe Moffat's suspicion of the engineers' motives for recommending the utility plant improvements. And like Joe they raised questions about the "finder's fees" that the financial consultant (yet to be selected) might charge. (Special bond-marketing consultants customarily charge their municipal customers a negotiated percentage fee for the printing of a prospectus, for legal counseling, and for helping the municipality solicit bids for its bonds.) At a city council meeting, Milton Starkman, a local attorney, city council candidate, and director of the Property Owners Association, rose from the audience to take the open microphone. In a smooth, deep-voiced, convincingly sincere manner he intoned that anyone who studied the engineer's report as carefully as he had would find that the $8.5 million proposal was "only the tip of the iceberg" and that "even more" construction would be proposed in future years.

A heated, free-wheeling debate ensued among the audience and the council members. Three council members loudly opposed the revenue-bond issue. Four of the council members were quietly impressed with the unanimous recommendation of their consulting engineers, their utilities finance expert, and their special legal counsel, but they seemed reluctant to speak to the merits of the recommended program.

Now the mayor turned to me and asked for the city manager's recommendation. I briefly reviewed my own work with the engineers, our auditor, and the circuit court and responded that I was in accord with the engineering, financial, and legal advisers.

The city council voted to adopt the rate schedule that would finance the recommended improvements, and they appointed a councilmanic committee chaired by Councilman Rubin to select a firm that would help the city market its revenue bonds. However, the four council members who appeared to support the improvement program also voted to hold a referendum at the next local election so that the voters could decide whether the utility should proceed with the $8.5 million revenue-bond issue. Though I didn't know it at the time, these same four council members had decided not to run for reelection. Their three council opponents would run, though, and their opposition to the water bonds would be their principal campaign issue.

The city attorney had advised the city council that the laws of Florida did not require a referendum election on the matter of whether or not the utility should issue self-financing revenue bonds, but the four council members who proposed the referendum question explained that they had made some promises to their friends in the community that they would allow the voters to decide the merits of the proposed water-revenue bond sale. After the city council had determined that a referendum would be held, the mayor, with the concurrence of the council, directed me to see that no city funds whatsoever would be expended to provide the voters with information about the meaning of the referendum question.

I had been city manager ten months when I received a letter signed by ten officers and directors of the Property Owners Association. They wrote that they believed "the City Manager has the basic ability and desire to do a good job for the City of North Miami Beach"; however, they wanted the city manager to refrain from getting involved in "policy making." Specifically, they mentioned the water-bond issue. The signatories were the husband of Councilwoman Marge McDonald (ex-Mayor Bill McDonald), the wife of Councilman Helfand (Democratic Party Committee Member Rosslyn Helfand), Mr. Ben Kurzman, Sam Opsheler, and several other citizens who had been drifting in and out of my office for ten months.

At about this time the utilities commission commanded Dr. Singley to appear and explain to them the meanings of many of the mysterious technical recommendations contained in his report. I introduced Dr.

NORTH MIAMI BEACH PROPERTY OWNERS ASSOCIATION

P. O. BOX 574
NORTH MIAMI BEACH, FLORIDA

February 14, 1975

Mr. Oliver Merriam
City Manager
City Hall
North Miami Beach, Florida.

Our Board of Directors believes that the City Manager has the basic ability and desire to do a good job for the City of North Miami Beach; however, we feel that the City Manager has shown a tendency to inject himself in the policy making process instead of concentrating on his duties of attending to the administration of the City's business.

It is not the function of a City Manager participate in the policy making process of the City Officials who are charged with that responsibility. We have observed the City Manager involving himself in a number of policy matters of the City, such as the Water Bond Issue, which is not within his province.

We request that you carry on as our Chief Administrative Officer and put into effect the policies as they are determined by our City Council.

Respectfully yours,

Officers and Members of the Board of Directors

[signatures]

cc: Mayor & Council

Property owners organization in North Miami Beach, Florida, objects to the city manager's participation in efforts to solve the city's water problems.

Singley to the commission at its next regular meeting, explaining that the consulting engineers were cooperating with Dr. Singley in the implementation of the recommended water-plant modifications. I further explained that these plant modifications were being financed with revenues produced by the recently adopted in-plant connection fees, and that the lifting of the moratorium would result in a number of new connections and fee collections.

Some commissioners did not appear too interested in Dr. Singley, the implementation of his recommendations, the financial condition of the utility, its rate schedules, or the status of the receivership litigation. The secretary and chairman of the commission, for example, seemed to be more interested in talking to me about their recent loss of authority to order supplies and services and to pay by writing checks against the utilities funds (the city manager's new purchasing regulations had terminated these privileges). But Joe Moffat had asked, and was prepared, for Dr. Singley's appearance.

"If we do all the things you think we ought to at the water plants," Joe asked, "will the water be clear?"

"Yes," Dr. Singley replied. "I think the water-quality problem can be cleared up."

"Well then, is there any reason why we need to implement the $8.5 million plant-improvement program that the engineers say we need?"

"My contract did not provide for that. The engineers are talking about future water demands and production requirements. I'm talking about what can be done right now to improve the efficiency of the chemical-treatment process. I'm a chemist, not an engineer."

"Well then," Joe pressed on, ignoring the fine distinctions between chemists and engineers, "don't you think we could get by with, say, a $4 million bond issue rather than the $8.5 million the engineers think we need?"

"I really can't say," Dr. Singley replied. "That wasn't a part of the study I contracted to do."

"But you do think that if we do all the things your report says should be done, we can have clean water?"

"Yes."

"That's all I wanted to hear." Joe was convinced that Dr. Singley had denied the need for the $8.5 million bond issue. (At least that was the claim in campaign literature later distributed by the Property Owners Association.)

A week after I got the letter signed by the officers and directors of the Property Owners Association, I received an invitation from their program chairman to speak to their next regular monthly meeting. I accepted immediately, and a couple of weeks later I addressed their general membership meeting. I told them about the considerable progress achieved in a number of areas since I had joined them as city manager eleven months before. I mentioned the new twenty-four-hour citizen-complaint answering service, the completion of the recreation center and the new municipal garage, the addition to the public safety building, several storm-drainage projects, the paving of dusty alleys, improved street lighting, new playgrounds and bikeways, a municipal nursery and beautification projects, a new day-care program for low-income mothers, a hot-meal program for the elderly, new fire-rescue equipment for heart-attack victims, a new police helicopter patrol, and (in response to the boat-owners' requests) a police marine patrol. Also, I pointed out that we had initiated several employee-training programs, including water-plant-operator training and an innovative truck-driver course for sanitation workers, cosponsored with North Miami. Through mechanization we were improving productivity in the collection and disposal of refuse, and we were introducing data-processing to the city. We had negotiated labor contracts with our three employee unions and were enjoying labor peace. Partly as a result of our tight-fisted management of public dollars and aggressive pursuit of state- and federal-assistance programs, we had achieved a balanced budget and also accomplished a significant reduction in the property tax. Then I reminded the audience that the average tenure of professional city managers in North Miami Beach was eighteen months and, in view of the directive I had received from their board of directors, I did not expect to remain in the service of the city too much longer. I then read to the general membership the directive their board of directors had sent me.

I explained to the audience that I believed that the quality of the public water supply was a proper concern of their city manager and that, in fact, the city council had directed me to do something about the deluge of muddy-water complaints we heard at the time I had started working for them. I then explained how the consulting engineers and I had developed a plan for utility-system improvements, and I invited questions from the audience.

A lady in the audience responded angrily that the traffic congestion and crowded conditions everywhere in the city were the fault of the surrounding condominiums. She wanted to know why we had to build plant facilities to serve the new developments. I expressed my appreciation of the problems brought about by rapid growth in the unincorporated areas but explained my belief that our best hope for rational control of development in Northeastern Dade County would be to pursue cooperative planning efforts with the Metropolitan Dade County government, and, concurrently, to seek annexation of the surrounding unincorporated areas. Refusing good-quality water to the unincorporated areas was a self-defeating strategy. This was so because the water distribution system was so interconnected that city and noncity customers alike would suffer if the city didn't authorize investments in needed water-plant improvements. To do otherwise would be like cutting off our noses to spite our faces.

I heard Joe Moffat mutter in the back of the audience, "Merriam's gotta go." And, like the echo of distant jungle drums, old Bill McDonald was murmuring repeatedly, "Yeah, he's gotta go, he's gotta go." I watched him shake his head from side to side, his way of showing friendly agreement with Joe.

Because election day was a city holiday, I spent the afternoon resodding the front lawn of the little house we had purchased in a quiet neighborhood about five blocks from the city hall complex. While I was standing in the front yard, shovel in hand, the mayor pulled up in his big station wagon and shouted a loud "Hello." The back of the wagon was filled with campaign literature. The mayor explained that he was out campaigning against Starkman, Helfand and McDonald (he called the latter two the Bobbsey twins because they always voted alike), and Taylor (whom the mayor disliked more than any of the others). He seemed confident of victory. Actually he was never more out of touch with the realities of the local political situation.

On election night, the city clerk, the municipal judge, and I served as a board of canvassers. We visited the polls, checked the voting machines, and tallied the votes registered on the machines. At about ten o'clock that night we returned to city hall to open the absentee ballots and announce the election results.

The impact of the property owners' superior campaign organization was obvious. In addition to months of dedicated doorbell ringing, the property owners' candidates had attended meetings in nearly every condominium in our eastern shores. They had enlisted the support of the Italian-American Welfare Club and the North Miami Beach Chapter of the Senior Citizens Association. And they had the benefit of campaign know-how contributed by members of the regular Democratic organization. All but one of the property owners' candidates were elected. Four of the successful candidates, including McDonald, Helfand, and Taylor, had actively campaigned against the water-revenue bond question, and the other three had promised that if elected, they would undertake a "serious study of the need for more water bonds." The bond proposal itself was soundly defeated by a two-to-one margin.

In the final weeks of his term, the mayor became much more friendly, almost sympathetic, to me. One of his last official acts was to write a nice letter of recommendation for me "just in case I might need it." I hadn't asked for the letter, but I thanked him anyway. Councilman Levy sent me a similar letter. He commended me for my professional nonalignment among the factious members of the city council.

The newly elected mayor and council members faced a dilemma of first magnitude. Even though the local voters had indicated their opposition to the bond proposed, clearly something had to be done about the shortage of water-production capacity. The dry season was upon us once again, and, in spite of recently completed improvements, the plants were still operating dangerously close to their peak production capacity. Construction of major new production facilities would take at least twenty-four months—once the city had decided to proceed.

Fortunately the new mayor exercised good judgment and displayed a capacity to reconcile the quarreling factions of the city council. He scheduled a series of joint meetings of the city council and the utilities commission. The city council normally met for an "executive session" on Monday nights preceding Tuesday night's "official" council meetings, and, happily, these "executive sessions" coincided with the utility commission meetings. The mayor sought assurances that Joe Moffat would be in attendance at the joint meetings.

At the staff level we continued to seek the assistance of the Metropolitan Dade County Water and Sewer Authority. The Authority's director had agreed that a major transmission main, serving the highly developed, unincorporated area between the ocean and the northern end of Biscayne Bay, could be financed by means of a special-improvement-assessment district. The properties in this area could thus be required to pay for the transmission main through a special assessment tax levied by Dade County. Even though the new transmission main would be a county-owned asset, the city would agree to maintain it and produce and pump potable water into it, and to service the meters and connections as if the main were a part of the city's own water-distribution system.

This arrangement allowed us to reduce our revenue-bond financing requirements by $3 million, to $5.5 million, and to complete the $8.5 million improvement program that the engineers had recommended in the first place. We proposed the new financing plan to a joint meeting of the city council and the utilities commission. It was accepted.

The plan was a face-saver. The property owners could explain to the voters how their efforts had resulted in a "savings" of $3 million, even though the same $3 million would be collected from the service district in the form of a tax assessment, and even though water-rate reduction had not been proposed. The stigma of bonded indebtedness had frightened many of the city's senior citizens who had not been told that the proposed revenue bonds were not solely their obligation but rather an obligation of the water users in the entire utility-service district.

A special election was called by the city council for consideration of a $5.5 million water-revenue bond issue. This time, with the aid of the Property Owners Association, the measure passed two-to-one. I reflected that this flip-flop was an outstanding demonstration of the polling-place clout of the Property Owners Association and of the power of the grey hairs they had pulled together.

My own position was precarious at best. One of the newly elected council members, Henry Harris, who had eclipsed Marge McDonald as the most outspoken council member, was clearly hostile to me. Worse yet, Harris controlled the advertising budget for a large regional shopping center in an unincorporated area that, like a hole in a donut, was an enclave completely surrounded by the city of North Miami Beach. When he wasn't altogether satisfied with the attention his frequent public statements were getting in local papers, Harris published a free paper of his own. That paper printed his statements verbatim, and lots of his pictures, too–all of which was financed by shopping-center advertisements. Interestingly, he referred to himself in these articles as "the new administration" and, though the shopping center would benefit from our efforts to gain the county's permission to annex our service area, Harris repeatedly denied that he was representing the economic interests of the center's owners.

Taking advantage of the vacuum created by the defeat of the former mayor, Harris had the council name him "liaison" with the fire and police unions. But the men and women in municipal service uniforms were not quite so willing to be represented by this stranger who called himself Henry Scott Harris. Smelling something a little fishy about him, police officers and firefighters searched their information sources, exchanged notes, and decided that the new councilman was not the famous graduate of the London School of Economics and Columbia University, the recognized genius listed in *Who's Who* as Harris said he was. Ex-Senator Harry Cain of the Metropolitan Dade County Board capsulized these suspicions when the local papers quoted him in bold headlines, "Henry Who?"

Unfortunately, the senior citizens in the Property Owners Association were not as cautious in their dealings with strangers. Harris especially sought Joe Moffat's support. He repeatedly flattered Joe. When Joe would release a statement at Monday night's utility-commission meeting, Harris would echo and amplify Joe's statement at the following night's council meeting. Harris, the first with hip shots and those the loudest, outgunned Mrs. McDonald as Joe's voice on the city council.

My second employment contract was scheduled to expire October 1, eighteen months after I had started work for North Miami Beach. The city council delayed their consideration of the renewal of my contract until October 1, when I was in Seattle attending the annual conference of the ICMA. Because the city charter required a twelve-month contract for the city manager, except for a newly appointed manager, to whom the city council was required by the charter to give only a six-month contract, the council decided in my absence I would be "officially" unemployed for one day (while I was attending the conference) and then "hired" again for six months, as if I were a newly hired city manager. The mayor telegrammed the Council's decision to me in Seattle.

Marge McDonald was becoming generally distant and occasionally vicious. Councilman Helfand was a complacent follower who was made most uncomfortable, to the amusement of his fellow council members, whenever the council changed the order of roll-call voting so that Helfand would have to cast his vote before Mrs. McDonald cast hers. Taylor was my strong supporter in spite of our differences on the water-bond issue.

He and Harris were both interested in becoming the city's next mayor. Their rivalry only strengthened Harris's animosity toward me. The mayor and Councilmen Littman and Cohen were noncommittal; the mayor was a compromiser by nature, and Cohen and Littman were anxious to promote a clublike feeling of comradery among their fellow council members.

The mayor was quite dissatisfied with the city attorney, who, besides being a potential rival for the mutually coveted judgeship, would spend the better part of each morning on the telephone with reporters for the numerous suburban papers. The mayor repeatedly attempted to silence the attorney, and although the attorney obliged by assuming a somewhat less prominent public profile, the animosity between the two did not lessen.

One day, the mayor came into my office and explained that Councilman Harris, who had joined the mayor's synagogue, also agreed to join with the mayor and other council members in terminating the city attorney if the mayor would, in turn, join Harris, McDonald, and Helfand in terminating me. The mayor told me he had agreed to this swap, although he would do whatever he could to assist me in finding another city manager position elsewhere. He suggested that I could submit my resignation to avoid the stigma of an involuntary termination, but I chose to continue working for the balance of my six-month "contract." In the meantime I completed the annual budget and various other projects, among them an investigation of an attempt by former Councilman Rubin to solicit $100 contributions from city department heads on behalf of Councilwoman McDonald in return for a promise to them of job security.

I also attempted a further mechanized refuse-pick-up system that promised to improve greatly the productivity and working conditions of our collectors. The residents in our demonstration area responded 85 percent in favor of the experimental system, but Sam Opsheler, a director of the Property Owners Association, was not in favor and, with the help of Councilman Harris, terminated the project following the completion of the successful demonstration.

When my six months were up, my employment with North Miami Beach was ended without a public hearing or any word of explanation from the city council as a whole.

My successor, Harvey Rose, survived for two years. I don't know if the city ever completed the water-plant improvement program I had initiated, and I don't know what the drinking-water quality is now. But I can guess. I do know that the city attorney, the personnel officer, the utilities director, the recreation director, the parks superintendent, and perhaps two finance directors were replaced soon after I left. Even the computer may have been replaced by a service bureau. Rubin became a judge; the mayor didn't. My former administrative assistant died of a stomach ulcer when Harvey Rose and the entire city council were attending a convention in Colorado. The building department director died of a heart attack a little later. I will miss them both.

What Do You Do When You Run out of Water?

Mildred P. McDonald

My first year as town manager of Southern Pines, a beautification-conscious, fast-growing North Carolina resort city, began with a crisis.

In 1977 we had the worst drought in years and faced both a raw-water shortage and limited treatment capability. The water superintendent's reports on the lake level and water in tank storage grew more alarming every day. Believe me, there is nothing more frightening than the prospect of a major fire without adequate water to fight it.

We tried every avenue for help—civil preparedness, the Army Corps of Engineers, and the nearby town of Aberdeen. None was productive. Finally I recommended to the council an ordinance prohibiting water use for car washing, filling swimming pools, watering shrubs, trees, and lawns, and all other unnecessary uses. Complaints poured in from car washes, service stations, and motels. We were criticized by people losing their expensive trees, plants, and shrubs. One gentleman threatened to sue us because his shrubs died. Ironically, this gentleman had just come into the city limits after hotly contesting the annexation but now was demanding that we cut off all water users outside the city limits. A month before, had the town gone that route, he would have been one of those cut off.

To protect the residents' health and safety, we stuck to our guns and kept the ordinance in effect. The police and fire departments patrolled day and night, with an eye out for offenders. Most citizen-reported violations turned out to be golf courses and hotels using their private wells for watering. We issued warnings, giving violators the benefit of any doubt that they had heard of or read about the ordinance, and took no one into court.

This was a temporary measure. What I needed was a permanent solution to the problem. Previously we had had an engineering firm do a water-feasibility study for both Southern Pines and the surrounding area. And just before the big drought, the county government had attempted to create a regional water system for our end of the county. But the bond referendum failed miserably. One big factor was the lack of county-wide zoning to protect the land use. Also, we have many environmentalists who do not want the streams tampered with or the county covered with water lines. Moreover, many folks alleged that we had no water shortage, that this was propaganda to encourage a regional water system. So now Southern Pines needed interim measures that would ensure adequate water until a decision could be made and implemented on long-range water sources.

Our consultants advised me that under the Drought Act of 1977 the U.S. Farmers Home Administration had emergency funds for distribution in North Carolina. Hastily we put together an application to fund several emergency water-source projects. With excellent help from our local FHA agent and from state-level people, we qualified and were awarded a grant (the only community in the state so privileged). With this money, some clean-water bond grant funds, and an appropriation from our own water and sewer fund balance, we were able to award contracts and get improvements under way. We leased and converted one existing privately owned well and added two new wells. We negotiated with the town of Carthage (thirteen miles from Southern Pines) to purchase water from a stream they controlled and to put in a raw-water line from their pumps to our reservoir. Also, at our water plant we installed a recycling system to save water used for sludge removal, water that previously had gone down the sewer.

These projects have given us enough additional water to take care of current normal use and growth and have bought us four or five years of time. In the interim we can decide which way to go—surface water or groundwater. Fortunately we did not have to restrict water use during the summer of 1978. The whole frightening experience makes clear how important it is to plan ahead of the community's needs, not letting growth outrun ability to provide services.

Part Three

The City Manager and the Social System

We think of the social system as the total of community organizations and activities that facilitate people's living and interacting with one another, as distinguished from the organizations and activities established and conducted primarily for political or economic purposes. The social system includes a range of conditions, arrangements, and interests that may extend from the morals and mores of the community, through the provisions for social accommodation of one another, to the means of satisfying a broad spectrum of human wants and needs. All three systems—political, economic, and social—overlap and interrelate in many ways, making it difficult to draw clear-cut distinctions among the three. For example, the views about morality held by a majority of the members of an elected public policy-making body can have much to do with the kinds of social activities conducted in the community; similarly, these same members of the political system can influence the local economic system: compare the hotel, motel, restaurant, and casino business activity in Las Vegas, Nevada, with the business activity in any city where antigambling laws are enforced.

Are city managers involved with the communities' social systems? They are, in countless ways—personally and officially. The reports from three city managers' wives, Sally Rowlands, Harriette Cookingham, and Agda Harlow, plus one city manager's story of how his ten-year-old son was affected by a crisis in his father's career, provide concrete examples of this involvement. These examples show that city managers don't live in ivory towers, far removed from the day-to-day concerns of other citizens in the community. On the contrary, they and their families take an active part and are affected by the kind of city they live in, by what goes on there. This helps the managers keep their feet on the ground and their values and priorities straight, both personally and professionally.

The episodes show how city managers sometimes get involved in such social problems as prejudice and race relations, inconsistencies between individuals' statements and their actions, relationships between government and the press, pornography, sex, and corruption.

Although city managers are neither politicians nor private entrepreneurs, they must be knowledgeable and sensitive about the political, economic, and social characteristics and changes in their communities. To be less than this is to decrease their usefulness to the public and the city councils they serve, and to increase drastically their professional management difficulties.

Family
Involvement

Life with a City Manager
Sally H. Rowlands

My husband, David, was city manager of one town and three cities—Mt. Lebanon, Pennsylvania; Eau Claire, Wisconsin; Tacoma, Washington; and Huntington Beach, California—from 1949 to 1976. Only Mt. Lebanon was near our original homes and families, yet we never felt at loose ends or rootless. This was because life as the wife and children of the city manager was interesting and exciting. It enabled all of us to make wonderful and lasting friendships with my husband's coworkers and with the council members and citizens of each community that David served. It involved our children both outside and inside our home. And it challenged me to make a secure and ready home for David and the children, yet also render useful community service.

We lived in Mt. Lebanon the year of the big snow. Dave was enjoying the ICMA annual conference in Houston's balmy weather the day we got thirty inches in twenty-four hours. Our house was on a hill, forty steps up from the front street. His office force trudged up through the snow to see how the kids and I were, even though the other citizens were ready to kill Dave for being out of town when they faced a calamity.

In Eau Claire, a delegation of French labor leaders toured the city, and after the reception several people hosted the men in their homes. Dave brought two home with him. Our children were ages two, four, six, and eight but were as much a part of family affairs as if they had been in their teens. Four-year-old Peggy really didn't speak English too plainly, and each evening her Daddy was in the habit of prattling a type of pidgin French to her as we sat around the table. When he first knew the Frenchmen were coming, he had assured her that she'd be able to understand them even though the other kids might not. But when the guests had arrived, and after sitting quietly in the living room, Peggy came to me in the kitchen and said, "Those men don't speak the French me do."

That was quite a night at our house. There I was, trying to handle the whole scene. Then, in the midst of my efforts to get dinner ready for the table, the Frenchmen came out to the kitchen. They were interested in the refrigerator and the basement, and then they asked who was preparing the dinner. When I said it was I, they were amazed; they had just assumed that everyone in America had at least one maid.

Another time a gentleman from Iran fascinated all the Rowlandses as we sat around the table. He led us through the similarities of languages in seven tongues. Maybe that was the beginning of our girls' interest in languages. (Jean attended the International Language School in Switzerland, and Peggy the University of Madrid. Both became bilingual in French and Spanish.)

How often I have heard Dave say at the time, and many years since, "Never will I have a city council of such high caliber as the men in Eau Claire." They were especially progressive about community development. Because parking was a problem in the central business district, the council instructed Dave to purchase and tear down an old hotel and construct a parking-garage facility. Eau Claire became a trailblazer in Wisconsin by forming a parking utility and obtaining a bond-attorney's opinion that permitted the marketing of revenue bonds, the first in the state. Other cities, including Milwaukee, sent delegations of officials to Eau Claire to learn how this was accomplished. My part in this episode was a bit different. Dave had me go down to try parking in the various parking stalls. He knew that if I could do it, anyone could!

During Dave's twenty-six years as a city manager, I never attended a council meeting. But when a Tacoma radio station began to broadcast the Tacoma council meetings, that was a different story. Every Monday from 4:30 P.M. until midnight or later, I was at the ironing board. For the next several months, I had the best-ironed clothes in the country. The angrier I got over the crazy antics at those meetings, the harder I ironed.

During this time, Dave was chosen Tacoma's Urban League Man-of-the-Year. The award citation was in recognition of his contributions to "harmonious and effective relationships between all groups in the community, with particular consideration of the position of minorities." When he resigned as city manager, the chamber of commerce and several other groups had a beautiful reception for him, where literally hundreds came to express their love and admiration for his thirteen and a half years of service to Tacoma. At another reception in which many citizens participated, our Presbyterian minister announced, "This is a party for the Rowlandses and tonight there will be no speeches. But we do have a couple of tokens

Tacoma, Washington, citizens demonstrate support for city manager. *Courtesy of Tacoma, Washington,* News Tribune.

for them—Jean and Peggy!" They had brought our daughters home from Europe for the party.

Some months after David resigned, five members of the Tacoma council (several of whom had made his life miserable), were recalled. Justice and honesty do prevail!

The Tacoma years were the most turbulent of Dave's career, yet they were rewarding for all of us. The children went through school, entered college, and did the European School bit. (At one time we had three in Europe at once.) I was involved in the nonpolitical community—church-school teacher, from day school little ones to programs for nursing homes; Salvation Army board member; president of the Goodwill Industries auxiliary; and a three-week summer typing class for our children and their friends.

Through all the years of Dave's career, he and our four children were naturally of first interest to me. And our family and home were an important part of his life. Our children were always helping with parties for city employees and their families, and for other guests, and they felt a part of the "organization." Many dinner-table discussions centered on the activities of his day. He would present a problem and see which of the children could come closest to a solution. A game it was that kept the whole family aware of what their father did when away from home. Often Dave called to announce, "I'm bringing someone home for dinner; we'll be

there in thirty minutes." It was not always convenient, but I always felt
good he knew it would be fine.

Recently Dave has rounded out his career by passing on his experiences to graduate students he has taught at California State University,
Long Beach. Who could dare to say that being the wife of one of the best
city managers has not been exciting, thrilling, and happy?

Between Us Wives

From my twenty-six years of sharing David's professional city manager
experience, I have gleaned the following views about life as the wife of a
city manager. I have shared them with other wives and am pleased to
share them with you.

1. First and foremost, the city manager's wife must be flexible—informed,
interested, and involved in her particular areas of interest (but not in politics). She must know that her husband is the greatest there is. If the citizens don't realize that, that's their problem.

2. There may be drawbacks to being the wife and family of the city manager, but the pluses always outweigh the minuses.

3. We considered every city we served to be our "home town." The first
step was to find our church home, a fact I believe helped us always to feel
at home immediately. Then locations of schools and activities for the
family (two sons, two daughters, Dave, and me). Every city was special,
with its own vitality. Wonderful people all along the way. I have always
prefaced every move with the observation that I have loved every city we
served in and would not have wanted to miss out on any of them.

We had no fear of moving, for the past had been so good, the present
so great, that moves held nothing but excited anticipation. It was, "Here
we go again," but the new city was always a challenge and a terrific place.

4. Although Dave, the children, and I were friends of his coworkers, we
were never intimate friends. Any intimate friends were outside the city
hall clan. My being socially involved with the wife of one of his men
could pose a problem.

5. We joined the City employees and their families for special events, and
at least once a year we entertained many employees and their wives or husbands in our home.

The holidays lent themselves to open-house entertaining, and I
remember the times of memorizing long lists of names. Before each party
that list was uppermost on my mind. How often I have laughed when
people commented on my ability to remember names. I could handle fifty
or sixty a night, but they never knew the ordeal I went through.

Shortly after we moved to Tacoma, Washington, Dave wanted me to
have the "girls" in for dinner. Of course I said, "Sure," but I didn't realize
that I would end up serving dinner for eighty-five women in three nights.
(After three nights of remembering names, I was numb.) Of course I used

the same menu throughout; I felt like a short-order cook before it was over. Mostly I recall doing the linens after each dinner because I didn't have enough to carry me through three nights. One guest came forty-five minutes early. I wasn't quite ready so I simply sat her down at the kitchen table while I finished my chores. I always felt that the two of us really got acquainted that night.

6. So many good things have happened to us throughout our lives, and God's hand has been in the midst of it all. One thing I know: Regardless of the circumstances, with faith some good always emerged from our experiences.

The Bitter with the Sweet

Harriette W. Cookingham

Looking back over my years as a city manager's wife, I could not ask for a better life. When the city manager first enters the job in a new city, all are curious about both the manager and his wife. This was especially true in Kansas City, where the former city manager who had served for thirteen years was a widower. There had not been a wife of the city manager in Kansas City before my husband came there. Naturally people were quite anxious to see what the wife of a city manager looked like and how she would act. This was interesting for me because in the other three cities that we had served there had been city managers' wives before me, so I had not been such a curiosity as in Kansas City.

The manager's wife is invited to many civic events, particularly when her husband is the luncheon or dinner speaker. This is a wonderful way to become acquainted with a city and its leaders of civic, business, religious, and cultural affairs.

As I became acquainted in a new city, I was asked to join numerous organizations. In the small cities my activities were mostly church oriented and in the local women's clubs. In the larger cities the women's city club immediately extended an invitation to participate. Also, the League of Women Voters asked me to transfer my membership to the local chapter, which I did. And I always resumed my activity in that organization.

In one city I became interested in the Rehabilitation Institute. I am still a member of the auxiliary, though not actively working. In Kansas City I also was active in the auxiliary of the Kansas City Museum of History and Science, the Kansas City Rose Society, the Kansas City Art Institute, the Children's Cardiac Center Auxiliary, and a number of others. Again, I am still interested in many of these organizations, attending some of their meetings and making contributions to their programs.

I learned early in my husband's career that a city manager's wife should not push herself into active participation in the local women's organizations; rather, she should wait to be asked and urged to become active. This lesson came because I learned of a city manager's wife who was a dynamic leader. Upon coming to a new city, she became more active than some of the local women leaders wanted the city manager's wife to be. I never tried to play a major role in any of the local organizations, although some of them urged me to take such a position.

As time goes on there are always a few more lessons to be learned. For example, you have to keep a few of your possessions packed up in case a landlord sells the house you have rented just when you get it cleaned up and nicely settled. We had to do this twice in one city we managed. We learned to keep a part of our things packed for just such occasions.

Sadness comes from parting with good friends. There is always quite a tug in my heart strings when we have moved from one city to another.

One less than happy day that I recall began at a mayor's prayer breakfast on the day the mayor was to be inaugurated for his third term. The mayor introduced everyone around our table but failed to introduce us or even mention us during the breakfast period. Then, when we arrived at the place of the inauguration, our reserved seats and those of outgoing councilmen had already been occupied by ward and precinct leaders of the group that had been elected on a platform opposed to a true charter government.

I remember well the campaign when my husband's first name came up for discussion. One candidate for mayor said the initial "L" stood for Levi. At that a reporter called and asked what the letter *really* stood for. Much to my husband's chagrin, because he always used L.P., I had to tell the reporter that it was an old family name—Laurie. But I also went on to say that it would not have mattered to me if his name had been Levi, because we had many friends named Levi, and I could not see what difference a name made. Perry says that statement led to the winning over of three to five thousand votes for the Citizens Association from persons whose given name or surname was Levi.

As a city manager's wife one must take the bitter with the sweet, but most of my memories are definitely on the sweet side.

From a Wife's Perspective

Agda G. Harlow

When my husband and I met in college, he had already decided that he wanted to be a city manager. Since then he has had three careers, all related to his early goal. He has been a city manager, a management consultant specializing in public-management problems, and a university professor of urban management, in that order.

Our family life during the city-management years was strikingly different from what it became when LeRoy was in private business or on a university faculty. I think of these differences: a goldfish-bowl existence, occasional threats to our physical safety, the unfounded rumors and deliberate lies that go with local politics, and job uncertainty. But offsetting these were unique opportunities.

Because the city manager is a public servant, his family experiences some degree of public scrutiny. Our arrival in a new city and our house hunting were publicized. Community drives and parades featured the family. A few days before our fourth child arrived, the following news item appeared in the Albert Lea, Minnesota, *Evening Tribune*:

WHO SAID IT ISN'T A WOMAN'S WORLD?

> One man who will breathe a sigh of relief when this week is over is LeRoy F. Harlow, city manager.
>
> To begin with, this is the week of the city council meeting which always means busy days thereafter. Then on Wednesday, Mr. Harlow will drive to Owatonna to meet with H.Z. Mitchell, editor of the *Bemidji Pioneer,* for a discussion of council-manager government and possible charter changes at Bemidji.
>
> From there he is scheduled to be a speaker at the 3-day conference of finance officers to be held at the University of Minnesota March 27–29. Mr. Harlow will speak on bases for salary and wage scales and municipal pension plans. . . .
>
> But the thing which may change that busy schedule is an appointment Mrs. Harlow has sometime this week—with the stork.

I was embarrassed by this prenatal publicity. Whose business was it, anyway? Furthermore, I was upset thinking that if the baby didn't arrive on schedule, there would be more unwanted publicity. Fortunately, Tom must have sensed my concern. He arrived on the exact day the doctor had predicted. This prompted another news report, this one titled "Obliging Stork Calls on Harlows" and giving details of where and when the baby arrived, how much he weighed, his name, and the names and ages of the other children and divulging that all the children had my maiden name as their middle names.

A few weeks before our sixth child was born, in Daytona Beach, Florida, a reporter and photographer came from the local paper to interview me and take a picture of us at our home. Again I was embarrassed to learn from the published story that during the interview the older children had found a way to climb onto the roof. That story was fittingly titled, "With Five Children, Mrs. Harlow has a Fulltime Management Job."

Although anonymity was not one of the blessings of city management, the goldfish-bowl existence was not a serious problem, only an occasional irritant. More difficult were the terror tactics that opponents of good government sometimes used to further their cause. For instance, on the night following the day LeRoy fired a police chief, we had very little rest. First, our oldest son became very ill and had to be rushed to the hospital for a midnight appendectomy. And then, when finally we were able to get what we hoped would be a few hours of unbroken sleep, we were wakened by a 2:00 A.M. call from a friend of the chief who told LeRoy he ought to be killed and vividly described the method.

In Daytona Beach, during a strike of city-yards employees, LeRoy was asked by one strike leader how he was going to like being carried out of town feet first, and another strike leader threatened death if the garbage trucks were moved. On the advice of friends, we moved the family to a safer location. Two years later, during the primary-election campaign, a man called the police department to say he was going to kill LeRoy as soon as he could find him. The police chief was concerned enough that he assigned bodyguards around the clock for several days, even while we ate Thanksgiving dinner.

After experiences like this, it wasn't surprising that I was alert to unusual night sounds. One late evening in Florida while LeRoy was out of town, I was reading in bed. The children were asleep and we were living some distance from neighbors. The only light in the house was my bed lamp. I was suddenly aware of footsteps beneath my window. I reached up and turned off the bed lamp, felt my way to the phone in the living room and called the operator, asking her to notify the police. What seemed like hours (but was less than fifteen minutes) I waited, trying not to breathe, hearing again and more distinctly in the darkness, footsteps. I was very much relieved when the police car drove up and two officers hurried toward the house with flashlights poised. They fanned out into the yard and into a nearby field and finally came to the house to assure me that what had seemed to me to be footsteps was the slapping tail of an armadillo. They had followed it away from the bedroom window into the field and were sure that there had been no human threat that night.

Usually we tried to ignore the rumors, misrepresentations, and deliberate lies about LeRoy, his salary and fringe benefits, his taking graft, and so on. In Daytona Beach he tried to counter them with a letter to the editor saying if *anyone* wanted to know *anything* about things connected with the city, all he needed to do was come to City Hall. It was frustrating to have to deal with an attitude of "Don't trouble me with the truth; my mind is made up," and with unfounded animosity, even apparent hatred.

A constant unpleasantness a city manager's family faces is job insecurity. If the majority of the citizens approve of the city manager's performance, there is a good chance he will be offered a better position in a larger city. There is only one job of its kind in each community, and the only road to advancement is to pull up stakes. On the other hand, if the majority of the citizens, or citizens' elected officials, disapprove of the city manager's performance (often because his administration is too honest and too efficient), he is likely to be asked to resign or to be summarily dismissed.

LeRoy was often asked to give talks explaining the council-manager concept. After describing the overall control by the council, he would outline the authority of the city manager and the reasons for it. But being aware of concerns about "dictatorship," he would explain that such power was balanced by lack of tenure. To make the point more dramatic, he often said, "The city commission could be meeting right at this moment to fire me." I knew the line well but didn't really take it seriously until I was the sole audience at just such a meeting, in Fargo, North Dakota, one October evening in 1949.

A few months earlier LeRoy had struggled with a difficult decision—whether to dismiss the police chief, knowing that such an action might well lead to his own dismissal. I urged him to do what he felt was right without regard to our personal economic position. I wanted him to feel the same freedom he would have had as a bachelor—to follow his conscience and not be restricted by concern for the welfare of a wife and five small children. With this assurance he did dismiss the chief of police. As I sat in the small commission chambers and heard the mayor ask for LeRoy's resignation, I was convinced that LeRoy's dramatic punch line—"They could be meeting right now to fire me"—was really the way the council-manager plan functioned.

However, according to North Dakota state law, the city manager could be dismissed only after a public hearing if the manager requested one. The night of the hearing I took the children out into the yard after an early supper. LeRoy has the rare skill of being able to nap for five minutes at any time, anywhere, and after a few weeks of preparing his defense and sending job applications throughout the country, he needed a nap so he could be clearheaded for the coming ordeal. Out in the yard, little four-year-old Christine looked up at me and asked a sobering question: "When are they going to burn up Daddy?" I hugged her, laughing and crying, and explained, "They aren't ever going to burn up Daddy. He's just not going to be city manager any more. That's what firing means."

My wish that the hearing would not be as lonely as the dismissal was generously granted. The court house chambers were crowded; people filled the window sills and corridors. If someone hadn't given me a seat near the front, I might have missed much of that wonderful evening. As the hearing progressed, it became plain that one of the five commissioners felt it would be a mistake to dismiss LeRoy and that the audience was unanimously of the same opinion, having come to see justice done. Though it happened almost thirty years ago, that public hearing at which the commissioners changed their minds remains a vivid memory. I have often had reason to be proud of my husband, and this was one of those golden moments. He had chosen the profession of city management with his eyes open to its risk and difficulty. He was skilled at it, dedicated to making the city government better serve all the people. On this night in Fargo a battle was won. Antagonistic men, adverse publicity, a hostile atmosphere were overcome. I shared my husband's faith that there are things worth fighting for.

Florida law did not require a public hearing before firing a city manager. And so, five and a half years after our triumphant evening in Fargo, another city commission convened in Daytona Beach and the first order of business was to fire the city manager. Unfortunately the recent election issue had become whether to keep LeRoy as the city manager. Two on each side of that issue were firmly decided. The pivotal, newly elected commissioner declared he would be fair and take six months to decide. We were happy about this. It might give the children a chance to finish their school year and LeRoy a chance to find another position.

But something had happened very quickly to change the commissioner's mind. The afternoon of the first meeting of the new commission he phoned LeRoy to say, "I'm giving you a chance to resign before the commission votes to fire you tonight." LeRoy thanked him and again declined to resign, preferring that the three commissioners be required to publicly vote out good government.

Our two oldest sons were in a dance program at the civic auditorium that evening, and I had taken them there before coming to the commission meeting, arriving a little late. Foot-stomping, cheering, and whistling accompanied wild applause in the smoke-filled room. I asked a police officer at the door what had happened. "They've just fired Harlow!" he replied, not recognizing me. LeRoy left his place at the commission table and joined me in the audience, and then we quietly left to go to his office and start packing his personal things.

Despite the drawbacks of public life in city government that I've mentioned, there are also unique advantages for the city manager's wife. In our first city I was invited to be the book reviewer for the library and a 4-H Club leader, both of which may have been partly attributable to LeRoy's position. One of the most enriching experiences, and also the most bizarre, was definitely tied to his job. One evening we were about to leave home for the city hall, where I would read while he worked, when the phone rang. A newspaper reporter was asking for details about a killing that had just happened on Main Street. I went with LeRoy to the city hall, intending to stay in the car. But when LeRoy saw the difficulty the state patrolman was having questioning witnesses and typing their statements, he volunteered my help. Soon the officer asked me to continue the interrogations while he went in search of the accused killer.

In an hour or so he had his man. He brought him to LeRoy's office, where the police chief, the sheriff, and the county attorney were now assembled. There, behind closed doors and away from the large, curious crowd, the young man told his story. I typed it as he told it, and he read it over and signed it. I count this experience a unique opportunity, because I became aware as never before how the stereotype of labels can distort truth. This man, a killer, was—of all who had been questioned—the most appealing, the finest. He told his story simply, with the ring of truth. I hoped that his plea of self-defense would be upheld. The mayor and the man's employer put up bail so he could be with his family over the holidays. When he came to trial, there were no accusers, and he went free.

In addition to the drama of that early experience as a city manager's wife, I had the opportunity to meet many interesting and outstanding people, sometimes when LeRoy was the guest speaker, other times (seldom) when I was asked to speak, or when we were invited guests. I recall most vividly two Daytona Beach events.

One year the Chamber of Commerce had Drew Pearson as speaker. I was a frequent reader of his column and was thrilled to hear him in person. But I remember the occasion because it also had a humorous and an embarrassing side.

It was a formal dinner, held in the beautiful Princess Issena Hotel dining room. A friend made me a new, long dress—except for my wedding dress, the first long dress I had owned since college. The children had never seen either of us in such finery and were duly impressed. Tommy, now an avid viewer of western movies, paid LeRoy in his rented tuxedo the supreme compliment: "You look just like the sheriff!"

We sat at the head table with a couple of dozen notables. As the banquet got under way, the master of ceremonies introduced all of us. When he announced "City Manager and Mrs. LeRoy Harlow," LeRoy got to his feet slightly before I did. He had stepped solidly on my long dress. I started to stand only to be yanked abruptly back to my seat by the pull on my dress. I felt, and I'm sure I looked, like an introverted Jack-in-the box.

Dr. Mary McLeod Bethune was Daytona Beach's most distinguished citizen, and she and LeRoy had developed respect and affection for each other through their joint efforts to make Daytona Beach a better place for both black and white citizens. One morning she telephoned LeRoy to ask if we would like to come to her home to meet Eleanor Roosevelt. She invited us to bring our six children with us.

I remember Mrs. Roosevelt's asking me if I didn't find it difficult to

The children of the Daytona Beach, Florida, city manager meet two great ladies, Eleanor Roosevelt and Dr. Mary McLeod Bethune.

take care of so many children (she could see there was another one on the way), and I believe I said, "Well, yes, Mrs. Roosevelt, but you had a large family, too."

On the way home, seven-year-old Christine sat in the front seat between us, sparkling with excitement at having met the two great ladies. She wanted to know which of the two *we* thought the most beautiful. I suppose LeRoy and I had not thought either of those over-seventy ladies beautiful. Exchanging glances over her head, we asked, "Christine, which did *you* think more beautiful?"

"They are both beautiful," she said unhesitatingly, "but I think Mrs. Bethune is a little more beautiful."

Our little daughter, with a child's wisdom, sensed Mrs. Roosevelt's reserve and Mrs. Bethune's genuine interest in meeting the children of her good friend, LeRoy Harlow. To this day, all of us treasure the photograph taken that day of Mrs. Bethune, her great grandchildren, our children, and Mrs. Roosevelt.

A final benefit I enjoyed as a city manager's wife was the privilege of attending the annual conferences of the ICMA. I was not able to go each time LeRoy went, but I enjoyed associating with other manager wives at the exotically beautiful conference settings in Chicago, Montreal, Mackinac Island, Kansas City, and St. Petersburg.

I have enjoyed the more than twenty years of anonymity since we stopped being the city manager's family, but I am very grateful that we did have that opportunity. Before LeRoy left his enjoyable position with the U.S. Bureau of the Budget in Washington for his first city manager job, an ex-city manager colleague at the Budget Bureau warned him, "When it's all over, all you'll have to show for it will be headlines and ulcers." We have had more than that, partly because of LeRoy's convictions about the importance of local government.

For the past dozen years LeRoy has been helping prepare future city managers. Recently a group of wives of these graduate students asked me to tell them what it was like out in the real world of public service. Among other things I told them I considered them fortunate if they were married to men committed to the public service and that there are several ways a wife helps her husband succeed as city manager:

1. By being as excited as he is about his first job as an appointed public official.
2. By being willing to live in the public eye.
3. By accepting the fact that he is not in a 9–5 job, and knowing that many times the burden of family life will be hers alone.
4. By being willing to move as many times as his career requires, whether he is leaving a city involuntarily or because of an opportunity for a bigger challenge.
5. By being a good money manager, able to plan ahead for possible periods of unemployment to give her husband a chance to wait a few months for the right job.
6. By being his sounding board, because she may be the only one with whom he can talk out alternatives and arrive at hard decisions.
7. By being completely willing for him to risk his job in support of his principles, if that need arises. (On this point, I reminded them that Dwight Ink, who was LeRoy's assistant at Fargo and later the national president of the American Society for Public Administration, had assured a similar group and their husbands that it was possible in the public service to be fired, to lose a job or two along the way, without failing to progress in a lifetime career.)
8. By believing in her husband's choice of professional public management and in him as a worthy representative of it, for sometimes she may be in a very small minority of people who do.

LeRoy left city management to join Booz, Allen, and Hamilton, Inc., a private management-consulting firm. In a conference with his tough, sophisticated boss before being transferred to a position with greater responsibility, LeRoy was surprised to have his superior give him this counsel: "Remember, there is strength in righteousness." Our years in city management, and the years since, have proven this to be so. I have found a special kind of adventure in being LeRoy's full partner in his chosen field, which he has followed without fear or favor.

A Ten-Year-Old
Feels Threatened

Bert W. Johnson

Ernest Walton Johnson, my thirty-year-old son, recalls that his foremost boyhood trauma occurred twenty years ago, when I was about to lose my job as the first city manager of Evanston, Illinois. The circumstances were these.

After a year-long study in which the fire chief had been fully involved, and with the chief's endorsement, I recommended to the city council a police-fire cooperation plan in which the fire department would train policemen to function to a limited extent in fire fighting. The council unanimously approved the plan, and we were ready to implement it.

However, after the chief went back to his officers and firefighters, not to mention his fellow fire chiefs in neighboring departments, he reversed himself. No longer was he the happy-go-lucky booster of our plan but a schizophrenic: denying our long, creative dialogue, he resolutely refused to carry out the plan. As a result, I was forced to dismiss this popular fire chief who had an unblemished performance record. The regrettable action precipitated a drive for a referendum on retention or abandonment of the council-manager plan.

Ernie was ten at the time, a fourth-grader who, like most of his friends, looked up to firemen as heroes. First he heard talk about the firing of a fire chief, then about firing the city manager. Although four teachers were telling Ernie's two brothers and two sisters, "Don't worry, we'll back your Dad," Ernie's teacher never reassured him, and I missed the opportunity to explain to him what was happening to me. He wondered, "Why doesn't my teacher say anything about my Dad?" He couldn't understand why his dad was in such serious trouble. (Probably we were not as concerned as Ernie sensed we were.)

The referendum campaign gave our citizens the opportunity to learn more about the increased protection and safety they would enjoy when their police were trained as fire fighters. Natural sympathy for the deposed fire chief was replaced by a general citizen approval of the plan, of me, and of the council-manager plan that brought me to Evanston. The prospect of a change in the fire service was no problem: Evanston was a community proud of its excellence. In fact, during the final weeks of the referendum campaign, the "Anti-Bert Johnson" group started soft-pedaling their opposition to the police-fire cooperation program. They changed their strategy to a more general one—that the council-manager plan was too costly, as well as un-American ("communism in disguise"). But our boosters took this in stride, stating that the council-manager plan was as "American as apple pie", having its roots in Staunton, Virginia, in 1908.

A highly significant campaign factor was the record established by Wayne F. Anderson, Evanston's first director of finance and comptroller. Three years earlier, after some struggle I had obtained permission to recruit Wayne. His fine rapport with a questioning city council and his wizardry in bringing order out of the chaos inherited in Evanston's financial machinery, brought pervasive praise and devastated the antimanager arguments relating to finance.

Accordingly I was confident of victory on election day, 7 April 1959. *The Evanston Review* gave superb coverage and editorial support, as did the now-defunct *Chicago Daily News*. Other metropolitan newspapers seemed noncommittal. The anticipated high voter turnout gave me and council-manager government a smashing five-to-two majority (higher than that achieved by Mayor Richard Daley in Chicago on the same day), doubling the margin of victory that the council-manager plan had enjoyed when adopted in 1952. The magnitude of victory is said to have killed any subsequent challenge.

On election night my Evanston neighbors came to celebrate. The telephone kept ringing to congratulate me. Our crisis had passed with a joyous ending. Son Ernie knew things were once again all right for his Dad. And he stopped worrying about me from then on.

I may have known it before, but I was reminded that Ernie's needs should have had better attention. In a similar manner, our citizens and their public servants need help understanding what can otherwise be terrifying threats of change.

Prejudice and
Race Relations

We've Come a Long Way, Baby!

James Joshua Mott

Four incidents that occurred while I was city manager of West Palm Beach, Florida, illustrate the kinds of prejudices that confronted this country when the civil-rights movement started.

In 1952 the women's toilet on the ground floor at city hall did not have a sign on it. One day I almost went in by mistake, so I had a sign put up on the door. This dismayed a female department head and others. I suspect the absence of a sign was intended to keep the toilet segregated by race.

Another time I advertised for a secretary for my office. After interviewing several applicants, I hired the one I found to be best qualified. My selection upset several people. Later, although it made no difference to me, I learned why: she was Catholic.

One night at about eleven o'clock, on my way home from the usual extra work at city hall, I came on two police cars at a large Hebrew tabernacle. Uniformed officers and detectives with flashlights were running all around. I stopped, asked if I could help, and got out of my car.

"Someone phoned there was a bomb planted here and about to go off. Here it is! I've found it! Here, hold this flashlight!" shouted a detective.

I was caught. Not exactly what I had in mind when offering to help.

Three feet away, in the light of the flashlight I now held, the detective was examining a black box that had tape around it and wire connections at the top.

The detective clipped some wires with pliers, heaved a big sigh, and kissed the pliers!

The bomb was a fake. But a good imitation, we all admitted.

The Palm Beach County School Board owned the football stadium across from the white high school. But the City of West Palm Beach maintained the field, the stands, and the lights.

There was another high school football stadium, at the "colored" high school.

Not long before a scheduled game at the colored stadium, the lights went bad. The repairmen had some difficulty locating the problem, and I was asked if the school could play their game at the white field if the lights weren't fixed in time. I said, "Yes, I think so. I understand Palm Beach Senior High School has no game there that night. But I'd better check with the school board. It is actually their property. I'll let you know."

The school board said all right. I gave the go-ahead for the white field to be ready and the lights on for the colored game.

Lo and behold, the mayor got wind of the agreement. He went directly to the city electricians and ordered them to work night and day to repair the lights at the black field.

All of this I learned a day or so after the game was played—on the field where originally scheduled.

For weeks the mayor was very chilly toward me, and the incident seriously damaged the relationship between the two of us.

Mother Power
Peter F. Lydens

I was city manager of Gastonia, North Carolina (population 47,000), on 4 April 1968, the day Martin Luther King, Jr., was assassinated in Memphis. For the next two days and nights our plans for dealing with civil disturbances were thoroughly tested. But, thanks to our regular city departments, the effective human-relations commission, and a half-dozen black mothers, we survived the ordeal with no deaths or injuries and minimum property damage.

Because the sixties were volatile times, when minority-group demonstrations were common, our police and fire departments had prepared plans and trained their personnel to deal with such occurrences. When I received intelligence indicating that we should expect one or more days of civil demonstration following the unhappy King event, I notified the police chief and fire chief to get ready. The two departments canceled all days off and leaves. The police department put all plainclothes personnel in uniforms and reorganized the total force into two twelve-hour shifts. The fire department issued defensive weapons to the ranking officer of each fire-fighting unit, the fire-prevention vehicle was assigned to scout each fire alarm to determine if it were valid, and other fire-department personnel were put on night patrol in the areas most likely to be affected by civil demonstrators.

The human-relations commission, composed of both black and white representatives with a good record of racial relations, was mobilized to provide the first response and initiate dialogue in an effort to preclude the need for law-enforcement officers to become involved. For instance, one commission member spent most of the first evening with a group of emotional young men about sixteen to twenty-one years of age. After talking with them for several hours, the member took them to a local soda shop and fed them milkshakes and cheeseburgers. Too tired and too full to create any problems, the demonstrators went peacefully to their homes without causing the city any trouble.

On the second day we were informed that the black community had scheduled a peaceful march from one of their churches to the courthouse lawn adjacent to the city hall. Although we had authority to deny a parade permit, we decided it would be best to work with the group holding the march. We assigned a police unit to go ahead of the march to scout possible problems, another unit to bring up the rear, two units to serve as roving flank guards, and officers on foot to provide escort protection.

The demonstrators marched the mile and a half to the courthouse and held their program without mishap. On the return march, while riding with the police chief, I spotted a person with a scoped rifle silhouetted against the sky atop the tallest downtown building. The chief immediately dispatched two units to investigate. At the same time we tried to step up the rate of the march without alarming the participants. Shortly we received a radio message that it was one of our police majors who had unilaterally decided the building was a good observation and tactical counterpoint position. I was relieved yet chagrined at this lack of communication among city officials.

Around eleven o'clock the second evening, the crisis seemed to be over. The mayor and city council members, who had been on the street continuously, decided that the alert status could be stepped down and that at least the human-relations commission members could go home for some sleep. Just then six young black men home from college decided to hold an impromptu demonstration on the courthouse lawn. They proceeded to link arms and sing in some disharmony, "We shall overcome." This triggered a counterresponse from the "redneck" element of the white community, including some from outside the city limits. Then other blacks began moving in from the periphery.

The mayor, our black mayor pro tem, some human-relations commission members, a sprinkling of law-enforcement officers, and I observed this development. The mayor asked me if I felt we should declare an official curfew and clear the streets to prevent further problems. I had just asked for a few moments to think that over when one of the black police officers recognized one of the six demonstrators as a classmate of his son. Quickly the other five were identified by the mayor pro tem, other police officers, and members of the human-relations commission. Someone suggested that instead of a curfew we notify the mothers of the young men and let them handle their sons. Transportation was quickly arranged, and the mothers were brought to the site. The mothers made short shrift of the demonstration and the demonstrators. In no time the crisis was resolved, and by morning the city was back almost to normal.

Our review of the experience showed that property damage totaled less than one thousand dollars. This was for the loss of a small store whose owner had been gouging the black community for years. The review also enabled us to refine our policies and procedures for handling civil demonstrations and racial relations—including no more police officers' stationing themselves atop buildings without their superiors' assent.

A Close Call
David D. Rowlands

In Tacoma, Washington, on Mother's Day 1969, at about 6:30 P.M., I received a call at home from a black woman who told me I had better get down to the city hall as quickly as possible. She said that in serving a warrant, two police officers had inadvertently knocked over an eight-months-pregnant black woman on her front porch. When the neighborhood learned of this, the more belligerent blacks marched on city hall, charging the police with brutality. About seventy-five to a hundred sixteen- to twenty-five-year-olds were involved.

By the time I reached the city hall, the crowd had dispersed. I had a fair notion of where they might have gone, so the captain of our detective division and I drove an unmarked police car to that neighborhood. Arriving at a particular intersection—and I must admit an eerie feeling seemed to pervade the atmosphere—we were ambushed. A 45-caliber bullet pierced the side of the car about eight inches below the window on my side, bottles and stones crashed through the windows, all the tires were slashed, and we were surrounded about five deep by angry black youths.

At this time my son was one of the stars and the only white player on the starting five of the high school basketball team. One young fellow in the crowd, about seventeen years old, recognized me as "Dixie" Rowlands' dad. He told me and the captain to move out of the area, that the people were very angry and not inclined to talk. He then explained to the crowd who I was—the city manager and Dixie's dad. The crowd separated so we could drive on, flat tires notwithstanding.

In a sense, I had been saved by my son.

After this incident, city officials did everything possible to resolve the minority problems in the community. The black community responded. Shortly after, I was chosen to receive the recently-formed Tacoma Urban League's Man-of-the-Year Award. The citation noted "[the recipient] has been an important voice in maintaining communication between the black community and city government in the face of difficulties." I consider this one of the greatest honors I ever received.

Inconsistencies

Poetic Justice
Richard G. Simmons

Winter Park, Florida, a wealthy residential community that labeled itself the City of Homes, was opposed to high-density zoning. While serving there as city manager, I witnessed an unusual zoning event.

A turn-of-the-century wooden hotel was to be torn down and a series of condominiums built on the site, one of our more beautiful lakefront points. Even though the condominiums would be expensive and the density low, community resistance to anything other than residential use ran very high. At a public hearing on the matter, opponents to the proposal were so numerous that the city commission had to adjourn to a high school auditorium.

Also located in Winter Park was Rollins College, a private college for the wealthy. The opposition to the condominiums had as its leader the college president's wife, a woman wealthy in her own right and a great art collector. She seldom came to public meetings, but this time she did come. And she expressed herself eloquently as being opposed to anything that smacks of commercialism on the lakefront.

Two days later I noticed in the newspaper an announcement that one of the college president's wife's properties, also on the lake front and only a few doors from the hotel property in question, was going to be dedicated as an art museum. Because of the wide community interest in such a cultural addition, the dedication and grand opening of the museum were to be a major social event. The newspaper gave all the details.

Among the details, the article pointed out that there would be a low admission charge to cover the expenses of operating the museum. This was very interesting: charging an admission fee made the museum a commercial enterprise and placed it in violation of the zoning law. The surprise among those who favored the museum but opposed the condominiums could be appreciated only by one who knew the characters.

It was poetic justice.

Small Incidents Beget Big Irritants

Thomas F. Maxwell

As assistant to the city manager in Kansas City, Missouri, I learned how little things can outrage the taxpayer. The following example has stuck in my mind:

One of the first steps taken to break the grip of Boss Tom Pendergast's political machine was to take the police department out of the control of the city government and place it under a board appointed by the governor. This was done just prior to L. Perry Cookingham's becoming city manager in 1940. When the reform government went in, it was determined in agreement with the board of police commissioners that all fixing of traffic tickets would stop.

A few months after I had been hired by the city, my wife and I were attending a bridge party. At the table next to mine sat a prominent merchant who had made large financial contributions to the reform party and given it his strong public support. I was astounded to overhear him complaining bitterly about having to pay for a traffic ticket. I heard him make the following statement (and I believe I am quoting almost verbatim): "I have just had to pay the first traffic ticket that I have ever had to pay in my entire life as a resident of Kansas City. I don't know whether this reform government was such a good idea or not!"

In deference to my host and hostess—but probably more out of respect for a stern warning glance from my wife's big brown eyes—I kept my mouth shut and did not give vent to the disbelief I felt which probably showed in my reddening face.

Miles's Law: Where You Stand Depends on Where You Sit
Thomas F. Maxwell

The policemen and firemen of University City, Missouri, worked hard to get the voters' approval of a pension plan that would give them and their families at least some economic security. (At that time coverage under the U.S. Social Security program was not available to local government employees.) The first tax bills that included the three-cent tax-rate increase to pay for the pensions were issued almost immediately after I took office as the first manager under the new council-manager plan. I expected to receive an avalanche of complaints. Perhaps councilmen and others did receive complaints, but I received only one, and that from an unexpected source.

A captain in the fire department came to my office and complained bitterly about the tax increase, even though it had been instituted to provide him and other firemen a pension. It seemed that he owned several rental properties in the city (although how he ever accumulated the money to purchase such properties on a fireman's salary is a complete mystery to me). As the owner of these properties, he found this three-cent tax increase a real hardship. My explanation that it was to be used solely and only for financing a pension fund for the firemen and policemen did not satisfy him in the least. I think of all city employees I have ever had contact with, and I had more than 5,000 in Norfolk and we had more than 6,000 in Kansas City, he was undoubtedly the most unreasonable employee in my thirty-three years experience as an assistant city manager and city manager. I simply could not convince him that his future pension benefits so far exceeded his tiny tax increase that he should be as happy to pay it as were all the other firemen and policemen.

Contradictions
LeRoy F. Harlow

Zoning is a delicate and sensitive matter that sometimes makes ordinarily honest people dishonest, and turns friends into enemies. On more than one occasion people who have signed a petition have asked to have their names removed. The pattern seems to be that a petition will be taken through a neighborhood in the evening, when both adults are home.

People will sign to satisfy a neighbor and avoid hard feelings, although they are actually opposed to the neighbor's proposition. Then the next day they will call city hall and ask to have their names taken off. My most bizarre example of this occurred when I was city manager of Albert Lea, Minnesota. It involved three men: Mr. Roberts, Mr. Hansen, and Mr. Edwards.

Roberts telephoned me one day to say the question of rezoning a parcel of property from residential to commercial use would be coming before the council. The applicant would be a Mr. Hansen, Roberts said. He added that Hansen had previously applied for the rezoning, but he (Roberts) and others had stopped it.

The next day Hansen came to see me. If he was aware I had been fore-warned of his interest in rezoning some property, he gave no sign of it. In fact, he didn't mention zoning. He said he simply had a suggestion: that we station police officers at a couple of intersections to direct traffic during rush hours.

About ten days later Hansen came back. This time he brought up the rezoning matter. He said that formerly he had been in the grocery business, having owned the building in which he had his store. Then he had leased his building to Edwards. At the time he and Edwards discussed the lease agreement, Hansen had agreed to a provision that he would not go back in the grocery business within a certain stipulated area surrounding the location Edwards had rented.

Edwards had the lease prepared and presented it to Hansen for his signature. Trusting Edwards that the lease read as they agreed, Hansen had signed it. He later discovered that the provision about his not going back into business described a much larger area than they had agreed on verbally. In response to my question, Hansen acknowledged that he had no proof of their original agreement other than his word against Edwards's.

Faced with this problem, Hansen had sought and located a suitable site for another store, outside the prohibited area. But the site was in a residential zone. He commenced proceedings for a rezoning with the understanding that if the city would rezone the site, he would purchase it and build a store there.

As required by the zoning board before it would even consider a rezoning petition, Hansen had visited all the neighbors within 300 feet of the proposed store site. He had obtained their written consent on a formal petition to the zoning board and city council. This had required considerable effort, because the owners of several properties within the 300-foot area lived out of state.

The zoning board had visited the site, talked with the neighbors, satisfied themselves that rezoning was in the best interest of the community and was favored by the people in the area, and had recommended to the city council that the rezoning be granted. The ordinance establishing the rezoning petitioned for by Hansen had passed council on the first of the three required readings, but got no further.

Hansen said he was going to try again but was being opposed by Edwards. He said Edwards, working through Roberts, was having another petition circulated in the same neighborhood where Hansen got his petition signed. Roberts had persuaded some people that rezoning would be bad for the neighborhood and had got them to sign a second petition asking that their names be taken off the Hansen petition.

Hansen cursed Edwards. He said that if he didn't get the rezoning he was going to force Edwards out of the building Edwards was renting from him. But, he said, the real reason he came to see me was to ask whether names on the petition favoring the rezoning could be removed by another petition, after the zoning board had recommended the rezoning and the city council had passed the rezoning ordinance on first reading.

He said that he couldn't get a local lawyer to handle the matter for him but that an outside lawyer had advised him the second petition was illegal and of no effect. Not knowing that the city attorney represented the city only, not private parties, he asked me to get an opinion from the city attorney. I explained to him that because this was not a matter involving the general public, I could not ask the city attorney to give him a legal opinion. He would have to employ his own attorney.

A few days later, Edwards, a pompous individual bent on making me understand he had great influence with both the zoning board and the city council, came to my office. He said he could get the rezoning through if he wanted to. Then he added this confusing touch to the picture.

He told me that Roberts had originally telephoned me from his (Edwards's) store when Edwards was there. Edwards said he appreciated all that Roberts had done for him. "But," he continued, "Roberts doesn't know my true feelings in the matter." Nor, after all Roberts had done for him, did Edwards want to tell Roberts how he really felt. Actually he wanted Hansen to get the rezoning so Hansen wouldn't evict him from the rented building. As to competition from Hansen, Edwards said he wasn't worried about that, not only because the property Hansen was trying to get rezoned was quite a distance from his store, but because he didn't think Hansen had money enough to build a new store.

Edwards closed our conversation with this: "My only interest in this is to protect myself. You can ask anyone in town. They'll tell you. We three—Hansen, Roberts, and I—are all the closest of friends."

Don't You, or Do You?

LeRoy F. Harlow

After the voters of Sweet Home, Oregon, approved the new charter recommended by the Oregon League of Cities, which provided for the council-manager plan, John Russell, the editor and publisher of the local
weekly, was not happy with the council's choice of a city manager. He
had wanted them to choose a local man, specifically a friend of his. In
person and in his editorials and local stories, he frequently criticized the
city. One time it would be the police, another time the city council. And
as city manager I got my share.

In one issue he ran a story about Tom Burgett, an exlogger who frequently contributed short pieces to the paper. John stated that Burgett's
ideas were so "logical" it almost seemed he should be appointed city manager. This was three weeks after Burgett had come to my office the second
time to give me "some helpful advice." His advice was that Sweet Home
should keep its money from "going through the Narrows" by providing
gambling, drinking, and prostitution—all high class—so the city could get
the revenue and build streets and sidewalks. He charged that we were permitting local money to be spent on prostitutes down the valley in
Lebanon. So much for logic.

As far as I know, John never came out in his newspaper against the
council-manager plan of government for Sweet Home. But a statewide
proposal to adopt a constitutional amendment that would permit counties
to have council-manager government gave him his opportunity. He could
express his opposition to the form of government without offending
Sweet Home residents who favored what Sweet Home had, several of
whom were large advertisers in his paper and had talked openly of starting
another paper in town.

Shortly before a fall election, he ran three editorials on one day and in
one column of the paper. The top editorial in the column was titled
"DON'T FAIL TO VOTE–VOTE AS YOU BELIEVE." The lead sentence read, "This newspaper during its existence has never told anyone
how they should vote." This was followed by sentences such as, "To vote
as you please is an inheritance of democracy. . . . Don't let anyone tell you
how to vote. . . . Keep America free. Vote as you believe on November
7th."

The editorial at the bottom of the column was titled "MANAGER
FORM OF GOVERNMENT." The closing sentence read, "Vote against
the proposed amendment."

Press/Media Relations

It's Easier from Outside than Inside

Richard G. Simmons

In my first city, Melbourne, Florida, in the early fifties, the radio news commentary was by a crusading and often critical news announcer. He often editorialized from the sidelines about what he considered to be the correct action that should have been taken on a specific matter. An ex-Marine from World War II, he took pride in teaching our excellent high school band close-order drill.

In one of his editorial blasts, he was critical because the city hadn't purchased a large and expensive tract of land for a park where he wanted the high school band to practice drill. He received some citizen support and decided to run for city commission to set things straight. He was the highest vote getter, which made him mayor.

After a few rough meetings in which he had to make decisions that weren't as popular as he would have liked, he realized that it was easier to editorialize after the fact than face the live music.

His first major test was the budget sessions. We spent all evening talking about police, fire, streets, and sanitation. And when we had taken care of these essentials, we had only one source of revenue for new parks—a considerable tax increase.

Shortly after the budget sessions he resigned from the city commission. But after that his news commentary had a decidedly different tone.

Only Conflict Is News
James Joshua Mott

In West Palm Beach, Florida, I considered having weekly meetings of just the department heads and myself. The aim was to provide a closed session in which these key administrators and I could update one another and improve communications, planning, and coordination. Other than in this proposed meeting we had a full open-door policy to the media, citizens, and employees. (In fact, the door had been taken off its hinges and stored away.) Also, we issued news bulletins from my office.

Nevertheless, I anticipated difficulty with the news media people, some fifteen of whom covered city hall representing local and metropolitan newspapers, radio, and TV. They might not think that the open-door policy and the bulletins gave them access enough to City Hall news. They might insist on access to the proposed department-head meetings.

I was surprised, then, when all but one reporter agreed to give the meetings a trial, depending on the city manager to give the media a full report immediately thereafter. One reporter, a Yankee, said, "No." He wanted to be present. I said, "All right, then, be present."

At the second department-head meeting, the assessor, who had thirty-five years of city service, asked the public works director, who had thirty-four years of service, if the garbage collectors could replace the lids of the cans after they emptied them. He thought it would keep the lids from blowing away, be less of a nuisance to the owners, less unsightly, and so on. The public works director replied, "Maybe so. We'll look into it and see what we can do. Thanks."

Next morning the local newspaper had a glaring headling: ASSESSOR BLASTS WORKS DIRECTOR FOR INEFFICIENT GARBAGE COLLECTION.

We had two more weekly meetings, with the one reporter present. Not one department head would open his mouth. I discontinued the meetings.

Conclusion: Headlines sell newspapers. When there are no wars, or not enough, the news media will generate conflict and controversy.

"Heil, Hitler!"
David D. Rowlands

Although I was city manager in Tacoma, Washington, from 1956 to December 1969, I want to discuss the period from 1967 to December

1969. During this time, the weekly city council meetings started at 4:30 P.M. and ran until midnight or later, with a recess at around 7:30 for a smorgasbord dinner. The audience usually included about forty little old men and women who brought brown-bag lunches. The meetings were always broadcast by radio; frequently they were televised.

The mayor, who was adept at creating controversy, tried constantly to ridicule and embarrass my staff members and me. Although the majority of the council members were supportive of programs designed to improve the city, unfortunately there were a few council members who generally sided with the mayor. At one council meeting held in front of a full house, a council member declared that three other council members (whom he named) and I should take a lie-detector test to determine who had planted the bomb that totally destroyed his wife's Cadillac the night before. The accusation was so ridiculous that we ignored it and went on with the other city business.

Among the important community issues were three major urban renewal projects in which the city was involved. To some ultraconservatives such efforts to clean up blighted areas and to provide better housing for the community's less-advantaged citizens are the work of the devil or of the communists. Tacoma had its share of these extremists, and they controlled KAYE, the radio station that broadcast the council meetings.

For months, at about 7:00 P.M. daily, KAYE played Nazi Germany's marching song, while the announcer told his listeners to bow to "Dictator Rowlands." And I was harassed regularly by telephone calls at three and four in the morning, with no sound at the other end of the line when I answered.

Fortunately, a couple of years after I had left Tacoma, the Federal Communications Commission received complaints about KAYE, and the subsequent investigations and hearings resulted in the revocation of the station's license. This forced a change in station ownership and broadcasting practices.

B-8— ••   THE TACOMA NEWS TRIBUNE

Martial Music Played At KAYE Hearing

By WIN ANDERSON
News Tribune Staff Writer

SEATTLE — Static-filled strains of marching music, described as "Nazi Germany's Horst Wessel Song" filled the tiny hearing room in the federal office building here Thursday as the Puget Sound Committee for Good Broadcasting (PSC) began to present its case against the renewal of radio station KAYE's license by the FCC.

The taped song was played over a voice described by PSC attorney Morton Hamburg as Dr. Jon Gold, KAYE commentator. The voice dedicated the song to former City Manager David Rowlands and described the council-manager form of government under Rowlands as "the most purely fascist form of government in North America." This particular excerpt, one of several played in the hearing, was allegedly recorded on Jan. 30, 1969.

COMMENT ON ROWLANDS

At a segment identified as commentary by station manager and president Jim Nicholls, associating Rowlands with black militants, saying, "he runs and hides or he falls on his knees and grants their every request . . . and encourages them by providing jobs." One of these jobs he noted was legedly recorded on Jan. 30, 1969.

The tape also played alleged broadcast swipes by Gold at Lynn Hodges, former Human Relations Commission director in Tacoma.

One of these jobs he noted was a $700 per month position to teach black culture in the parks.

The voice distinguished blacks from Negroes, saying that blacks were not American and blessing Negroes.

The tape was not heard by KAYE attorney Benedict Cottone, who left the hearing room after protesting the playing of the tape as improper and prejudicial. He said the proper method to introduce the evidence was through written transcripts and after being admonished by FCC examiner Ernest Nash for his conduct in departing the hearing room, Cottone in a parting jab said: "I am willing to have my conduct judged in any proceeding other than one over which you are presiding, sir."

PROTEST OF MOVE

In preliminary matters, Cottone requested that since the hearing had to be moved from Tacoma at the request of PSC attorneys that for the convenience of all it might as well be moved to Washington, D.C. Nash said it was not within his authority to deal with the request and that it would have to be taken up with the chief examiner.

The taped excerpts and transcripts were prepared by PSC with the analysis prepared by Dr. Ralph Jennings, of the Office of Communication of the United Church of Christ. Dr. Jennings was to be called as PSC's first witness to testify to the methods of preparation and study.

In connection with the taped broadcast week, Hamburg says it was made starting Aug. 1, 1968, and that it contains approximately 33 personal attacks as described under FCC rules.

FCC rules say that if during the presentation of views on controversial subjects of public importance, if persons, groups or organizations are attacked, the station licensee must within one week notify the person or group attacked and deliver a tape or transcript of the program and offer the opportunity to respond.

Nicholls has testified that no such personal attacks were made and therefore the procedure was never followed.

Radio attacks on city manager prompt citizen response and action.

A New Chief in Town
Buford M. Watson, Jr.

In 1961, when I became manager of Muskogee, Oklahoma, the city had had a long history of internal problems in the police department. Only the year before, a large group of police, including the chief, had been indicted by a grand jury. The chief was removed for illicit activities with prostitutes. Several policemen convicted of grand larceny had been placed on probation by the court.

The officer who was chief when I became city manager was a gentle man who had been with the department for twenty-five years, having advanced through the ranks from rookie patrolman. He was a good policeman but not a good administrator, and after a short evaluation I knew I wanted a new chief, from outside the department.

The present chief and I had several discussions, and he indicated his willingness to retire at my request or when a replacement was available. I began secretly interviewing candidates from outside the city, so that when I located a suitable successor I could take quick and decisive action. Finally, I made a choice from among the candidates. But before I could make an announcement, someone bombed the present chief's car in front of his house. As a consequence, to avoid the appearance of a "scared" change, I decided to delay action on the new chief's appointment, and the chief candidate agreed to wait sixty days for action.

The Muskogee city charter required appointment of a city resident if there was a qualified candidate on the eligible list. My plan was to make a provisional appointment for three months and, during that time, to establish an eligibility list. So about sixty days later I called the chief candidate to ask if he was still interested in the position and if he would accept a provisional appointment. He was interested and willing.

Much to my shock, the next morning the local newspaper editor called me and asked, "When are you announcing the new police chief?" When I responded with a "no comment," he said, "You'd better get going on the appointment: the full story hits the streets in fifteen minutes."

Immediately I called in the present chief. After explaining the change of events and the "leak" to the newspaper, I had to ask for his resignation or retirement along the lines we had discussed. This proved to be an emotional time for him and a difficult one for me, but he did agree to retire. My apologies for the way the story had broken were small solace, I am sure.

Then, wondering how the private conversation on my telephone might have been intercepted, I checked to see if my phone was "bugged." But I found no evidence. Finally, the telephone company discovered what had happened and told me: An operator had overheard the conversation and told a newspaper reporter.

The newspaper leak and my resulting action set off a whole series of problems. The police union appealed my actions to the merit board. The merit board ruled that in this instance I did not have authority to make a provisional appointment. After having moved to town, the new police chief learned of the merit board's decision. There were threats of violence. And on and on. My only support came from the city council. But that, fortunately enough, was all I needed.

I began the selection of a police chief, in accord with the requirements of the merit system, by setting the job qualifications. This allowed me to narrow the field immediately to two men: a local police administrative assisant and the man of my choice. The test results were close, but (fortunately for me) my man had the better psychological test results. This made possible my appointment of the new chief from outside the city, as I had planned.

Summary: The appointment of a police chief is a difficult decision, and secrecy is almost impossible. The city manager has many publics to satisfy, and even though he may want to improve a department, many citizens will not appreciate the need. Furthermore, the newspaper can make the job even more difficult. Most important to the city manager is the support of the city council, because in the last analysis they control the management of the city government.

Pornography
and Sex

Two Can Play That Game

Richard G. Simmons

We were getting complaints about a downtown store that was selling pornographic materials. The store was a major newsstand in the community and sold newspapers and periodicals to a number of influential people. To find out what was going on, we had the police department send a fifteen-year-old boy to buy materials, then showed to the city commission what the boy was able to purchase. The commission members were aghast at the materials and demanded that we do something to stop this activity. Of course the newspapers covered the commission's actions with a great deal of publicity.

I called the bookstore proprietor for an appointment when the city attorney and I could come down and discuss with him the problems we were having. About an hour before our appointment, I got a call from some individual who implied that he was from out-of-town, that he had stopped at the bookstore, and that the proprietor was putting secret recording devices around the store because, "the SOB city manager is coming down, and I'm going to trap him."

When we left for our appointment, I had my own tape recorder with me. I indicated to the proprietor that I understood his store was bugged, so to be sure that we got everything correct, I would ask him to speak directly into the microphone. He was shaken by this turn of events and denied that he had hidden microphones.

The attorney and I pointed out to him that his arrest and the ensuing publicity would not help his business, since by his own admission 75 percent of his business was newspapers and conventional paperback books.

We acknowledged that because of Supreme Court rulings we might not be able to win in court, but we also realized that the newspapers would thoroughly cover a local trial, and during the ensuing publicity any respectable person who bought newspapers, periodicals, and books would stay away from his store. If he were to lose this business, as a result of the publicity on the trial, he would go broke.

The city commission then attempted to pass an antipornography ordinance. On the first evening we had peddlers of pornographic materials from three counties in the commission room, demanding that the commission not pass the ordinance because it would violate their constitutional liberties. They came early and in such numbers that there was no room for people who supported the ordinance to get into the commission room.

Recognizing that we needed political support, between the first and second readings of the ordinance I arranged for speaking engagements with a number of senior-citizen and parent-teacher organizations. I took the books with me. I said that I did not want to offend anyone but that if anyone after the meeting wished to come up and review the materials, they were welcome to do so. Many of the people had never seen material of this type and were alarmed at the contents.

At the meeting for a second reading of the ordinance, the people supporting the ordinance came early and packed the auditorium and the halls so that the pornography peddlers could not even get into the city hall. The ordinance went through on a five-to-nothing vote.

The local bookstore proprietor threatened to sue me for a million dollars for implied threats. However, with the tape recordings I had, he backed down and dropped his line of offensive materials.

"——, I Can't Believe it!"
William H. Parness

On a weekend evening the telephone rang at my home. It was one of the police captains, calling on behalf of all the department's command officers–three captains and one lieutenant. Could they have a private meeting with me soon?

Next evening these four officers sat facing me. One of them began, "There's a problem in the department. It concerns the chief. We have reason to suspect that he has been engaging in illicit sex acts with young boys."

The officers proceeded to give me the reasons for their suspicions:

intervention by the chief in departmental investigations involving young boys who had been victims or suspects in sex crimes or misbehavior; the chief's standing order that he be notified immediately whenever one of these young boys was brought to the station; his taking the youngsters into his private office and giving orders that he and they not be disturbed; abruptly adjourning other meetings when one of his young male friends came in; his secretary's report that after the chief's thirty- to forty-five-minute "counseling sessions" with the youngsters, invariably the toilet in his private office was flushed and then the chief ushered the young visitor out and bid him a warm farewell; and a recent instruction from the chief that the secretary order through the city purchasing office a medical journal relating to sexual practices between men and boys.

My first reaction was to say, "Where's your proof? Show me some tangible evidence." They had none—nothing but suspicions, allegations, and rumors. Each of the officers separately had been suspicious for some time, but only within the past few days had they all jointly communicated their individual beliefs.

One of the captains added, "Mr. City Manager, as you can imagine, our suspicions about the chief are common knowledge within the department. We are amazed that the rumor has not broken loose and run rampant throughout the city. In fact, one of our more vocal and dissatisfied officers is threatening to reveal the entire thing to the press unless the city's management takes some action immediately. We aren't sure how long we can keep this guy silenced." At the same time, they cautioned against calling in the district attorney, fearing that his office was so large that leaks would occur.

What a bombshell! And, what a predicament. As the person responsible for administration of city affairs, including the police department, I had a problem that needed action before some dissident revealed "juicy" allegations that would tarnish the police department's (and the city's) image and lower departmental morale even further. On the other hand, the evidence was only circumstantial. If I brought accusations against the chief, they could unjustly destroy his reputation and credibility, even his career.

At this point, I decided I needed outside advice. I availed myself of a relatively new device in the field of urban management. I called in two "range riders," those retired city managers who are now available as consultants to active city managers faced with difficult professional problems.

After I recited my problems to them, they both advised me to retain the services of a private investigator to conduct a confidential investigation of the operations and management of the department. I took their advice, and with their help engaged a retired police officer who had served some thirty years in one of the area's major departments.

In the succeeding weeks, the investigator interviewed some fifteen department members and five other people. With the knowledge and consent of the interviewees, he taped more than eight hours of testimony. He frequently reported his findings to me, and occasionally he had me listen to the tapes. Although somewhat revealing, none of the information contained evidence that would support a charge that the chief was practicing illegal sexual conduct. Here are a few examples of what we learned:

• A young boy had been booked on a minor charge of possessing marijuana. Upon learning of the boy's incarceration and record of indecent exposures, the chief had the boy removed from the jail and brought to his office, where he talked to the boy about sex for thirty to forty-five minutes. He interrogated the boy about his past sex experiences with other boys or men and with girls or women. He then had the boy remove all his clothes. According to the boy's statement, the chief didn't touch him. He just looked at him, and after a while told him to get dressed— that he was going to call the boy's mother and release him to her.

• One incident involved a youth who was AWOL from the army. Military police had reported the absence and a federal court had issued a warrant for the youth's arrest. The chief intercepted the warrant and, to the amazement of the departmental investigating officers, destroyed it.

• A juvenile officer reported to the watch commander that informants had revealed the location of a stolen motorcycle. An investigating officer filed a report that he had found the main parts of the stolen motorcycle and also had found potted marijuana growing on the premises. The location was the home of one of the chief's young male protégés. The chief countermanded an order to confiscate the stolen property, and when investigating officers visited the premises, not only had the motorcycle been removed, but every trace of marijuana as well. The staff was convinced that the chief had been responsible for alerting the occupants.

• More than once the chief insisted upon being given cash from the department's undercover fund, which was administered by a detective sergeant and was to be used only for necessary dope buys. The chief was giving the money to his young friends.

Although I concurred with the investigator's opinion that any of these examples of gross misconduct could be the basis for severe disciplinary action, including discharge, there still was no tangible proof or testimony of illicit sex acts. Almost in desperation, I finally insisted that the investigator arrange a private interview with one of the chief's boys, a known sexual pervert and the most regular visitor to the chief's office. (Until then the investigator had resisted talking to this boy because the boy would reveal the discussion to the chief.)

The investigator made the necessary arrangements with the boy's mother and stepfather, but the interview gained us little. We learned that the boy had had weekly "counseling sessions" with the chief for seven or eight months. But the boy maintained that the chief had committed no sex acts with him; in fact, he argued that the chief was a beautiful person and was his dear friend.

About two months had passed since this fuse had been lit, and I could sense the growing discontent within the department. The captains, who had been keeping in touch with me, advised me now that some managerial action must be taken as soon as possible.

The following weekend, while I was away from the city on business, the investigator reached me by phone. He said, "You'd better get home. Your local newspaper editor has been alerted by someone, and he's asking questions about the investigation." I told him I would be in my office Monday.

When I arrived Monday morning, the editor was waiting for me. In a somber mood—and with pencil and pad in hand—he shot out at me, "A very reliable source has told me that an investigation is being conducted within our police department and that it involves some sexual misconduct by the chief. I want your comments."

Taken back by his demand and with full cognizance of the volatile nature of the entire problem, I stumbled a bit, but responded, "I cannot reveal anything as yet, except to admit that an investigation of the department is being conducted. It is not true that the chief has been engaging in illegal sex acts. I am going to meet privately with the city council tonight, and with their approval I'll have a full story for you tomorrow morning. Please be patient." Thank heavens he agreed, although reluctantly.

That afternoon I arranged a meeting of the private investigator, our mayor, and me. With her strong character, superior intellect, and political savvy, our mayor had earned a great deal of respect from her city council colleagues. Following introductions, I alerted her to be prepared for a shock. And then, for the next two hours, the investigator and I unfolded the distasteful report—interspersed with several taped interviews. He revealed information I had not heard before. Over the previous weekend, in the chief's absence and with the help of the departmental officers, he had entered the chief's private office and searched his desk. His main goal was photographs, but none were to be found. What he did find were a couple of dozen pornographic magazines showing males engaged in sex acts and a large, commercial-size jar of petroleum jelly—half used!

At the end, the mayor sat in stunned silence. At first her complexion was drained, but now she was florid. She exclaimed, "My God! I can't believe it! Of course you've got to tell the council the whole story tonight."

She agreed that we must maintain total confidentiality and that, later, any statement would come from me.

That night the full city council gathered in a private executive session. I introduced the investigator and briefly explained the reason I had retained him. For the next two hours the only display was when one council member would look at another. The investigator concluded by informing all of us that one of our department's shift personnel reported witnessing the chief removing several armloads of material from his private office and placing them in his automobile during the very early hours of the previous Sunday. It seemed obvious that he was aware of our investigation and a tightening noose.

I expected personal chastisement for withholding such important information from the council, and for the professional violation of hiring an investigator without prior council review and approval. However there was none. Unanimously–and almost in a unified voice–they stated, "Mr. City Manager, you have no choice. He's got to go–immediately." And the mayor added, "He shouldn't be allowed to enter the police station again."

All were kind in offering their support and sympathetic understanding of the problem facing me.

The next morning, I phoned the chief and told him to report to my office within the hour.

He came as directed and obviously was nervous.

Carefully choosing my words, I began, "Chief, because you have been spending an inordinate amount of time with several youths in the community, very serious internal-management problems have arisen within the department, problems that I believe are intolerable.

"First, let me make one thing quite clear. I am not accusing you of having committed any illicit affairs with these young people. Rather, there are several incidents that I have had documented, some of which are patently illegal and cannot be condoned. These have caused the severe disruption of law-enforcement efforts in our community and a serious decline in personnel morale."

With his facial muscles twitching, he listened intently, wringing his hands. When it appeared that I had ended my indictment, he blurted out, "I can't believe my ears! I demand to know what these so-called incidents are! I demand a chance to rebut. Please, there must be some mistake."

"No, Chief," I replied. "There's no mistake. All these charges are well documented." I displayed an eighteen-page record of all events, interviews, and findings prepared by the private investigator. "Things have progressed too far. No purpose would be served by your trying to refute these charges. They have been reviewed in detail by the city council. The council has concluded unanimously that you must vacate your position with the city."

His voice quavered, and sweat broke out on his brow. Then he responded. "This is unreal. I can explain any of your charges if given a chance. You're asking me to cancel my career. Impossible!"

I replied, "Look, Chief, this is the hardest task I've ever had to face. I am fully aware of its consequences. There is no alternative. As you know, a private investigation has been conducted on you and on internal departmental affairs."

Displaying impressive poise, he quickly responded, "What do you mean 'investigation'? I don't know anything about an investigation."

I continued, "I have no alternative but to ask you to submit your resignation. If you refuse, I shall order your immediate discharge. It's your choice, but I want your answer by 5:00 P.M. today."

He wiped his brow and pleaded, "Please, give me more time. I need to discuss this with my wife. I'll let you know first thing in the morning."

I set an appointment for 9:00 A.M. the next day.

That afternoon, in anticipation of the inevitable confrontation by the press, I drafted a resignation news release. As the hours wore on, a nagging thought kept me tense. "He may refuse to resign. If so, I'll have to discharge him, which means that the whole dirty mess—departmental management defects and youth relationships—will have to be dragged out and aired openly. This would ruin not only this man's career, but his personal reputation and that of his attractive young family as well. Then, too, it would be extremely embarrassing to the city in general, the city council, the department, and me.

The following morning he appeared at my office as agreed. At my insistence, the investigator was present, more for moral support than for physical protection—although the thought had crossed my mind that the chief carried a gun, was undergoing a tremendous shock, and was probably suffering from mental imbalance anyway.

The mayor, who asked if she could be present, was relieved at the presence of the investigator, because she feared for my safety.

Looking out an office window to the sidewalk adjoining the city hall, I was startled to see fifteen or twenty news-media people, and several television cameras. Every major TV channel in the metropolitan area was represented. Word came to me that they insisted upon a news interview with the mayor and me.

At about this time an acquaintance of mine entered my office and asked permission to remain. He was a local private attorney and a close personal friend of the chief. I sensed complications.

I began by asking the chief what he had decided to do. He replied, "I'll resign. I need your secretary so I can dictate my resignation."

I arranged for the dictation. As soon as the chief had signed his resignation, I suggested to the mayor that she and I face the news media who were clamoring for an audience outside my office door.

The chief stated his intention of confronting the press. His attorney friend urged him to leave by another exit, arguing that the press would cause him great harm and embarrassment through their questioning. Fortunately, the chief heeded his advice.

When the mayor and I met the press, we got a shocking blast of television strobe lights and were bombarded with questions. When calm was restored, the mayor read the press release. In essence it admitted to the conducting of a private investigation of the internal affairs of the police department which revealed several complex managerial defects. These prompted the resignation of the police chief, just filed with my office.

These media people were the "big-time metropolitan news pros" as contrasted with the small-town, suburban cub reporters who usually frequent city hall beats. One probed, while shoving a television microphone in my face: "Mr. City Manager, did you, on your own, initiate a private investigation into the affairs of the police department and the personal conduct of the chief?"

I answered, "Yes, I did."

Another continued, "Were some of the charges concerning sexual misconduct by the police chief?"

Suddenly there was dead silence and all eyes and cameras turned on me. (I was told later I had a deathly pallor about me, and it looked that way as my wife and I viewed the TV broadcast later that night). I hesitatingly answered, "The investigation was into all phases of departmental operations, its management, personnel morale, and personal conduct of its principal staff members. The news release read by the mayor adequately states our position."

The commentator continued to press: "Is the police chief being accused, or has he been found guilty of practicing illegal sex acts with youngsters?"

I answered unequivocally. "No. There is no truth or foundation to those allegations."

With that, the mayor and I retreated into the solace and privacy of my office.

What an ordeal!

My next step was to appoint one of the captains as acting chief, and I promised him full administrative support in his efforts to bring order to the departmental chaos.

That night the television newscasts and airwaves were full of the story. The following day each of the three local newspapers and the neighboring metropolitan press devoted most of their front pages to the subject.

The chief cloistered himself in his home and would not answer his phone nor a caller's knock.

The following day the mayor called and suggested that I immediately contact the district attorney and invite his investigation and counsel. I made the call right away, and the DA expressed his gratitude that I had initiated the request. He said his criminal investigator would visit my office in two days. By the next day, word of the DA's impending investigation had spread through the police department. And that evening the acting police chief called me at my home. He said, "We have just gotten some new evidence that you should be aware of before you meet with the DA's investigator tomorrow."

Next morning the acting chief and I met in my office. Smiling and relieved, he said, "Apparently when all the news stories were released about the chief's resignation, one of his little boyfriends felt liberated and

Tri-Valley *Herald*

Vol. 103, No. 204   Dublin, Livermore, Pleasanton, San Ramon, California, Wednesday, February 8, 1978   36 Pages

Lindgren is charged in teen boys sex case

By JUDITH SHERARD

LIVERMORE — The district attorney Tuesday morning filed a complaint charging former Police Chief Ron Lindgren with three felony counts of oral copulation and one misdemeanor count of child molestation involving four teen-aged boys.

Lindgren, who has been on a leave of absence since his resignation under fire Jan. 13, was booked at the Santa Rita county jail after he surrendered with his attorney. The 39-year-old Lindgren was released on $1,000 bail pending arraignment on the charges Feb. 15 in Livermore Municipal Court.

The three incidents of oral copulation allegedly occurred last August, September and December in Lindgren's private office at the Livermore police station on Pacific Avenue, according to an affadavit filed in support of the complaint and arrest warrant.

Two of the three victims, ages 15 and 17, allegedly had their first contacts with Lindgren were in 1976.

One of the youths also told investigators that Lindgren offered him money on two occasions to perform oral copulation, the district attorney's affidavit said.

The affidavit stated that the money allegedly used to pay the teen-ager came from the special undercover fund of the vice, narcotics and intelligence division, and that receipt books were kept on amounts checked out to Lindgren.

Two days before his resignation, Lindgren allegedly asked for the receipts books and then ordered them destroyed because he was "doing some housecleaning," according to police personnel affidavits. The records were shredded.

District Attorney Lowell Jensen said that no additional charges against the former Livermore police chief are being contemplated and he said that a charge of misappropriation of funds will not be filed.

Although six paragraphs of the affidavit deal with the use of undercover funds and their destruction on Jan. 16 at Lindgren's order, Jensen said, "We did not find anything that justified anything other than the charges that were filed." The district attorney also stated he was satisfied that the investigation is completed.

Lindgren, on separate occasions, allegedly called the boys into his office and showed them magazines and pictures depicting naked men engaged in homosexual acts, the affidavit said. The boys also told investigators that homosexual activity reportedly was discussed during their meetings with the chief.

The child abuse charge, a misdemeanor, stemmed from the chief's alleged strip-search of a 15-year-old boy who had been arrested and the chief's alleged discussions of homosexual acts with the teen-ager.

Formal charges against Lindgren, who served as the city's police chief for 5½ years, was the culmination of a two-week investigation by DaVega, investigator Don Jones and members of the police department.

The district attorney was brought into the case two days after Lindgren's resignation at the request of City Manager Bill Parness, who was under press and public pressure to reveal the contents of his private investigation into the internal affairs of the police department and Lindgren's professional and personal conduct in office.

Parness and City Attorney Gary Reiners declined Tuesday to publicly air the contents of the city's probe, stating that Jensen had requested they not release any information pending a plea on the charges by Lindgren.

"I am not trying to be coy about this at all," Parness said. "I wish we could relieve ourselves of this burden, and, at the proper time, we will."

Parness responded to the allegation that he and the city council were engaged in a

coverup of the activities within the police department relating to mismanagement and morale.

"How can anyone say that there's been a coverup when we've just gone through what we have (the private investigation and the hand-over of the report to Jensen) and all just one month before a city council election!" Parness exclaimed.

Reiners claimed that Lindgren's resignation was called for on the basis of what he termed substantiated information that the chief's administration and management of the department was deficient and that serious morale problems existed.

Reiners contended that there was nothing improper about ordering an outside investigator to look into allegations and problems brought to Parness by the police captains several weeks ago.

Acting Police Chief Jack Essex Tuesday reiterated declarations by Reiners and Parness that, at the time of Lindgren's resignation, "there was no evidence to substantiate criminal charges against the chief."

Lindgren began his 18-year law enforcement career as a Livermore police officer in 1959. He served as the police chief of Union City before returning to the city in 1972 as chief. He is married and has two young children.

Lindgren has been active in youth groups and in 1977 was president of the 300-member Bay Counties Police Officers Association. This year, he is president of the Alameda County Police Chiefs and Sheriff's Association.

In addition to his police department activities, Lindgren taught law enforcement classes at Chabot College's Valley Campus and at the Livermore and Granada High Schools. He resigned from his teaching duties last week.

confessed his entire relationship with the chief to his mother. His mother was distraught. She called the department yesterday and requested an interview on the subject. Two of our men met with her. Without her knowledge, they tape-recorded the interview."

He played the tape for me.

The next several minutes were some of the most heart-wrenching moments of my career. This mother stated that her sixteen-year-old son had been seeing the police chief on regular weekly counseling sessions for almost a year. According to her son, these sessions were in reality nothing but sex orgies whereat masturbation and oral copulation had been committed for the chief.

The mother broke into sobs and was barely able to finish her statement that before the chief resigned, her son had been afraid to confess for fear of recrimination from the chief.

For some selfish reason, I was delighted to hear the tape. It constituted pretty good evidence that our suspicions were true. It served to bolster my conviction that although we had no proof of illegal acts by the chief, my action in removing him from office was justified.

Later the DA's investigator read our private investigator's written report and listened to several parts of his taped interviews. Also, I played the mother's interview for him.

At the end, he sat back and shook his head, saying, "I've been investigating crime and fraudulent behavior for twenty-three years. This is the most sordid, disreputable mess in my experience."

He promised to proceed and conclude his work at the earliest possible time.

From then on the newspapers were unrelenting in pressing for every aspect and detail of the story. Some reporters and editors, convinced there had been a "city hall coverup," refused to accept my first public statement that no evidence could be provided that would convict the chief of having committed illegal sex acts.

Later, based upon the mother's testimony, I revealed that "new evidence" had come to our attention that illegal sex acts may have been committed. But this served only to reinforce their supposition that this "evidence" was known all the time. Despite my protestations and repeated explanations as to the circumstances, the local editor who had initially contacted me about the story deeply resented the fact that he had been scooped by the metropolitan press and TV after withholding the story at my request. He began with bitter editorials berating my performance on the whole affair, claiming that the city council had a duty to invoke disciplinary action against me for my "indiscretions".

As is inevitable, crank letters-to-the-editors came seemingly from everyone who ever had a problem or a denial of any kind from the city government. All were extremely critical of the city manager's tactics and decried this horrid blasphemy against such a fine, upstanding, youth-oriented police chief. Some argued that the proper course was not to discipline the police chief but to fire the city manager.

Fortunately, throughout these very trying five or six weeks, I was supported by a very considerate and sympathetic wife and family and mostly supportive city council.

Unfortunately, this mess occurred at an unpropitious time, namely, about a month before a city council election. Some of the present council members were seeking reelection; hence the matter was bound to become an election issue.

In the meantime the DA's investigator, who, together with other investigative teams, had been at work for more than six weeks, notified us that the DA had enough evidence to level seven criminal charges—mostly felonies—against the chief. Any one of these, upon conviction, could mean a prison sentence.

At this point the local attorney friend of the chief was joined by another attorney from the metropolitan area who had a reputation for criminal legal defense.

There followed lengthy plea bargaining between the DA and the defense attorneys. (In this process, if the prosecution will drop several of the more serious charges, the defense will consider a guilty plea—all in the interest of saving considerable time and expense on both sides.) It was the DA's responsibility to determine the limits of the plea bargaining so as to insure that expediency would not overrule justice.

Finally the DA presented his case to the grand jury. After due deliberation, that body returned indictments against the chief on three counts of committing oral copulation with a minor, and on one misdemeanor.

Again, the news media had a field day. And again the healing public relations wounds were reopened. The question I pondered was: "How will the chief plead? If he pleads guilty, as is expected, his career will be ruined, as will his personal reputation and presumably his marriage. If he pleads innocent, he may not have anything to lose. The burden of proof will be on us—his employer—and the DA. The DA was relying heavily on testimony given by some fairly disreputable young boys—many of whom had previous police records, and none of whom would be considered too reliable or stable as witnesses when confronted by a sharp, probing, articulate defense attorney.

There was more waiting until the plea could be entered, more controversy—bitter editorial attacks, letters to the editor, news columns, on and on.

Finally, some three weeks later, the superior court heard the matter.

Entering the courtroom hand-in-hand with his lovely wife, the chief was on all the area's TV newscasts.

Following the traditional court introductions, the judge asked "How does the defense plead?"

The defense responded, "Nolo contendere to all counts." No contest!

Technically, this was not an admission of guilt, but for all practical purposes, that is what it amounted to.

The judge set a future date for sentencing, instructed that in the interim a probation investigation and report be done, and ordered that the defendant be examined by one of the area's top clinical psychiatrists.

More waiting. It seemed interminable.

About a month later the fateful day arrived. In the interim I had discussed the matter with the DA. He confided to me that his office would not seek a jail term. He contended that there exists a very firm and inviolate moral code among convicts. First, they don't like ex-police officers—particularly a police chief; second, they could never coexist with a child molester. The DA was convinced that if the chief were interned in a state prison, his life would be in serious jeopardy.

In court the judge noted the psychiatrist's review and opinion that the chief was almost schizophrenic—one side believing that his conduct had been acceptable and appropriate, the other yearning to be apprehended. This assessment fit the chief's behavior.

The judgment was rendered: three years probation and one year of donated community service.

Could it be that this terrible experience was ended?

Apparently not. At this writing, the mother of one of the involved youths has begun litigation against the chief and the city in a multimillion-dollar damage claim.

Perhaps this episode is far from complete!

Corruption

Cutting Off the Tip-Off
Richard G. Simmons

When I was city manager of Haines, Florida, in the late fifties. Polk County—in which Haines City is located—was dry, by virtue of a local-option election. This meant that beverages of greater than 2.8 percent alcoholic content could not be sold anywhere in the incorporated or unincorporated areas. Because Polk County was surrounded by counties where alcoholic beverages could be sold, we faced a variety of policing problems.

For instance, one of the local newspapers had an ad for "Champale," with the slogan, "It is more than a beer." Because beer was legally a 2.8 percent beverage or less, I asked the owner of the store featuring Champale to prove that the alcohol content was less than 2.8. If he could prove it was less than 2.8, I pointed out, he would be in violation of the state statute on misleading advertising because Champale was *not* "more than a beer." After an independent testing laboratory revealed that Champale was 3 percent alcohol and higher, sales were discontinued immediately.

A major policing problem was the bootleg or illegal sales of alcohol in the community. One day one of our young, progressive police officers came to my office and asked to talk to me privately. He had come to report that he believed the chief of police was tipping off an establishment that sold illegal whiskey. This concerned me, but it also posed a problem of how to get the evidence needed to prove or disprove the officer's allegations. When I suggested we might go to the county sheriff, he reminded me that the sheriff was suspected of cooperating with certain of the bootleggers. I knew, too, that the sheriff was strictly political and could not be trusted to refrain from telling the police chief about any secret investigation. The state beverage department was not much help, either.

Further, this was a local matter, not federal. It was up to us to determine what to do next.

I considered several alternatives and finally settled on one that, although not entirely satisfactory, seemed the only way to get the information we needed. With the officer's help, I got a mutual friend from the telephone company to isolate the two cable pairs that went to the Police Chief's house and to run two small, almost invisible copper wires from the cable through the middle of an orange grove. I borrowed a 6-110 volt converter from a dictaphone salesman, took my office dictating equipment out into the back of my car, parked in the middle of the orange grove at about ten o'clock at night, and hooked the small copper wires to the recorder so I could record any conversations.

We had arranged that the young officer would call the chief and tell him he suspected illegal activities and wanted to pull a raid. Shortly after 10:30 the phone call came through. The young officer told the chief that whiskey was being run into the "red house" and asked permission to raid it immediately. The chief thanked him and told him that he should call two or three other officers and raid it in about fifteen minutes. After that call was completed, the dial tone came on and immediately another number was dialed. The chief contacted someone and said, "Police are about to raid the 'red house.' Please notify them."

Of course, I realized that my tap was illegal and could not be used in court. Moreover, it was scary as the devil, sitting in the middle of the orange grove by myself, without other police officers knowing why I was there. But I had a serious problem that had to be resolved. Early the next morning I called the mayor, played the transcription to him, and told him of my findings. I then called in the police chief, played the recording for him, and asked him if he would like it played at the next commission meeting or would he prefer to resign. To this day, very few people know why the Chief resigned.

A sequel to this story involves my wife. We were newly married, and during the incident with the police chief she was exceedingly concerned about my safety. In the meantime, I had forgotten to tell her that I had been talking to our parks director, who had a small nursery of his own, about having a Florida everbearing lime tree in our yard. So, one evening he brought by a little potted tree without my knowledge and placed it at our front door. About two weeks later, because I had said nothing, he asked what I thought of the lime tree. I told him I hadn't seen it and guessed that somebody had stolen it.

That evening I asked my wife if she had seen a small lime tree outside our door. She blushed. "Oh, is that what it was?" She had interpreted the tree as possibly a threat to me, like the crown of thorns placed on the head of Jesus. So as not to worry me, she had thrown it into the vacant lot next door.

We retrieved the tree and planted it.

Local F(l)avors
Robert M. Tinstman

Abilene, Texas, was my first city manager post, and at the age of thirty-two I was more than pleased to take on the responsibility in a city of approximately 100,000 population.

One of the more interesting episodes in my first few weeks as city manager of Abilene occurred when a Texas Ranger walking down the midway of the West Texas Fair closed down some of the booths because of gambling activity. His appearance was unannounced and not graciously received by some business leaders. A few days later, the mayor and city commissioners called an executive session with the chief of police, whom they had appointed under the then existing city charter. I was invited to attend as the new "professional" city manager.

The local elected officials suspected that the chief might have invited the Ranger specifically to stop the gambling, and they needed assurance that the chief of police was in no position to instruct or restrain the Texas Rangers. This I was able to give them. Probably the episode reinforced the chief's support of a new city charter which placed his position under the supervision of the city manager.

On another occasion I had to inform a city commissioner who ran a grocery store that he was expected to observe the same driveway-opening and permit policies as other citizens and businessmen in the community. When the street in front of his business was being paved, he insisted on "lay-down" curb the full length of the corner property. When I informed him of his limitations, he tossed his store keys at me, saying, "Take the damn store!"

In executive session with him and the other commission members, we reached a compromise, but substantial compliance was realized with vertical curbing at the corner and one or two other locations. I returned his keys.

Instant Repentance
Richard G. Simmons

When I was city manager of Winter Park, Florida, an incident took place that is laughable now but was then a serious in-house matter.

I have always been a strict disciplinarian when it comes to accepting gifts. The one exception (allowed because enforcement was impractical) was the residents' practice of giving gifts of money to their garbage collectors at Christmas.

The week before Christmas the sanitation director came into my office with a very serious expression. I knew that something was wrong because 6'6" Dave ("Digger") O'Dell, was always cheery—especially at Christmas. Digger said he had personnel problems and expected real trouble, and he wanted advice.

It seems that one of the crews went on the route only to find that someone had collected the garbage before they got there. Of course, all the Christmas gifts were gone. We decided to tell the crews that the police were investigating.

The next morning before the crews started, Digger put his 6'6" frame on a large elevated platform for a departmental meeting. In his most serious tone he told of the events of the previous day. He stated that the police were investigating and, at that time, were fingerprinting garbage cans on the route in question. Digger said he would be gone for two hours and his office would be open for any messages or notes anyone wished to leave. When he returned, he had no notes, but found an envelope containing slightly less than $100. We don't know if all the money was there, but the deprived crew was happy because it was more money than they had expected and they didn't have to pick up garbage to collect it. The event was not publicized by the press, but it was number one on the grapevine.

Money Talks (Back)
Richard G. Simmons

Once at Winter Park, Florida, we took bids on an expensive fire pumper. A member of our volunteer fire department, who was also quite influential in the community, was contacted by a representative of a major fire-equipment company that was bidding for the contract. The representative indicated that if his company won the bid, there would be $5,000 in it for the volunteer. The volunteer reported this to the fire chief with the understanding that he would not be identified. The chief reported the matter to me.

I wasn't sure how to handle the problem, so I decided that the best thing would be to take the offensive. I said nothing about the bribe until the bids were opened and presented to the city commission for award. I casually announced that one of the bidders had offered a bribe to one of our volunteers for purchase of this equipment and I wanted to take that bid off the list. Each commissioner attempted to make a motion, and each attempted to second it, and it was unanimous that the bid should be disqualified. Two days later the president of the company called and demanded my apology. I refused but said that if he wanted to go to the state attorney and have an investigation, I would be happy to cooperate. Needless to say, the item was dropped.

Part Four

Functions of a Professional City Manager

As noted in the Introduction, some seventy years ago Dr. Richard S. Childs conceived a plan of local government that would merge the two essentials of effective democracy. These essentials were, and still are: (1) control of the government by the people, through their elected representatives; and (2) an organizational mechanism that will assure effective functioning of the governmental machinery. He probably borrowed his concept from the familiar business model. This model featured logical structure combined with the principle of specialization. This combination in the private sector had made America a magnet that drew millions of people across the seas to share in a better life through creative freedom and a higher standard of living. It was a combination that thrust America into a position of world leadership.

Dr. Childs structured his plan around a chain of responsibility and authority at three levels. At the top are the sovereign people of the community. Next, the people's elected representatives, who enunciate and carry into effect the wishes of the electorate. Then, a trained and experienced manager to administer the policy decisions of the representatives.

This division of labor calls into play the principle of specialization. The special function of the people is to know what they want their local government to do, to select qualified representatives to carry out their will, and to communicate their wishes to these representatives. The representatives should be men and women skilled at reconciling competing interests within the community. Their special function is two-fold: to reconcile competing interests for the greatest good for the greatest number in the community; and to select, direct, monitor, and control the city manager. The manager is chosen on the basis of proven executive and administrative ability, whether a local person or not, and without regard to the manager's political preference. He serves at the pleasure of the council of elected representatives. His special function is to apply professional managerial skills to the business of the local government, for the benefit of all the people.

This structure has been maintained for nearly three-quarters of a century in the council-manager plan of local government. The people served by this form of government have generally benefited thereby. Their approval is manifest in the steady growth in the number of communities that have chosen council-manager government, or some modification of it, to serve their people.

In the meantime, society has experienced change, has grown more complex, and has placed greater demands on local government. The governments have tried to respond. Consequently, although the basic design of the council-manager plan remains unchanged, the roles of both the council and the manager have expanded. They are required to spend an increasing portion of their time on economic problems, the social concerns of various individuals and groups, and the growing inter-relationships among the political, economic, and social systems within the community.

With increasing demands but no more available time, what does the manager do to accomplish all he should? What functions of the city manager are similar to those of executives in other fields, and how is his job different?

Much has been written on the functions of executives in general, whatever their titles—manager, supervisor, executive director, administrator. By definition an executive or manager is one who gets things done through other people—by a distribution of responsibilities. In my opinion, an effective manager performs the following functions: (1) he develops the *plans* for achieving the organization's objectives; (2) he divides the work to be done into parts, assigns to each part the needed and available human, material, and financial resources, then assembles the parts—*organizes* them—into a going concern that will function smoothly; (3) he *staffs* the organization with qualified and dedicated people, giving personal attention to the selection of people for key positions; (4) he *trains* his immediate subordinates, or provides training for them and others in the organization; (5) he *decides* among alternative courses of action open to the organization; (6) he *delegates* to the heads of departments—entrusts to them—part of the responsibility, authority, and accountability the governing board has delegated to him; (7) he *directs,* in general terms but sometimes in specific terms, the persons in the organization directly responsible and accountable to him for accomplishing the organization's work; (8) he *represents* the administrative organization in its relations with the governing board and outside agencies, and when requested by the governing board he represents the organization in its relations with the public; and (9) he *reports* to the governing body, and through them to the owners or the public, on past performance, anticipated future conditions, and proposed goals and actions.

These functions are common to all managers. Specific examples from city management are planning for the physical and social improvement of the community, including preparation of the annual operating budgets and the longer-range capital improvement budgets; recruiting, examining, and appointing a new police chief and other officials and employees to the city staff; training department heads, firemen, and clerks; deciding on policies to control personal use of city vehicles; directing the water superintendent to undertake a study and recommend a more equitable water-rate schedule; representing the city in wage negotiations with an employee union; and preparing an annual report of accomplishments, future needs and programs, and the city's financial status to the city council and the public.

How does city management differ from private management? Three or four differences are readily apparent. First may be the unique and varied purposes which the city is attempting to serve, as compared with the single or limited purposes of a private organization. Even the smallest city provides the basic services of police protection, fire protection, street construction and maintenance, drainage and flood control, and refuse collection and disposal. No other agency, public or private, offers all these community services, each of which requires special kinds of personnel skills, facilities, equipment, and procedures. The list of city services rendered by larger municipalities can easily reach a hundred or more, including airport operation and maintenance, auditoriums, schools, public health and hospital services, parks, libraries, public recreation, water, sewers, electricity, gas, public transit, and an increasing number of regulatory activities.

Second may be the method of financing city operations. Virtually without exception, private management provides goods and services only in response to desire on the part of the user. No one is required to either purchase or to pay for an item or service he does not want; the choice is left to the purchaser. In contrast, residents may be required to accept and pay for certain public goods and services, whether they wish them or not (e.g., water, sewers, and refuse collection). Also, they may be required to pay for services they never use, or feel they get little or no benefit from (e.g., schools, libraries, parks, and cultural and recreational facilities). Consequently, instead of enjoying the pleasure of freedom of choice, the taxpayer may—and often does—vent his resentment of the coercion to which he is subjected on the public manager who has the duty of imposing it.

Third, willing sellers and willing buyers determine the value of private goods and services, and profit or loss determines whether the private enterprise is a success. In contrast, a city has no single, quantifiable, generally accepted "bottom line" to determine the value of its goods and services, or the success of a program. What is the value of the life of a child or an invalid saved from a burning building, or of anyone who was saved from tuberculosis or undulant fever because the city inspected the community's milk supply? Or how can we precisely measure the success of a juvenile-delinquency reduction program, a mosquito-abatement program, or a sewer-repair program?

Another significant difference is the relative privacy and independence enjoyed by private managers and their families, as compared to the public exposure characteristic of public management. Little of the activity of a private company is known to the stockholders, most of whom may live thousands of miles from the company's operations. Nor is every user of a private company's goods or services also a voting stockholder and therefore eligible to criticize and take action against the management. Theoretically the private manager's employment can be terminated by the stockholders, acting through the elected board of directors. But this is not likely to happen, if for no other reason than the simple bottom-line measure mentioned above. If the numbers on the bottom line are big enough to protect the stockholders' investment and provide them an ample dividend, that usually is all the stockholders expect and require of management.

The city manager's situation is noticeably different. Virtually every recipient of the city's goods and services (whether the recipient wants them or not, or is pleased with them or not) is a stockholder in the municipal corporation, with voting privileges. All these stockholders need do to take a reading on the city's operations is look out the window. They can see instantly whether the garbage is picked up, the pothole in the street is repaired, or a police patrol car goes past as often as they would like. Collectively these stockholders who are so close to the city's operations have the power to force termination of the manager, by changing a majority on the city council.

In the episodes that follow, more than half the city managers listed in the Who's Who at the front of the book describe how they have performed their management functions in this environment. What they relate ranges from innovative improvements in the management of cities to personal threats against them. A few of their experiences are amusing, all are informative, and some are dramatic. Such episodes as the American Nazi Party's confrontation with Skokie, Illinois, the rioting and burning in Washington, D.C., following the assassination of Dr. Martin Luther King, Jr., and the decision to locate the United States Air Force Academy in Colorado Springs, Colorado, may be familiar because of the national and international publicity these events received.

Crisis Management

The Village of Skokie versus
The American Nazis

John N. Matzer, Jr.

On 20 March 1977 an emotional fifteen-month struggle over the First Amendment began between the Village of Skokie, Illinois, and the National Socialist (Nazi) Party of America. On that day the Skokie police chief received a letter from Frank Collin, the Nazi Party leader, announcing that his organization planned to demonstrate publicly in Skokie from 12:00 to 12:30 P.M. on 1 May 1977. The purpose of the demonstration was to protest the Skokie Park District requirement that the party supply the district with $350,000 worth of liability insurance before holding a rally in a park. Another Collin goal was to bring to Skokie the message of free speech for white-power advocates. The Nazis had singled out Skokie, Collin said, because, "A lot of Jews live there. The Jews have been the mainspring of opposition to our organization, and Skokie is synonymous in the minds of most people with Jews."

Community response to the announced May 1 demonstration was swift. Several Jewish organizations reversed the initial position they had taken to ignore the rally, and decided to encourage people to hold a peaceful demonstration against the Nazis. On April 25 a Skokie resident and member of the Janusz Korczak Lodge of B'nai B'rith (the Jewish cultural, educational, and social organization) appeared before the village board. He said, "We'd like legal action to be taken before we show up and tear those people apart." (The Korczak Lodge of B'nai B'rith consisted of survivors of the Nazi holocaust.) We at the village hall responded to the public concern by filing suit in the county circuit court for an injunction to halt the proposed march. The suit stated that the march constituted a grave and serious threat to peace because 40,000 of the 70,000 people in Skokie were persons of Jewish religion or ancestry. Moreover, hundreds of Skokie residents were survivors of Nazi concentration camps, and thousands of others were relatives of the victims. Our suit pointed out that the purpose of the rally was to antagonize and excite people to whom the swastika represented a horrible nightmare and to incite racial and religious hatred.

On Thursday, April 28, Judge Joseph Wosik granted an injunction prohibiting the march on May 1. The judge expressed annoyance with Mr. Collin, who said during the hearing that his group would march in Skokie at the end of May regardless of the court ruling. The judge was quoted as saying, "He told me, in effect, to go to hell. He said, in effect, that he doesn't care what I do, that he's got other plans." The court ruling was immediately appealed by the American Civil Liberties Union (ACLU), who represented the Nazis.

After the Illinois Appellate Court sustained Judge Wosik's ruling on April 29, Frank Collin rescheduled the proposed demonstration for Saturday, April 30. On the day of the proposed rally, Circuit Court Judge Harold Sullivan, in response to our request, issued a temporary restraining order from his home in Skokie. The order was issued as a crowd of more than five hundred angry people were gathering outside the village hall. Members in the crowd carried signs with such headings as "Smash the Nazis" and "No More Auschwitz." Prominent in the crowd were about thirty yellow-helmeted, well-padded members of the Socialist Workers of America, some of whom carried flags mounted on four-foot 2"X2" sticks.

Skokie police were prepared to handle the situation and were assisted by the county sheriff's office, the state police, and police officers from neighboring departments. Thirty-five members of the Nazi Party, dressed in full Nazi uniforms, including high black boots and swastika armbands, were stopped by the police as they exited the expressway in three cars at the border of the village. After being served the injunction, they departed peaceably and scheduled another demonstration for May 22. Direct costs to the village for security was $4,426. This did not include the costs incurred by other police agencies who assisted.

On May 2 the Skokie board of trustees suspended the rules to adopt three ordinances regulating demonstrations. One ordinance prohibited demonstrations by members of a political party wearing military-style uniforms. A second ordinance banned the dissemination of material that incited hatred against any group because of race, creed, or nationality. The third ordinance required that parade sponsors post a $350,000 bond if more than fifty spectators or participants were expected. Sponsors were required to file for parade permits at least thirty days ahead of the scheduled date. We planned to use the ordinances to block future demonstrations if the court injunction was overturned.

Skokie, Illinois, residents protest planned assembly and march by the Nationalist Socialist (Nazi) Party of America. *Courtesy of North Shore, Illinois, Suburban Trib. Photo by George Thompson.*

The American Civil Liberties Union appealed Judge Wosik's injunction to the Illinois Appellate Court and the Illinois Supreme Court. Both courts refused to lift the injunction pending appeal. Following this action, the ACLU filed a request with U.S. Supreme Court Justice John Paul Stevens asking for a stay. On June 15 the U.S. Supreme Court voted five-to-four that Skokie could not bar the group from publicly demonstrating. The court said that the state courts must suspend the injunction pending the appeal. But that decision did not affect the village's ordinances.

Immediately following the U.S. Supreme Court decision, Frank Collin announced his intent to march on July 4. Tension and emotions increased in the community. Rabbi Meir Kahane, head of the militant Jewish Defense League (JDL), arrived in Skokie from New York and announced, "We will stand along the route of the march, and when the Nazis show up we will charge them and break their heads."

On June 23 I received a request from the National Socialist Party for a permit to demonstrate from 12:00 to 12:30 P.M. on July 4. The application said the group would not be able to obtain the necessary insurance and that thirty to fifty Nazis would march in single file back and forth on the sidewalk, wearing uniforms with swastika emblems or armbands.

While the plans for the march were proceeding, Sol Goldstein, a prominent Skokie citizen, assisted by the Chicago Chapter of the Anti-

Defamation League of B'nai B'rith, filed a class-action suit in Cook County Circuit Court, on behalf of all Nazi holocaust survivors, asking that the Nazis be permanently banned from marching in Skokie. His suit included an affidavit by a University of Chicago psychiatrist, who said, "Such a march would cause various emotional injuries to the Jews, including an urge to respond pathologically to the reenactment experience."

In a June 25 letter to Collin I denied the permit application because it violated the village ordinance prohibiting a demonstration by members of political parties wearing military-style uniforms. The July 4 rally plans received a further setback when the Illinois Appellate Court said it would not hear until July 8 any argument over the legality of efforts to ban the march. Although Collin postponed his rally, anti-Nazi groups staged demonstrations on July 4. Five hundred people gathered at the Mayer Kaplan Jewish Community Center in Skokie to hear Rabbi Kahane, who was accompanied by 100 uniformed and helmeted JDL members who had arrived on two buses from New York City. At the village hall about thirty members of the Workers Defense Coalition conducted a demonstration. Again elaborate police plans including mutual-aid assistance went into effect. Fortunately they were not needed, but direct costs to the village amounted to $9,469.

On July 12 a three-judge panel of the Illinois Appellate Court reversed portions of the earlier injunction by ruling that the Nazis could march in uniform in Skokie and distribute their literature but could not wear swastikas, which the court described as "a personal affront to every member of the Jewish faith." This decision was immediately appealed by the ACLU, and Justice Stevens of the U.S. Supreme Court denied their petition to overturn the ruling. Frank Collin said he was "very pleased" with Justice Stevens's ruling: "The more this case is dragged out, the more publicity and attention we get." He was quoted as saying, "I don't give a damn about Skokie. Skokie is just a means to an end for us. We know they wouldn't ever let us march there. If they did, we'd never have had the publicity we're getting now. All Skokie is for us is a chance to spread the word." There was little question that the matter received widespread publicity. Newspapers and TV networks across the nation and internationally outdid each other in overdramatizing the situation.

On 27 January 1978 the Illinois Supreme Court reversed the Illinois Appellate Court decision and ruled that the Nazis had a constitutional right to wear and display swastikas during marches in Skokie. In an unsigned opinion the court decided that the display of the swastika was guaranteed by the First Amendment's freedom of speech clause. In part, they said, "We accordingly, albeit reluctantly, conclude that the display of the swastika cannot be enjoined under the fighting words 'exception to free speech,' nor can anticipation of a hostile audience justify the prior restraint." Skokie Mayor Albert Smith immediately announced that the ruling would be appealed. We received another setback on January 30 when the Illinois Supreme Court ordered the dismissal of the Goldstein class-action suit.

Following this latest Illinois Supreme Court ruling, the Nazis announced that they would march in Skokie on April 20, Adolph Hitler's birthday, if the U.S. District Court approved an ACLU request to issue a preliminary injunction blocking enforcement of the village ordinances.

Less than a month later we encountered another obstacle when U.S. District Court Judge Bernard Decker struck down major portions of our three ordinances. He said that the ordinances violated the First and Fourteenth Amendments to the Constitution and continued, "The ability of American society to tolerate the advocacy of even hateful doctrines is perhaps the best protection we have against the establishment of any Nazi-type regime in this country." Announcing that the decision would be appealed, Skokie Mayor Smith said, "It is unfortunate that today's decision ignores the First Amendment rights of thousands in favor of the alleged rights of a few." The village continued to contend that the march posed a threat to the well-being of the community because many organizations were planning counterdemonstrations.

Meanwhile numerous organizations began to plan for a counterdemonstration. Illinois Governor Thompson supported such a march and said that he would be present if it was in a place distant from the Nazi march. The counterdemonstration plans were supported by the Chicago Chapter of the Antidefamation League of B'nai B'rith, and the Janusz Korczak Lodge, who said they hoped to attract 50,000 participants to such a countermarch. The president of the lodge said, "There will be a confrontation, but we intend to meet hate with love." The public-affairs committee of the Jewish United Fund, representing thirty-four major Chicago Jewish organizations, announced it would support a countermarch and a week-long education program on the holocaust. Not all Skokie residents were supportive of the counterdemonstration. A *Chicago Sun Times* poll showed that 60 percent of the residents questioned felt the counterdemonstration should be held some place other than where the Nazis planned to march. Sixty-five percent said they would try to avoid both the parade and the counterdemonstration. However, Mayor Smith received hundreds of letters from all fifty states, Canada, and foreign countries supporting the village's position and offering comfort, encouragement, and suggestions for handling the matter. One letter writer suggested that the Nazis be permitted to march, but that the village remove all the manhole covers just before they start. Another writer suggested that the village send its public works trucks to farms to collect all available manure, and put the manure in a spreader, and let the spreader lead the Nazis down the street.

On March 17 we received some good news when Judge Bernard Decker issued a forty-five-day stay of his January 26 ruling declaring the village's ordinances unconstitutional. The stay came in response to a plea by Corporation Counsel Harvey Schwartz that, "The possibility of turmoil and violence outweighs any hardship that might come to the plaintiff."

Despite this reprieve, community groups continued to make plans. On March 24 representatives of the Christian clergy of Skokie, who were members of the Niles Township Clergy Forum, announced that they would sponsor an interfaith, open-air worship service on Sunday, April 16, at Skokie's Niles West High School. Reverend Thomas O'Connor, Pastor of St. Peters United Church of Christ, said that the open-air service was intended to "emphasize the solidarity of the Protestant, Catholic and Jewish community." Three thousand people, wearing armbands bearing the Star of David, attended the interfaith service, which was covered by the national media.

On April 12 I received a letter from Frank Collin requesting a permit to demonstrate on June 25 from 12:00 to 12:30 P.M. in front of the village hall. The application said that fifty to a hundred Nazis and their supporters would participate. Some or all of the demonstrators would wear uniforms, including a swastika on the uniform or on an armband. They would carry a party banner and placards bearing the words "White Free Speech" and "Free Speech for the White Man." There would be no speeches or distribution of handbills. I responded that the village would delay issuing an application until a decision was made by the U.S. Court of Appeals.

Closely following the Nazi application were requests for permits from the Public Affairs Committee of the Jewish United Fund and United Jewish Organizations of the Sheerith Hapleitah ("Remnant of Those Who Escaped"). Both groups wanted permits for June 25.

Opposition to the proposed June 25 Nazi demonstration was expressed in other ways. United States Congressman Abner Mikva of Illinois announced that the correct course was "to find a constitutional way of stopping them." State Representative Calvin Skinner of McHenry County introduced two bills to keep the Nazi demonstrators from marching. State Senators Howard Carroll and John Nimrod sponsored bills in the state senate to block the Nazi demonstration. Senator Carroll's bill was based on a group-libel law upheld by the United States Supreme Court in 1952. The law prohibited defamation of any ethnic, racial, or religious group. Both bills passed the senate but were defeated in the Illinois House.

On May 22, by upholding the district court decision ruling the village's ordinances unconstitutional, the U.S. Court of Appeals affirmed the right of the Nazi group to march in Skokie. The three-judge panel stated unanimously, "The First Amendment right to free speech protects even minorities whose views may be unpopular at a particular time or place." Judge Robert Sprecher, in a separate opinion, disagreed with the majority of the court on whether the parade's sponsors should have to post a bond. He said Skokie could require a bond because "the Village has a right and duty to protect its citizens and property in this reasonable manner." The Judge further said, "Seldom before has the Federal Court been faced with a situation embracing such powerful cross pressure as has been created in this case."

The day following the U.S. Court of Appeals' decision, Frank Collin announced that he might not march in Skokie if three conditions were met. One was that the village rescind its three ordinances. The second was that the legislature stop action on the two antimarch bills. The third was that the Chicago Park District abolish its insurance requirements, and allow him to march in Marquette Park. We immediately advised him that we would not negotiate. State legislators and the Public Action Committee also announced they would reject any arrangement, agreement, or deal.

On May 26 I issued a permit to the Nazis allowing them to demonstrate at the village hall at 3:00 P.M. on Sunday, June 25 (at noon there were church services in the vicinity). I stated in the letter that the group would be required to comply with all Illinois statutes and village ordinances and called attention to the section of our code on disorderly conduct. I also announced that a permit for a counterdemonstration would be issued to the Jewish Federation of Metropolitan Chicago, which would serve as an umbrella group for the three Jewish organizations requesting permits, consisting of the Federation, the survivors group, and the Jewish War Veterans.

The decision to issue the permit to the Federation came after considerable discussion among the members of the board of trustees, some of whom were concerned that multiple demonstrations would aggravate an already volatile situation. The permit was issued to the Nazis because refusal to do so would have meant possible contempt charges in federal courts. I did deny one request for a permit: an individual asked permission to bring a plastic enclosure and twelve water moccasins, rattle snakes, and cobras to the village hall during the proposed demonstration. He said he would invite the Nazis to come into the enclosure with him and stand in the midst of the deadly snakes.

On June 5 the federal appellate court denied the village's request for a stay of the lower-court ruling permitting the march. Two judges voted to deny this stay, while one judge voted to grant it. Harvey Schwartz, the village's corporation counsel, immediately moved to request the U.S. Supreme Court to grant the stay. In a terse, one-sentence order, the U.S. Supreme Court denied the village's request. In a decision dissenting from the majority, Justices Harry Blackmun and William Rehnquist said that they would have delayed the march pending the outcome of Skokie's appeal.

After the U.S. Supreme Court's order, extensive planning began for the proposed counterdemonstrations. The public-affairs committee predicted that 50,000 people would assemble. Their proposed counterdemonstration was scheduled for Niles East High School, approximately five blocks from the village hall. They planned a symbolic delegation of sixty to a hundred community religious and interfaith leaders who would confront the Nazis at village hall by standing and reciting the Kaddish Jewish prayer for the dead, and reciting the names of death camps where millions of Jews and non-Jews were killed. The committee also announced that they expected the demonstrators gathered at the high school to participate in a march around the village hall. Federation representatives made arrangements for a field hospital, for 200 off-duty law-enforcement officials from the Fraternal Order of Jewish Policemen to serve as marshals, for special transportation arrangements, for emergency rooms at the local hospital, and for legal observers from the Decalogue Society (to insure that the counterdemonstrators were not deprived of their civil rights). Similar arrangements also were being made by the survivors group and the JDL.

We began to finalize elaborate security plans involving approximately three hundred police officers, including 140 from Skokie and twelve neighboring municipalities, as well as approximately eight hundred state police and national guardsmen and Cook County Sheriff's officers. A decision was made to establish a police line, cordoning off a one-square-mile area around village hall from 8:00 A.M. to 6:00 P.M. on June 25 and permitting only autos of residents through four checkpoints. Cars would be searched for weapons. Pedestrians would be permitted to walk into the area. Another police line would cordon off several blocks in the immediate vicinity of the Nazi demonstration. Only Nazi demonstrators and working press would be permitted in the area.

A press room was established at Niles East High School, the site of the proposed counterdemonstration. Arrangements were made for the issuance of press passes, the establishment of a triage team with paramedics, and the use of seven national-guard helicopters for surveillance and emergency use. Mass-arrest procedures were worked out with the sheriff's office, and court arrangements were coordinated with court personnel. A command center was established at Niles West High School about eight blocks from the village hall. Five hospitals were put on temporary emergency duty, and the park district closed all facilities from 10:00 P.M. Saturday to 6:00 A.M. Monday. Aaron Cushman and Associates, the village's public-relations advisor, took charge of media relations.

We were very concerned about our ability to handle the large group of people expected to participate in the counterdemonstration and about their intent to place a symbolic delegation fifty-five feet from the Nazi demonstrators. The potential for violence was considerable. We worked closely with representatives from the governor's office in an effort to reduce the chances of violence. And we tried to persuade the counterdemonstrators to change the time of their demonstration, thereby decreasing the likelihood of a disastrous confrontation. But our efforts to persuade them failed.

While we were preparing, I received a letter from Niles Township Clerk Louis Black directing me to revoke the Nazi permit. The members of the Board of Trustees of Niles Township released a statement saying the letter was not written or authorized or sanctioned in anyway by the trustees or the supervisor. The clerk filed suit in county circuit court saying that the village erred in authorizing a permit because the party was not a legitimate Illinois organization and failed to list a phone number or an address in applying for the permit. The court denied the request for a temporary restraining order.

As village and counterdemonstration plans began to solidify, behind-the-scenes efforts were being made to stop the march. Since the beginning of the year, the U.S. Justice Department Community Relations Service–Midwest Region had been working behind the scenes to find an alternative to the march. Midwest Director Richard Salem and his staff had been meeting with me and other village officials, representatives of the Jewish organizations, the ACLU, and the Nazi planning personnel. Much of their effort was directed at finding a face-saving way for the Nazis to call off the march.

In a *Chicago Sun Times* article on June 9 the Midwest director of the service was quoted as saying he was so pleased with the talks that there is "a distinct possibility" the march will be called off. On June 14 the federal officials announced that they had received a letter notifying them the Nazis would demonstrate on the Federal Building plaza in downtown Chicago on Saturday afternoon, June 24. Because it was federal property, no permit was needed. In a newspaper article, a Nazi spokesman said behind-the-scenes negotiations petered out when Justice Department officials would not agree to put pressure on the Chicago Park District to permit assemblies. He said the federal officials promised only to try to influence the state legislature to defeat the bill against ethnic defamation, if the Nazis would call off the march.

In a letter to Frank Collin, Richard Salem said that the Chicago Park District officials would agree to count only Nazi party members and not outsiders as participants in a demonstration. If there were fewer than seventy-five, no insurance would be needed. Initially park-district officials denied any commitment had been made, but later they reported that they had offered to let the Nazis demonstrate in Marquette Park in Chicago on July 9 without a bond, provided that the Nazis limited participation to seventy-five uniformed party members. (In the summer of 1977 the Nazis had won a ruling in the federal district court declaring unconstitutional a Chicago Park District requirement that rallies of more than seventy-five persons be covered by insurance policies of $350,000 or more. As a result of the ruling, the park district had lowered its insurance obligation to $60,000, which was still unacceptable to the Nazis.) The Nazis rejected the offer because they didn't want to set a precedent that would limit the size of future demonstrations. Richard Teodor, deputy leader of the Nazis, said, "It is possible that the system may give into our demands for a no-strings-attached demonstration and, in that case, we would not demonstrate in Skokie." Community Relations Service personnel felt that the park-district proposal and the planned rally on the federal plaza combined with developments in the U.S. Supreme Court and the Illinois Legislature and progress in pending litigation, made it clear that the Nazis' First Amendment rights were being protected.

Hope for the postponement of the Skokie march improved on June 20 when Federal Judge George Leighton directed the Chicago Park District to issue a permit for a march on July 9 in Marquette Park on Chicago's southwest side.

On June 21 Frank Collin called off his plan to march in Skokie unless the Chicago Park District obtained a stay of the judge's ruling. At a press conference, Collin said, "It does not mean I forego any future demonstration in Skokie. It means only that this one has been canceled."

Following Collin's announcement, I immediately revoked the demonstration permit, and the counterdemonstration sponsors canceled their rally. Even though the demonstration was canceled, we still incurred costs of $13,898.

Concurrent with the cancellation of the demonstration, we dismantled our security plans and returned to normal. On Sunday, June 25, all was quiet in Skokie. Five JDL members, who were standing on the steps of the village hall waiting for a ride, and a Niles Township Jewish Congregation service for 200 Jewish supporters who had arrived from California were the only remnants of the proposed massive demonstrations.

Reactions in the community were mixed. Many felt that the principles should have been upheld in court, that free speech, as represented by the Nazis, was not covered by the First Amendment. Others pointed to the increased solidarity among the Jews and Christians. Many felt that Collin had held Skokie hostage and had obtained $1 million in free publicity. Skokie Mayor Smith said, "I don't think our community will ever forget the Nazi thing. We took a stand for what we thought was right and still do."

The intricate series of legal maneuvers by Skokie and some of its residents was concluded in October 1978 when the U.S. Supreme Court, with two justices dissenting, let stand a lower court ruling that the Skokie ordinances were unconstitutional. In his dissent, Justice Harry Blackmun protested that the high court should have used the dispute between Skokie and the Nazis as a means of deciding "whether there is no limit whatsoever to the exercise of free speech." Blackmun wrote, "When citizens assert, not casually but with deep conviction that the proposed demonstration is scheduled at a place and in a manner that is taunting and overwhelmingly offensive to the citizens of that place, that assertion deserves to be examined."

In another decision the U.S. Supreme Court without dissent, declined to review an Illinois Supreme Court decision that a group of Jewish survivors of the Nazi holocaust could not constitutionally obtain an injunction against a Nazi march in Skokie. These decisions marked a substantial victory for the ACLU. The Court's decisions do not set a binding precedent nationwide, but the lower-court ruling will remain in effect throughout Illinois, Indiana, and Wisconsin and could be cited as authority elsewhere, if some other community tries to curb demonstrations in the way that Skokie did.

Ironically, the importance of the Skokie issue was cited in December 1978 when Justices Byron White and Harry Blackmun listed twenty-seven cases which raised important questions of the law that could not be heard by the U.S. Supreme Court because its work load was too heavy. Skokie's case was included.

Village government was severely affected by the Nazi episode. Important village issues and internal-management operations were neglected and priorities significantly modified. Elected officials were forced to postpone decisions on urgent policy matters. Mayor Smith spent countless hours meeting with community groups and media representatives. Other negative aspects of the Nazi episode included the surfacing of opportunists who used the incident to promote their own interest, and the excessive publicity given the small band of Nazi troublemakers.

On the positive side, the experience brought all components of the community closer together. Coalitions of Christians and Jews were formed to combat the threat peacefully. The community strongly supported the village government's policy of pursuing a legal remedy for stopping the proposed march. Even the local press, which had opposed some of the village's actions, complimented the local officials on the calm and careful manner in which they conducted themselves. While the fifteen-month episode left many scars, it also proved that such a conflict can have a positive impact on a community.

Weslaco, Texas, versus Hurricane Beulah

Cecil E. Massey

Beulah has turned in a northerly direction. The latest location indicates that Beulah will strike near Brownsville, Texas, still moving at 12 mph with 160 mph winds at the eye, with hurricane force winds extending out as far as 90 miles.

The above bulletin was the first indication that Hurricane Beulah would strike our city, Weslaco, sometime Tuesday night or Wednesday morning, 19–20 September 1967. Following is an abbreviated description and summary of the next week's events, day by day.

Tuesday, September 19

At 10:00 A.M. the city commission met with key city personnel to provide all the advance planning humanly possible to meet the approaching hurricane. Both the municipal employees and the people from the other agencies knew they had their work cut out for them.

As information about the hurricane spread, our police dispatcher received these citizen calls:

> We are going into our bomb shelter. Please check once in a while to see if anything falls on the door.

> Check my house during the storm since I am bedridden and cannot go to a shelter.

> If the windows in my business blow out, call me in time so that I can get things out.

> Check on children stripping tape off windows.

> People in shelters need food. Some shelters are already full.

Several municipal employees spent the night at city hall listening to weather reports and preparing for emergency food from the Red Cross.

Wednesday, September 20

According to the police department log, Beulah hit Weslaco at 4:05 A.M. Wednesday. Her advance winds from the north were moving at 75–85 mph. Our dispatcher received more calls:

> Trees down on Kansas, Iowa, East First, Casa Blanca, Witmer.

> The signal system and cable are swinging three feet off the ground at Texas and Highway 83.

> Burglar alarms ringing at Texsun Plant and Williamson-Dickie.

> Electric lines broken at Plaza, Second, South Texas, Kansas, Bridge and Casa Blanca Streets.

At daybreak I called for a police car to take me on a survey of the damage. When we were driving on Bridge Street at 30 mph, a wind gust brought our car to a halt. The driver had difficulty dodging fallen trees and flying garbage cans and carports. On our return I sent emergency vehicles for the mayor and commissioners to bring them to the control center that had been established in the city manager's office.

Shortly after 8:00 A.M. the electricity went off all over town, creating a problem we had not anticipated would happen so soon. Because of the increasing wind and rain, it was essential that we stay in touch with the citizenry. The local radio and television station was now on auxiliary power and had set up their operations in the electric cooperative office. We immediately transferred the mayor and the mayor pro tem to the station, where they could make announcements and appeals to the people throughout the day. Here are some examples of their messages:

The Weslaco shelters are at all public schools, all churches, and the Weslaco Civic Center. It is estimated that these shelters will accommodate 5,000.

Schools will be closed all day, and the school administrators and other personnel will be on hand to operate the shelters. Citizens are encouraged to make plans to utilize the school shelters nearest their homes.

The city manager has reported that those people planning to spend the night in the operated shelters should make arrangements to move in without delay and certainly before the night.

All merchants with broken windows at their places of business should make their own arrangements for guarding and protecting their property, since the police and national guard will be able to provide general protection only.

All citizens of Weslaco can be a real help to the city crews if they will attempt to keep the leaves and brush off the storm-sewer grates in front of their homes at intersections to keep water from backing up.

Those citizens who start moving brush should pile it in front of their homes, near the curb. Try not to put it in the streets. With hundreds of trees down, the city crews will be able to clear the streets in a few days.

Please do not tie up city lines to report trees down in the street. The city police have a record of all these areas in Weslaco, and they will be moved on a priority basis in order to open major streets first. All streets will be opened as soon as possible.

Now that the rain has slacked up, the Weslaco Fire Department and volunteers are operating tractors throughout the city to move trees out of the streets. So, please be on the lookout if you are driving on the streets.

There appear to have been no injuries in Weslaco. It has been estimated that all damage in Weslaco may exceed $100,000, disregarding the hundreds of trees blown down and damage to other plants. The important thing at this time is for all citizens to remain in their homes or shelters until all danger has passed.

The county health nurse has announced that the citizens of Weslaco will be offered typhoid shots as soon as the rain is over, probably on Saturday, if it becomes necessary.

As of 3:30 P.M. it is estimated that 2,500 have already moved into the various centers.

As was preplanned in case the power went off and the waterplant went out of operation, the water superintendent moved to shut the valve so as to hold the water in the overhead storage tank. But the valve was inoperable. As a result, by 5:00P.M. the water storage was completely drained.

Later in the evening the mayor broadcast the following message:

Cecil Massey, Weslaco Civil Defense Director, announced at 6:00 P.M. that as of now Weslaco has had much damage. A survey of the business district produced aluminum awnings blown down and plate-glass windows broken by the strong wind. Mr. Massey urged the Weslaco citizens to stay in their homes. There is nothing to see downtown.

Thursday, September 21

In the morning we informed the public that the thirteen shelters in Weslaco had housed 2,900 people through the night, and we urged everyone to remain in the shelters or at home.

By now, we estimated, 1,100 trees were down or damaged. Volunteer firemen and citizens, with some twenty farm tractors they had parked next to the city hall twenty-four hours in advance, put log chains on the trees and began clearing the streets by dragging the trees to vacant lots, parking lots, and unused streets.

Other towns reported that debris and leaf-covered storm sewer grates had caused widespread flooding in their communities. Our citizens had helped us avoid that problem by responding to the mayor's appeals, sometimes working in torrents of rain to keep the grates open.

It rained all day, with reported amounts ranging from eleven to seventeen inches. As darkness approached, new problems were reported to the control center.

The lack of street lights will make it difficult to patrol the business district.

Food brought in by truck in advance is running out.

Houses in the northeast part of town are flooding.

Sewer lift stations are flooded.

The national guard responded to some of our needs by providing seven men, including two policemen and a water-plant operator. In addition they provided large self-powered floodlights that they towed throughout the business district. Local representatives of the Salvation Army took over the task of supplying the school superintendent with food for the thirteen shelters.

Friday, September 22

The rain continued. We spent the day moving citizens from flooded areas to shelters, sandbagging major lift stations to get the sewer plants back in operation, and moving trees and brush to clear thoroughfares. The welfare building had flooded, which necessitated our moving all supplies to higher ground. We used school buses.

We continued to appeal to citizens to stay out of the streets and to respond to calls for help from official sources only. (Fortunately calls for help from unauthorized persons were minimal.)

As Friday drew to a close, we thought the worst was over. Schools were returning people to their homes and supplying them with food and clothing. Our next task was to start the massive cleanup. Looking back over the four days, I recalled events ranging from the almost amusing and the unreasonable to the heartwarming and reassuring. Here are some:

• With water well over knee deep in all parts of town, we got a call that a lady had fallen into a well.

• We were requested to advise people to put out pans to catch rain water to flush their toilets.

• At the height of the storm, when all available radio equipment was in use, a lady insisted she be supplied with a walkie-talkie radio.

• Faced as we were with the acute problem of finding places for people to stay, we were asked by a lady caller if we could let her store her furniture in a shelter.

• Another lady insisted that she and her daughter be allowed a school room for their private use.

• Could we send two men to the neighboring town to help a lady load her furniture?

• Could we help a lady get a plane to fly over Corpus Christi, not to stay but just to see if her folks' house was O.K.?

• Why can't we do something; the books are getting musty in the library?

• Did you know they have not picked up my garbage all week?

On the other hand, the news media performed a tremendous service. Though naturally spectacular in style, their reporting was factual and reasonable. Their assistance in keeping the public informed of conditions could not have been better.

The telephone service also was great. Fortunately, by using auxiliary batteries, the telephone company was able to keep telephones in operation for most of the city. The operators must have sent, relayed, and received hundreds of urgent messages.

It would be impossible to single out all the organizations and individuals who responded magnificently to the need for help.

Saturday, September 23

The day started with a call from officials near Nuevo Progreso, Mexico. The Rio Grande was rising. Could we take care of 1,500 refugees from old Mexico?

With our shelters still housing local and area citizens, and food supplies dwindling, this request created both concern and confusion. However, with the aid of the county commissioner, we acquired the county labor camp. School officials rushed vehicles to the county welfare for food, and the Salvation Army again set its wheels in motion. As the day wore on and with the crisis in Old Mexico changing hourly, the school superintendent sent buses to the international bridge to await developments. Finally about a hundred people were permitted to cross the bridge seeking food and shelter. The border patrol set up a post at the labor camp shelter to assist us.

Sunday, September 24

At 11:37 A.M. we received the following message: "A floodgate has blown out south of Mission. All people should be ready to evacuate immediately. The International Boundary and Water Commission is enroute to repair the floodgate."

This floodgate opened into the boundary and water commission's internal floodway system from the Rio Grande. Having been designed to move drainage water from the cities of the Lower Rio Grande Valley to the Gulf of Mexico, the system had so far proved adequate. But the addition of uncontrolled water from the flooding river was another matter.

At about the same time, someone discovered a near breakover of the floodway levee at Mile Two West, southeast of Weslaco. We sent out an urgent call for help to sandbag the levee, and some six hundred citizens responded.

The levee at Mile Two held on the north side when the crest reached the Weslaco area, but the weir dam on the opposite bank went out, sending the swirling floodwaters on to Harlingen, eighteen miles away. Contributions of citizens and organizations that Sunday and the following day were well presented in this *Weslaco Mid-Valley News* account written at the end of our second crisis.

Bone-weary teams of volunteers worked around the clock starting last Sunday in a hard-fought battle to contain flood waters which threatened the area between Weslaco and Mercedes.

As many as 200 men at a time stayed on the job day and night, sandbagging the levee in the Mile Two vicinity.

They were still fighting the swirling, debris-filled flood waters Wednesday when most expressed the opinion that the reinforced floodway would continue to hold.

At 2:30 A.M. Wednesday, the County Commissioner reported to the nerve center at City Hall that the water had dropped approximately six inches from its previous peak. Actual depth at crest had not been determined at deadline, but the muddy flow at one time was estimated at some 1600 feet in width and was level with the embankment on both sides.

A control center was set up on Sunday when flood waters first became a serious threat in the Mercedes floodway system. The City Manager—working with police, civil defense, the highway patrol and volunteer agencies—called for male volunteers to sandbag along the low spots, a plea which resulted "in a remarkable turn-out of people willing to spend long hours helping other people."

From Sunday through noon Wednesday, men and boys from Weslaco, Donna, and the Progreso area had lugged some 20,000 sandbags weighing 80 pounds apiece into position wherever the flood waters threatened to breach.

They filled in soft spots caused by the seepage.

City crews, aided by volunteers with borrowed equipment and materials, even built and graveled a road alongside the levee in order to gain access for heavy equipment.

Meanwhile, the workers were fed, quite literally, by the citizenry.

The Salvation Army headquarters at McAllen sent in truckloads of food supplies. Students of the Weslaco High School home-economics classes prepared sandwiches, and cookies by the thousands. Women employees at city hall worked through the long days and nights making coffee for the full complement of workers on duty there.

Some of them—the Police Chief and Civil Defense Chief—stayed with it 36 to 48 hours with no sleep.

The Mayor was on the scene directing volunteers and city youth corps workers most of the first two days and nights of the threat.

City Commissioners—usually impeccably dressed—helped the sandbagging crews and showed up at control with mud ankle-deep on their boots.

On Tuesday—as floodwaters from the swollen Arroyo Colorado crept over Harlingen—evacuees began to pour into Weslaco from several directions.

First to arrive were some 75 persons from the Mexican side of the still-open border who were housed in the Labor Camp north of the city.

By mid-afternoon Tuesday, almost every form of mobile vehicle began bringing more flood refugees—from Santa Rosa, Mercedes, La Villa, Harlingen and various points in between.

One family of 11 persons was among the second wave of evacuees who arrived from the flooded area, according to a police sergeant who shepherded the truck load of refugees to the labor camp for temporary care.

Shortly after 4:00 P.M. Tuesday, helicopters and buses transported more than 110 patients from the Harlingen Tuberculosis Hospital to Knapp Memorial Methodist Hospital here and another group to Grandview Hospital in Edinburg.

Weslaco's public schools were alerted and on standby, ready to resume their role as shelters for the homeless if needed.

Weslaco, Donna, Mercedes and surrounding areas took a beating from Hurricane Beulah and its subsequent floods. But as of Wednesday presstime, it appeared that we had won.

During the crises of Hurricane Beulah and its aftermath, mistakes were made, rumors were spread, feelings were hurt, citizens became impatient, and the city's public servants became weary. If any good can come to a community from such an experience, in my opinion the good was that all agencies and city departments worked together with great harmony, and more than a thousand citizens got together—even if it was on the levee at Mile Two.

Summary

When it was all over, I prepared a report on our experience. The summary was as follows:

We must add a final word concerning the people—the citizens of Weslaco. Mere eloquent phrases and high sounding praise can not adequately express our thanks to the hundreds who served.

Their oath of office failed to mention the manifold and at times even hazardous jobs that would be performed by the Mayor and every City Commissioner for over a week. A simple thank-you would not be enough.

The 3,000 or more people who availed themselves of public shelters during our week of Beulah must surely feel a deep sense of gratitude to the school administrators, the faculty who doubled as bus drivers, and even the janitorial personnel who all worked for their concern and welfare.

How can we thank the women and young people who prepared staggering quantities of food for a job well-done without seeming to burst with pride at the caliber of our citizens.

To the volunteer fire department—the men, their wives, and even the children, we again feel a mere thank-you is inadequate. You who performed such a never ending variety of tasks, from the all important message nerve center, to sandwich-making, sand-bagging, tractor-driving, and even setting up a complete hospital wing for TB patients, to scouts and young men from high school and the business world who manned tractors moving the mountainous piles of twisted and uprooted trees and metal awnings to provide that vital factor that kept our streets passable and the storm sewers flowing to the last possible moment, a tremendous vote of thanks goes to this seemingly unfatigable group.

Many people worked hour after hour overtime at their regular jobs in order to serve the personal and public needs of our community. Grocery men with only candles to light their stores; policemen and all city employees from office workers to water, sewer and street personnel; lumber and hardware people who tried valiantly to supply emergency repair materials; utility repairmen who began restoring service before the winds had even subsided; the news media who at times became tongue-sore and hoarse from hours of endless talking to keep people informed . . . the list goes on and on.

After a week of crisis and imminent disaster from wind and water, maybe we shouldn't say thank-you at all. Maybe it really isn't necessary, for each person who served must have felt as the community united itself against the elements that each and every one of us was just grateful we lived in a town called Weslaco.

My City Is Burning
Thomas W. Fletcher

It was early July 1967, six weeks before I unexpectedly became the first deputy mayor (in effect, city manager) of our nation's capital. Also, it was my first night in Washington, D.C.—in a rented efficiency apartment because my family was still in San Diego—and my first occasion to see why the district is known as the "City of Demonstrations."

The local TV newscaster had spent about one minute covering a march of 5,000 women led by Jeanette Rankin to Capitol Hill, protesting the Vietnam War. Later in the evening that short news item struck me forcibly: I realized that I knew who Jeanette Rankin was. She had been a member of Congress from Montana and was one of a handful who voted no on declaring war in 1917 and was the only member of Congress to vote no on declaring war in 1941. And now she was leading 5,000 women to the Hill, and the local TV was devoting only a minute to the coverage. Had this happened in San Diego, where I had just been city manager, there would have been massive coverage that would have received the attention of all our city government. But here in Washington, D.C., it appeared to be a normal everyday occurrence. Next day the *Washington Post* gave the march a mere few inches on an inside page.

During the next few months I witnessed demonstrations almost daily—including the demonstration against Walter Washington and me the day after he and I were sworn in as mayor and deputy mayor of the District government.

The new mayor had given a brief talk at the annual meeting of the Federal City Council. The theme was his goals for the new government, one of which was a "balanced" transportation system. The next day more than fifty demonstrators confronted us in our office, objecting because they felt that a balanced system included highways and they were against any more highways in the District. Walter seemed to take this in stride. He had been a public official in D.C. for better than twenty-five years, and he saw this as a normal way of doing business. For me it was new and unsettling.

A larger demonstration began just one week later. I was called to the White House to meet with Steve Pollack, President Johnson's staff man assigned to District affairs. Steve advised me that there was to be an anti-Vietnam demonstration in the District and around the Pentagon in the next couple of weeks. The demonstration would probably involve more than 100,000 participants. He assured me that everything was being done to take care of this demonstration and for us not to worry. Recognizing that we had just taken office, he felt that it would be better for him to handle this one, but he wanted me to be an observer so that we could take care of the next one, which he pointed out would be our responsibility. That demonstration in October 1967 did involve more than 100,000 participants and was held without major incident.

These experiences lulled me into feeling that the District could handle almost any emergency. Despite the urban riots that had taken place in other cities in recent years, the District had had only one race riot, and that in 1919. Almost everyone felt if a riot did occur, we were well prepared to take care of it. I was to discover that "almost everyone" was terribly wrong.

In early 1968 Mayor Washington did express some concern about our disaster preparedness. He asked me to chair a committee of District officials to determine our state of preparedness and to recommend any needed improvement. This committee had representation from the police, fire, health, welfare, and national guard departments. We proceeded without any sense of urgency, perhaps because of the feeling that we were pretty well prepared and organized to take care of almost any problem.

Police Chief John Layton had already made extensive plans for riot control. The plans were designed for massive police presence but using minimum force. The lesson had been learned in Watts, Newark, and

Detroit: violence only produced more violence. The chief also assured us that the operating relations with the military had been worked out, that there had been substantial joint training exercises between the police and the military assigned to our area in case of civil disturbance.

The fire chief assured us that his department was also well trained and equipped to take care of any problem. He also said that we had a good working relationship with all the neighboring departments for mutual aid. In fact, all department heads gave us assurance of their preparedness.

On the evening of 4 April 1968 the mayor and I were having one of our usual late evening meetings in his office. With us, as usual, were Charlie Duncan, our corporation counsel, and Julius Dugas, the head of our economic development department. Just before eight o'clock the mayor's hot-line telephone rang—an urgent call from the White House. Joseph Califano was calling to tell the mayor that Martin Luther King had just been assassinated in Memphis. We sat in stunned silence for a few seconds, then we started for the phones to alert our key department heads.

As soon as the news of King's death reached the streets, rioting began. Within an hour, we doubled our police force by calling our midnight patrol early and keeping our evening patrol on duty. The military and the national guard were alerted, although they were not used that evening. By 3:00 A.M. the city had quieted, but we had suffered substantial property damage, looting, and a few fires. There had been more than two hundred arrests and two deaths.

The city appeared quiet, but we were not fooled. We all expected a renewal of trouble that evening. Studies of other cities' experiences during riots told us that most of the real trouble took place after people got home from school and work. We called the school superintendent and urged him to make sure the schools stayed open and that every effort was made to calm the students. We suggested memorial assemblies for Dr. King.

To get ready for the trouble we expected that evening, Pat Murphy, our public safety director, set up a morning meeting with the military commander assigned to the District. The mayor met in the White House with the President, congressional leaders, and civic leaders, and then proceeded to the National Cathedral for a noon memorial service. I was left back at the District Building to monitor our cleanup activities and to watch for other developments.

During the noon hour, Police Chief Layton called to tell me, "It's starting up again and it looks bad. The kids have all left school and are breaking windows, looting, and setting fires in scores of locations. I don't think we can handle it alone." The chief explained that there were fewer police on the streets than normal because he wanted his men to rest up for the evening. I immediately tried to get word to both Pat Murphy and the mayor. I finally located Pat, who was having lunch at the Pentagon,

Functions of City Manager

and asked him to call Chief Layton at once. I left a message with the Secret Service to deliver to Mayor Washington when he left the memorial services.

Calls started coming in from everyone, with rumors, questions, demands, even threats. People kept coming into the mayor's office asking what was going on and what I was doing about it. I didn't hear from the mayor, the public safety director, or the chief of police for almost an hour. It was the longest and loneliest hour I ever spent.

We learned later that the rumors were spreading by telephone and it was almost impossible to get calls through. We also learned from our traffic engineers that a massive traffic jam was starting because everyone was leaving work and trying to get home. I called the U.S. Civil Service Director and suggested that the departures of the federal employees be staggered to relieve the highway congestion, but he told me it was too late. The reports (or rumors) were that large groups were rioting along 14th, 7th, and H streets already and that large fires were burning out of control. When I could finally get through to the school superintendent, he confirmed that the schools had started to clear out just before noon. And when I asked him why he hadn't let us know, he said that he hadn't been able to get a call through.

The mayor called on the hot line to get the latest information I had and said he would be over shortly. He asked me to have our corporation counsel draw up a statement for him that would justify the President's calling in the army and federalizing the national guard. When the mayor arrived back at his office, we all went down to Room 10 in the District Building. This was the facility that our highway department used when we had difficult traffic problems, such as heavy snow (anything over one inch) or parades and demonstrations. It was a small room, equipped with radio transmitters and large detailed maps of the city. From there we were able to establish an open line to the police chief's office so that we could update our information continuously. We also had several highway department mobile radio units reporting from the field. This information confirmed most of what we had already heard—the city was burning, and the riot was almost completely out of control.

The mayor signed a request and justification to the President for bringing in the army. Our messenger brought it right back from the White House because the President wanted it signed by the police chief and our public safety director. The President was protecting his rear as well as the District. At about this same time one of our aides came up to me and said that the President was on the phone asking for me. When I said, "You must mean he wants the mayor," he said, "No, he asked for you specifically." When I picked up the phone and identified myself, the President asked, "Fletcher, what the hell is going on?" After I gave him an update on what we knew, he asked if we wanted the help of Cy Vance. After checking with the mayor, we said yes: Cyrus Vance had been the

President's representative in Detroit during that city's 1966 riots.

Cy Vance appeared within an hour, which I thought strange, because I knew that he had been in New York earlier that day. (I found out that the mayor had cleared this with the President several hours earlier on a standby basis. It was another example of the President's concern that his actions be justified.)

The President ordered the army in and federalized the national guard at about four o'clock. At about the same time, the mayor established a 5:30 P.M. to 6:30 A.M. curfew and stopped all sales of alcohol, firearms, ammunition, and gasoline or other flammables until further notice.

With Cy Vance, we went first to the mayor's office and then to the police chief's office (in the municipal building) so we could be closer to the action. On my way back to my office on the north side of the District Building, I saw the fire and smoke for the first time. It has to be the most frightening sight I have ever seen. I ran back to get the mayor, and when he came in, we stood in awe for minutes.

We spent the rest of the night in the chief's office. Cy Vance took over the direction of the military and established close relations and coordination with our police department. He left the mayor and me to take care of all support needs, which had become difficult because of our limited communication capacity. By Saturday morning there had been at least five hundred reported fires, and at one time in the early evening we had two hundred going at one time. This was way past anything our fire department could handle, even with the help of the suburban departments. The only thing we could do was to save lives when possible and try to keep the fires from spreading.

The rioting lasted through Saturday, but by Sunday we had it pretty much under control. By then we had suffered more than a thousand fires and twelve deaths (ten from fires) and had made more than 7,500 arrests for looting or curfew violations. Better than 13,000 troops had been committed.

One scene I shall never forget from those three days occurred early Saturday night. I went out in a police patrol car to feel for myself what was going on in the city. When the patrol car got to the center of the intersection of Connecticut and K Street, I asked the driver to stop. This is one of the major cross streets in Washington, normally jammed with cars and people on Saturday night. But this night there was not a car or a person to be seen in any directon—except an occasional soldier dressed in full battle gear. It was like one of those end-of-the-world movies.

We continued to drive through some of the riot-torn areas, where now there seemed to be a spirit of revelry. Although it was after curfew, there were still many people on the streets. They seemed to be having a good time, running whenever the police or army started toward them, then reassembling when the coast was clear. We saw many arrests, but again everyone seemed happy. Some fires were still burning, and the results of the looting were everywhere: empty stores, broken windows, empty boxes and crates strewn over the streets. We could even see people rummaging in the debris to see if anything was left. For a public official it was like a picture of hell.

As our activities slowed down, I turned my attention to what we had done wrong and how we could learn from our experience. Everyone was telling everyone else we had done a pretty good job, and even Cy Vance said that we had handled the situation better than any city he was aware of that had gone through riots. But I knew we had made errors, including some bad ones.

The first challenge was to find out what had happened. Until we really knew what had gone wrong, we wouldn't know what we ought to fix. In a moment of inspiration I called Dr. Kermit Gordon, president of the Brookings Institute, and asked him if he could immediately assign some of his people to study the situation and tell us what really did happen. Dr. Gordon agreed to try, and the next day he had at least twelve of his people spending Sunday afternoon out interviewing everyone from top officials down to some of the rioters and looters.

Several weeks later, when their study and report was finished, it became obvious that we had made serious mistakes. For one thing, we had been primarily reactive—trying to follow up after the problems had developed. The army, the police presence, and the curfew were effective, but they had been established only after the major damage had been done.

Our key failure was the failure of communications. We just didn't have an effective communications system. One of the more startling revelations in the Brookings report was that, although we had a civil-defense communication system, none of us had thought to use it during the entire three days!

During this recovery period the mayor and I had one additional problem: Committees and individual members of Congress wanted to talk to us about the riots. In most of these meetings, held behind closed doors, the main point seemed to be that we had not been shooting looters. We explained that studies of other riots had shown that shooting by the police and army just produced more shooting by the rioters. We pointed out that although we had experienced heavy property losses and damage, we had had only twelve deaths—10 of those from fires. We also pointed out that there had been 7,500 arrests, far more than in any other city, and that those arrests seemed to be the major force in quelling the riot. They still felt that we should have been shooting from the beginning. Perhaps the only thing that restrained members of Congress from blasting us publicly was that our police chief stood behind us completely.

When we had returned to something approaching normal operation, I began looking for what we could do that would let us profit from our experiences. Of course it was obvious that we had to improve our communication and control system. Then I remembered a visit the previous

March from representatives of the Institute for Defense Analysis Corporation (IDA), a semipublic research agency created by the Department of Defense. The IDA representatives were seeking ideas for work they could do for urban governments, to broaden IDA's operations. In March I hadn't been able to come up with any ideas to match their capabilities, but I had one now. Could they help us set up a command center similar to a military system but oriented to our urban needs? Accompanied by our civil-defense staff, I talked to IDA. They saw the advantage of the idea and set to work at once, using their background and our analysis of the April riots.

A command center was designed and established in the Municipal Building on the same floor as the police chief's area, but separate. It consisted of three major facilities. First was a complete communications center, including radio transmitters and receivers (both fixed-base and mobile) on a variety of frequencies, teletypes, telephones, and a complete broadcasting facility that could be patched into all the major radio and TV stations in the metropolitan area. We had learned that people hunger for official news during any emergency. They want information from the mayor and other top officials directly, not screened through the news media. By the Friday night during the riots we had started putting the mayor and others on radio and TV and had received a good reaction.

The second facility was an information-gathering and -dissemination center. When fully operational, it had working representatives from our police, fire, welfare, health, transportation, school, and general services departments. It also had a representative from the Washington Metropolitan Area Council of Governments, with direct links to all suburban governments. (We had learned that these governments had to be kept in direct contact about what was going on and how it might affect their areas.)

As part of the information-gathering and -dissemination setup, we established a rumor center. We placed a representative of the rumor center in the command center, where he or she had a two-way function—to log and summarize incoming phone calls and advise the mayor and others of us in the Command Center about the kinds of calls, and to pass correct information from us and other units to the rumor center. The rumor center operated on a separate line of phone numbers. Whenever a problem started to develop, we broadcast these numbers over the radio and television networks. Because in any potentially threatening situation, rumors can cause many kinds of problems—traffic jams, disruption of the phone system, general breakdown of control—the rumor center may have been one of our most important innovations.

The third element in our command center was the center in which the mayor and his staff operated. It had all the facilities for information gathering but was also away from the confusion and noise of the other facilities in the center. In the main room of this center was a table that

had two slanted boards, one facing each side, with more than forty telephone buttons that gave hot-line access to everyone we needed to reach
quickly. Two people could use the equipment at the same time. There
were separate hot-line phone buttons giving us direct contact with the
White House, the attorney-general's office, and D.C. military headquarters. Using phone jacks and headsets, we could listen in on all radio frequencies that might be in use. A bank of four TV sets allowed us to
monitor all major TV broadcasts. A large magnetic map of the District
allowed us to track any action. The room was soundproofed to give us
maximum access to information with a minimum of confusion and noise.
A small adjoining room could be used for private conversations, as well as
for rest and sleep if needed.

The command center was manned by at least two civil-defense
employees twenty-four hours a day, seven days a week. They kept in close
contact, giving us any information they felt we would want to know. We
even organized a group of ex-convicts under one of the mayor's aides, to
keep us advised of anything that might be brewing. Several of us were
equipped with radio transmitters in our offices, our cars, and even in our
bedrooms. We always told the center where we were going.

During the first year, representatives of the IDA were present every
time the center was activated. They continued to make suggestions for
improvement. During the next few years the Center proved its worth over
and over again. Even before it was completed it was being used to monitor the activities of the Poor Peoples' Resurrection City, particularly
when we had to close that "city" in June 1968.

Two other examples will show how the command center functioned.
In early 1969 there was a sit-in at Howard University, within the District.
When the president of the university ordered all students to leave the
buildings by 6:00 P.M., we knew we were in for a major confrontation.

Our first step was to persuade the university president to modify his
order. Then, with our communication system in complete operation, we
were able to control the situation without any major problem developing.

We had already determined that any appearance of either the police or
the fire department at the university might set off a riot. Consequently,
we had both chiefs under direct orders from the mayor not to put uniformed officers on the campus without the mayor's express order. A small
fire started in a wooden shed on campus, but our information indicated
that it would not create any hazard if it were left to burn. However, without the mayor's authority, the fire chief sent in one of his trucks. The
truck had barely pulled up when students surrounded it, pulled off the
firemen, and set it on fire. We lost one of our $75,000 trucks.

Initially the police chief was not too happy when we set up a communication center separate from his. But he had started coming down to the
command center when anything big seemed to be happening, so we provided a place for him to sit and a phone tied to his center.

The chief was in the center when our sources reported that a police car had arrived at the scene of the fire on the campus and was beginning to throw tear gas. This was the one thing we didn't want; obviously the fire had been started solely to provoke police action. When we confronted the chief with this information, he immediately contacted his communication people, who assured him there had been no such incident. I radioed our people and was able not only to confirm that it had indeed happened, but also to give the chief the car number and the badge numbers of the two policemen who had done it. The chief called his people and the information was reconfirmed. Either our system was faster than his, or he was being deliberately misled. After that experience, the chief seemed much more willing to work with our command center.

The second illustration involved the "New Mobilization March" of anti-Vietnam War demonstrators held in November 1969. The White House had expressed deep concern to us about this demonstration and had taken extraordinary measures for their protection, including ringing the White House and the Ellipse Park with buses, bumper to bumper. Our experience on communications had told us that demonstrators were as liable to be spooked by rumors as anyone—if not more so. Consequently, we decided to give the leaders of this march walkie-talkies tuned to our civil defense frequency.

By adding this communication link to our system, we were able to handle a demonstration by more than 300,000 people, most of whom had come by bus from other cities, and to avoid any large problem. For example, after the march was over, a large number of the demonstrators started to mill around in the downtown area. When some got carried away and broke a few windows in the area, the police moved in fast and laid down tear gas between the demonstrators and the White House. This trapped the demonstrators, cutting them off from their buses, which were parked at the Tidal Basin, more than a mile away.

We were able to get in direct contact with the New Mobilization leaders. They wanted no part of any trouble, but just to get back to their buses and out of town. We asked them to control their groups as well as they could and said we would bring buses to them, so they could get back to their own buses without having to go through the police lines. We tried to get the White House to release their buses for this purpose, but they refused. We found a bus company in Maryland that could provide the buses on short notice but would do so only if they were sure of being paid. Fortunately, one of the innovations we had built into our command center was to have a representative of the business community with us at all times. He was able to convince the bus company that the business community would stand the cost.

The Maryland buses took the groups back to their own buses without incident. Over our radio I could hear the cheers at the Tidal Basin when our buses brought the rest of the demonstrators back safely.

In December 1969, when I was getting ready to leave the District to become city manager of San Jose, the D.C. government's management club asked me to speak about how it felt to be the first deputy mayor of the nation's capitol. About halfway through my talk, I started to describe my part in the April riots. As I began to tell them about how I first saw the smoke and fire from my office that Friday night, I cried. I had been too busy to cry at the time, and afterwards I had been occupied with trying to see that we never got into that kind of situation again. This was the first time I had relived that moment, and I realized, as I tried to express it, what a public official feels when he sees his city burning.

Confrontation(s)!
Thomas W. Fletcher

It was Sunday morning in the summer of 1971 in the City of San Jose. My new police chief called me to tell me that at about four o'clock that morning one of his patrolmen had killed a citizen. But he assured me, "Don't worry Tom. It was a good shooting." He told me that he would have it checked by internal affairs and that the policeman would be suspended with pay until the completion of the investigation. He went on to explain that after the patrolman had stopped a motorist for a traffic offense, a scuffle had occurred in which he had had to use his police dog and Mace because "deadly" physical force had been threatened. He then shot in self-defense and killed the man.

By Monday morning I began to realize it was not a "good" shooting (if there is such a thing). I had started receiving calls from community leaders expressing shock and anger at what had happened. I had also learned that the victim had been a black research scientist at IBM, a man well respected by all his associates and active in many community activities. The general manager of the San Jose IBM plant had called and assured me that something had to be "terribly wrong." His employee just wasn't the type to get involved in something like this.

The morning paper had carried a small article reporting the shooting and quoting the chief as saying that the shooting was "completely justified" and praising the policeman for good work.

Later that morning several policemen who were active in the police union came to see me and expressed their concern that the department might be in some trouble over the incident. It was their belief that something very "wrong" had happened. It was then I learned that two other policemen, off duty at the time, had also been involved.

I was especially concerned because the chief had been in office only about four months. Appointed from outside the city and therefore the subject of some controversy, he was still "on trial" within his department, the city council, and the community. I asked him to come over for a conference.

By the time he arrived, he knew he had been ill-informed. As we talked, he confirmed that more than one policeman had been involved and that there was additional information being developed that was raising serious questions about the incident. But he still felt that internal affairs could, and should, take care of the investigation. During this meeting the mayor came in and told us that the minority community was in an uproar and that because of the chief's quote in the paper they were convinced that there was a coverup going on, that even if an investigation was made they would not trust it.

With this additional information, I called the county district attorney and asked if he would take over the investigation with the understanding that if the evidence warranted it, he would turn the results over to the county grand jury for possible prosecution. He agreed but insisted that no city action be taken until the investigation was complete.

That afternoon we were told that there would be a community protest activity at our city council meeting that evening.

By seven o'clock that evening the council chambers were overflowing: Almost five hundred people were crowded in a room equipped to seat only 250. There was no way that the council would be permitted to go through its regular agenda. Those people represented a broad spectrum of the minority community. They wanted to be heard—and *now.*

Their basic demands were: (1) that the policemen involved be fired and prosecuted for murder, (2) that the chief apologize for his rash and false statement to the media, (3) failing the apology, that he be fired, and (4) failing the chief's firing, that the council fire the city manager.

Before the meeting I had told the city council members the facts as I knew them and that I had turned over the investigation to the DA. I also emphasized the DA's insistence that the council take no action until after the completion of that investigation, which he had estimated would take no more than three weeks.

This information did nothing to calm the audience. Their demands were loud and continuous. They just did not trust government, whether at the city or county level, and they had clear evidence of its insensitivity to their people. They wanted action now—tonight.

The city council, city manager and city attorney went into executive session in the small room behind the chamber. The noise and shouts of the audience could be heard as our very nervous group discussed what to do. I indicated that in my judgment we must abide by our agreement with the DA and that even an apology from the chief, which he was willing to give, would be construed as a prejudgment of the investigation.

We returned to the chamber, but in no way did our statements satisfy the audience. The demonstration continued for three more hours.

This was not the first time there had been a major confrontation in the city. Several years earlier (before my tenure) the city had created an annual fiesta to celebrate the city's Spanish heritage. The Chicano community was split over this celebration. The younger, more radical members objected strongly to the "Spanish" flavor, which they felt insulted their Indian heritage. During the fiesta parade, this group disrupted the ride of the "conquistadores." They had also demonstrated before the council and had picketed the homes of council members. But this shooting was the first issue in San Jose's history that had united the two principal minority groups (Black and Chicano).

The next two weeks witnessed the same strident confrontations at each council meeting. By the end of the third week we were advised by the DA that his investigation would take at least three more weeks! (This was probably a direct result of his growing concern over the reaction to the results of the investigation.)

As expected, this news frustrated and angered both the city council and the protesters. There was some acceptance of the necessity to complete the investigation, but action was still demanded. Now the focus was on the police chief and the city manager. The minorities' position hardened on the fact that the chief had obviously prejudged the situation and without investigation was willing to not only justify the incident but compound it with praise and commendation for the officer involved. I was in total agreement that the chief had erred—probably because of his concern about his lack of acceptance by the department during his short tenure.

I had requested the chief to write out a letter of apology in which he admitted his error in judgment. But even this action was rejected by both the DA and the city attorney as being inappropriate under the circumstances.

Members of the council made several attempts to adopt some action expressing council disapproval of the chief's behavior. But the city attorney cautioned the council that they were bordering on a violation of the city charter relative to the authority of the city manager.

This moved the focus to me and my personal lack of action. Even the fact that my daughter had been involved in a police incident in Washington, D.C., was used as evidence of my lack of action—a classic case of convoluted thinking.

The additional three weeks we waited for the DA in no way lessened the pressure and confrontation at our council meetings. All during this period the rest of the community seemed reluctant to get involved. The religious and business communities were notably absent, having made no apparent effort to find out what was going on, let alone to offer support or (at least) mediation. Certainly there was no shortage of available information. The incident and the confrontations were well covered by the local press and media as well as by the major Bay Area press and TV.

During this entire period I was receiving continuing information on the progress of the investigation. Our police department internal-affairs section had continued their own investigation. Their investigation, coupled with the findings of the DA, indicated a series of events and actions that bordered on the ludicrous, if not the hideous. The following is as clear as possible a description of the incident as established by the two investigations.

At about four o'clock Sunday morning the officer observed a car commit an illegal turn. (It was determined later that it was not an illegal turn.) Using his red light and siren, the officer pursued the car into the driveway of an adjacent apartment house, where the motorist lived. The motorist remained in his car, declining to get out when asked by the officer. He did turn over his driver's license for inspection.

The officer returned to his patrol car to call in the name and license plate number for a routine check. The police-dispatch recording of this transmission indicated that someone interrupted the officer in the middle of his call. Evidence indicated that this occurred when a sports car pulled up next to the patrol car. The two occupants identified themselves as off-duty San Jose policemen and inquired whether the officer needed any backup assistance. The officer indicated that none was needed. The next step in the scenario is hazy, but apparently the sports car moved ahead and adjacent to the stopped vehicle. There, without identifying themselves as policemen, they said or did something that angered the motorist. He came out of his car with a tire iron in his hand. (Subsequent testimony indicated that he carried the tire iron under his front seat because of his concern for his safety.) However, as soon as the occupants of the sports car identified themselves as policemen, he dropped the iron to the pavement. (The tire iron was not discovered until the next day when it was revealed that one of the off-duty policemen had thrown it into the back seat of the victim's car.)

The officer in the patrol car had witnessed the confrontation and, according to his own testimony, felt that a dangerous situation had developed. He emerged from his car accompanied by his police dog. The dog attacked the victim. While the victim was attempting to avoid the dog, the officer sprayed Mace in his face. It was determined later that the Mace was double strength and therefore, under state law and departmental rules, illegal for use by police officers.

After the Mace was discharged, the victim started to run toward his apartment house. The policeman followed and shot him in the back just as he reached the front door.

This was evidence enough to indicate disciplinary action, if not actual criminal charges, against all three policemen.

The DA's investigation finally concluded that the evidence warranted his submitting it to the county grand jury. In less than one day the grand jury brought down a manslaughter indictment of the officer who did the shooting.

That night at the council meeting we had our first evening of relative tranquility in six weeks. In our executive session that night I advised the council that I would release the chief's statement of apology. I also advised the council that it would be difficult to get a jury to find the officer guilty because of the rule of reasonable doubt. The next day the judge ruled that no statement could be made by the city until after the trial—so the chief's statement still could not be released. (It never was.)

The case was brought to early trial, and within hours of its being submitted to the jury they found the officer innocent of the charges.

As soon as the verdict was known, I met with the police chief and members of the internal investigative staff. After this meeting I issued an order to fire two of the policemen (the one who had done the shooting and the one who had removed the tire iron) and suspend for thirty days the other policeman, who had left the scene after the shooting (his excuse being that his pants' zipper was broken). In my public statement relative to these actions, I emphasized that these three disciplinary actions were being taken because of their violation of department rules and conduct unbecoming policemen and not because of the alleged criminal acts.

Now came a confrontation of a different sort. On one hand, the minority community was only mildly satisfied. They still felt that action should have been taken against the chief and that we should have moved faster. On the other, the police union was up in arms: their brother had been found innocent and the other two brothers had not even been indicted. In their judgment, my action was double jeopardy. Calling for my resignation, they filed an immediate appeal from my actions before the civil service commission, and hired one of the top defense attorneys in town to represent them in this appeal. I was able to convince our council that we should also hire a top attorney to represent the city in view of the fact that our own city attorney had been a participant in our previous actions. We were sustained on the two firings but not on the suspension (apparently a broken zipper was sufficient excuse).

And then one more confrontation took place. A few days after I had taken my disciplinary action a group of prominent businessmen called on me to tell me that they disapproved of my action and were going to protest to the city council. I finally lost my cool. After eight weeks of almost solid pressure and confrontation—after eight weeks of almost no governmental business being done—after eight weeks of feeling alone and unsupported—I *now* had these businessmen telling me that they didn't approve of my action.

I asked them where the hell they had been for the last eight weeks. I asked if any of them had been in the council chambers during our confrontation. They said of course not—they weren't going to be subjected to that kind of harassment. Then I asked why they hadn't called or come in to see me or the council to find out what was really going on and ask what they could do to help. Their response was that it did not seem necessary. I asked them if they had taken the effort to investigate the circumstances behind the incident. Again their response was in the negative. Then why, I asked, in a fairly loud and strained voice, did they have the nerve to come in now and tell me that what I had done was wrong. They felt that the bad publicity might be bad for their business. I assured them that people tend to have short memories (including their own) and then asked them to leave. They did not reappear.

And what had I gained in all of this? What was the lasting result of this? What had anyone gained? Probably nothing—really more was lost than gained. Two policemen had lost their jobs, and probably would always be hurt economically. The policeman who did the shooting must always live with that fact, and with a stigma that affects not only him but also his lovely wife and two small children.

The police union was further alienated from city government. The city council would never quite forgive the city manager for getting them into the mess. The police chief would probably never gain the acceptance he so badly wanted in his department and the community.

The minority community still felt that nothing had really been done to their satisfaction—they were further alienated. And now the business community was also alienated.

After twenty years of service to local government I felt it was time to look elsewhere—why should I and my family have to go through this any more?

And as for Mr. Smith, the IBM research scientist, all was lost.

Looking back over the intervening years, what could I have done differently? What did I learn?

In the first place I should have been more alert to the potential problems when I received the first call from the police chief. How could he know so quickly that it was a "good" shooting? I should have cautioned him not to make any judgmental statements to the press until the investigation had been completed.

I probably should have been more involved in letting other segments of the community know what was happening.

My learning resulted in taking a closer look at some of the psychological problems of members of the police department. Shortly after this incident, the city did hire a psychologist.

Decision-Making

The Air Force Academy
Comes to Colorado Springs
John M. Biery

In 1950 a brief newspaper story gave Joe Reich, restaurant owner and chamber of commerce president, an idea. The story said General Hoyt S. Vandenburg, U.S. Air Force chief of staff, was proposing a separate academy for the air force. Joe reasoned that since his community, Colorado Springs, Colorado, already had Fort Carson, Ent Air Force base, and the North American Air Defense Command, why not have the Air Force Academy too? Within days he had appointed a chamber of commerce military-affairs committee to sell his idea to the air force.

Headed by Russell Law, owner of the Law Mortuary, and Thayer Tutt, a hotel manager, and including three retired generals, three businessmen, a bank president, and John Love (who later would become the governor of Colorado), the committee spearheaded a cooperative effort among the Denver, Pueblo, and Colorado Springs chambers of commerce to get the Air Force Academy for Colorado Springs. Eventually they succeeded. In the meantime they produced for me the toughest decision I ever had to make as a city manager.

A prime factor in consideration of any site for the new academy was an adequate and reliable water supply. Recognizing that its water supply was insufficient for the current population, and that it would be in bad shape if the air force accepted its offer of a site, in 1950 the City of Colorado Springs began an adjudication in court and the construction of a tunnel through the Continental Divide for the transmountain diversion of the Blue River some 120 miles west of the city. In addition, it committed itself to provide the academy a firm supply of two million gallons of water per day.

On 1 February 1952 I assumed the job of city manager, including responsibility for operation of the city's water, electric, gas, and sewage departments. At that time, the city was a long way from delivering the Blue River water to the city. In fact, the district court had turned down a request for water rights on the Blue, a decision we would appeal to the state supreme court. Moreover, we had yet to construct the dam for a storage reservoir at the lower end of the Continental Divide tunnel and the 120 miles of pipeline.

However, by June 1954 much of this construction was under way, a million dollars worth of 30-inch steel pipe was being stored for coating, and the supreme court had reversed the district court, entitling us to the diversion. But I'm getting ahead of my story.

In March 1954 Congress directed Harold E. Talbot, secretary of the air force, to appoint a five-member commission to advise him on the academy's location. If the commission was unanimous on a site, the secretary was required to accept their recommendation. If they were not unanimous, the commission must submit three sites, one of which the secretary must select. The site-selection commission consisted of Air Force General Spaatz, Lieutenant General Hubert Harmon, Dr. Virgil Hancher (president of the University of Iowa), Merrill C. Miegs (vice-president of the Hearst Corporation), and Charles A. Lindbergh.

At the same time that the site-selection commission was considering some four hundred possible sites, and traveling more than eighteen thousand miles on inspections, we were experiencing severe water shortage problems in Colorado Springs. The early 1954 spring produced little snow runoff into our four reservoirs on Pike's Peak, while the water demand for domestic and irrigation use had reached a rate of 30 million gallons per day. To deal with the problem, I first reduced all irrigation for city-owned parks and boulevards, which meant that by June the grass in these areas was brown and trees were dying. The day before the site-selection group was to arrive in Colorado Springs, my utility director reported that the storage in our reservoirs was almost gone, that unless we immediately cut water consumption to a minimum, in a few days we wouldn't have water enough to wash our teeth. We had to reduce or eliminate irrigation of private lawns, shrubbery, and gardens.

The decision to restrict water was the city manager's. But I had the mayor call the city council together for an informal information meeting. They all agreed I must stop the use of water for irrigation. Realizing the effect of a newspaper announcement of restrictions on the day the academy site-selection commission was to arrive, I met with Mr. Law and Mr. Tutt to explain what I must do. They were astounded. Couldn't I wait a week or two? If not, the city manager—and he alone—would be held responsible for the loss of the Air Force Academy to Colorado Springs and of the committee's four years of work and expenditures of more than $50,000.

The site-selection commission arrived that evening. Next morning they were greeted by two-inch headlines in the *Free Press* stating that the city manager had put restrictions into effect, limiting lawn watering to two hours a week and then only during early morning hours. From their hotel windows, the commission members looked out on the thirty-six-hole Broadmoor Golf Course, now brown with shrubbery dead or dying. They reacted by asking how the city could furnish water to the academy when it couldn't even keep up with the needs of its parks, boulevards, and citizen requirements. Of course we answered, through our consulting engineers, that before the academy would need it, our Blue River water would be here in sufficient quantity for all projected needs.

That day, pondering what my decision may have meant to the future of the city, I felt lower than a snake's belly. In the evening, my wife, young son, and I went out north of Colorado Springs to the Flying W Ranch for a barbecue and a little relaxation. After supper, cowboys assembled around the open fire to sing western songs. When they sang "Cool Clear Water," I retired to the bushes, thinking I might upchuck my meal. For me there was no cool water anywhere, only little muddy ponds at the bottom of our reservoirs. Never before or since during my forty years of municipal responsibility has a decision been so tough to make or had such an effect on me.

On 3 June 1954 the site-commission members announced that they had been unable to agree on a site and so offered Secretary Talbot three locations: Alton, Illinois; Colorado Springs, Colorado; and Lake Geneva, Wisconsin. For the next three weeks I had doubts that being city manager of Colorado Springs was worth the responsibility the job carried. During this twenty-one day period our utility department and consulting engineers submitted good and sound engineering proof that we would have a firm water supply for the academy. This, together with a million-dollar appropriation by the state legislature for purchase of a site, turned the trick. On June 24 the secretary announced that Colorado Springs had won.

A week later I received a letter signed by all twelve members of the chamber of commerce military-affairs committee, thanking me for my part in obtaining the newly created United States Air Force Academy for Colorado Springs. I have often wondered what my future as city manager of Colorado Springs would have been if the result had been negative.

The water rationing and the cooperation of the citizens in using dish and laundry water for lawns and shrubbery and in abiding by the rationing hours saved enough water that we survived the summer. By taking temporary measures and speeding up construction of the Blue River diversion project we were able to furnish the needed water to the Academy.

All's well that ends well. I retired from Colorado Springs in the Fall of 1966, after several more years of service to the city. But even now I get a chill down my back when I think that I personally might have been responsible for the loss of the Air Force Academy to Colorado Springs.

Managing Facilities
and Equipment

Insuring the Government
LeRoy F. Harlow

When I became city manager of Daytona Beach, Florida, in 1953, the city owned some seventy-five buildings and 2,500 acres of land. In addition to the usual city hall, fire stations, recreation facilities, and utility structures that most cities have, Daytona Beach had acquired from the federal government the former Women's Army Corps Training Center and a former naval air station with not only the runways, administration building, and hangars, but also several auxiliary buildings. (The city had converted some of the air-station land to first-class baseball diamonds, which became the spring-training camp for the Cleveland Indians' farm teams.)

On inquiry, I found that nobody really knew what the city owned: that some of the buildings were occupied by squatters, others were being rented or leased at give-away rates, and some were just falling apart. Further, our insurance program was a puzzle. We didn't know whether we were underprotected or overprotected.

Under a commission-approved reorganization plan, we established a purchasing division within the city manager's office. In addition to central-purchasing responsibilities, the division was to be in charge of rental, lease, assignment, and maintenance of city-owned real estate, and the management of our insurance program.

When we were able to hire a qualified purchasing agent, one of his first assignments was to inventory our holdings, finding out how much land and how many buildings the city owned and where they were, what they were worth, whether the city was getting the rent it should, and how much land was lying idle—whether we were making the best use of our real estate.

Next we tackled the insurance problem. Like a private individual, a city is pretty much at the mercy of the insurance agents when it comes to the small print and estimating a reasonable coverage for the risks and hazards involved. But the individual has one distinct advantage: the freedom to choose the company, the agent, and the contract that pleases him or her. Not so with the city.

Virtually every insurance agent is a local taxpayer. He feels "entitled" to part of the city's insurance business. The easiest way out is for the city to say to the local insurance men, "Look, fellows, we don't have time to talk to all of you. Get together; choose one of your men to represent all of you. We'll deal with him, and he can split the premiums among you."

This is common practice, but it does not satisfy all the agents because some represent investor-owned (stock) companies and some, policyholder-owned (mutual) companies. The two kinds of companies operate differently. Thus, although the stock-company agents might agree on one of their number to speak for them, and the mutual company local agents might do the same, the city is still between the two.

Then there is another factor—degree of coverage. Traditionally municipal corporations have enjoyed some of the sovereign power of government. Consequently they have enjoyed immunity from some types of liability. Although the distinctions are not clear, courts generally have distinguished between what are called "governmental" functions and "proprietary" functions. Speaking very broadly, when a local government is engaged in a governmental function (firefighting, for example) it enjoys an immunity it does not have if engaged in a proprietary function (operating a water system, for instance). It would be a waste of taxpayers' money to pay insurance premiums for protection the city already had under its partial sovereign immunity. Unfortunately, not all insurance agents know where the line of distinction is, if they know at all this principle of municipal law; and no one knows what the courts will hold in a specific situation.

After a country-wide search, I finally located (in Indiana) a firm of insurance consultants. They didn't sell insurance; they served organizations that had to buy insurance but felt at the mercy of the insurance salesmen. The consultants' job was to identify the client's hazards and liability, define the insurance needs, give counsel on how to draft specifications for insurance coverage to meet those needs, and suggest alternative approaches to buying reasonable protection. With city commission authorization, we engaged their services and got a useful report with recommendations. From then on I felt more comfortable about our insurance coverage, both its adequacy and its cost.

Finances

Finding Additional Revenue

Thomas F. Maxwell

In 1947, shortly before I became the first city manager of University City, Missouri, the firemen and policemen had obtained voter approval of a first-time pension plan for those two services, and a three-cent additional real-estate tax to finance the plan. Because state law limited cities to a real-estate tax of $1.50 per $1,000 of assessed valuation, this three-cent increase was 2 percent of our allowable tax rate. That, plus postwar inflation and the need to catch up on long-neglected services and facilities, pointed to higher property taxes. But I was determined to reduce taxes, not increase them. And that meant I had to find additional revenue sources.

First I found that the utility company serving University City was also serving St. Louis at identical rates but was paying St. Louis a 5 percent gross-receipts tax and University City a 0.5 percent gross-receipts tax. But my part-time city attorney (quoting the famous Dartmouth Case) said that couldn't be changed because a previous council had given the utility company a twenty-year franchise at 0.5 percent.

At about this time, Clarence E. Ridley, executive director of the International City Management Association, came down from the association's Chicago headquarters to a meeting of Missouri city managers. During that conference I learned that the Missouri Supreme Court had held in a somewhat similar case that one council could not bind future councils.

Armed with this information and the backing of the four lawyers on council, the council passed an ordinance requiring a 5 percent gross-receipts tax on collections in University City. That alone brought in enough money to increase salaries and reduce taxes. The utility company took the city to court on the issue, but the city won the case.

Also I found that merchants, businesses and professionals were paying only token business licenses. We adopted a new, equitable rate and audited their books to make sure they complied. Strangely, with a few outstanding exceptions, this procedure was not tremendously objectionable to the business community. They realized that they were all being treated the same, whereas in the past those in favor with the mayor had paid very little while others paid much more.

I also required payment of personal property taxes before issuance of an auto license. This increased our personal property tax collections from 15 percent to 90 percent.

Thus, the Council was able to reduce the property-tax rate, although when I arrived in University City it looked as though that could not be done.

The Norfolk Story
Thomas F. Maxwell

Norfolk, Virginia, was one of the first cities in the nation to adopt the council-manager plan of government. Its first city manager was Charles E. Ashburner, who had been the first city manager in the country when the plan was formulated in Staunton, Virginia.

In September 1918 Mr. Ashburner took office as the Norfolk city manager. Although he was derided by some as Mr. Cashburner because he had the foresight to build a bridge over the Lafayette River (opening up a new residential area which is still one of the city's finest), he served until 1923, when he left Norfolk to take a similar position in California. From then until 1946 all the Norfolk city managers were local people—personal friends and associates of the various city council members under whom they served.

During most of this period the council members probably were associated with the Byrd organization, which generally controlled Virginia politics. Although the Byrd organization was politically strong, it was not a machine of the Pendergast type; rather, it was noted for the rectitude of its elected officials and freedom from corruption. It can best be described as an association of gentlemen with similar political philosophies. Nevertheless, at the local level, 300-year old Norfolk suffered from mildly protected vice, political favoritism, physical deterioration and other evils usual in old port cities.

These problems increased enormously during World War II, when thousands of navy personnel poured into the area. During this period the city developed an unsavory reputation with the navy people because of the housing shortage, protected vice, rent gouging, and generally bad wartime conditions. Moreover, the permanent residents of Norfolk were not generally hospitable to these strangers. Later I found that some people who had served in the navy during the war still resented the Norfolk residents and city government.

At the end of the war, the physical and moral deterioration of the city led to the formation of a coalition of highly respected businessmen determined to improve the city government. Led by Pretlow Darden, who was elected mayor, the group gained control of the city council, and in November 1946 they brought in Mr. Charles A. Harrell, the first professional city manager since Mr. Ashburner. The reform council gave full support to Mr. Harrell's successful efforts in reorganizing the city government along professional lines. He eliminated much of the political favoritism that had been rampant, brought in qualified personnel, appointed a new police chief to clean up the vice and corruption, and in general performed in a manner to be expected from one of the most respected city managers in the nation.

At the end of their four-year term, however, Mayor Darden and his colleagues declined to run for reelection. I recall Mr. Darden's telling me that in a council meeting a lady berated him at length and concluded by saying she would never again vote for him. Mr. Darden's reply: "Lady, you will never have the opportunity to vote for me or against me again, as I agreed to serve only one term when I ran for this office."

In the ensuing election, another coalition of outstanding businessmen was elected. This group was led by Mr. W. Fred Duckworth, a successful automobile dealer and former Ford Motor Company plant manager, who was elected mayor. Mayor Duckworth was an exceptionally vigorous, intelligent, and strong executive, and although he had no background in municipal affairs, he became an excellent mayor.

This second coalition group did not run on a platform of firing Mr. Harrell, as did other tickets in the election, but neither did they offer him strong support. Consequently, in 1951 he left Norfolk to become the first city manager of San Antonio, Texas. From 1951 to 1955 the city-manager position was filled by the director of public works, an engineer with no experience in other elements of city government. He was totally dominated by the competent and persuasive mayor, who provided the executive leadership for the city.

On 2 January 1956 (a holiday in Columbia, South Carolina, where I was serving as city manager) I received a telephone call from Mayor Duckworth inviting me to come to Norfolk immediately for an interview about the city-manager position. I knew that just six months before, Sherwood Reeder (who had been the first and very successful city manager in

Richmond, Virginia) had been appointed in Norfolk, after his voluntary absence from the profession. So I asked what had happened to him. I was stunned when the mayor said Sherry had suddenly died of a heart attack about a week before.

Between the shock of learning of Sherry's death and the unexpectedness of the call, I said I would need some time to consider his invitation, especially since I was very happily situated in Columbia. However, the mayor insisted that I let him know within twenty-four hours whether or not I was interested. He said the salary was $25,000 per year (among the highest for city managers at the time) and that they were eager to make a new appointment without delay.

I knew nothing of Norfolk except that Mr. Harrell and Sherry Reeder had served there. But I felt that Sherry, having been in Richmond for many years, knew the situation in Norfolk and would have refused the Norfolk position had he not felt that it could be handled by a professional city manager. Therefore, I accepted the invitation and, on the following weekend, had a long interview with the Norfolk city council.

I was impressed. The council members, all successful businessmen, demonstrated a strong desire for progressive city government and an improved image for the city. I stayed overnight in the city, and the following day the mayor offered me the position. Again I pleaded for time to discuss it with my wife and give it further consideration; again he insisted on a prompt answer, which I promised to give him within forty-eight hours.

The $7,000 salary increase and, more important, the opportunity to rebuild an old and deteriorated city represented an opportunity and challenge I could not resist. With some regret and trepidation I left Columbia and moved to Norfolk. Upon my arrival I reiterated what I had said to the mayor and city council in our original conference: my philosophy was that the city manager and council must work as a harmonious team if Norfolk were to become a rejuvenated, progressive city. They were in agreement. And from that day until my retirement, the cooperation between Mayor Duckworth, his successor (Roy B. Martin, Jr.), their city councils, and me enabled us to make enormous progress in restoring the vitality and physical facilities of this old port city.

Among cities of our size, we had the largest and most successful slum-clearance program in the nation, building extensive public housing, developing and attracting industry and commerce, and all the time keeping the city on a sound financial basis. We built a new $10 million civic center without issuing bonds, thus saving $2 million in interest cost. We won the All-America City award for developing community cooperation and support for slum clearance and public housing. Our bond rating was increased from A to AA, saving millions of dollars in bond interest. We built the famous MacArthur Memorial, a new jail and library, and a $30 million convention center and theater, and we provided water and sewer service to the one-fourth of the city that had not had such service. We built a new $20 million airport and new schools, brought employees' salaries up to a reasonable level, eliminated protected vice, and developed a large and competent planning department (which the city had never had). We created an entirely new complex of office and bank buildings around a beautifully landscaped mall that added hundreds of thousands of dollars to our tax revenue and created much employment. I estimate that our city-financed capital improvements totaled about $100 million during the fifteen years I served, and we kept real-estate taxes at next to the lowest among all cities of 300,000 or more.

That seeming financial miracle was accomplished by the use of a unique sales tax that I devised. It was a 2 percent tax with a $5 limit on any single purchase. The limit was necessary to keep auto, appliance, furniture stores, and the like from being driven out of business by competition from the three surrounding and immediately adjacent cities of Portsmouth, Virginia Beach, and Chesapeake. It provided revenue equal to a 40 percent increase in the real-estate tax. The tax was imposed primarily to finance a quality education program (which required an additional $4 million appropriation).

Before the tax was levied, we carried out a massive public-relations campaign, explaining what the money would be used for (mostly improvements in the school system, including higher salaries for teachers, smaller classes, and new facilities; the balance was to be used to improve city employee pay, which was inadequate, and attract candidates for the police department, which had been unable to fill many vacancies). In the election immediately following the imposition of the sales tax, an opposing political slate that used opposition to the tax as its principal issue was soundly defeated and all members of council were easily reelected. One of the losing candidates said the winners took a lemon and made lemonade out of it.

The imposition of this tax was the most controversial issue I ever faced as a city manager. When I first recommended it, the news media supported the idea for *one day*. Then they heard from their advertisers and launched a vicious campaign against me and the proposed tax. They were joined by business leaders in the community, as well as by politicians who claimed it was a tax on the disadvantaged people of the community. I defended my recommendation by stating the following facts, which I had carefully researched and analyzed.

1. An increase in the real-estate tax would mean higher rents for the lower-income families—an increase they could not avoid, because shelter is a prime necessity. Statistics proved that the lower the income, the higher the percentage of such income was required by shelter cost. Thus, if we were to raise the real-estate tax, low-income people would be trapped by high shelter costs that they could not avoid. By con-

trast, because they could choose alternatives in their other purchases they would not be so hard hit by a sales tax.

2. People were not stupid enough to take the time and pay the transportation costs to drive to surrounding communities to save a few cents on small purchases, or the maximum $5 on a major purchase such as an automobile.

3. An increase in the real-estate tax would be a greater burden on retired people on fixed incomes than would the limited sales tax I proposed.

4. A sales tax would provide funds from visitors, conventioneers, and vacationers from other states (who were accustomed to the sales taxes in effect in almost every state but Virginia).

I estimated that the revenue to be derived would be $6 million, and much to everyone's surprise (including mine), the estimate was within $50,000 of the actual revenues. Our merchants also enjoyed splendid business, and as a result, all opposition to the sales tax disappeared. For one of only two times in my career, the newspapers editorially admitted that they had been wrong!

The following year all the surrounding communities and most other cities throughout the state adopted an identical tax.

The more equitable forms of taxation such as a piggy-back on the graduated state income tax or a local payroll tax for localities were prohibited by state law. I am sure the state would have prohibited a local sales tax had the legislature believed that any city would have the courage to impose such a tax.

For Norfolk and all cities in the state the most important thing about our bold leadership in adopting the limited sales tax is that when the state imposed an unlimited 4 percent sales tax three years later, the state was forced to share it with the cities because it had become imbedded in city budgets as a principal source of revenue. Had Norfolk not furnished the leadership in the sales-tax field, I am convinced cities would have received not one cent of the state sales tax and would have had to continue to increase the property tax, which is the most regressive tax that cities are forced to use and which nourished Proposition 13 in California and similar movements throughout the nation. Cities simply must be afforded less dependence on the real property tax; otherwise they must curtail services to an unacceptable level.

On 1 January 1971 I retired as Norfolk city manager, never having regretted the more than thirty years of my life that I devoted to being a public servant. Although I believe that almost any successful city manager could accumulate more worldly goods with fewer trials in private business than as a city manager, for me—and I think for all of us—the satisfaction of serving the public to the best of our ability is reward enough.

Taxes and Television
Richard H. Custer

In 1957 the city of Zanesville, Ohio, won an All-America City award for the successful campaign organized and conducted by a group of citizens to adopt the council-manager form of government. On 1 January 1958 I became Zanesville's first city manager, but only after considerable hesitation.

I hesitated because I felt the All-America City effort might have come too late, that the city might be beyond redemption—a feeling shared by a former Zanesvillian who wrote the newspaper that he considered his former home town "the nadir of civilization."

Located where two rivers join, the city was noted for a Y-shaped bridge that spanned the river junction. Zanesville also had been once known for its flourishing pottery industry, but this had declined seriously. Because most of the pottery workers were unskilled, new sources of employment were slow to enter the area. Although several major manufacturers had branch plants in the area and the city was the commercial center for an area much larger than that of most cities with a similar population, Zanesville was not prosperous.

Economic woes were compounded by a history of local-government neglect and mismanagement. The city had neither a building code nor a zoning ordinance. More than half the streets and alleys were unpaved. The water supply was unreliable and unsafe, being distributed mostly through wooden mains. Nor was it metered. There were practically no sanitary sewers. Equipment was antiquated. And the city had only one part-time engineer on its staff.

On the other hand, the vote to adopt council-manager government had been decisive, with strong support from the local newspaper and the TV station. The first council showed promise of being outstanding: the three incumbents, who were serving their first term, had been instrumental in establishing the manager plan; the four newcomers, all in their first public office, were manager-plan supporters. Of the seven, five were businessmen, one was a medical doctor, and one a certified public accountant. These positive indications coupled with persuasions of the retiring council president, who had spearheaded the campaign for the new government, convinced me to accept.

Before my acceptance, and to avert virtual bankruptcy of the city's water utility, the outgoing council had enacted a new ordinance increasing water rates to two and three times the existing flat rates and requiring installation of water meters within a year. Of course the first part of the legislation alleviated an immediate financial problem that otherwise would have fallen on to me to resolve. But the second part posed a large and immediate administrative and public-relations task—to organize and oversee a twelve-month program of purchasing and installing meters in about twelve thousand homes and businesses.

The sanitary sewer system and its financing also demanded my early attention. The state health department had ordered the city to construct a system of trunk sewers and a primary treatment plant. The city had engaged a reputable consulting engineering firm to design the facilities and devise a schedule of sewer service charges to finance a $5 million construction program. Sewer service charges would be a percentage of a customer's water bill and were to be collected with the periodic water bills.

Unfortunately the city also had a contract with a financial "consultant" of lesser qualifications. The outgoing mayor had hired a free-lance, self-proclaimed expert on municipal finance to set up the bond issue and sale on a negotiated, noncompetitive basis with a Cleveland investment firm.

Keep in mind the nature and potential effect of a municipal bond sale. It is a carefully prescribed procedure, subject to state law, by which a city can borrow large amounts of money for particular projects. It is a local government IOU. In return the city promises to repay the bondholder the amount of the bond plus interest at an agreed-upon rate over a predetermined number of years. The city gets its payback money from general taxes and/or charges for specific services such as water and sewer services, plus miscellaneous other city revenues.

The repayment schedule and the interest rate are critical factors: The wrong combination of these elements can double or more the amount originally authorized to be borrowed. Most city managers know about the importance of proper debt administration; hence, my experience told me that although the Zanesville contract for negotiation of its bond sale was legal, it was not only unnecessary but unwise. If the negotiated interest rate on the bonds was only the seemingly insignificant amount of 0.5 percent above what could be obtained through competitive bids, the added cost to Zanesville taxpayers could total hundreds of thousands of dollars over the twenty-year life of the bonds.

My doubts about the contract were reinforced when I reviewed the consultant's suggested repayment schedule. He proposed to defer repayment of major amounts of principal until later years. The result would be excessive interest costs. Accordingly, I recommended to the council that we extricate ourselves from the contract in any possible legal way and handle the bond issue through my office. With the certified public accountant member strongly supporting my recommendation, the council agreed, and I had another significant task on my hands early in my days of office. But at least we now had the financial problems of the water and sewer systems under some control.

In the meantime, opponents of the new water-rate ordinance successfully challenged the ordinance in the Ohio Supreme Court. Also, it was increasingly clear to me that the city must have more general revenue if it were to meet its steadily increasing pension and insurance costs, make a start on rehabilitating its deteriorated physical facilities, and support even the present minimum levels of fire and police protection, street maintenance, refuse collection and disposal, public health service, park and recreation program, and operation of the civic auditorium and municipal airport. As I stated in a speech to the local Zavi Shrine Club, the amount the city was receiving to pay for all these vital services was about the price of two packages of cigarettes per week for each Zanesville citizen.

The revenue crunch was the product of several factors. One was the Ohio constitutional provision that limited municipal property tax levies to 1 percent (10 mills) of the property's assessed value. County government officials did the assessing and levied and collected the taxes. First they paid the principal and interest on debts owed by the county, the school districts, and the municipalities in the county. From what was left of the 1 percent levy, the county officials decided how much each of the governments would receive. While the constitutional tax limit and the system of administration imposed rigid discipline on spending by local officials—which was the intent of the original authors—in Zanesville it was making the patient comatose.

The state government administered a sales tax and a gasoline tax, part of which were returned to the counties where collected. Again, county officials then distributed these funds among the county, the school districts, the municipalities and other local governments, according to their respective needs as determined by the county officials. As might be expected, county needs got highest priority when the county officials allocated these tax revenues.

To top off all the above, in 1957 the voters had approved a measure that reduced the police work week from forty-eight hours to forty and simultaneously rejected a special tax levy that would have made it possible to maintain the force at its existing strength. In November 1958 they approved a petition-forced referendum that reduced the work week for city firemen. To prevent a budget deficit, I had to close two of the city's five fire stations.

While the Ohio constitution put municipal officials in a financial straitjacket with its 1 percent property-tax limit, it also provided a degree of home rule to local voters by allowing them to vote for additional tax levies if they chose. Such levies were limited in purpose, amount, and duration, but they were options that could relieve financial pressure. One such option was a city income tax. This tax was not to exceed 1 percent of the gross income of all persons who lived in a city regardless of where they worked, and all persons who worked in the city regardless of where they lived. The rate was uniform on all income, and there were no exemptions or deductions; hence, it was a tax easy to understand and relatively simple to administer through payroll withholding.

At the time a few of the state's larger cities had adopted the municipal income tax, but the smaller cities had been reluctant to present it to their voters. As I got into my second year's budget preparation, I became convinced that the city's only financial salvation was enactment of a local income tax. During informal council sessions, I presented my conclusion and we discussed my reasons therefor. The new council president, Dr. Gordon "Doc" Gifford, and the other members encouraged me to prepare the necessary legislation and a timetable and strategy for enacting and implementing such a tax.

A major policy decision was whether to propose to the voters the full 1 percent allowed, or a lesser percentage. The council members expected that in referendum-prone Zanesville if they enacted the tax, it would be subjected to a referendum. Nevertheless, they unanimously rejected the idea of adopting a lesser tax rate that might be sufficient to maintain services but not to make improvements.

Backed by council support and with legal advice, we drafted a 1 percent income-tax ordinance. In April 1959 I submitted my proposed budget, the income-tax ordinance, and supporting legislation that empowered me to borrow short-term funds against the first three-month anticipated proceeds from the tax. The council approved the items, which would become effective the following July 1.

This strategy gave us necessary lead time for organizing and installing the new tax, and several months' experience in collecting the revenue before the anticipated November referendum. Also, it provided some badly needed funds for immediate use on street improvements in the spring and early summer months.

Only 74 miles of Zanesville's 189 miles of streets and alleys had a permanent surface. Moreover, because of the large and cheap deposits of clay in the area, most of the downtown streets and many others were covered with nothing more than loosely mortared red brick. Consequently, the council considered a street-improvement program our most urgent priority. Judging from the citizen complaints, the public agreed. Accordingly, after reopening the two closed fire stations, we concentrated use of the new money on street and alley improvement.

We rebuilt the city's inoperable street sweeper. Acquiring a second sweeper on a lease-purchase plan, we instituted what citizens told us was the first systematic sweeping program in the city's history. We cured two notorious chronic storm-drainage problems that had blocked permanent street improvement in their vicinities for years. We engaged a private contractor to apply a mixture of reclaimed motor oil and 20 percent liquid asphalt to stabilize dusty surfaces. This provided—again, for the first time—summer-long dust control on every unimproved street and alley. During all these activities we displayed prominent signs on equipment and job sites: "This work made possible by the proposed income tax."

Although these visible improvements received favorable comment, there were also signs of growing opposition as the date approached for the tax to go into effect. A small but vocal group of citizens, headed by an elderly man named Harry Conn and calling themselves The Citizens and Taxpayers League, denounced the proposed tax as unnecessary and circulated flyers urging opposition to it. Although Conn's known following was small, and although many people thought him misguided if not irresponsible, past history indicated that his influence could not be taken lightly. (It was Conn's group that had successfully challenged the city's new water rates in the Ohio Supreme Court.)

I suggested to the council that they take the offensive and conduct an informational and promotional campaign in behalf of the tax. Agreeing to this, they asked me to arrange anything I thought appropriate. Fortunately, the private TV station in Zanesville, WHIZ-TV, enjoyed a wide local audience, and its part-owner and manager, Allen Land, had remained strongly supportive of the new government and its efforts to improve the city. While the local newspapers, the *Times Recorder* and *The Signal*, also were supportive, I felt that TV coverage of the city's high-quality council members would be the most effective way to offset the rumors, innuendoes, and half-truths being circulated by opponents of the tax.

Land agreed. Together we developed a program in which, for one hour of prime time on five consecutive evenings, the entire council and I would respond to questions or comments called into the station by the public. The program would be live and unrehearsed and questions being called in would be screened only for propriety and to reduce repetitiveness. Time for the series would be donated by WHIZ.

The council, having seen at close hand what we had been able to accomplish with the added funds in a short time, was enthusiastic. We proceeded. Public response was heavy, with most of the initial calls being (as we expected) critical. As the series progressed, however, "Doc" Gifford's contagious good nature and the entire council's sincerity and knowledge of the city's needs and of plans to meet those needs had their effect. By the time of the last evening's program, the calls were overwhelmingly positive.

I believe it was largely due to television that we were able to install and implement the new tax as planned and with a minimum of non-compliance. Although Conn was able to force the expected referendum, by that time we were able to fulfill many of the promises for improvement we had made in the TV series. In the referendum the people voted two-to-one in favor of continuing the municipal income tax. A year later, after we had been able to repave most of the downtown streets and major arteries, and aided by a parade of new city equipment that was purchased from income tax money—and prominently so labeled—another referendum resulted in a three-to-one majority in favor of continuing this vital new source of revenue for the city.

City Revenue Equals 2 Packs
Of Cigarets Per Citizen

Revenue foreseen now for Zanesville's general fund this year amounts to the price of two packs of cigarets a week for each citizen, City Manager Richard H. Custer declared Wednesday night.

Custer, addressing members of the Zavi Shrine club at the YMCA in one of the first in a series of town meetings on the city's sagging income, said the money — totaling $920,110 — is earmarked for 9 different city services and activities.

Referring to Councilman Roy Wilson's call Monday night for consideration of a city income tax as a possible new source of revenue, Custer cited these points:

"We have 120 miles of streets to maintain in Zanesville, and the money we have available to do it with amounts to only 2 cents a day or 7 dollars a year for each person in the city.

"Because of lack of funds, we are operating our street department with six fewer men than we had a year ago, and, in addition, all of the street crew men are working fewer hours per week than a year ago.

"To place our existing paved street system in what might be called even good condition, and to do it over a two year period, would call for a rate of spending almost four times greater than our present funds permit.

"The money allotted to the city by the County Budget commission from the sales tax is expected to be less this year than it was eight years ago — in 1951.

"The amount of your tax dollar which must be earmarked to pay debts of earlier years will be more than double this year over what it was in 1957.

"The city's charge for garbage and refuse service will not pay the full cost of that service in 1959 unless the charge is increased by 25 per cent," Custer said.

"The councilmen further knew that, with these problems of

City Manager Richard Custer is shown here as he addressed Zavi Shrine club members Wednesday night on Zanesville's sagging revenue.

shrinking or stable revenue, our costs of living were increasing," he continued. "For example, they knew:

"The cost of police, fire and other employe pensions has increased by one hundred thirteen since 1957.

"The cost of workmen's compensation insurance on all city employes has been increasing

steadily, and in 1959 will be 200 per cent higher than it was in 1952.

"In 1957 a system of automatic salary increases for police and firemen was started, based on length of service, so that each year our salary costs will be higher with the same manpower."

Zanesville, Ohio, city manager addresses a local civic club on the city's financial problems.

You Shall Not Steal—
Neither Electricity nor Elections

Bert W. Johnson

In 1937 Clarence A. Dykstra, city manager of Cincinnati, Ohio, became president of the University of Wisconsin. I was an undergraduate majoring in accounting, and student chairman of a lecture series. I interviewed President Dykstra, who was to be our first lecturer and was so impressed by his contagious excitement about his previous work that I changed my major to city management. Following short periods with three research organizations, World War II navy service, and two years as finance director of Winnetka, Illinois, I got my first city manager job. My employer was Lebanon, Missouri, a small Ozark city with a municipal power plant but with limited public services and a skeleton public work force to serve the 6,800 residents—quite a contrast to Winnetka, the wealthy Chicago suburb with superb municipal services.

Lebanon was in financial trouble—$51,000 in the red. But it had an excellent city council of five of the community's best citizens, who had been virtually drafted for office and were determined to get the city organized and balance its revenue and outgo.

Shortly after my arrival, Chief Lineman Opel Lawson told me I could stop worrying about city revenue if I would support a street-lighting system. He explained that in lieu of regular street lights, Lebanon relied on home porch lights, fed by a direct series line from the municipal power plant. The home owners often tapped this porch-light circuit to supply their household heating and lighting needs, thus reducing their use of metered electricity.

I did some comparative checking. At that time Winnetka householders were billed for an average of 100 kilowatt hours and Lebanon householders an average of 25 kilowatts. During a selected period, demand on the Lebanon plant was up 200 percent, its consumer billings up only 18 percent. Obviously, the city was losing revenue some way.

We designed and installed on a competitive bid basis a complete new street-lighting system, including 241 poles equipped with 2,500 lumen lighting fixtures. We disconnected the porch-light line from the light plant, because the line was no longer needed. Consumption of metered electricity skyrocketed and soon began to match the municipal power-plant production.

These changes had two major impacts. First was the almost immediate improvement in services. With the newly available revenues, we were able to provide higher pay for the work force, a new swimming pool, a renovated park, and a stepped-up street-maintenance program. The other impact was delayed about a year, until the next elections.

The state, national, and local elections of 1948–50 had unusual interest for Lebanon's voters for a particular set of reasons. In the 1948 race for governor of Missouri, both major candidates–Democratic nominee Phil M. Donnelly (who won) and Republican nominee Jean Paul Bradshaw– were from Lebanon. (Interestingly, Lebanon voters cast identical numbers of votes for each of their hometown candidates. A gracious fix? Could be.) Then Missouri's Harry S. Truman was unexpectedly reelected President of the United States.

The local primary and regular elections of 1949 and 1950 gave me further reasons to doubt the election process. The city was divided into four precincts of approximately the same number of voters. However, the fire-station precinct turned up 50 percent more voters than any of the other three. If there were to be any irregularities, this was the precinct to watch.

The spring 1950 primary and regular elections were to be crucial for my survival. Ostensibly the issue was the outsiders who headed our city government: the city manager, the new chief of police, and the new director of utilities. The real issue was citizen resentment at no longer being able to tap their porch-light circuit for free electricity. The primary turned out 1,800 votes as compared with 426 the previous primary. And as expected, the regular election drew a record turnout.

Civic, church, and business leaders whom I had learned to admire were apprehensive. They knew that as a committed professional city manager I would not become involved. Therefore, it came as a shock to me when the editor of the *Lebanon Daily Record* called on me for help.

"They're stealing the election, Bert. What can you suggest?" he pleaded. "Election clerks at the fire house are clearing repeat votes and those who live outside the city limits, and there is a long, long line waiting to vote. Come on, Bert, we need your advice."

Hearing the editor's scenario, I came up with the suggestion that he consider stationing his photographer to take pictures of each person in this line. This might scare some away who were not legal.

The editor responded, "But, Bert, I can't afford the film."

I retorted, "Why use any film. Just pretend!"

The *Lebanon Daily Record's* box camera was prominently set out to "take" pictures of each would-be voter. What I thought would happen did happen: the long lines dwindled, as second thoughts came to haunt dozens in line who may have been pondering the title of this vignette, "YOU SHALL NOT STEAL–NEITHER ELECTRICITY NOR ELECTIONS!"

Two months later I became city manager of Boulder, Colorado.

A post script. Eight years after I left Lebanon, their voters decided to abandon the council-manager plan of government. This development was the subject of some perceptive comments from the famed Louis Brownlow. At a luncheon in Arlington, Virginia, some twenty members of the chief administrator section of the Washington Council of Governments were inspired by nearly an hour of yarn-spinning analysis by this eighty-four year old presidential advisor, author, and past president of the International City Management Association. He discussed some aspects of my then twenty-three-year career. Lamenting the events in Lebanon (which he had followed closely because he was born in nearby Buffalo, Missouri), he made this analysis: "Bert Johnson came from serving the rich folks in Winnetka, to serve the poor folks of Lebanon, Missouri. I think it is ironic that poor folks require good local government so very much, yet too often are cheated in getting it. Winnetka folks, as Bert knows, can do much for themselves, but insist on the bargain of good local services."

This was Louis Brownlow's final public service. As he was concluding his speech, he collapsed and died.

Fire
Protection

City Manager to the Rescue
James Joshua Mott

One Sunday afternoon in Big Stone Gap, Virginia, while I was working on the budget, I heard someone shouting, "Fire! Fire! Lordamercy! Somebody help me!"

The shouts came from one of the two jail cells on the second floor of the town hall, right above where I was working.

When I raced upstairs I found a woman, the only inmate in the jail, quite alarmed. Smoke was coming from the empty, but locked, cell next to hers. The smoke was from a mop bucket in that cell.

Perhaps I did not have to call the volunteer fire department (it would cost the town money). Perhaps I did not even have to locate the chief of police or any of his five officers. Perhaps I could put out the fire. Managers can do anything. ICMA tells us so.

Downstairs in a hurry, I found an empty bucket and filled it at a basin. But to get it out from under the faucet I had to tip it and pour out all except about a cupful.

Never mind. That was a start. Upstairs in a rush I tossed the water at the smoking bucket—which was at the far end of the locked cell.

Downstairs! Upstairs!

My aim was not so good, and the bars on the door split the effectiveness.

It did not take me long to decide that a better system should be arranged. Good managers are always devising systems for their government's operations.

Eventually the fire in the bucket was put out. The lady in the adjacent cell calmed down. She had no mattress or pillow, so she could not (if she still had matches and had thrown a match in the first place) set another fire.

Downstairs that night, I returned to my work on the list for town hall improvements. After "New paint job" (the last painting apparently had been done two score years ago), I added, "Hose to reach the jail."

When the Fire Bell Rings, Will Anyone Answer?

Richard H. Custer

Fort Fairfield, Maine (1940 population 6,000, spread over seventy-eight square miles) is bounded on the east by Canada's New Brunswick. When I became town manager in February 1946, the town was a thirteen-hour train ride due north of Boston, then ten miles (riding backward on a siding) from neighboring Presque Isle. A rural community in the heart of Aroostook County's potato-growing country, Fort Fairfield claimed, "More potatoes are grown in Fort Fairfield than in any other town in the world."

Each potato farm had one or more barnlike buildings—"potato houses"—set on heavy masonry foundations built well into the earth. Farmers stored the harvest in these houses, pending spring shipment to Boston's wholesale markets. To prevent freezing during the severe Maine winters, virtually every farmer placed a lighted but unattended salamander (portable kerosene-fueled heater) in each potato house.

Unfortunately a huge mound of potatoes is structurally unstable. Consequently, a passing truck or other force frequently shifted the mounds, which upset the salamanders and set off fires that illuminated the rural landscape.

Adding to the rural fire risk was the town's business center—a collection of squeezed-together two-story frame buildings reminiscent of a western frontier settlement. The only exception was the three-story Plymouth Hotel, which sat alone in a block at the north end of the main street.

The town government provided fire protection for the seventy-eight-square-mile area with a forty-member volunteer fire company and two pieces of apparatus housed in the ground-floor garage of the town hall. Annually the volunteers elected one of their number chief of the department. The current chief had the distinctive first name Flavel (his surname escapes me.) Flavel was the genial manager of the local "green front"—the state-owned package liquor store.

I soon noted the high incidence of major and spectacular fires, particularly of potato houses. Also, I observed that upon return to the town hall from each major fire, the company held a celebration featuring consumption of the wares that were the chief's stock in trade. My observations led me to wonder whether the chief wasn't mixing his vocation with his avocation. Further, my navy training and experience led me to question the basic competence in and knowledge of fire-fighting techniques of the chief and some volunteers.

My concern was enhanced on receipt of a letter from the Boston-based New England Fire Insurance Rating Bureau. This private agency, an arm of the insurance industry that classifies communities according to their fire-protection abilities and exercises considerable influence on the amounts of fire-insurance premiums property owners must pay, wrote that Fort Fairfield's fire losses had become excessive. Unless the town instituted listed improvements, it would be downgraded and fire-insurance premiums increased.

I discussed the situation with our board of selectmen and suggested they authorize me to visit the rating bureau manager, Mr. Percy Charnock, in an effort to negotiate on some of the listed requirements. My bargaining chips would be (1) a plan whereby I would appoint the next chief of the fire company, who would become directly responsible to me, and (2) a plan to hire a qualified full-time fire inspector and training officer. The selectmen concurred, and in a few days I was en route to Boston.

Unfortunately my absence was hard to disguise. News of my mission and plan circulated throughout the town, and upon my return I was faced by an angry Flavel. He informed me that the entire fire company would resign if I persisted in implementing the proposed plan, and that he fully expected to be reelected when his current term expired.

With trepidation I awaited the next developments. The prospect of handling a fire without the volunteers was not reassuring. We had agreements with the fire companies in our neighboring towns of Caribou, Limestone, and Presque Isle to assist each other when the need arose, but the nearest of these was thirty minutes away. Meanwhile, there would be only me, our three-man police force, and one or two maintenance workers to man our apparatus.

My fear reached its zenith late in the afternoon of Flavel's last day in office when a letter of resignation, signed by all members of the department, was delivered to me. That night was one of the longest I can remember. But the fire bell did not ring. The next morning my pulse returned to normal when about half the volunteers showed up at my office to retract their resignations. They said they had felt obliged to sign out of friendship for Flavel but that they would have responded to any alarm the previous night. These were the more desirable men in the department, and among them was one whom I had planned to appoint as chief. I did that on the spot.

Under his leadership the company attracted some new, young members. With his cooperation I subsequently hired as a full-time training officer a lieutenant from the Bangor Fire Department. A year later, with full acceptance by the volunteers, the training officer became the town's first full-time chief. These events, and our fulfilling some of the physical improvements on Mr. Charnock's list, forestalled the downgrading of the town's fire-insurance rating. This saved local residents from higher insurance premiums, at a relatively modest cost, one part of which was the addition of a few gray hairs to the manager's twenty-eight-year-old head.

Is *Now* the Time, and *This* the Way?

John C. Crowley

In Monterey Park, California, in 1953, after months of trying to help the police chief plan departmental operations, improve his staff, direct his subordinates, and measure the effectiveness of his department, I demoted him to patrolman, the level from which he had been directly promoted years before. At the same time the fire chief was preparing for his scheduled retirement. In this unique situation, I asked myself whether this was the time to try a version of police-fire integration.

I consulted an old friend, City of Los Angeles Fire Chief John Alderson. He advised, "It's an idea that deserves a trial; it was successful in Sunnyvale [California], and it should work in a medium-sized city, especially the way you have planned."

What I had in mind was dual training exclusively at the firefighter–patrolman level, keeping the forces completely separate at the level of sergeant, fire engineer, and above (except the chief). Even at the first level, I expected to maintain a modest distinction between fireman and policeman. It seemed logical to provide training so that routine fire *and* police response could result regardless of who arrived first at an emergency. With or without two-man police cars, such dual training would increase field effectiveness far more than it would the budget.

Of course, I had ready at hand the long list of obvious advantages of the scheme. But, I had naively overlooked the effectiveness of the firefighters' union (police seem rarely to resist as much).

The rest of the story is largely political.

At first blush the city council was unanimously enthusiastic. I successfully recruited John Cordell, who had been public-safety chief in Sunnyvale after holding several posts with the City of Los Angeles Fire Department. Chief Cordell was a commanding figure; respect from the forces, both police and fire, was virtually automatic.

The city council next endorsed my recommendation that four recruits be hired and trained in both disciplines.

But one councilman with political ambition (he is now a Congressman) sensed a political advantage in separate negotiations with the fire fighters. So my council vote changed to four-to-one. Next he persuaded our one young lady councilperson that her chances of reelection would be improved if she joined him in opposition.

Within a few weeks a third councilman, responding to passionate objections from fire-fighters' union representatives, said, "Let's try it for a year; if at the end of the year a majority of police and fire personnel don't like it, we'll abandon the program." That was the kiss of death. The whole enterprise was stopped before it was well started.

Following the political debacle, however, a committee was appointed to analyse the duties of policemen and firemen. The questions to be answered were several:

1. What kinds of duties should be carried out exclusively by a policeman?
2. What kinds should be carried out exclusively by a fireman?
3. What functions do firemen engage in that a policeman could do equally well?
4. What functions of a policeman could a fireman also handle?
5. What kinds of things do either police or fire personnel undertake that any other field person on the City staff could do equally well?

Cooperating in good faith, professional fire and police officers, a couple of appointed citizens, Chief Cordell, and I produced some detailed and exhaustive lists. We also clarified degrees of importance of duties of policemen and firemen, which inspired more respect for the two emergency and protective forces.

Alas, those detailed lists are long gone, and largely forgotten. But the process was almost more important than the product. The single most important point identified was the following:

> If *every city employee* could be motivated to be aware of police and fire
> problems and hazards, recognize incipient or suspicious circumstances,
> and just *report* the facts, both crime prevention and fire prevention
> would take a vast leap forward. Correspondingly, if every policeman and
> fireman could be motivated to report problems and opportunities affect-
> ing other city departments, similar benefits would be achieved in those
> departments.

Some examples:
● Anyone driving about the city can spot construction that is taking place without a permit.
● On fire inspection, a health hazard can be identified.

- An abandoned vehicle can catch the eye of a building inspector who drives past it several days running.
- If a public-works truck were equipped with a police-band radio, the driver could report a fire or a suspicious vehicle.

The list could go on and on.

A postscript. Currently (1980) I am a member of the elected city council of the City of Pasadena. The consolidation of public-safety department heads (only at the top) into a new city "agency" is a contemporary controversy. In a city of this size (over 100,000 population), there seems little merit in asking that policemen carry fire axes and firemen, pistols.

But it does seem inescapable, in this era of budgetary constraints, that the fire service participate in new ways of producing more for the pay received. A few possibilities:

- New and improved methods of building inspection
- Installation and maintenance of smoke detectors*
- Repair of water meters

Although integrated consolidation of the emergency services is not a viable objective of most cities, higher productivity among firemen should be an essential objective in local government.

---

*A novel experiment now budgeted in Pasadena involves the installation of phone-line-connected smoke detectors that will call paramedics or police. All signals so received at central dispatch are expected to display the address and telephone number of the source of the signal. The fire crew may arrive before the householder wakens. The ambulance can be called with a portable signal device.

Innovations

Cloud Nine
Thomas W. Fletcher

When I first went to San Diego, in June 1955, City Manager Humphrey ("Hump") Campbell did not know quite what to do with me. I was the first assistant *to* the city manager his office had ever had. (There had always been an assistant city manager, which was the classic line position.) Hump had decided to activate this newly authorized position after he had lost his budget director, but he was not too sure of the capacity of his new appointee.

I had been city administrator of Davis, California, for two and a half years and had expressed to the League of California Cities my interest in becoming an assistant in a large city. It was unusual for a city manager to want to go back to being an assistant once he had become a manager, regardless of the size of the city. I was having the time of my life in my first manager job and was in no trouble, but I had set a career path for myself shortly after I left college and had gone to work in San Leandro, California, as an assistant city manager. My plan was to be a city manager in a small city, an assistant in a large city, a manager in a medium-sized city, and finally end my public career as manager of a major city. The proposed move would further my experience and education in city management. When Hump contacted the league, they recommended me, and I was interviewed and appointed.

On my first day at work in San Diego, Hump had lunch with me and suggested that I spend my first month just getting acquainted with the various departments, their department directors, and their staff.

At the conclusion of that month I reported to Hump my findings and recommendations. One recommendation was that we needed to fill a number of assistant department-head vacancies. Of our twelve major line departments, five were without assistants. One vacancy had existed for more than three years. These vacancies were my first vague clue to a potential problem in governmental management. In every department in which such a vacancy existed, the department head had held the assistant's job before his promotion.

Hump asked Ed Blum, the assistant city manager, and me to help the department heads recruit the "best young men we can find, both within the departments and in California." Within six months we had filled the vacancies, including three from outside the city. Within two years, three department heads had retired, and Ed and I helped again in the recruitment of assistants.

The result of all this was that within the first three years I was in San Diego I had helped recruit nine of the twelve assistant department heads in the city government. Because of my involvement with their recruitment and appointment, I had taken a certain proprietary interest in their activities. And during the next few years some of these assistant department heads were not performing up to my expectations. There seemed to be a problem in their motivation. We had made it a point to recruit those who had shown strong line-management experience and potential for leadership. But our idea was not working out: We began to lose some of them to smaller cities as department heads.

I wasn't sure what the reason was, but I assumed that the principal cause was their lack of promotional opportunity because most of our department heads were many years from retirement.

In 1960 a departmental reorganization helped clarify some of the problems. Our new city manager, George Bean, was dissatisfied with part of the current organizational structure of the city. He particularly disliked the fact that our public-works activities were divided into three departments: the public-works department (including the sewerage division), the water department, and the engineering department. George felt that all these functions should be under one department. Therefore, we tried out a consolidated department of public works and utilities, with the three former departments acting as divisions within this new structure. We promoted the water director to head this new department. The two remaining department heads and the assistant water director became division heads. Because these division heads were relatively new, and because of the potential difficulties of a reorganization of this type, we decided to bring all the new division heads together with the new department head in his office area and leave the assistant division heads with their divisions to take care of the day-to-day activities.

Six months later George asked me to analyze the results of this reorganization. It had not worked as well as we had expected, primarily because of personality problems. We decided to break up the super department except that we combined the old water department with the sewerage division of public works into a new utility department.

During my analysis I discovered that although the plan had not worked, there had been some good results. The former department heads did not like the reorganization, but they did enjoy the freedom from day-to-day administrivia—details that had plagued them as department heads. When I checked with the assistants who had been left back with the divisions, I found that they too had enjoyed their relative freedom and increased involvement.

This discovery led me to analyze further the relationships between department heads and their assistants. I found that traditionally the position of assistant department head was not a line but a staff position. If they had a choice, division heads and departmental employees would always go directly to the department head rather than to or through an assistant. This created two problems: The department heads were so involved in the administrivia of their departments that they didn't have time to do the more important things that they really wanted to do as department heads. Frustration was the obvious result—for assistants as well as department heads. All these assistants, appointed from line positions, were disgruntled to find themselves in a staff role.

But how to correct these frustrations? Simply telling people to change their roles and habits doesn't work. Given a choice between taking your problem to a department head or to an assistant there will always be a tendency to go to the top person. Heading off that option when the department head is sitting right there frustrates everyone. The need was to differentiate clearly the roles of the two positions. The logical way would be to make the assistant responsible for day-to-day administration and let the department head be responsible for longer-range departmental needs.

As I kept thinking about this problem, I remembered another comment that the department heads had made about the six months they had worked together. Each had mentioned enjoying the ability to communicate and work together in the same area.

Some months later the pieces came together in what I've since called the "Cloud Nine" concept. George Bean had left, and in September 1961 I became city manager. One of my first major responsibilities was to start construction on a series of new city buildings aimed at revitalizing the economy of the downtown area. One of the buildings was to be our city hall.

In my preliminary planning for space requirements and assignments in the twelve-story structure, I started with the top floor, which was to be the council chamber and city clerk's area. The eleventh floor was for the mayor and the city council. The tenth was for the city attorney and his staff. The ninth was for the city manager and his staff. But now I had a slight problem. We would need less than half the floor, but our budget and management staff was too large to fit in the remaining area on that floor. Splitting a group between floors was something we wanted to avoid. Who, then, should occupy the same floor as the city manager?

Suddenly I recalled my department-head problem, and a wild idea struck me. Could I solve my department-head and floor-space problems at the same time? Why couldn't I bring all my department heads up to the ninth floor with me and leave their assistants back with their departments? You just don't do things like that, of course. What department head would want to be away from the department on a permanent basis? Who would be held responsible for departmental performance?

But suppose we could give the department heads something they wanted or needed to compensate for the physical separation? There were three possible inducements: (1) freedom from day-to-day administrivia, so that they could function more as department heads, (2) the opportunity to work in close proximity with fellow department heads, (3) a close working relationship with the city manager and his staff.

The way to allow the department heads to retain responsibility lay in the way the city manager and his staff would work with department heads and assistant department heads. Although department heads would be freed from the normal everyday problems of their departments, they would still want to be in direct contact with them, particularly those that might be of interest to the city manager or his staff. The way to assure this was that the city manager and his staff would always work with the department heads and avoid the temptation of going directly to the assistants. If we worked with an assistant—even on one small problem—we would find the department heads back with their departments.

The theory sounded good, but would it fly? I first talked to the three department heads who had been involved with our superdepartment experiment several years earlier. They accepted the idea immediately and with some enthusiasm. They still remembered the good aspects of their six months together.

Given their acceptance, it was not difficult to convince other department heads to give the idea a try. I had decided that I would not include the police chief or the fire chief in this move because their semimilitary positions required a different command approach and because their departments were not moving to city hall. The city librarian would not be included: We had just built a new central library (her life's dream), and it seemed inhumane to take her away from it.

The only real difficulty I had was with the head of the building department. Herb was not convinced that his department could function without his constant presence. At my third or fourth meeting with him, he still resisted, saying he would go only if I ordered him to. That was something I did not want to do. Herb's assistant director was with us at that meeting. I had helped to recruit Bill and knew him to be a good administrator but one who had become completely subservient to Herb. I had never heard him disagree or assert himself around Herb. In desperation I finally turned to Bill and asked him if he thought they could get along without having Herb with them at all times. Bill sat up straight and said, "Damn right!" This comment coming from Bill so shocked Herb that he put up his hands and said, "I give in."

There was still one major problem. I had convinced my department heads to move, but what about the three department heads not under the city manager? The planning director and the personnel director were under their commissions, and the auditor/comptroller was directly under the city council. It would have been easy to leave them out of the plan, but their work related so directly to everything we did that it would be difficult not to have them with us.

The planning director and the personnel director had no problem accepting my invitation as soon as they learned that the other department heads had already accepted. The auditor/comptroller was not so sure. He had no problem accepting the idea in his role as comptroller (finance), but he was concerned about preserving his independence as auditor. He agreed to try it for three months.

In 1965 we occupied a suite of nine identical offices for the department heads on the ninth floor. Cloud Nine was in operation.

Three months later I went around to each of the department heads and asked them if they were happy with the new arrangement. They all expressed complete satisfaction. They commented on how much more productive they had become. They were also impressed with the collaborative results they had achieved with their fellow directors. The city engineer was particularly impressed with the fact that nonengineering minds had been able to help him solve some of his more difficult problems. The independent department heads were particularly pleased with the new arrangement. They felt they were increasingly being accepted as part of the management team. When I reminded the auditor/comptroller that his three-month trial was up, I asked him if he were happy. He said "No." When I asked if that meant he was going to return to his department, he again said "No." Then he went on to explain: "I've never worked so hard in my life. Getting me out of the routine problems of my department has meant that I have been able to concentrate on the more important problems of the department, and that's tough but very productive work. You couldn't get me to leave now with a twenty-mule team."

But the real proof of any experience is how long it will last. Did it work only because I was the originator and supporter of the plan? Today, fourteen years and four managers later, it not only is still working, but now the police chief, the fire chief, and the city librarian are with their fellow department heads.

Whether this idea would work in other cities, I don't know. The theory still seems sound, but there is one big problem: putting it into effect. The very idea of change is frightening. We had two advantages

going for us in San Diego. First, there had already been an experience
with it in the superdepartment experiment. But more important, everyone
was going to have to move into the new city hall anyway, so the move
was not so drastic. I tried a modified version of this idea in the District of
Columbia and in San Jose; in both places I brought together a limited
number of department heads on a project basis, only to see them return
home after I left. I believe at least one other city manager in Southern
California has also tried the idea, with some success.

Interdepartmental Relations

My Department Heads Are Retreating
Thomas W. Fletcher

My first experience in department-head meetings was in San Leandro, California, in the early 1950s. Wes McClure, the city manager, held them every Wednesday from 10:00 a.m. to noon. Wes would bring us up to date on the latest council activities, and then each of us would discuss some of our current activities. These meetings were not only informative but set an atmosphere of camaraderie that was important to all of us. The only discordant note was that one of Wes's negative council members, Frank Canasero, would stick his head in at each meeting and say something like, "What are you doing here. Why aren't you working?"

In Davis, where I was city administrator from 1952 to 1955, I used the same system of department-head meetings.

When I went to San Diego in 1955, as assistant to the city manager, I found a very different situation. San Diego was a big city, especially when compared with Davis, and the departments—some of them—were as large as whole city governments in the towns I was used to. San Diego didn't have routine department-head meetings. When I had been there several months and had accumulated several items that needed discussion, I mentioned it to City Manager Hump Campbell. He told me to set up a department-head meeting, but when I mentioned this to his secretary, she wanted to know who should be invited. I told her to invite the ones who always come to department-head meetings. That's when I found out that there hadn't been such a meeting in more than two years.

San Diego needed such a meeting, so I went ahead and set it up for the next week in the city manager's office. But even though all twenty-two department heads showed up, the meeting seemed dry and unproductive. I came out with the same problems I had gone in with. Departments didn't understand each other's problems; sometimes they just got in each other's way. On the theory that they just weren't used to the process, I set up another meeting several weeks later. The results were worse. Nobody talked unless Hump or I asked a direct question. At that point, I was willing to believe that department-head meetings were mostly for small governments and that we would just have to accept the fact that what worked so well in San Leandro and Davis wouldn't work in San Diego.

But I still felt that there had to be an answer to the problem, and when George Bean became city manager, I suggested a new idea for department-head meetings. I felt that part of the problem was the fact that the number of department heads meant they had to sit in three rows in front of the city manager's desk. It was just too formal. I suggested that we have breakfast meetings instead, so that there would be a sense of social as well as a business environment. We tried it out and, after some experimentation, found that the best format was a meeting on the first Friday of each month with the staff-department heads, on the second Friday for the line departments, and on the third Friday for all department heads.

Although this seemed to be a lot of meetings every month, all of us, department heads included, found the time well spent. Whenever we brought up a question as to whether or not to continue this format, everyone insisted that the meetings be continued.

These informal breakfast meetings were so successful that when I became city manager in 1961, I decided to experiment with a much larger version. Mr. John Rohrbaugh, assistant personnel director for the navy in San Diego, had been talking to me about some new theories in interpersonal relations (ultimately known as "organizational development" and "team building") and had suggested that he would be willing to work with us to try them out.

Two months after I became manager, John and I convened a day-and-a-half meeting—a "retreat"—with my department heads, at a resort about forty miles away from San Diego. The retreat lasted all day Friday and ended at noon on Saturday. The agenda was fairly open ended, consisting primarily of a group discussion about our individual, group, and organizational goals.

As we were ending the meeting, John asked each participant what he or she had gotten out of the day and a half. Almost everyone felt that it had been useful and wanted another such meeting. When it came my turn, I said the biggest thing I had noticed was that: "Clara called me Tom." For seven years I had called our library director "Clara," and for seven years she had called me "Mr. Fletcher." But on Friday afternoon, in the middle of a heavy discussion, she started to call me Tom. To me that meant that the dynamics of the day had produced a sense of participation that we had not been able to develop before.

This first retreat was so successful that we continued to have them twice a year for the five years that I was city manager. As an example of what such a meeting can do, let me explain what happened about the personnel department. In San Diego, as in some other cities, the personnel department does all the testing and hiring for the city. The other departments hated the personnel department. Sometimes it seemed as though the only obstacle to prevent San Diego from becoming a paradise was the obstinacy of personnel. Naturally the personnel department staff felt not only unappreciated but downright abused. So we scheduled a retreat at which we would discuss that problem, and only that problem. I warned the head of the personnel department what to expect, and sure enough, it happened. From the beginning of the meeting until late Friday afternoon, the anger and abuse that poor chap had to endure—and did endure—was astonishing.

But an odd sort of thing began to happen toward the end of Friday afternoon: People started hearing what they were actually saying to the head of the personnel department. They began to be aware from their own statements that they were blaming personnel for too much. By Saturday morning they were willing to work out some solutions to problems they faced *and* to problems faced by personnel. I won't say it turned into a love feast, but by the time everyone went home there was a strong sense that what had been seen as purely personnel problems were actually city problems for which everyone had some responsibility.

Another spinoff of this type of meeting came about almost inadvertently. In the spring of 1962 I was preparing my first budget for the city council. We were still substantially out of balance and had only a short time left before our deadline. I decided to take my key staff members to a hotel meeting room for a full day to see if we could resolve our problem. The morning was fairly unproductive, but by late afternoon we had solved our problem. After several more experiments of this type, I realized that the process of getting out of the office for an entire day could be highly productive. I then instituted a system in which I would meet with my staff the last Friday of each month in a board room in Balboa Park.

When questions were raised about the amount of time we were spending in each meeting, I was able to say that the production we achieved was greater than if we spent the same amount of time in a series of shorter meetings. We really needed the extended period in a remote location to reach the peak of creative thinking.

There was still some unrest among our mayor and council members. Consequently, I decided to invite the mayor to our next retreat. Although there was some early unease, by the afternoon he had been accepted as a full member of the process. Later I started inviting members of the council. Their attitude and participation was valued by everyone.

In Washington, D.C., we had more than fifty department heads, so we were unable to use the same system. We divided the departments into five groups and met with them that way.

In San Jose I used the San Diego system with equal success.

Personnel
Management

The Personnel-Application Form

Peter F. Lydens

In 1962, within the first six months of my service as the first city manager of Mount Airy, North Carolina, I had set up a formalized personnel-management system. This included revamping the personnel-application form, which had violated principles of sound personnel management—not to mention federal and state regulations on types of information that could be required.

About three months after the new form had been put into use, it came up for discussion at the end of a meeting of the board of commissioners. An old-time commissioner, who was very politically oriented, heatedly questioned my motives for changing the form. His final question related to why I had removed the "political affiliation" box from the form. I explained that under the council-manager form of government, the applicants' qualifications for a particular job were the guiding light. He harrumphed momentarily, then said I was certainly making the screening of applications much more difficult. After all, on the old form if someone marked "Republican Party" as his political affiliation, the application could automatically be put into the wastepaper basket, thus cutting down on the number of applications to be considered.

I was chagrined to think that the board of commissioners still had a member who was that old fashioned or that politically oriented, but as years went on I realized that for many elected officials a local arm of the national political organization was the basis of their campaign organization at the municipal level. It points out the need for managers to explain the obvious to elected officials. After all, what is obvious to a manager is not always so obvious to the local governing body.

The Skokie Police Uniform Strike

John N. Matzer, Jr.

On 10 March 1975 the village of Skokie, Illinois, began negotiating salaries and benefits with the union known as the Combined Counties Police
Association. Little did we know then that we would have to contend with
a ten-day uniform strike, occupation of the village hall by women and
children, the dismissal of thirty-four police officers, and extensive litigation in federal courts.

After seven negotiating sessions with the union, we realized that they
were not interested in an early settlement. The union representatives took
initial offers to the membership, inquired about our final offer early in the
negotiations, postponed meetings, failed to make significant headway, and
unilaterally increased the size of their negotiating team. In their attempt
to organize the village's public works employees into an affiliate called the
Association of Independent Municipal Employees, the union retained as
their attorney John Burpo, an employee of the International Association
of Chiefs of Police.

Negotiations became stalemated on May 21, after we had made our
fourth economic proposal—as compared with the union's one counter-
proposal. Following that session, the union bypassed the negotiating team
and made an appearance at a board of trustees meeting requesting an
opportunity to negotiate with the board. This request was denied, and
negotiating sessions were held on June 18 and 27, at which time we made
our final offer of 7.4 percent (a 5 percent salary increase and 2.4 percent in
benefits). (Fire and other employees previously had agreed to settlements
of 7.5 percent.) As part of our package, we included the removal of
annual step increases for twelve members of the ninety-two-member
patrolmen unit. The police negotiators rejected the offer, demanding a
package in excess of 10 percent, including an 8 percent salary increase.

On June 26 the police voted to authorize a job action. This was the
same union which five years earlier had conducted a successful five-day
blue-flu strike against the village. (Union representatives termed it a "recognition dispute," but the fact is that the strike occurred *after* the village
had recognized the union.) In 1970 the union also had been involved in a
strike in Waukegan, Illinois, where the entire force was fired and replaced
by new recruits.

A Uniform Strike

After our final offer and the union's repeated efforts to persuade the board
of trustees to negotiate, the union stated publicly that they were planning
a job action. Such a job action materialized on the 11:00 P.M. shift of July

3, when patrolmen appeared in civilian clothes. They were advised that they were in violation of the rules and regulations of the police department, which required patrolmen to appear in uniform. The supervisors informed them that if they did not put on their uniforms and report for duty, they would be put on a no-pay status and charges would be filed against them before the village fire and police commission.

Five patrolmen appeared in uniform and were assigned to beats. Supervisors were also assigned to fill the vacant positions along with two patrolmen from previous shifts. At each subsequent shift change, patrolmen continued to report in civilian clothing. After someone tampered with police cars in the police garage, the patrolmen were barred from the station. They sat in lawn chairs outside the station, played cards, skimmed Frisbees, and worked on motorcycles. Most continued to wear their guns and holsters. And they drew support from the Chicago chapter of the Southern Christian Leadership Conference. Two members of the conference came to the police station and yelled to passersby, "Call the mayor. Call the mayor. You have no police protection."

During the job action, which was to continue for ten days, adequate police protection was provided through the use of twenty-four supervisors and thirty-four patrolmen who did not participate. All police personnel worked twelve-hour shifts seven days a week. Numerous offers of assistance were received from neighboring communities, but it was not necessary to utilize them.

On July 7 Police Chief Kenneth Chamberlain prepared charges against the protesting patrolmen. They were charged with two violations of regulations, including failure to report for roll call properly uniformed and failure to obey an order to change into uniform. The charges were delivered to the men who continued to report for roll call out of uniform. Fire and police commission hearings were scheduled to begin on July 14 for fifty-eight patrolmen and one sergeant who participated in the strike.

Board Meeting Disrupted

On the evening of July 7, at the regular board of trustees meeting, a large number of nonuniformed patrolmen, some of whom were armed, and their sympathizers were in attendance. We had anticipated their attendance and earlier had requested assistance from Cook County Sheriff Richard Elrod, who refused our request for protection of the officials at the board meeting but offered to serve as a mediator and to patrol the village. His offer was rejected.

During the regular agenda, Leonard Jaglarski, an officer of the union, approached the trustees, entering through the gates separating the public from the board, and engaged in a pushing and shoving match with sixty-three-year-old trustee Robert Morris. At that point, the meeting was adjourned, and the officials went to an adjoining conference room. A director of the union urged the crowd, "Go in there and get them." Members of the group blocked the exits to the conference room, while others shouted for an immediate discussion of the dispute. A call was made for the chief of police, who, along with one captain, came to the village hall and escorted the mayor and his wife from the hall to their car. After approximately an hour, the officials left the building.

Outside the building, a *Chicago Tribune* photographer was assaulted by several men who stripped him of his camera, tore out the film, and threw the film to the ground. He had been taking pictures of a fight between one of the men and a citizen accused of assaulting one of the strikers' wives. The entire demonstration in the board-meeting room had been televised by a number of local stations.

Secret Meeting

The following day I was contacted by John Burpo, the union attorney, who asked to meet with me that evening. At our meeting I was advised that there was a threat of violence. The attorney mentioned Waukegan and said that the violence here would be greater. He indicated that they had not gone far enough in Waukegan but would not make the same mistake in Skokie. I was told that women and children would conduct a sit-in at village hall and that the husbands/fathers would watch to see how we responded.

However, the attorney said, the men would return if the board of trustees met with them. He suggested that the chief of police drop the charges against the men, that we mediate the charges, and that we not pay the men for the days off. I was further informed that he was leaving town for eight days and would not be able to control the men while he was away. Finally he said that if we were willing to accept mediation, the union would drop their interest in organizing our public-works employees as part of their affiliate, the Association of Independent Municipal Employees, and that if the dispute were resolved, the public-works employees would not strike.

I made no commitments during our discussion, indicating only that I would discuss his proposals with my elected officials. I did review the proposals with the board, but we concluded that because the charges had already been filed, we were not in a position to negotiate.

Women and Children Seize Village Hall

The following morning, my secretary informed me that about fifty women and children were filing into the village hall with bedrolls, pillows, TV sets, radios, food, games, and infant supplies. They said they were going to sit in until officials met with them to discuss the dispute. I decided to make no effort to remove them. They stayed throughout the day and were careful to not disturb either the citizens who came into the building or the employees in the offices. At the end of the day, village personnel left and I permitted the women and children to remain. I decided to leave a custodian in the building overnight.

At 6:00 the following morning, I received a call from the public works director advising me that the women refused to permit the day custodian to enter the building. I called the village attorney, and we immediately went to the building and were advised by the women, who were blocking the entrance, that they would not permit employees or citizens to enter. Assistant counsel Gilbert Gordon attempted to enter the building and injured his back as he was pushed away.

On the afternoon of July 10, Harvey Schwartz, the village attorney, presented a petition to the county circuit court asking for the removal of the women and children. With much reluctance Judge Nathan Cohen ordered children under the age of 15 to leave the village hall that evening. The parents complied with the judge's order. He refused, however, to issue a temporary restraining order requiring that the wives and other adult sympathizers leave the building.

In refusing to order the adults from the hall, the judge said that such action could result in violence. He said, "I think it's reprehensible. I in no way condone it. But I'm also disturbed about the callous attitude of city officials who refuse to conduct meaningful discussions with the police group." The judge asked to serve as a mediator, but we told him that we didn't go to court to seek mediation. He was incensed at our attitude.

Finally, on Friday, the judge issued an order requiring the adults to vacate the building by 7:00 P.M. Judge Cohen stipulated that his order must be enforced by Skokie Police and that he would not order the Cook County Sheriff's police to evacuate the building. This was highly unusual because the sheriff's police had always been responsible for enforcing court orders. In issuing this order, the judge said that the village had the power to enforce the order. We replied that it would create an inflammatory, provocative situation. In response, the judge said, "If anybody is creating an inflammatory situation, it is the Skokie trustees through their intransigence and refusal to mediate the dispute."

After the issuance of the order, we returned to the village hall where the village attorney, Harvey Schwartz, posted the judge's order. The women indicated that they would have to be removed physically. Our next step was to appeal the judge's decision to refuse to have the sheriff's office evacuate the building.

During the occupancy of the building, the women refused entrance to a Commonwealth Edison meter reader who was booed and hissed. However, during the entire time, their husbands and officers of the association were permitted to enter the bulding to deliver food and other supplies. The women continued to ignore the court order until Sunday afternoon, when the police union announced that the men were returning to work.

At the time the announcement was being made, the women left the building. I immediately inspected the hall and found it had been left in a clean, neat, orderly manner. The only damage was a broken glass door.

During the time that the hall was occupied, we set up emergency offices at the health building and the village office on aging. Emergency phones were installed, and the media were asked to notify all residents that village business was being conducted at these locations. Although it was difficult, we continued to provide services and even prepared a payroll with the assistance of the local banks. Our failure to remove critical financial and other records at the time we left the hall presented the most serious problem.

Strike Ends

On Sunday, July 13, union members met at the Holiday Inn in Skokie. Two votes were taken on whether members should return to work in uniforms. A majority voted both times not to do so. Those who voted in favor of returning to work made it plain they would do so irrespective of the majority vote. On the advice of the union attorney, all decided to return.

That afternoon Chief Chamberlain received a call from the union attorney, who informed him the men would return to work on July 14. The chief said he wanted the men to return at once. But Burpo said the men were going to have a party on the night of July 13, that they needed this type of recreation and would therefore return on July 14.

Some of the men returned on July 13, but many of them did not return until 6:00 A.M. on July 14. During the ten-day strike, twelve men returned before the group voted to end the job action.

Throughout the strike and for a period after the strike, the village experienced an increase in vandalism, false police and fire alarms, bomb threats, and picketing. An estimated $10,000 worth of business and car windows were broken in three nights of vandalism by shots from pellet guns. Threatening and abusive anonymous phone calls to village officials and nonprotesting police personnel included threats of physical violence.

During the ten-day period, the police officers not engaged in the strike were subjected to verbal attacks by protestors, threats of physical violence, slashed tires, and broken windows. A window on the first floor of village hall was broken, and a homemade black-powder pipe bomb was placed in an office. A loaded shotgun with a hair trigger was placed on the lawn of a trustee. Bomb threats required frequent evacuation of the village hall. One board meeting was adjourned because of a bomb threat; another was delayed until the building could be searched.

The net cost to the village of the ten-day strike was $10,738. For overtime and meals, the village paid $46,236 to policemen who remained on the job. This cost was partially offset by $29,938 in salaries not paid to striking policemen and $5,560 in salaries not paid for special details cancelled during the strike.

Disciplinary Hearings

On July 14 the board of fire and police commissioners began hearings on the charges against the patrolmen and the sergeant who had participated in the uniform strike. Fourteen days of hearings produced more than 3,000 pages of hearings records. During the hearings, the three-member board of fire and police commissioners suspended twenty police officers, found one not guilty, and discharged thirty-four other officers. Those who were suspended for periods ranging from two days to thirty days pleaded technically not guilty and signed stipulations of fact wherein they admitted they had refused to perform their duty in uniform and that they had disobeyed orders to put on their uniforms and perform their duties. These twenty were not represented by an attorney. After mitigation and aggravation hearings, the board suspended them. Those discharged had been represented by a union attorney and had pleaded not guilty.

The commissioners considered varying circumstances and numerous factors in determining whether the return of the men would be detrimental to the discipline, efficiency, or morale of the department. Each case was considered independently, with attention given to such factors as the seriousness of the violations, the length of time the violations existed, the attitude of the officer toward defiance in the future, testimony of the chief and others, demeanor and credibility of witnesses, how the accused pleaded to charges, and at whose direction they returned to work.

During the hearings Captain James Halas testified that on July 9 he began to receive phone calls from protesting officers who wanted advice about what to do. He told them that an effort would be made to save their jobs if they returned to work no later than July 13. The time and date when protesting policemen returned to work was one of the factors, but not the controlling factor, that board members considered before deciding to discharge. Board members felt that to preserve discipline and require loyalty to the department, they could not allow the union or its attorney to dictate whether or when the men should abandon the strike and return to work. Those returning on July 14 were discharged.

One interesting aspect of the hearings was a motion by the union attorney, John Burpo, to disqualify the chairman, William Elliott, from hearing cases on the basis of extreme bias and prejudice. Mr. Burpo testified to a conversation he had had with Mr. Elliott on 13 March 1975 regarding Mr. Elliott's attitude toward police discipline. At that time an employee of the International Association of Chiefs of Police, Mr. Burpo had been interviewing village officials in connection with a study he was making for the chiefs association. Burpo's move to disqualify Elliott was denied by the commission.

While the hearings were taking place, a bargaining session was held at the request of the union, but it proved nonproductive. However, at the request of thirty-one patrolmen, the village implemented the same pay and benefit package for the police officers that had been given to the other village employees. This action was taken after a legal opinion had been obtained as to the legality and appropriateness of granting such an increase. It was made retroactive to May 1.

Civil-Rights Case

Shortly after the conclusion of the fire and police board hearings, the police union filed a $4.2 million civil-rights suit on behalf of twenty-seven dismissed police officers. The suit named the village, the board of fire and police commissioners, and thirteen officials (the mayor, six trustees, three fire and police commissioners, the village manager, the village attorney, and the chief of police). The suit alleged that during the discharge proceedings, the police officers had been deprived of certain constitutional rights guaranteed in the First, Fifth, and Fourteenth Amendments. The civil-rights action was filed in the United States District Court for the Northern District of Illinois. Later the suit was amended to include thirty-two of the dismissed officers.

The plaintiffs alleged that most of the men who were suspended had been contacted during the protest by a ranking officer and encouraged to return but that none of the men who were fired had been contacted. In addition, the suit alleged that the men were denied a hearing before having been suspended. Included in the suit was a request for an injunction to prevent the village from hiring replacements for the dismissed police officers and requesting that the village be ordered to reinstate temporarily the dismissed officers.

After filing the civil-rights suit, the union filed for a Cook County Circuit Court review of the action of the board of fire and police commissioners under the State of Illinois Administrative Review Act.

Judge Orders Officers Reinstated

In response to the motion for a temporary injunction, Judge Joseph Perry held a hearing on 30 September 1975. On October 2 he ordered that the village reinstate the police officers temporarily as of October 6, and he prohibited the village from hiring new officers but allowed us to give tests and preliminary training. Judge Perry felt an emergency situation existed and that the public interest was better served by having a full complement of police during the time the case was being heard. This decision overlooked Chief Chamberlain's testimony that an emergency situation did not exist.

On October 3 the village attorney appealed the judge's decision to the

U.S. Court of Appeals. Our position was that the grant of the injunction was premature because the plaintiffs had not exhausted their state remedies to review the administrative decision that discharged them and failed to prove extraordinary circumstances in that there was no immediate danger to public safety.

In his decision Judge Perry had found that the police officers were engaged in an illegal strike, that the taking over of the village hall was an illegal action, that the village officials throughout the strike acted properly and commendably, and that the policemen and the union acted reprehensively and against the public interest.

A three-judge panel of the U.S. Court of Appeals stayed Judge Perry's order, stating doubt that the policemen could prove they suffered irreparable damage by their discharge. The suit was sent back to Judge Perry, and the court asked him to expedite the hearing. In its ruling, the court said, "It is also important to remember that it is the duty of the elected officials in Skokie to determine what is in the best interests of the citizenry, including as to the safety requirements. This duty does not rest within the jurisdiction of the Federal courts or the plaintiffs."

District-Court Rules

On December 8 Judge Perry began the hearings on the civil-rights case. Before the case began, the union attorney dropped the charges against the mayor, the trustees, the village manager, and the village attorney. The damages were reduced from $4.2 million to $600,000. On December 22 Judge Perry cleared the members of the board of fire and police commissioners and the chief from personal liability, stating that they had not engaged in willful acts of malice or bad faith. This left the village and the board as parties to the suit.

The village attorney argued that the board of fire and police commissioners determined the cause for the discharges and that the decision was not to be disturbed by the court unless the court found it arbitrary and unrelated to the requirements of the department. He further argued that the courts had no power to inquire as to whether a penalty imposed by the board is too harsh. During the hearing Chief Chamberlain testified that the men who returned to work after July 13 were responding to outside sources and in so doing were destroying the command function of the department. He felt that they could not function again effectively.

On 3 February 1976 Judge Perry ordered the village to reinstate the dismissed patrolmen, effective February 17, and dismissed the suit for $600,000 in damages. The judge said that the advice given the plaintiffs by their counsel was patently incorrect and that the action was in violation of well-settled law. He wrote that policemen have no constitutionally protected right to strike and that the plaintiffs had brought about a state of government chaos and near breakdown in law enforcement.

The judge said that the failure to give all fifty-nine striking police officers notice that they would not be discharged if they reported for duty in uniform on or before July 13 constituted a failure to provide equal protection of the laws to the plaintiffs within the meaning of the Fourteenth Amendment. He further stated that the discharge was in part a result of the policemen's having been deprived of equal protection under the laws in that they were discriminated against (1) for exercising the right to be represented by counsel, (2) for pleading not guilty and contesting their guilt, and (3) for not stipulating that they had reported for duty out of uniform and had refused to obey rules to put on their uniforms after reporting. Judge Perry ruled that the board applied the statute governing discipline to the policemen unequally and in an intentional and unreasonably discriminatory manner.

The judge said that all the defendants acted in good faith without any malice toward any policemen involved in the strike. He found the conduct of the village officials to be beyond reproach, stating that despite the most adverse circumstances they exercised calm and good judgment and tolerated unwarranted abuse and threats cast from persons in sympathy with the illegal strike.

On the other hand, he found the conduct of the plaintiffs and other striking policemen inexcusable. He found that they were shamefully misled by the officers and the attorney for their union, Mr. John Burpo, who gave them advice which led them to believe that they were acting within their legal rights when such was not the case.

Judge Perry ordered the village to reinstate all the plaintiffs retroactively to July 4, with full rights to all seniority, back pay, other benefits, and any or all pay increases they would otherwise have received. However, he deducted from the back pay their salaries for the ten days during which they had engaged in the strike and for an additional thirty-day suspension period, $3,423.80 for damages suffered by the village, any wages received by those who worked full-time during the period, and the total amount of unemployment compensation received from this state.

We felt that Judge Perry had substituted his judgment for that of the board of fire and police commissioners as to punishment. He did this by reinstating each officer and directing that a thirty-day suspension be substituted for the discharge. Basically we felt that the judge had reinstated the men on the basis of procedural errors. Our attorneys contended that the court had no power to determine what disciplinary action the board of fire and police commissioners should have taken, particularly when the court found that the board was correct in determining that the plaintiffs were guilty of repeated acts of insubordination and violations of rules.

In our opinion the district court had intruded improperly into the statutory responsibility of the Skokie Board of Fire and Police Commissioners. Therefore the village appealed and requested a stay of Judge Perry's order. The plaintiffs cross-appealed, seeking a reversal of the

$3,423.80 penalty against each officer and an award of additional damages for violation of the plaintiffs' constitutional right of equal protection and due process.

Court Orders Return of Officers

On February 15 the U.S. Court of Appeals for the Seventh Circuit stayed Judge Perry's ruling until the appeal was decided. Oral argument was held on June 11. On September 17, in a two-to-one decision, the court affirmed the decision of the district court and set October 8 as the deadline for rehiring the dismissed police officers. Justices Luther Swygert and Robert Sprecher held that the plaintiffs' actions were in violation of department rules and under Illinois law would be cause for discharge. They felt that there was a constitutional problem of a fair and impartial hearing. In their opinion, the justices stated,

> It seems obvious that contrary to Illinois statute as interpreted by the
> Illinois courts and contrary to the due process and equal protection
> clauses of the Fourteenth Amendment, the defendant Board and its
> individual members acted in a wholly arbitrary manner in purporting to
> distinguish between suspension and discharge. Actually, they were dis-
> tinguishing between employing or not employing counsel.

The judges felt that the plaintiffs had been penalized for asserting the right to be represented by counsel. However, Judge Harlington Wood, Jr., dissented, stating,

> I do not believe, however, that this record is sufficiently clear to justify
> for constitutional reasons the intervention of a federal court into the
> solution of this local problem of utmost importance to the welfare of
> the community after Village officials made a good faith and satisfactory
> effort to resolve it for themselves. I do not believe that we should now
> substitute our judgment for theirs in the administration of their police
> department under the circumstances we find here.

After reviewing the decision, the Skokie Board of Trustees elected not to petition the U.S. Supreme Court for review because of the potential financial liability that would be incurred by the village as a result of the anticipated long time it would take for the Supreme Court to hear the case.

Impact of Uniform Strike

The court decision was costly for the village. These costs included $159,297 in excess payroll costs and $65,832 in other expenses, including $23,125 in attorney fees. In addition, the total cost of back pay was

$274,882. The gross back pay was $646,429. Deductions from this amount included $105,553 in pay received by members for full-time employment, $109,562 for the penalty of $3,429.89 per man, $55,783 for the thirty-day suspension and ten-day strike pay, and $100,669 in unemployment compensation. The costs were financed from the city's fund balance.

A special training program was established for the returning police officers, to acquaint them with changes in the law and departmental procedures that had occurred during their absence. Considerable tension existed between the returning patrolmen and those who had been working. Many returning patrolmen were given the silent treatment by other officers. Moreover, patrolmen who did not participate in the strike asked for backup from other nonstriking patrolmen because they did not trust the returning men. Hard feelings between the men existed for some time. During the following months, some returning men resigned from the force and others became involved in disciplinary action.

Throughout the fifteen-month period, village officials received considerable support from the community. Much of this support is explained by the fact that the village distributed three issues of its newsletter to 25,000 residents assuring them that adequate police services were being maintained and presenting the village's position on the dispute. Certainly the deplorable behavior of many of the union members at the July 7 board meeting, the wives' sit-in, and the disruption of village business cost the police officers the support of many residents. Our experience during the work stoppage demonstrated the importance of contingency plans, the advantage of decentralized operations, and the need to inform the public of the municipality's position and the level of service being provided. We further learned that we could have prevented federal-court intervention by dismissing all officers involved in the illegal action, instead of suspending some and dismissing others and thus denying the latter equal protection of the law.

Park Your Car
Thomas W. Fletcher

On 6 July 1967 I became deputy assistant secretary of Housing and Urban Development for subsidized housing. Six weeks later my wife called me from San Diego with the news that our house had just been sold, but on condition that the new owners could take immediate occupancy. I advised the HUD Secretary's office that I would have to fly to San Diego that weekend and spend the next week bringing my family back to D.C.

Friday evening, while I was waiting for the plane at Dulles Airport, I was paged for a phone call. It was a call from Joe Califano's office in the White House. They had just heard that I was going to be gone for the next week, and they were disturbed because the White House and HUD had just announced that week the results of the Kaiser Commission on public housing, which called for more private-sector involvement—a plan that came to be known as "Turnkey." They wanted to be assured that my absence would not cause a problem. I assured them that nothing was going to be done on this until I returned.

The following Monday my wife, daughter, younger son, and I started our trip back to D.C. Because it was August, we decided to use a northern route, through Utah, Montana, and South Dakota. We had not left an itinerary with anyone because we had not made any reservations and didn't know our exact route.

Thursday morning, after visiting Mount Rushmore, we were going through Rapid City, South Dakota. As I waited for a downtown street light to change, a man came running up to our car and asked, "Are you Tom Fletcher from Washington, D.C.?" When I said I was, he identified himself as an FBI agent and asked me to park my car in front of the Post Office—which I did immediately. When I got out, he said, "I'm sorry to stop you, but you have a call from the White House."

Since I assumed this was about the Kaiser report, I told my family it would probably only take a few minutes. I was wrong.

I made the call from the agent's office and was connected directly to Mr. Joe Califano, then assistant to President Johnson. When Joe found out where I was calling from, he asked when I could get to D.C. I told him I would be there Monday. He said, "No! How soon can you get here today?" I asked: "Why?" He said: "I can't tell you. Just check the airline schedules and call me right back."

I checked the airline schedules, called Joe back, and told him that Rapid City was not the easiest place to get out of. The earliest flight was the following morning.

"That's not early enough, it's got to be today. Sit right there, and I'll call you back in a few minutes."

As we waited I asked the agent how he had been able to spot my car and how he knew I would be driving through his city at this time. He told me that he had a description of my car but that it was just by chance he had seen us waiting at the signal when he came out of his office. He told me there was an all-points bulletin out for me in the entire middle third of the United States with every FBI office, city police department, and highway patrol in a dozen states. (I learned later that relatives in Nebraska had even heard the announcement over the radio in their area.) I was beginning to realize that something unusual was happening.

Ten minutes later Joe called back and told me that an air force plane would be landing at the Rapid City Air Force Base shortly. I was to get on that plane, and they would fly me to Andrews Air Force Base, where a White House car would meet me and bring me to his office.

Within the next hour the FBI agent had put my family into a motel, got my suit out of the suitcase and had it pressed, lined up a guitar contest for my son that night, driven me out to the air base, and made sure I was on the plane. At 9:00 P.M. I was in Joe Califano's office where I learned that I was being considered for appointment to the position of deputy mayor of the District of Columbia government.

In the previous weeks I had become aware that a government reorganization was going through for the district government. Under the Presidential Reorganization Authority, President Johnson had sent to Congress a plan that would do away with the 100-year-old, three-commissioner form and create a mayor/council system. This reorganization plan not only created a mayor and a nine-member city council; it also called for the position of deputy mayor to serve as chief administrator under the mayor. All these positions were to be filled by presidential appointees. This plan had become law during that week.

Joe explained what he knew about the position and some of the problems he foresaw, and then he asked me if I would be interested in the appointment. I told him I was interested (the city manager of the nation's capital!) but was concerned about changing jobs so fast after only six weeks over at HUD. He said casually, "That's one of the things you'll have to take up with the boss." That comment didn't sink in for a few minutes, and when it did I asked who he meant by "the boss." His reply was, "There's only one boss." "When do I see *him?*" I asked. Joe looked at his watch and said, "Ten P.M.—in about fifteen minutes."

While we were waiting, I asked Joe to tell me how my name had come up and why they had gone to such effort to get me there when they knew that I would be back the following Monday. He told me that the President had requested names from a number of public-interest groups and that my name was high on some of those lists. He said that when they discovered I was already working in Washington, D.C., the choice seemed logical. Anyway, Joe said that the President had told him on Wednesday that he wanted to see me tonight (Thursday). Even when they found that I was "somewhere in the middle of the United States," they decided it was still better (and I guess easier) to find me than to try to explain to the President why I wasn't there when he wanted me.

At ten o'clock I was led into the Oval Office, where I met President Johnson. He wanted to know if I had had dinner. When I told him no, he invited me to join him. He walked over to an alcove off his office and went through the door. Assuming this was the way out, I followed him but quickly stopped when I realized that it was his bathroom. I stood there in some shock because he started to use the facilities without closing the door and kept right on talking to me. I noticed Joe smiling, so I assumed this was a regular scene.

When he was finished, Joe and I followed him up to the small second-floor dining room in the mansion. Lady Bird joined us, along with Jim Jones, one of the President's aides. All during the dinner the President talked about the District of Columbia and what his hopes were for the new government.

He finally got around to asking me whether I wanted the job if it were offered. I told him I was very interested but (as I had told Joe) was concerned about changing jobs after such a short tenure at HUD. He gave me a Presidential answer: "Fletcher, you work for me now; if you turn me down when and if I ask you to be deputy mayor, I'll fire you." That seemed to settle the matter.

After dinner we all watched the eleven o'clock news on three different stations on three different sets with the President controlling the sound. I then followed him into his bedroom, where I was motioned to a rocking chair at the foot of the Presidential bed. Joe and Jim were standing at the wall by the windows, and the President was out of my sight behind me. After a few minutes Lady Bird entered wearing her nightgown and robe and got into bed. At about the same time a gurney was pushed into the room. It had a thin mattress and two pillows at the front end. In front of it was a small table with a large stack of folders and papers and a lamp.

The next thing I saw was the President walking by me stark naked! He got up on the gurney, and a chief petty officer from the coast guard came out of the shadows and started to give the President a massage. At this point I think my cumulative shock almost overwhelmed me. Six hours ago I had been driving with my family through South Dakota. Since then I had been stopped by an FBI agent, flown to Washington, D.C., in an air force jet, been told that I was being considered for one of the choicest jobs in my profession, watched a President use his bathroom, had an intimate dinner with the first family, sat in the President's bedroom (the First Lady in bed), and seen the President of the United States nude.

The President went through the papers on his table and gave orders to Joe and Jim, with an occasional aside to me so that I could better understand what was going on. He also added comments about the district from time to time.

At about one o'clock the President completed his work, and while he was waiting for his dog to be brought to him, he suggested that I find a bedroom up on the third floor of the mansion and then come back and have coffee with him at eight.

The next morning I was ushered into the President's bedroom. Lady Bird was already up, dressed, and getting ready for a trip back home to Texas. The President was still in bed in his pajamas, with the morning papers spread across the bed. He was going through his morning schedule with Marv Watson, his appointment secretary. They asked me to sit in the rocking chair again, and I was served a cup of coffee.

A few minutes later, Marv had left and I was alone with the President. Our discussion about urban government and the district went on for almost half an hour. I found him not only knowledgeable about urban problems, but also concerned. He seemed to have a strong interest and concern about the district and its residents. He claimed that the district was really his home because he had lived there more than in Texas.

The only interruption during our conversation was when the President received a call from Defense Secretary Bob MacNamara to give him the morning report on the Vietnam war. When I heard the President ask, "How many of my boys did I lose last night?" I again realized the strange situation I was in.

At the conclusion of our talk, the President told me that he had already asked the FBI to do a thorough background check on me, and if that came out all right he would nominate me (and Walter Washington as Mayor) in the next two weeks. But he also told me that if he read about my name being under consideration or about my having been brought to D.C. the day before, he would never nominate me and would probably fire me from HUD.*

I was driven back to Andrews Air Force Base in a White House limo, which drove clear out to the taxiway, where a Lear jet was sitting. As I went up the gangway I was saluted by the pilot and copilot, a full Colonel and a Lt. Colonel. That tickled me almost as much as having been in the White House, since I never got higher than army PFC.

When the plane landed back at the Rapid City Air Force Base, I was met by the base commander, who gave me a review of his troops. I guess he thought that anyone important enough to be flown to meet the President was important enough to be given a review.

I was then taken back to my family after the most extraordinary twenty-two hours.

After I got back to work at HUD the next week, I was asked to go see Secretary Weaver. He expressed disappointment at losing me after such a short time, but he made it clear that the President would not tolerate any objection from him. HUD found this was particularly difficult because they had held this job open for several months while I was being recruited and had even paid my moving expenses—almost unheard of for the federal government. (I may well have been the last one.) The crowning blow, however, must have been when the White House sent HUD a bill for $800 to pay for the cost of my round trip by air force plane.

---

*A year later this story came out in the *Washington Post*. When I checked with Joe Califano, he told me that he had released it because it was so unusual.

Policy-Making

The Duncraig Story
Mildred P. McDonald

I had hardly been moved up from my regular position of assistant town manager to interim town manager for Southern Pines, North Carolina, in March 1973, when the Duncraig matter surfaced. Before it ended three years later, it had become a controversial political issue that divided our citizens, offended many nonresidents, reduced our ability to carry on our regular town functions, cost the town a large sum for legal fees, and put Southern Pines in the national press and radio.

The issue was whether Duncraig Manor, a lovely estate in an affluent neighborhood zoned for single-family dwellings, should be used to provide a homelike center for treating emotionally troubled children. In sympathy with the project were our mayor (a banker who was also financial adviser to the owner of Duncraig Manor), the owner's attorney, the state department of human resources (which had entered into a lease of the property through the Southeastern Mental Health Center), the director of Duncraig, and many citizens who favored the center. This group presented several arguments: that there was no violation because schools, day nurseries, nursing homes, and hospitals were permitted in single-family residence zones, and this facility combined those functions (certainly it was not a correctional institution); that a trained married couple would live in the facility to make a homelike atmosphere; that a trained psychologist would be available; and that the children were neither delinquent nor violent. In short, they argued, the center was essentially a foster home with foster parents.

Opposing the center were our building inspector/zoning-enforcement officer, the town attorney, a vocal town councilman, and another group of citizens. These people contended that the state had already violated the town's zoning ordinance by establishing the center and placing some children in it; that Duncraig Manor would adversely affect the neighborhood and reduce property values; that in one case at least, one of the boys had frightened a lady when he knocked at her door because he "looked funny."

I was in the middle. It was my job to enforce the town's ordinances, but at the same time I sympathized with the state's efforts on behalf of those children and their families. Both the building inspector/zoning-enforcement officer and I were under great pressure, between those citizens who wanted to block the project and those who wanted to allow it.

There followed a series of actions involving the town council, the planning board, the attorneys on both sides of the issue, the state legislature, and the courts. I can best describe them in chronological order, with some side observations.

1. The center was advised that it was in violation.

2. A request was made to the planning board to permit child-training centers in residential agricultural districts (outside the town limits, but within the town's planning jurisdiction).

3. The planning board recommended to the council that the requested amendment to the zoning ordinance be denied. The board gave the following reasons for its recommendation:

    a. This use is not acceptable to the residents of the immediate area.

    b. It is not in keeping with the long-established character of the neighborhood, which is strictly residential.

    c. They had established the institution without first obtaining approval from proper town authorities, and had continued to operate it after having been notified (by the zoning-enforcement officer) of the violation.

4. The Council voted unanimously to accept the planning board's recommendation and to notify Duncraig to vacate the premises within fifteen days.

5. Having heard from some citizens that fifteen days was too short a time to vacate, the council called a special meeting to reconsider. A motion for a time extension that would allow the children to complete the school year died for lack of a second. The owner's attorney expressed the view that the issue should be tested in court.

6. Another special council meeting was called to hear a report from the town attorney on the Duncraig Manor situation. He reported that the town had been dealing with the Southeastern Mental Health Center, that no notices had been served on the property owner. He and the owner's attorney had not been able to reach agreement on a compromise time extension, and the owner was going to file suit against the town. How-

ever, the state had advised the center that it would be closed and the children moved as soon as possible. Therefore, the town attorney recommended an extension of about ninety days. This would show that the community members were reasonable, not the cruel monsters they had become in the media.

7. A motion to extend the time to the date recommended by the town attorney failed on a two-to-two vote. After some citizens opposed to the center spoke in favor of extending the time for vacating, the date recommended by the attorney was adopted. (By now the owner of Duncraig Manor had taken the matter to court.)

8. At the next regular council meeting, the town attorney stated that his previous recommendation was based on written assurance that the center would be moved within the extension period he had recommended but that the assurance had been overruled by a higher state authority. Therefore, he now recommended that the council rescind its time extension and engage another attorney to assist him, and that the two attorneys be authorized to proceed as they felt proper to enforce the town's zoning laws. By unanimous vote, the council rescinded the time extension, engaged the additional attorney, and empowered the two attorneys to proceed as necessary to protect the town's ordinances.

9. The town brought a suit against the State of North Carolina for violating the town's zoning ordinance. The case was tried at the county seat. The judge ruled in favor of the state.

10. After lengthy consideration of the merits of the case and also of the cost of appealing the decision, the council decided to appeal.

Except while I was ill, I served both as town clerk and as interim town manager during this maneuvering. My office was flooded with newspaper reporters, citizens, and attorneys who were querying me about the case, looking up minutes, checking records, and reading the ordinances. Virtually no other town business got done. The case had become "the tail that wags the dog."

There were potential economic repercussions, too. Because Southern Pines and nearby Pinehurst are resort communities, we depend heavily on the trade of out-of-town visitors who come annually for golf, tennis, and equestrian activities. Because of the wide adverse publicity given the case, we received many letters from past visitors who wrote that they would never set foot in the town again. Not one letter supported the town's position.

In the meantime the state legislature enacted a law protecting the rights of disadvantaged or handicapped people to live in residential zones. Citing the new legislation, the state's immunity from legal action, and our own ordinance definition of a single-family residence, the court of appeals ruled in favor of the state on every count. This was three years and a month from the day the building inspector/zoning-enforcement officer came to my office to report he had a complaint about "some sort of training school or treatment center" that "might be in violation of our zoning ordinance."

The Duncraig story illustrates how, in local-government affairs, personalities and emotions often obscure the real issue, which in our town was zoning. Fears were expressed, panic ran rampant in the neighborhood, parents who felt their children might be harmed protested the presence of "disturbed" children.

How has it all turned out? Since the court's decision, Duncraig Manor has operated quietly with none of the anticipated incidents. On 29 August 1979, five years after the controversy erupted, our local newspaper, *The Pilot,* ran a front page story describing the "phenomenal" success the center has had. By providing a disciplined but loving homelike environment for dozens of children (a first-time experience for most), Duncraig Manor has given them a new outlook on school, family, marriage, and the community. During the average stay of seven to eight months at Duncraig Manor, a child's intelligence quotient often increases remarkably. And the community has likewise gained a new appreciation of Duncraig Manor.

Conquering a "Now" Water Problem in Boulder

Bert W. Johnson

Scenic Boulder, Colorado, was a frustration and agony for me and some twelve other city managers who tried to understand and work with its strange politics. The city council that hired me in 1950 included a liberal member who was director of the University of Colorado School of Journalism. He kept badgering his colleagues and me about buying out the Public Service Company of Colorado. A conservative member, who was a baker at the university, had the feeling that the less done in any direction, the more money would be saved. They illustrate the wide spectrum of community opinions that created a volatile political brew. Then (and now, I am told) Boulder's citizens were more committed to winning a fight against other community factions than to making substantive progress.

Yet there was a community malaise or apathy (I am uncertain which) about needed local-government services. Frontier aspects obtained. There was no municipal refuse system; a bad network of poorly drained and rough-surfaced streets without curb and gutter; an inadequate water supply; no local planning staff to assist city, county, and school-district officials; a town-gown syndrome, with the university more often an adversary than a partner; and a newspaper with extensive coverage of city affairs but no editorials. The *Boulder Daily Camera* had no editorial policy; it was committed more to nostalgia than to rational civic progress.

Boulder was (and still is) an enigma. As recently as February 1979, in a *Harper's* article titled "Spiritual Obedience," Peter Marin confirmed that even before my time as city manager, Boulder was a puzzling mix of lively political activity and community mesmerism. Marin concluded that Boulder is "a complex and curious place, as is all of Colorado. Nature is so overpoweringly present that one feels as if one has escaped the ordinary and arrived at a place more beautiful and innocent. But that is not the case."

And escape from the ordinary was not the case in 1950. With a population of 20,000, Boulder had water rights for only 17,000. When water-supply issues were raised, the response was largely negative. Some opinion leaders thought a major issue was whether to cover or pipe the ditches carrying mountain runoff water. These rapid streams, they argued, were an attractive nuisance that endangered life. To many there was ambivalence and a certain myth about water: It was abundant in those ditches—even if the right to use it or trade it was not Boulder's to enjoy.

Among old-timers in city management it is axiomatic that solutions to water supply and drainage would head any list of needed improvements. But local, nonprofessional old-timers despaired and suggested that to pursue this matter would require a sense of fearlessness. I did not despair. Rather, I relied on the advice of two former city managers of Colorado Springs—Earl Mosley and C. H. Hoper. Mosley was chief engineer for the Denver Water Control Board; Hoper, a consulting engineer. Two others urged me to "do it alone," if that became necessary. These were Royce Tipton, a consulting engineer, and Robert Dille, the respected head of the Northern Colorado Conservancy District. All said the time was *now* for Boulder to get voter authorization to tax themselves for Colorado–Big Thompson water (a U.S. Bureau of Reclamation project that regulates and diverts some 300,000 acre-feet of water via a 13-mile tunnel through the Rocky Mountains).

Although back in 1937 Boulder had ignored the opportunity to join the Colorado–Big Thompson Project, fortunately the city got another chance. On 10 January 1953 the Northern Colorado Water Conservancy District authorized a contract with the City of Boulder for 12,500 acre-feet of water for delivery to begin in 1956. In return, Boulder voters were required to add their property to the district, pay millage assessments back to 1937, accept a mill levy on all their real property in perpetuity, and construct 11,000 acre-foot Twin Lakes Reservoir and other improvements by 1955. Complicated? Yes. But our new, young city attorney (now a highly respected and leading water-rights attorney for the Boulder-Denver area) ably walked us through the sequences.

The timing for a referendum on joining the huge and controversial federally financed project proved to be a good one. Boulder's municipal boundaries had been enlarged 41.8 percent in three years. A long-sought 17.3-mile toll road between Denver and Boulder was then a reality. A major new center of the National Bureau of Standards was under construction. Other relocations of federal agencies were due to be approved for Boulder. A new municipal building had been constructed and dedicated on 9 August 1952 to reduce (in my opinion) the siege mentality of a docile city-government staff.

Even so, aided and abetted by the failure of the *Daily Camera* editor to give his blessings, the Boulder city council dragged its feet on the water-supply issue. When the city council finally approved my recommendation for a referendum in 1953, I concluded that our gloomy editor had agreed "not to oppose" the referendum. But the campaign drew no editorial support. I had to be grateful for "no opposition" and for the skillful, comprehensive coverage by reporter Robert C. Looney, whose loyalty to his employers and to the Boulder community makes him one of my favorite unsung heroes.

In receiving city council approval for going to referendum and getting authorization for a $2 million bond issue, I realized that the burden for selling the complex issue was fully mine. In forty-two speeches I repeatedly needled my audiences by saying, "Without this project, Boulder will die!" I used an excellent General Electric Company 20-minute color film on water supply. The film's recurring theme was the song "Cool, Cool Water." My assistant and successor as Boulder city manager, M. Don Harmon, tested the film before every showing, and presented it without a flaw. He and I took our message to every audience we could cajole to invite us, including the youngsters in every public school (despite their ineligibility to vote). The school visits were arranged for me by the school superintendent, Natt B. Burbank. This was the first and last campaign for voter approval on a civic cause that I felt compelled to wage personally. I believed the stakes were high.

To me it is a great source of pride that we achieved the 1953 victory we so earnestly sought. Now, as Boulder approaches a population of some 80,000, the community is assured of having an adequate water supply.

But to me, Boulder will always remain an enigma.

Public Relations

Super Service
Thomas F. Maxwell

One day in University City, Missouri, I received a telephone call from a lady who was very upset. An hour ago a dog had been killed by a car in front of her house, and the dog had not yet been removed.

As I assured her that I would have the dog removed promptly, she asked me to hold the phone for a minute.

When she returned to the phone, she said, "My goodness sakes, you certainly do give wonderful service. They are out there picking up the dog right now."

Obviously someone else had telephoned the sanitation department earlier, but apparently she felt I deserved credit for an instantaneous response.

If You Don't Smoke, You Can Chew
C. Eugene Perkins

In Winston-Salem, North Carolina, a group of local business and civic leaders calling themselves the "Committee of 100" were instrumental in getting voters to adopt the council-manager plan and to elect a mayor and a board of aldermen from among the committee members. In 1947 I received the appointment as the first city manager.

The board members wanted me to become acquainted with business and civic leaders, industrialists, and others in the community as quickly as possible. This led to an amusing incident.

One of my first calls was on the officials of the Reynolds Tobacco Company. This firm not only furnished employment for thousands of local citizens, but also paid more than 40 percent of the city's taxes. Being a nonsmoker, I wondered how that would be received. So when I arrived at the company's executive offices for my appointment, I was feeling a little uncomfortable.

I was escorted into the office of Mr. S. Clay Williams, chairman of the board, where I was welcomed by Mr. Williams and John Whitaker, the president of the company. After a few of the usual pleasantries, Mr. Williams took a carton of cigarettes from his desk, handed it towards me and said, "Have a pack of Camels, Mr. Perkins."

With great trepidation I replied, "No thank you—I don't smoke."

Mr. Williams turned to President Whitaker and said, "By George, John, we'll have to teach him to chew Brown's Mule!"

That was all there was to that, although from then on I did keep a cigarette box on my desk for any visitors who wished to smoke. Years later, on my first day in office as city manager of Glendale, California, I was visited by a Reynolds representative. He brought me, with the company's compliments, a carton of cigarettes for my desk.

Woodman, Spare Those Trees!

Richard G. Simmons

Winter Park, Florida, where I was city manager for eight years (1959–67) was a high-income bedroom community with more than ten thousand oak trees lining the streets. Many of the more outspoken and influential citizens loved the trees, and to them each tree was a sacred shrine. There was an especially protective group of ladies who suspected that the city was there only to slaughter the trees. In fact, I was told that a couple of years before I became city manager, when the county had proposed to remove fifty or sixty trees for a road widening, some of these women chained themselves to the trees to prevent their removal. After much local and national publicity and a standoff for a number of days, the county commissioner from that district got his crew out at two o'clock in the morning and pushed down all the trees before daylight. The road was finished—and so was the commissioner, who was defeated in the next election.

Many of the trees were water oaks. They grow fast, reaching maturity after about fifty years, then deteriorate, rot, and fall. At least three large trees had fallen in the street. One fell on a Rollins College student's Volkswagen a moment after he had left the car to go into his dorm. The tree smashed the car flat with the road. People were becoming concerned about the potential liability, and the city's insurance carrier told us we had to take action to remove these hazards or they would cancel our policies. But neither these hazards nor the advice of a nationally known tree surgeon that the commission had called in to mark trees that should be removed made much impression on the opposition. The trees remained, rot and all.

Racking my brain for a solution, I finally called the University of Florida's School of Forestry for assistance. The dean of the school was most cooperative, saying he had the very man to help us, a Professor Silverculture. In a few days the professor called me. As the first order of business, he wanted to meet with the ladies of the opposition. This surprised me, because I felt that he should review the trees first. But I complied with his request and set up the meeting. The day arrived, as did the professor, a greying, small man of sixty-five with a twinkle in his eye. The meeting was held at the women's club, and tea was served. He commented on the tea and the graciousness of his hostesses. He talked of the beauty of the oaks and congratulated the women on their fight to save them. After about an hour he had singled out the most troublesome women and invited them to accompany him on a tour of the problem trees.

He pointed out rotten spots on the trees and showed the women how to detect a rotten tree. He explained how we could save certain trees by wise pruning. And he also pointed out that failure to do something about the problem would probably lead to a revolt that would require all the trees to be cut.

After hearing the old professor and receiving my assurance that before we cut any controversial tree I would call her for advice, the leader of the opposition apparently decided that the city was trying to act in the community's best interest. Three days later she called to say she had found two trees in bad shape and she wanted to use them as examples of what had to be done. One was in front of the women's club and the other in front of the president's office at the college.

I was concerned when she told me where the trees were, but I really had no reason to worry. When our forestry crew and I arrived, she was there with the press and key members of the women's club. She made a speech about saving the good trees, cutting the bad ones, and planting young ones in their place. After the speech, she posed with an ax and turned the chain saws loose.

From that point on, we cut the bad trees with few problems. She asked me to call her if anyone objected and she would personally investigate. When a problem did arise, she would travel with the truck and tell the facts to the persons who were objecting. We never really had any objections after that because she had the kind of verbal presentation which made opposition futile. We got rid of hundreds of old rotten trees, planted new young trees, and solved our problem. We were surprised that year when we won an honorable mention in the annual awards of the Florida Public Relations Association. This was one of those good lessons, where I learned if you can't beat them, join them.

From Disaster to Delight

Richard G. Simmons

Many of the satisfactions a city manager receives from serving the people of his community get scant or no publicity, are little known to the residents, and may even need to be held in confidence. A small example of this kind of satisfaction can be drawn from my experiences in my first city, Melbourne, Florida.

Melbourne had a causeway extending across a river to an ocean-front community to the east. The causeway was not well landscaped, but it did have a magnificent strand of trees and shoreline.

One morning an active Garden Club member came into my office and loudly protested the installation of ugly black poles in the middle of our causeway. I told her I was not aware of what this was and that I would check it out.

When I arrived on the scene, I found that the power company had installed a new major transmission line to serve the beach community. It had placed the actual transmission line in the edge of the water but, to obtain proper support, had extended a large guy cable onto the causeway over some black wooden poles. I agreed that the poles ruined the appearance of the natural causeway.

Immediately I contacted the manager of the power company and told him of the visit of the articulate spokesman of the garden club. I was a young manager at that time, but I was knowledgeable enough to know that the fires of hell would be preferable to having that particular woman at our next commission meeting. I received little solace from the manager of the power company. He assured me that they had to use the guy poles to insure the safety of the major transmission line. And, as I knew, their franchise with the city allowed them to construct facilities on city rights-of-way. He of course recognized the power of this garden clubber; he too had seen her in action.

As we talked, an idea came to me. What about installing street lights on the guy poles and following immediately with picnic tables and landscaping? The power-company manager was delighted with this suggestion and said that lights would be installed in a week even though a job this size would normally take three months.

I then called the woman and told her that I had been planning improvements for recreational facilities for some time but that the power company had moved more rapidly than we had anticipated. (This was not a complete falsehood: I had been thinking of putting picnic tables along the causeway and landscaping the parkway. However, I had not ordered lights.) To my surprise, she was delighted and agreed to help with the landscaping and beautification. The power company moved very rapidly to put in the lights, and what started as a disaster turned out to be a delight. After that I became very friendly with the garden club, and its members were very helpful in my years of service there.

I had occasion to visit this city about twenty years later. Strangely, the first thing I wanted to see was the causeway, and sure enough, it was as it had been twenty years before. This is one of those small incidents about which the public was not really aware but which gave me considerable satisfaction.

Flying High!
Richard G. Simmons

In 1977, while on a committee charged with planning activities for the Royal Palm Festival (an annual county-wide event to liven up the summer season in the Palm Beach, Florida, area), I was visited by the promoter of the movie *The Great Balloon Race*. This was a full-length picture based on a flight from Bimini in the Bahamas to the Florida coast. They were looking for a spot to fly their balloons to publicize the movie.

Because part of our festival program was to be competition between city and county officials, I asked the promoter if he was interested in a balloon race. He was, so I fired off a challenge letter to the county administrator. In it I noted that we were both full of hot air but that I felt I could control mine better than he could his, and that the race could be fair provided he didn't fly over the courthouse and get an extra burst of hot air. He accepted my challenge, with a threat to shoot me down.

In the preflight parade, dressed in Red Baron early-day flying togs, I rode on a City of West Palm Beach street sweeper, symbolic of my intent to make "a clean sweep" of the race. The county administrator rode in a garbage truck, alleging that I was "full of it." On arrival at the midtown launching site, our city police made a last minute search of the county administrator for weapons he might use against me and my balloon.

The official race course was scheduled to the west, but the county administrator went too high, caught a wrong breeze, and floated eastward to the sea. My craft drifted north and slightly west and landed in a football field, where a group of students were practicing for graduation. This gave us a ready-made crowd of 200 people, plus the television crews. After a slight descent, the county administrator's balloon drifted many miles northward, and it nearly knocked a man off a tee while landing in a North Palm Beach country club golf course.

It was a lot of fun, created interest in the local festival, and got an immense amount of publicity both locally and nationally. The challenge letters and race pictures were featured in *Public Management* magazine, and the race was also covered in an article in *Government Administrators* magazine. If there is a moral in this, it must be that what a city manager or county administrator may consider his greatest professional accomplishment is not what gets the most publicity.

There's Many a Slip
Thomas F. Maxwell

In Columbia, South Carolina, an elderly lady called me to complain that there were bats in the attic of her home, and that they were a nuisance and concern to her, and that she thought the city ought to do something about it. Although I doubted we could do anything because the problem was on private property and did not affect the health and safety of the community, I told her I would check to see if there were any way we could help her. As I was quite sure they would, both the health director and the city attorney said it was a private problem and that we had no authority to spend public funds to solve it. In a later conversation I explained to her as courteously and sympathetically as I could the reasons the city could not intercede.

A short time later I was invited to be the banquet speaker for the annual dinner-dance of the University of South Carolina chapter of Alpha Kappa Psi, the business and public-administration fraternity of which I had been a member at the University of Missouri. I tried to make my short speech light by describing some of the incidents that involved problems which I was helpless to solve. To add a touch of humor, I mentioned what I called the "Bats-in-the-Belfry Case." To my great embarrassment, a young lady approached me after the dinner to announce with some feeling, "The lady you talked to about the bats in her belfry is my grandmother!"

On the Street where You Live
Thomas F. Maxwell

Three brief incidents may throw a little light on human nature. In Columbia, South Carolina, I was invited to a cocktail party at the large and luxurious home of one of our most affluent citizens. After locating the house and parking our car, I noted that we and a number of other people were having difficulty making our way to the home because there were neither sidewalks nor streetlights. I was not surprised at the lack of sidewalks because they were not provided in many of the best residential areas. The residents preferred the appearance of a suburban road to that of a city street. Furthermore, in these affluent areas about the only pedestrian traffic was domestic servants.

After the party, it occurred to me I could do our host and the entire neighborhood a favor by installing a streetlight at the intersection, in keeping with city policy of lighting every street intersection. I ordered a light installed.

Much to my amazement, I received an angry call from my host. Complaining bitterly about the installation of the light, he demanded that it be removed. That put me in a predicament, because if others in the neighborhood wanted the light (to which they were entitled), I would have to leave it.

I solved the problem by leaving the streetlight but having it turned off. Nobody ever asked to have it turned on, so I suppose everybody was reasonably happy with what was admittedly not a totally satisfactory solution.

In the same city I received a lot of complaints about streetlights shining in people's windows. We devised a shade that partially obscured the offending light from the window in question. We installed the shades on request and left them in if the neighbors didn't complain about them. The hassle came when someone else objected to the shade. At that point I had to remove it and put up with the continuing complaints from the first complainer, sometimes suggesting he pull down the shades.

At four o'clock one morning I received a call from a gentleman who complained that the streetlight in front of his house was out and requested that I have it repaired. Although I managed to remain polite, his lack of consideration kept me awake the rest of the night, and I went to the office in a foul mood.

The first thing I did was make sure that the light was repaired and that the repair crew called me back as soon as the job was completed. I then called the state penitentiary, where the man had told me he worked (and had given as his reason for calling at such an odd hour, because he slept during the day). I found out his scheduled work hours, figured out what time of the day for him would be the equivalent of 4:00 A.M. for me, and called him precisely at that time to inform him that his streetlight had been fixed.

Lo and behold, I was denied my revenge. His wife answered the phone, but refused to awaken him to speak to the city manager. At four the following morning he called me again, to thank me for having the light repaired! That strengthened my resolve to try never to outwit a taxpayer.

Reorganizing

A "Before-and-After" Picture

Thomas F. Maxwell

I went to work as an assistant to L. Perry Cookingham in July 1940, two months after he became city manager of Kansas City, Missouri, following the defeat of Tom Pendergast's political organization, which has been called the most corrupt American city government. After seven years with Mr. Cookingham, and after two years of military service during World War II, I became the first city manager of University City, Missouri, a prosperous St. Louis residential suburb of about 40,000 population.

University City had no slums, no organized criminal element, limited services, high property values, and low property taxes. From the city's founding, municipal affairs had been run by part-time mayors and a city council.

A coalition of outstanding community leaders and the League of Women Voters promoted the council-manager plan, which was adopted in a low voter turnout. The plan was not actively opposed except by a local weekly newspaper, which was a one-man operation. The editor was vicious in his opposition to the plan and to me when I arrived as city manager. During my entire three-year tenure, he referred to me as a "Pendergast politician", although he well knew that the administration I worked for in Kansas City was the one that had destroyed the Pendergast machine.

The newly elected city council was composed of top-grade people. Four of the seven members, including the mayor, were successful St. Louis lawyers. The council met twice a month, and the council members were paid $10 per meeting. The new charter was a city manager's dream.

When I arrived in University City, the city had no budgetary system, no classification and compensation plan for employees, no central purchasing, no established lines of responsibility (not even an organizational chart!), and no central executive control. Each department head ran his little empire as he saw fit on whatever appropriations he could persuade the council to give him.

There was no civil-service plan. Employee pay rates were disgracefully low and, consequently, municipal services were inferior. Many of the city employees lived in St. Louis because they could not afford to live in University City.

The public works, finance, health, police, and fire departments were sadly neglected. In contrast, there was an excellent park commission. It received all the money it wanted because it was composed of prominent citizens. Also, there was a library commission which operated under the same circumstances.

In three years, without outside consultant help, I established an accounting and budgetary system that won the Municipal Finance Officers Association's Achievement Award. Also, I prepared a complete compensation and classification plan, established a civil-service commission, obtained new zoning and building codes, increased employees' salaries substantially, and reduced taxes. When I left at the end of that time, the city had a sound, well-organized and amply financed government. A move to abandon the council-manager form of government obtained so little support that the dissidents did not carry the question to a vote. The entire council was reelected by a four-to-one margin over a slate that advocated abandoning the council-manager plan.

Some Dos and Don'ts of Organizational Change

James Joshua Mott

I was city manager of West Palm Beach, Florida, twice—1952–54, when I was interim manager while the regular city manager was on active national-guard duty for the Korean conflict, and again 1958–60, when I was called back by the city commission from a U.S. Department of State technical-assistance position in Iran.

The city commission consisted of five elected, overlapping-term members, each serving for a two-year period, and one of whom was chosen by the commission each year to serve as mayor. The administrative service was divided into fourteen departments. Most of the department heads had worked for the city since the thirties. Deep South traditions prevailed, and there was no desire for any so-called "flashy modern procedures" or changes.

One of the first things I did as interim city manager was to improve the place where the city commission held its meetings. It cost less than $50 and made a considerable difference in decorum, in hearing the public, in promoting respect for the city commission, and in speeding up the discussions.

Some details of the improvements are as follows:

- A 6-inch platform to elevate the table where the mayor and the rest of the city commission sat
- Special front-row places for the news media
- Central places, at floor level, for the city clerk/recorder and the city manager
- Special seats for the city attorney and the city engineer (and other department heads on invitation from the city manager or the city commission for special projects or particular occasions)
- A well-lettered name and title plate for each official

Another early change was the successful consolidation of the city's health department with the county health department.

The city physician, Dr. W. E. Van Landingham, was well-known, well-liked, and well along in years. He had been a city employee since 1925. He had a staff of two nurses and four sanitation inspectors. The principal duty of the doctor and the nurses was to give first aid and minor health services to employees during working hours. The inspectors checked restaurants and other food-handling establishments. Their laboratory was extremely small and was isolated from the general municipal functions, and their office space was very limited.

Upon the retirement of Dr. Van Landingham as city physician, I realized that something might be done to utilize the facilities and staff of the larger and more modern county health department, which was located in a more desirable downtown area. With this possibility in mind (and knowing that the retiring city physician had no objection), I made observational visits to the county's health department and strengthened my personal contacts with their staff. The professional ability and pleasant personality of the county physician, Dr. Brumback, were definitely favorable factors. He ran a good department. Quarters and office and laboratory, vehicles, and supplies were of high quality. He held and encouraged in-service training sessions and staff meetings. Unlike the city health inspectors, his inspectors were all college graduates in public-health fields. Whenever the transferred city inspectors retired, replacements would have to meet the same high standards the county already had.

I did not have to argue that city and county health departments were combined in other places; that was well known. My informal discussions with the city commission appeared favorable. The commissioners simply wanted assurance that the cost of health services would not increase.

There were no personnel problems apart from guaranteeing retention of retirement benefits and status accrued by members of the city's health department who would be consolidated with or transferred to the county. The nurses and inspectors wished to continue working, and two of the inspectors were due to retire in a year or so.

Fortunately the county had taken advantage of optional provisions of the State of Florida retirement system. The city had chosen to keep its own various retirement systems (police, fire, and general retirement). With the help of the city attorney, the state, and others, details were worked out whereby city health department employees who were transferred to the county would not lose any future benefits nor suffer any loss of prior contributions to the city's general retirement system.

Financial arrangements were not difficult to negotiate, nor were they complicated. The county commission and Dr. Brumback were agreeable— they would not gouge the city on costs.

The city agreed to pay its share of the expense of a consolidated operation, with salaries, overhead, and the like at standard figures. Mutually acceptable adjustments could be made in subsequent budget-preparation periods. Either party could cancel the agreement. The last hurdle was overcome.

Discussions, proper investigations, unhurried legal arrangements—all paid off. Because we suffered no personality problems that they could play up, the news media left us alone. Quality of service, such as inspections of food-handling establishments throughout our urban area improved considerably. The taxpayers saved money, and no employee was hurt. And twenty-five years later the consolidation of the city and county health departments is still satisfactory.

At about the time that consolidation of the two health departments appeared to be well on its way, I decided something should be done to improve voter registration.

A citizen had to register at the city hall to vote in the city elections and had to register at the county courthouse to vote in all other elections. This was a nuisance, generally a duplication of operations, and of course an unnecessary expense for the taxpayer. The number of city and county clerks involved in voter registration was small, but there was also the expense of supplies, file cabinets, and minor equipment. Mechanical systems could improve the procedures, but with separate offices we could not justify the installation and other costs.

No one appeared alarmed at the suggestion of combining the registration of voters. The city clerk, Mrs. "Jimmie" Gardner, and members of her department were glad to be relieved of the operation. They had other, increasing duties to perform, and no one would be discharged or have a cut in pay if the function were given to the county. The city would pay the county a small sum (and even that eventually was forgotten).

Combining city and county voter registration proved easy. In retrospect, I think this may have been the reason: I was told if I would just forget about my soundings for possible consolidation of city tax assessing and city tax collection with those operations of the county (as had long been done successfully in nearby Fort Lauderdale), and be quiet for a spell, I would be allowed to consolidate voter registration. And I settled for the time being for that.

Fourteen department heads constituted too broad a span of control. Directing, coordinating, and controlling left little time for other functions of good administration: planning, public relations, training, reporting, and liaison with the policy-making body. Some consolidation of services was needed, in both staff and line offices.

Formal research on the subject was negligible. I had no staff or funds for the purpose. People in the city government, especially in the city commission, knew when particular organizational changes should be made, and they awaited only a city employee's retirement or some other timely event. The city commission wanted changes, but some of them also wanted their "pets" to retain power, and their favorites, qualified or not, to be given new positions. For instance, when I came back to West Palm Beach as the regular city manager, I found that there was now an assistant to the city manager, called coordinator, who had no particular training or education for the position. My problem was what to do with him. People seemed to like him, and he was a favorite of the current mayor. I proposed that he be made director for the annual Seminole Sun Dance festival and musical. (The first Sun Dance had been a fiasco of overspending of city monies by the unbridled Jaycees.) But the mayor did not like that change in title.

I then proposed to the city commission and mayor that the assistant city manager be made general superintendent of both parks and recreation and of the marina and the heliport. I also guaranteed that the new general superintendent would take a correspondence course in parks and recreation administration from the International City Management Association's Institute for Training in Municipal Administration. (The correspondence course idea began with other newly organized in-service group-training courses in public works, fire-department administration, personnel administration, and finance.) Before making the proposal, I had told the assistant city manager that he had to take and pass the parks and recreation course, that if he did not, he would not get the job. He passed. (And today he continues in the management profession.)

At the time, the parks service had a department head, a naturalized German who had been a city employee more than thirty-two years. Recreation also had a department head—an employee with better than twenty years of service. There was even a department head in charge of the separate Fishing Club program, and another for the marina's docks.

Parks and Recreation both had two bosses—the city manager and the parks and recreation commission. The marina seemed to get along the best it could from day to day. No one particularly cared about it, even though the new heliport (one of the first three downtown helicopter ports in the United States) was part Parks and part Marina.

The city commission concurred in the consolidation plan, and although the newly combined department still had two bosses, thereafter the work of both the parks and recreation commission and the city manager suffered less than previously from clique influence and rivalry. There was still a fishing club, but it was more social than administrative, conducting its own sailfish and other tournaments and sporting awards. Boating and fishing became a separate division in the new department, and the marina, a city business of docks, was a third division.

I felt that all financial operations should be under one head, but without in any way interfering with the outside auditor's direct responsibility to the city commission and without detracting from the city manager's responsibility as treasurer of the city.

Now, because the time seemed right, I began to reorganize the financial operations.

A selling point was that the city had grown so, and the budget had become so complicated, that while I could do without an assistant or a budget director, I did need help, and a finance director would be just the thing. And because most department heads who were approaching retirement lacked strong, trained assistants or deputies, I recommended that we hire an entirely new person—a professionally qualified finance director who could do many things: in-service financial-operations training, and such. The city commission approved my request for a finance director.

But . . .

After a wide, national search for a qualified finance director, the best one I found was a Catholic Yankee with a foreign-sounding name (D'Ippolito). Nevertheless, I selected him and so informed the city commission. Eventually the repercussions died down.

He would supervise the divisions of the comptroller, the tax assessor, the tax collector, purchasing (which had considered itself a part of the informal hierarchy of the department of public works, in whose facilities purchasing was housed), and the basement print shop. Supplies and purchasing were to be sections under purchasing. (For a short while, purchasing for the large water and sewer department had been combined with purchasing for the rest of the city, but because of personality conflicts, they had to be separated.)

Statistics and other reports had been prepared to help combine city and county tax assessing and tax collecting. And my personal investigations through field trips to other cities and counties showed such combinations working very well, notably in Fort Lauderdale–Broward County, just to the south of us. But the decision was no go. Absolutely not. Thirty-five and thirty-six years of city service cannot be conducive to combination with the county when the long-service people are top level and will be around for a few years.

During the period of financial consolidation the personnel director resigned, and the time was then ripe to move pensions (three separate systems) from the comptroller's shop to personnel and to formalize the relationships of the personnel director with the city physician, whose function was to assist in pension claims.

I felt also that city planning should not be the responsibility of the city engineer but that there should be a separate city-planning department for a city of our size (over 50,000 population) and growth rate.

Except for opposition from one commissioner, who objected to my including traffic engineering under the city planner, it was a simple matter to sell the city commission on the organizational innovation. A budget was prepared for the remainder of the fiscal year, money was found for it, and an old, unused parks building near the public-works department was easily renovated for the planning office. And fortunately a former city policeman who had left the city's service for the University of Florida and had received a degree in city planning, applied for and received the position. His name was Bill Dale.

Previously traffic engineering had been divided between the police department and the electrical section of the public-works department. Traffic engineering was given to the new city planner, who had training in the subject, and who had the good personality and West Palm Beach acquaintanceship that would help him handle the transition.

Dale soon had an admirable, modern sign shop in operation and an efficient public service, including all the proper liaison with taxpayers and other city departments. But I knew he would be subject to considerable pressure in his new job, partly because the same commissioner who objected to having traffic engineering in the planning department also objected when I appointed "an outside man." There would be other kinds of pressure, too. A note in my personal file of that time reads,

> City Commissioner Ray Behm came down and asked for about $60
> worth of signs for his private parking lot (garden supply business). I
> told him, "Sorry, I can't do it. It is city sign property." Behm said, "I
> am ordering you to do it." I replied, "Sorry, I cannot."

Nevertheless, I had confidence that Dale would stand his ground when necessary. And he did.

The organizational changes described here took place during my two two-year periods, the principal changes occurring when I had a regular appointment and therefore was more sure of myself and my authority.

I cannot claim all the credit for the shifting of functions and the improvements in personnel. Many times, the human-relations factors were fortuitous and "the time was ripe." On the other hand, it was not all easy.

I did not observe the Rule of Four: first year, look around; second year, decide what to change; third year, make changes; fourth year, check the changes, modify, amend, strengthen, supplement, or revert. I was too impatient. I pushed too hard and too fast. This may have been a mistake.

Coping
with Threats

A "House" Is
Not Necessarily a Hotel

James Joshua Mott

West Palm Beach, Florida, was (and I believe still is) one of only four cities of approximately 50,000 population to have an elected chief of police. Under this arrangement, the city commission and the city manager have virtually no control over the police chief, except for slight influence through the budget. In fact, chiefs have told city commissions, in effect, "Go to the devil. I got more votes than you did." Instead, there is danger of favors to supportive voters, revenge or neglect of responsible voters, politicking within and by the police department, and nonprofessionalism throughout this important law-enforcement agency.

While I was city manager, the city commission found it necessary to appoint a crime commission to study conditions involving the police department and related affairs. (The commission's official title was "West Palm Beach Police Department Commission.") The city attorney and I were members of the crime commission, which held many meetings, questioned many witnesses, undertook some investigations, and was a point of real interest to the media.

During one investigation, the madam of a house of ill-repute was subpoenaed for questioning about her activities, which took place in a large downtown building.

"My client runs a hotel," said her attorney.

"If you are a hotel, where is your hotel sign and hotel license?" I asked. Surprisingly, this simple question caused them visible alarm. The next day the building had a big new hotel sign, and application had been made for a hotel license.

During the crime commission's activities, one person who had been beaten up by persons unknown was interviewed by the crime commission while in the hospital. He died soon thereafter. I too received many male and female telephone calls at my home, obscene and threatening, and at all hours. Consequently, I decided to use my U.S. Civil Service retirement funds (accumulated during my government service) to send our ten-year-old son to an out-of-town military boarding school.

Four months after it was appointed, the crime commission completed its assignment and filed a thirty-two-page report. The report dealt with organization of the police department, use of facilities and equipment, and extent of dissension and discord. The commission listed and explained eighteen principal causes of dissension and discord, and concluded with this statement: "The system of electing the chief of police, in our opinion, is fundamentally at fault and making the office appointive would, we believe, greatly lessen and possibly remove the other causes we have mentioned."

Release of the report ended the delight of the media at such newsy goings-on. Shortly thereafter the elected chief of police resigned.

Garbage, Garbage, Who Hauls the Garbage?
Richard G. Simmons

In West Palm Beach, Florida, commercial garbage—from restaurants, stores, hotels, businesses, and office buildings—was collected both by the city and by private collectors. Each had their own customers. This meant that we knew only our customers and that the private collectors knew only theirs. We would drive a truck up to two containers and empty one, and a private collector would drive a truck up to get the other one. And I guessed that many people didn't pay the commercial collection fee to anyone.

We did an evaluation of this system and found that economies could be gained by having one operator collect all the commercial garbage. Of course, the private collectors felt strongly that the city should not interfere with free enterprise. I felt equally strong that either the city or an individual should be the sole collector. Either could do it more cheaply than under the present system.

To get around the free-enterprise argument, I proposed to put the commercial collection out to competitive bids and solicit the three largest companies in the nation to bid, along with the local private collectors. One of the local private collectors who had a piece of the action in our city refused to bid but kept feeding the commission information about problems the major companies were having. All the allegations were unsupported. As a consequence, I implemented my proposal, recommending to the city commission that we accept the lowest bid by a private individual or firm and award the winner a contract for collecting all commercial garbage.

One evening I received a call from the principal of the small private collector, who told me that I would be a ghost in a year if I pursued this recommendation. I reported this to the police department in the event something happened, and they made an investigation of this company. The police chief urged me to be exceedingly careful, because these people had direct Mafia connections. For the next month or so it was a common joke around city hall that the interns would take turns starting my car in the morning.

I am happy to say that nothing came of the threat. The commission decided that the city would not be involved with private contractors, that the city would do all commercial collection. And my guess proved correct: We found that more than four hundred commercial concerns were paying no garbage-collection fee at all. Not only were we able to improve the efficiency of the operation, but we were also able to eliminate the inequity of having some pay and some not.

Part Five

Personal and Professional Philosophy

City managing is sometimes a tough and lonely job. It can create overwhelming stresses on an individual. Therefore, it helps any citizen interested in improving local government to know in advance what kinds of situations to expect, or to see how others—managers, council members, and private citizens—have coped with similar situations. Also, concrete examples of positive attitudes may be helpful to any public servant who has become confused or discouraged, or who has temporarily lost sight of his goal to render significant public service to others.

In this final group of episodes, several managers share with us the philosophies that have enabled them and others to avoid difficulties, to meet the challenges of the job without abandoning or losing their personal and professional values. One writer compares the present with the past. Another takes a look into the future. Finally, a couple of managers describe what makes it all worthwhile, why the idea of professional management for the benefit of all the citizens in our democratically controlled local governments continues to gain adherents.

Enthusiasm Pays

L. Perry Cookingham

When I became the first city manager of Saginaw, Michigan, in 1936, that was one of the choice openings in the country, and the city council had received forty or more applications for the position.

I did not apply for the Saginaw job because I did not think I was qualified to move from Plymouth, Michigan, where I was serving in that 6,000 population city, to a city of more than eighty thousand. However, one of our Plymouth citizens had a relative who was active in Saginaw civic affairs. The Plymouth man urged me to submit an application, or at least write to his relative, because he had told his relative that Plymouth had the best city manager in Michigan (a statement that I doubted). To please him I wrote the relative and inquired about the city-manager position. The relative gave the letter to the chairman of the council committee that was reviewing applications, and the chairman in turn sought the advice of Harold D. Smith, executive director of the Michigan Municipal League. Harold Smith told the chairman that talent could be found in a small city as well as in a large city, and he suggested that they interview me.*

The day I was interviewed, the committee interviewed another manager, from a larger city. I was certain that because of his longer and larger-city experience I had no chance. But later I was called back for an interview by the entire council, and then was chosen.

After I had been on the job several months, I asked the mayor how I came to be selected over the other person interviewed that day, when he had had more experience as a city manager and in a larger city.

The mayor said, "Do you really want to know?"

"Yes, I would."

"During your interview, your lips turned up; during the interview with him, his lips turned down."

The mayor added that my enthusiasm and interest in attempting to do the job was as much responsible for my appointment as was anything else. In other words, I smiled most of the time that I was being interviewed, and the other man did not have the enthusiasm I had. This

---

*Harold D. Smith was director of the U.S. Bureau of the Budget (now the Office of Management and Budget) in the Executive Office of the President in 1943. I was on the bureau staff. Before I left Washington, D.C., to become city manager of Sweet Home, Oregon, Mr. Smith gave me this added version of the above incident about Perry Cookingham, whom I then knew only by reputation. He said Cookingham came to him saying he was "scared to death" to become city manager of a city more than a dozen times the size of the city he was then serving. Smith told Cookingham, "Take it. You'll find Saginaw easier to manage than Plymouth. In the small cities the manager has to fill several different jobs himself: city engineer, building inspector, volunteer fireman, city clerk. In the larger cities you'll have competent professionals to handle those jobs."

Then Mr. Smith also gave me some advice: He counseled me to guard against the danger of getting "small-townitis," now that I was going to a very small town from a job where I had been dealing with annual budgets that totaled billions of dollars. —Ed.

taught me that perhaps the personality of the candidate is as important as is his technical ability.

The Power of Example
Thomas F. Maxwell

I wish only that I had the talent to record Perry Cookingham's transformation of Kansas City, Missouri, from the worst-governed city to the best of its size in the nation. I do know that my experience there inspired me, and about forty other young men, to feel that I was something of a knight on a white horse charging into each city in which I subsequently served as city manager, my mandate being to give to the people good government in the broadest sense: equitable treatment for every person. I think the only difficulty I ever had with any city council was warning them that if they adopted a course of action that seemed benevolent in a certain circumstance, I would insist that *every* person in the city receive the same treatment under the same circumstances, but that, as they knew, the city did not have the resources to provide this special treatment to every person in the same circumstances. I suppose that many times this made me appear hardhearted, because everybody wants to help a person damaged by the zoning, health, sanitation, and other regulations that every city must impose. But never, publicly or privately, did I tell a city council that they shouldn't give an individual special relief. I said only that if they did take such action I would consider it a precedent to be followed in all similar cases, and that because it would therefore necessitate amending city ordinances, I would feel it my duty to recommend such an amendment.

Father Was a City Manager
Duane W. Koenig*

What does a son remember of his father as city manager? A variety of things: Father's philosophy about city management; characteristics of the profession; problems he faced; and some dramatic and amusing episodes and interpersonal relationships.

*On our way from Washington, D.C., to my first city manager job in Sweet Home, Oregon, my wife and I stopped at the wartime ICMA conference in Chi-

My father, Adolph J. Koenig, was one of the early professional managers in the United States. Having taken a master's degree at the University of Michigan in 1928, he went on to serve as manager of towns ranging from Milford, Connecticut, and Jackson, Michigan, to Anchorage, Alaska. His ideal was the city manager as nonpartisan technician (as prescribed then by the International City Managers Association), but his career demonstrated the difficulty of achieving that ideal in the confusion of local politics. He believed honesty is required of a manager. He always said that he hoped they caught him when he stole the first postage stamp.

A manager might not be able to store up much in the way of this world's goods, but he saw a lot of the country. And the towns where he served varied in sophistication. In some the only new faces that ever appeared were the city managers, the teachers, and the preachers.

Father had two trifling liabilities. He had been in teaching for eleven years before entering city management. His professor at Michigan had told him, "You are as yet too much the schoolmaster to be a successful city manager." Whether his instructor's observation was suitable may be questioned, but certainly management requires flexibility when one must serve simultaneously as manager, public-safety director, city clerk, assessor, and treasurer—which happened in some small towns. Also, Father was a Roman Catholic, which irritated people in many of America's small towns.

As village manager of Jackson, Michigan, in 1928, Father was expected to join the volunteer fire department at every fire. I can remember the excitement when the fire siren would sound. After calling the telephone operator (as did everyone else, unfortunately), and learning the fire's location, Father would speed off in the manager's car. Now and then I went along. While his obligations at the fire were informal, Father tried to make himself useful. He commented on the fire to reporters and answered taxpayers' questions.

Police matters were curious. A bank robber in Jackson who was frightened off by the prompt arrival of the police chief ran through the snow several blocks before giving himself up. When apprehended, the criminal had no gun, but he had displayed one in the bank. Father thought over the matter, traced the path of the chase, put his hand into a hole in a snow bank, and returned with the missing weapon.

Another time the police picked up a tramp who spun a remarkable tale. He said he had been sleeping behind a hedge near the lovers' lane

cago. One of the veteran city managers and his wife who went out of their way to welcome and encourage us were Mr. and Mrs. A. J. Koenig.

Mr. Koenig served nine cities and was a vice-president of ICMA. When I invited a number of managers and former managers to share the highlights of their professional experience in this book, I did not know Mr. Koenig had passed away. To Mrs. Koenig and their son, Dr. Duane Koenig, a long-time professor at the University of Miami, we are indebted for the above article. —Ed.

where the Hall-Mills murders took place. (Hall-Mills was the famous case of "the minister and the choir singer," involving Reverend Hall and the wife of the church sexton. The minister and Mrs. Mills were victims of a ritual-type killing in 1922 near New Brunswick, New Jersey.) Unobserved, the tramp had witnessed everything and could name the guilty party. His story was strengthened by the fact that he had a notebook containing information not in the press and a gun supposedly found on the spot. But when Father contacted authorities in the East to inquire about the murders, he could arouse no interest in this "new evidence." Apparently the case was closed.

Following their audit of a certain public hospital, the auditors reported to the manager that they had discovered shortages of $163,000 in the hospital receipts. Father's investigation revealed a peculiar story.

An old-maid cashier in the hospital had begun stealing money two decades before. She did so simply by listing accounts paid to her in full as uncollectible. In that file they were ignored. When the auditors came around, she "helped" by running up balances on her machine and making herself useful. Until eight years before her exposure, she had continued to thieve. Then, after having taken $163,000, she stopped. The money went to finance a bar and grill for a boyfriend.

By the date the defalcations were discovered, the statute of limitations applied. The woman could not be prosecuted or her name mentioned in the papers. And beyond firing her, Father was helpless. But fate intervened. The boyfriend's business failed, and he jilted the lady.

One of the city manager's chief liabilities is the councilman who would like to be a political boss and give the manager on-the-spot orders. One such individual, a naturalized American, made life difficult for Father. This man was mayor, and he badgered, posed, and blustered. Then suddenly, to everyone's surprise, he became silent and cooperative. This is what happened.

One day Father happened to be examining voters' lists. Noting that the mayor had been voting for years, he also remembered that the man had become a citizen only recently. The rest may be imagined. The mayor learned by bush telegraph of the disadvantages, penal and public, of having voted before becoming naturalized. He stopped heckling the manager, hoping that the matter would be overlooked. No more orders bypassed the council.

During the Great Depression many towns were urged by water engineers and generator salesmen to set up local water and power plants instead of depending on private utility firms. In one city a councilman planned to make political hay of such recommendations. However, observing that Father was friendly with the director of the private utility, and therefore assuming that the manager would be against city ownership, the councilman plotted Father's downfall.

The councilman asked that Father investigate water and power rates, with a view to local production. When the report was due, Father was ready. His opponent sat at the table with demands for resignation of the city manager in hand. My father had only to oppose public ownership of utilities. But that he did not do. He reported to the council that the city could operate the water utility at the same rate as the private firm. The private investors were making no profits and would be glad to get rid of the water business. As for electricity, rates were about as low as could be expected, even with home ownership. An independent engineer verified this.

The councilman was completely subdued. In anger he tore up his request for the manager's removal. He voted acquisition of water and rejection of electricity. Years later this man admitted to Father his regrets for his game.

Simple bad luck may dog a manager. Years back Father planned to attend the annual meeting of the International City Managers Association. He was vice-president. No sooner had he arrived at the meeting than telegrams came to him reporting that an unexpected hurricane had hit his city. He should go home immediately. He flew back to face an outcry that the manager should be able to predict the weather and should not have left with a storm threatening. When it came down to facts, the emergency procedures he had instituted had functioned perfectly in his absence. Disaster had been averted. But nobody noticed this. The city manager who was away on professional business should have been at home.

The manager is always in the public eye and is fair game for private as well as public hazing. This happened thirty years back. Some of the councilmen invited Father out to hunt pheasant. He dressed in old clothes and came with his shotgun. As a trick, the councilmen had hidden a farmer in ambush with a red rooster. When Father appeared, the farmer freed the chicken. Everyone shouted "fire!" Father did so, and the chicken was dead. Now the farmer came forth and, in pretended outrage, demanded a substantial sum for his prize Rhode Island Red. To everyone's amazement, Father just happened to have cash in his pocket and paid off quietly without protest. The next day the councilmen, disappointed in their scheme of ridicule, confessed and returned the money.

Would I recommend that a person follow my father's profession? Yes and no. The faults of professional management are obvious: absolutely no tenure, time without pay between jobs, moving a family here or there, meetings every night of the week, being in the spotlight of newspaper attention along with his wife and children, and frequently being obligated by city charter to live within the city limits instead of in a more attractive unincorporated suburb. On the other hand, Father was comfortable during depression and war. And he provided a university education and trips abroad for my brother and me. But, perhaps most important of all, he had a good time. His job was fun.

What's Wrong with the Goo-Goos?
LeRoy F. Harlow

In Daytona Beach, the young attorneys were generally aggressive and ambitious, but one of them was even more energetic than the others. He often appeared at city commission meetings, usually defending someone charged with violating a city ordinance and making a great show of how unjust the laws were and how his client had been abused, treated unfairly, or oppressed. He would address the commission and the audience as though he were attorney for the defense making a plea to the jury in a murder trial. Whenever I saw him in action I was reminded of the principal character in Budd Schulberg's novel *What Makes Sammy Run?*

This attorney was a good-looking man, always stylishly dressed, articulate, and positive. I didn't know him personally, so I was taken somewhat by surprise when he paid me a visit a few weeks before the primary-election filing deadline.

To break the ice, I asked him about his background. He talked freely. He had come from humble economic circumstances in one of the large northern cities. Apparently he saw Florida while in the service and decided he wanted to live there. He described life for his wife and himself in a one-room trailer while he went to Stetson University Law School. He said they were so poor he had to steal vegetables after dark from nearby truck gardens just to live.

I had noticed that he drove about the longest Cadillac in town and remarked that things seemed to have changed for him, and he acknowledged he was doing all right.

Turning to the reason for his coming to see me, he said he was thinking of running for the city commission. He said he was ready to run with and support either side—the present administration or those opposed to the administration. It didn't make any difference to him.

I didn't ask him what inducement he expected, to get him to throw his support one way or the other. Rather, I suggested he contact the mayor or one of the commissioners, because I had nothing to do with who would run for the commission. He said he would get in touch with them, but he also took the occasion to express some feelings about my saying I had nothing to do with who would be candidates.

"Harlow," he said, "do you know what's wrong with you goo-goos?" (*Goo-goos* is a derisive term for good government advocates.)

I replied, "I can think of several things, but what do you have in mind?"

"The trouble with you is that you make the rest of us feel dirty."

I protested that we certainly had no intention of making anybody feel dirty. I said we simply had some ideals about America and wanted to do our bit to see those ideals fulfilled. We saw government as the servant of all the people; we felt that all the facts about government should be presented fully and honestly to the people; we thought government services and regulations should be administered impartially; and we thought that whatever the people decided they wanted government to do should be done as efficiently as possible.

I said I realized others saw government differently. I had no doubt about their sincerity. They honestly believe that in government the end justifies the means. The end is spoils and rewards for the victor, and whatever means it takes to attain the spoils is fair. To them government is all a game, with no rules except those the competitors make up as they go along. If it takes lying to the public, stealing votes, threats or actual physical or economic injury to individuals, twisting or ignoring the law, or administering it for the benefit of those in power, that is all part of the game. The important thing is winning, staying on top. If, after winning, the victor abuses or destroys the losers, that's too bad; that's part of the game too.

I doubt that my differentiation between the views of the "goo-goos" and the "to-the-victor-belongs-the-spoils" people helped the young attorney feel any less "dirty." He did file for a city commission seat. He was eliminated in the primary, then declared his support of the administration candidate in the runoff election.

Lessons on Installing New Forms of Government
C. Eugene Perkins

Although I had more than twenty years of management experience, most of it in the private sector, Winston-Salem was my first city-manager experience. The lessons I learned in Winston-Salem may help other first-time managers, and proponents of the council-manager plan.
• After adopting a new charter and form of government, those responsible tend to feel that their work has been done, that they can now direct their efforts and interests to other matters. They should realize that the adoption of the new charter is only the first step toward accomplishing their objective.
• The recruitment and support of competent elective officials who support the new form of government is important, not only for the first election, but on a continuing basis, particularly until the new government has had an opportunity to become fully effective.
• Those who have opposed the new form of government do not change

their viewpoint because of election results. Rather, they will often attempt to discredit both the legislative and the administrative officials and their programs. This is why we so often see a second election to abandon a new charter after two or three changes of aldermen or councilmen.
- The ward system of choosing legislative representatives makes it easier for a political machine to place its representative in office than when they are elected at-large.
- The election of a mayor by the electorate, rather than by his peers on the legislative body, is a concept supported by many as providing greater "political leadership," but it is also more likely to produce friction between the mayor and the city manager.
- When the first city manager carries out a program of reorganization and economies, he steps on many toes, and those adversely affected may become bitterly resentful. They may, in all sincerity, feel that mistakes are being made, and they may attempt to discredit the programs among their friends and acquaintances.
- Although in almost every community there is a power structure, the number of votes influenced by the structure may be minimal. Therefore, the voters in all walks of life and in all segments of the community must be made aware of the goals of the city government, their importance to all of the community, and the need for legislative representatives who will support those goals.
- And perhaps as a final cautionary word to first-time city managers, move *slowly*! Traditional reorganization activities common in the private sector cannot be accomplished with the same dispatch in the public sector. Timing is all-important, and the skills the manager uses in planning and promulgating his programs and economies and getting public acceptance may help determine his effectiveness and tenure.

Lessons from Old City Managers
James Joshua Mott

Paul Morton had been city manager at Alexandria, Virginia, at Lexington, Kentucky, and at Trenton, New Jersey. At Trenton he enforced the law of "no slot machines" and instructed the police to confiscate and destroy some $10,000 worth of the machines. The city attorney and the courts ruled against him, and he was held personally responsible. It was his stories and some newspaper clippings of his municipal experiences that led me to study for and become a manager ten years later.

My master's thesis in political science at the University of Kentucky in 1947 was a vindication of his record as a manager at Lexington. For this research, I interviewed many of his Lexington, Kentucky, friends and enemies. One person said, "Paul's fault was that he embarrassed his friends. He would get up in the middle of the night and catch firemen and other city employees asleep when they were supposed to be awake and on duty."

When to bide your time was the issue that George Bean discussed with new and prospective managers at the 1949 ICMA conference in Palm Beach, Florida.

After having been the manager for several cities, George went to a certain Michigan city. There he was shocked at the open red-light district in violation of city ordinances. He discussed the matter with his wife, saying he intended to move in with city forces and clean it up.

"No," said his wife. "Wait a while. Bide your time. Concentrate on the things you know best, George—parking meters, garbage collection, water, sewers, streets, budgets. I don't think you know anything about red-light districts. Besides, the district is owned by two of your present councilmen."

George Bean said he took his wife's advice and was pleased at the compliments he received for the progress he was making in the city affairs he knew most about. And then, at the next election, the two councilmen were defeated and George was able to clean up the red-light district.

I remember well another old city manager. In 1950 I asked a friend, Sherwood "Sherry" Reeder, city manager of Richmond, Virginia, for any last-minute advice. I was leaving the staff of the Richmond City Planning Commission to be town manager of Big Stone Gap, Virginia. Among several excellent suggestions was one piece of advice I wish I had better remembered and practiced: "Don't go overboard in promoting industry for your municipality. Don't be too prominent in beating that drum of the local chamber of commerce, despite the loud endorsement of some of your councilmen at city hall. People make big noise for new industry, for new business. It sounds good to voters. But they don't really want new competitors in the labor pool."

Always Remember!
Thomas F. Maxwell

I had six happy years as city manager of Columbia, South Carolina, and had difficulty deciding to leave for a more challenging, better-paying position in a larger city. As in my experience serving elsewhere, before and after Columbia, I was blessed with excellent and supportive councils and with citizens who were kind to me.

One interesting sidelight from my Columbia experience: People did not realize that the mayor was the official representative of the city for all ceremonial occasions, and they were not sure where the city manager stood in this regard. The result was that both of us, with our wives, were always invited to cut ribbons, welcome distinguished visitors, attend the governor's receptions and dinners, and be guests at civic club affairs. This was time consuming but very pleasant.

But for years I kept on my desk a reminder that not everyone in Columbia was happy with me. The reminder was an unsigned postcard. The writer gave no reason for writing. He or she simply said, "There are six trains, four planes, and fourteen buses which leave this city each day, and I will be happier when you take one of them."

He Who Fights and Runs Away
Richard H. Custer

When on the evening of 28 August 1952 Nicholas Wade, president of the Kenosha, Wisconsin, city council, telephoned me that the council had unanimously approved my appointment as city manager, I knew the job would present a challenging test of my abilities.

A heavily industrialized city of 54,000, it had a record of instability and, most recently, corruption in its local government. Although it was Wisconsin's pioneer council-manager city, having adopted the plan in 1924, it had hired and fired six managers since that time, alternating between outside professionals and local appointees.

I would be succeeding one of the latter, a former city clerk who had been promoted to the manager post and who had resigned following a grand-jury investigation that had resulted in the indictment of the council president and two councilmen for complicity in organized gambling operations in the city.

I was encouraged by indications that the new council, under "Nick" Wade's leadership, was sincerely interested in honest and professional city-government administration. However, subsequent events were to pose for me that dilemma so often faced by city managers—when to fight, and when to run away so as to be around to fight another day.

An omen of things to come occurred even before I started my new duties. On my arrival two days before I was to start work, I was met by Mr. Wade and two council colleagues who informed me that the union representing all city employees except police and firemen had voted the previous evening to go on strike the following day. The reason: dissatisfaction with a position-classification and salary plan just completed for the city by the state personnel department. (The city had no personnel officer or department of its own.)

A classification plan is a basic tool in local-government personnel administration. It groups positions with similar duties and responsibilities into position classes, and it prescribes the training and experience required for persons to be appointed to perform those duties and responsibilities. Its major importance to employees is that it is the basis for a salary plan in which pay levels and rates are set for the various position classes. Apparently the employees' strike vote resulted from a feeling that a number of the pay scales in the proposed new salary plan were inequitable.

With Mr. Wade's concurrence, I arranged to meet that evening with John Serpe, the union president, and some other union members whom I suggested he select. Serpe proved to be reasonable and intelligent, and at the meeting I obtained his agreement to defer any strike action for at least two weeks, during which time I promised to review the state study and to undertake negotiation of the union grievances with him.

On my first official day of duty, I met informally with the city council. I invited them to join me in the ensuing negotiations, but (as I had hoped) they declined, authorizing me to proceed in my own way.

Fortunately we were able to work out the differences, and the strike did not materialize. But this one problem occupied virtually my full attention in my first days on the job—and long days they were—to the detriment of many other things I should have been doing as a newly arrived city manager.

This experience helped me resolve to establish the position of personnel director as soon as feasible. There were other reasons as well. For one thing, the police and fire departments each also had a union, so it was important that grievances and salary negotiations with the three union groups be handled professionally. Furthermore, the existing practices for recruiting and giving competitive examinations to new employees were crude; there were virtually no organized training programs for any city employees, and the payroll system was decentralized and lacked adequate controls for the prevention of fraud or abuse. All these factors reinforced my belief in the need for a full-time personnel officer.

Because of other priorities, I did not move toward this goal for a couple of years. In 1955 I included it as one of my major budget recommendations. The council concurred and appropriated funds to establish the position. However, council members who had been elected with strong organized labor support were clearly reluctant to have me recruit for the position from outside the city.

While assuring the council that any apparently qualified local applicant would remain under consideration up to the point of final selection, yet stressing the professional nature of the position and the importance of a comprehensive, modern personnel program, I proceeded with a nation-wide recruitment effort.

The technique I used to determine the final selection was a group interview. All finalists—I believe there were nine, including union president Serpe and three other local applicants—were brought in as a group and asked to discuss in their own way, without guidance or intervention from the three-member panel of examiners, a set of prepared questions given to them as they entered the room. This procedure enabled the examiners and me to observe and evaluate all nine applicants simultaneously in a three-hour period, rather than depending on nine separate interviews of perhaps three-quarters of an hour each.

At the conclusion of this process, the three raters and I were unanimous that one applicant stood out clearly as superior to the others in the group. Our choice was Robert D. Krause, then personnel director of Oak Ridge, Tennessee. I hired him. Subsequently, Serpe graciously told me privately that he believed I made the right choice. Bob Krause's later career accomplishments, including presidency of the International Personnel Management Association, are well known to government personnel professionals.

One reason I moved slowly on the matter of the personnel director was that our property-revaluation project had consumed my time. Records indicated that there never had been a systematic city-wide revaluation of property for property-tax purposes. Increasing complaints from business and industrial leaders about inequitable assessments led me to conduct a study that convinced me of the need for such a revaluation, both to avoid threatened lawsuits and to eliminate obvious inequities among residential, commercial, and industrial properties. Accordingly, later in 1953 I recommended to the council that a professional firm be hired to perform a general revaluation. Basing its decision on our presentation of the facts, the council agreed. After a competitive process, the firm of E. T. Wilkins & Associates was engaged for the project, with their work to be completed in time for use in preparing the city's budget for calendar 1955.

Revaluation of property and creation of a personnel department may seem unconnected, but subsequent events proved there can be a connection. As the revaluation neared completion, several local leaders began to express publicly their concern about the wisdom, if not the equity, of the entire revaluation program. Through their union-supported newspaper, *The Kenosha Labor,* they speculated that the result of the program would be increased residential property assessments and decreased commercial and industrial property assessments. They hired a respected University of Wisconsin economics professor to analyze the revaluation process. He confirmed the probable accuracy of their speculation but in his public report refrained from criticizing the equity of the new values being established. Nevertheless, local union organizations stated that they might take legal action to prevent the revaluation from taking effect.

The date the city council was to adopt a budget based on the new valuations happened to coincide with the dates of my previously scheduled attendance at the annual ICMA conference in St. Petersburg, Florida, and a subsequent short vacation. Consequently, I was not at the meeting when the council, by majority vote, approved the budget.

Word reached me that the council meeting had been crowded and that the budget was adopted amidst shouts from the audience to "fire the city manager" and "get a mayor." A fellow city manager and conference attendee, Carleton Sharpe, then city manager of Hartford, Connecticut, asked me if I planned to leave the conference and return to Kenosha to defend myself. I responded that I believed the revaluation project had been well conceived and competently conducted, that in adopting the new budget, apparently a majority of the council agreed with me, so I saw no necessity to return. I thereupon dove into the pool for a refreshing swim.

Perhaps this symbolized my decision not to enter a fight at that point, so as to be around to fight another day. Eventually the revaluation controversy diminished, the program was implemented without lawsuits, and only a few taxpayers appealed their new assessments. But seeds of dissension had been sown. They bore fruit in the April 1956 city-council election.

Three incumbents who generally had supported me were up for reelection. Opposing them were three representatives of organized labor—a state assemblyman, an active union member who worked in the American Motors Corporation plant, and a person who had served on the council before my appointment and was now an outspoken critic of the revaluation and most other aspects of my administration.

The three labor representatives were elected. With .the incumbent council president, a union official at Simmons Manufacturing Company, they constituted for the first time in my tenure a clearly labor-oriented majority on the council. I attended the first meeting of the new council prepared for anything, including a request for my resignation.

What did happen was that the assemblyman/councilman, who had stressed government economy in his campaign, introduced a resolution calling for the immediate dissolution of the personnel department along with a freeze on all expenditures for attendance of city officials at state and national conferences. The other two new council members supported him, but the council president and three incumbents voted to defer action on the resolution. I thought to myself, "A reprieve; but I see another decision coming up—whether to fight or run away."

In the following weeks Bob Krause and I discussed the situation, concluding that we should "play it by ear" while continuing to perform our jobs as professionally as possible. It became increasingly clear, however, that the deferment of action on the personnel department was only temporary. The majority of the council was committed to accomplishing their purpose by eliminating the department's appropriation in the next budget.

Accordingly Bob submitted his resignation to take a position with the Milwaukee city government.

Should I have fought harder to prevent this from happening—resigned, if necessary? I've often wondered, and still do.

The Way It Was, and Is
Richard G. Simmons

Often I am asked how I can stand the pressures and the unusual and unexpected events that happen in a city government. I always attribute my ability to "roll with the punches" to my basic training on my early jobs.

When I first started in city government, in the early fifties, we had no government in the sunshine, no open records, and no federally mandated requirements for advertising. But we really had community participation. This was before television, and in the small towns there was little in the way of entertainment. The city-commission meetings were covered live by the local radio station because it was the most exciting thing happening in the area at that particular time. In addition, the chambers were always full because it was always better to see it play-by-play than to hear a broadcast.

The participants in the early days often divided themselves into very specific, very active groups. For instance, in the first city where I worked as an assistant, the manager was most progressive and was serving as manager under a reform council in a city not used to change. The manager had made many necessary changes in department heads, had reappraised all the property for tax purposes, and in general had set about putting the house in order. He had done this in the scant period of less than a year. Citizens had chosen sides because he was a controversial manager. One day when I came to work, he showed me a letter he had received the day before. The letter simply stated that he must leave town by the end of the month or something drastic would happen. There was no signature, but across the bottom was a drawing of a fiery cross, the obvious implication being that the letter had been sent by the Ku Klux Klan.

This type of response was not typical, and it took a manager with a strong constitution to bear up under it. The manager that I worked under at that time made no public comment on the letter, but on the evening of the day he was supposed to leave, he opened the city hall, turned on the lights, and stayed there alone until midnight to show that he had no fear. Not every manager was of this type. I know of one manager from the North who came to a Florida community in the early fifties when Northerners were called Yankees. After receiving a similar letter and having decided that that was not the type of citizen participation he wanted, he left in the middle of the night about a week after he arrived. The following day the commission found a note that he was no longer interested in working for their town.

This type of citizen participation has always led me to expect the unexpected. In recent years, what have seemed like problems to new managers have often seemed fairly routine to me.

Today Florida is a progressive state, and citizens are generally tolerant of all groups. We have government in the sunshine and open-records laws, so that the media can cover every event and search every record to assure the public of what is going on in government. The name of the game is public and neighborhood participation. To meet the federal program requirements for public meetings, we have to appoint advisory groups, post meeting notices on the door of each neighborhood residence, and advertise in newspapers of general circulation.

Yet we are in a period of complacency. We have to strive to get people to participate in government. Recently, to achieve the required participation in hearings on a state-mandated master plan, we notified every resident of the city of the hearing by personal letter. We asked such leading questions as, "If you live at the end of a jet runway, does the noise bother you?"—this to get people to the hearing even though we could do little about jet noise.

Tenure Does Count:
My Thirteen-Year Climb over Molehills
Bert W. Johnson

In the 1980s it is almost certain that "survival" will be the name of the game for the city-manager profession. Inflation hits local government with a greater impact than society as a whole. Citizens are alienated as they adjust to the erosion of their standards of living, and the energy/gasoline crisis brings new tensions. City managers are attractive scapegoats, despite the fact that they are in a position to mitigate citizen malaise. In the years ahead, my thirteen-year tenure (1962–76) in Arlington, Virginia, may be looked upon as most unusual. My experience, with four changes in majority persuasions, should be emulated in other localities. I will provide a singular example of progress requiring persistence over a long time.

A curtailed service in my first manager post, Lebanon, Missouri (1948–50), cost their citizens my crusade for honesty and competence. The employment (no recruitment) of a series of nondescript managers saw the abandonment of good accounting practices, good personnel practices, and finally the abandonment of council-manager local government.

In Boulder, Colorado (1950–53), my departure cost this beautiful city a continuation of the standards of excellence that would have more adequately prepared Boulder for its inevitable growth pressures. The return to "quiet government" after Bert Johnson was not in Boulder's best interests.

In Evanston, Illinois, the lack of continuing tenure for Bert Johnson, albeit in my interest, was not as significant because it was a nine-year tenure (1953–62) and because of the magnificent performance of my successor, Wayne F. Anderson. However, I believe the police-fire cooperative plan would have survived had I continued as city manager.

Arlington, Virginia, is located along the Potomac River overlooking Washington, D.C. I was recruited without application as its fourth manager in 1962, only three having served before me since council-manager was voted in 1932. My Arlington service means an average tenure of eleven years in forty-four years. Progress in Arlington is ample demonstration that manager tenure does count.

Stated another way, Arlington's prestige emanates from tenured accomplishments made possible by citizen support for effectiveness in their local government and for the managers selected to head their local administration. Arlington's 174,000 citizens are highly educated, have a near record high per-capita income, and bring talent from throughout the nation. Critical to the need for manager tenure is the fact that Arlington citizens are highly mobile, some one-third of its residents moving every year. Half of its citizens are employed within Arlington, most of the remainder working in our nation's capital. Civilian and military jobs in Arlington number 130,000—75 percent of the residents. All these factors argue for continuity of local governance.

By court ruling no cities or towns may be incorporated in Arlington County. In state and federal highway designations, Arlington is treated as a city. Thus, as county manager I was, in fact, a city manager, and the county board is as a city council would be. Five members are elected on an at-large basis with elections held each year (every fourth year two are elected) for four-year terms. This highly volatile political situation is an argument for a tenured manager. Arlington has seven postal zip codes. Most elections see the election of candidates from one zip code, 22207. This too has been unsuccessfully challenged in the courts by those appealing for a return to the ward system for choosing members. Manager tenure assures a balanced and professional delivery of services.

In my first public appearance in Arlington, before a southside civic association in 1963, I tried to allay the fears that there was a northside bias

(22207 is northside) by suggesting that we should "try on for size" the development of a southside complex. Ears pricked up: the new manager was making a proposal. (I had learned that a major fire station was located in the path of a street improvement. A branch library was horribly inadequate. Similarly, a recreation/community center had been promised but not built because no agreement could be reached as to location.) I did not second-guess civic needs and aspirations. My solution was that all these new and replacement facilities be located in one general site. I suggested that a campus-type arrangement could be more than a group of functional units joined together. The center would be more than a sum of their parts, so as to be a focal point that would rekindle neighborhood pride.

My audience did not wait for me to finish my remarks. Hands were raised, and I heard outrage: "It's immoral to locate librarians and firemen so close together." "The noise of recreation and the quiet of a library won't mix." "That's a dumb idea and I will certainly fight all the way." "We'll go to court. It's another stab in the back for this area." "It will never be accepted." I quickly assumed that, in prestigious Arlington, my honeymoon was to be a short one.

As I completed my Arlington service, thirteen years later, the complex I had proposed on my arrival was ready for bids. Two years later I was the dedication speaker for the completed project. A visitor center and an air-pollution monitoring unit were added to make five facilities at one location. In my brief talk I reminded the large numbers of enthusiastic citizens that it was the late and beloved senator from Michigan, Phil Hart, who said that progress in the public sector is the capacity to climb molehills.

Because I had a thirteen-year tenure I was able to persist, to climb ever-present and changing molehills: the continuing citizen opposition and lawsuits that thwarted decisions to locate replacements elsewhere; a bond-issue referendum; extended political debate—all brought us back to the central-location idea. We climbed the molehills that brought agreement and success. "We did it ourselves!"

The Joys of Management
Dale F. Helsel

A story I tell about something that supposedly happened to me when I was a city manager of Painesville, Ohio, seldom fails to get a smile from other city managers. Seated next to me at a bar in nearby Cleveland was the archetypal hippie. He asked me where I was from. I replied, "I'm from Painesville." After a pause, he said, "Like, man, ain't we all?"

City managers like to describe their problems and talk about the pains of managing an urban community: the irresponsible press, city councils that don't know the difference between policy and administration, bureaucratic incompetence, the pressures of time. The litany is heard from managers of cities of all sizes and from all parts of the country. It is enough to discourage anyone from becoming a manager.

There is, however, satisfaction and joy.

Savoring the victory over paperwork, red tape, and bureaucratic roadblocks brings a thrill to the manager watching the first ball game at the new playfield. The justification of a host of activities in the budget office, tax-collecting section, civil-service board, and purchasing operations can be found when a manager sees the firefighters saving a building. There's a good feeling that comes from organizing and developing a program that performs what it was designed to do.

There is a deeper satisfaction found in the ancient Greek definition of happiness: exercising talent, along lines of excellence, in doing good. Every day city managers have opportunities to exercise their talents. Using the mind as an instrument of precision, managers attempt to understand problems, define solutions, and choose alternatives. Gifts of speech, writing, and persuasion are used along with talents of feeling, understanding, and empathizing with other people.

The complexity of the problems managers deal with requires excellence in meeting those problems. Managers have opportunities to improve through activities in our professional association, periodicals, university courses, and library research. For example, managers can receive assistance in learning how to write memos (which, in addition to being grammatically correct, must be written so the recipient understands the thoughts expressed). Reports, memos, letters, and conversations need to be understood and related to the history and purpose of the organization. Managers who need to improve their skills in this area have many sources for learning how to do so.

Many city managers think their job is to deal only with facts, figures, and scientific principles. They are uncomfortable with terms such as *good, love, duty, right,* and *morality,* and they think they can leave these terms to others. But when they do, they miss a major part of their responsibility.

Through religious teachings such as, "Love thy neighbor," "Feed the hungry," "Visit the widows and orphans in their affliction," civilization helps define the term *good.* Social and ethical philosophers such as Kant, Rousseau, and Hume wrote about our joining together to confer benefits on one another. There is no dearth of teachings that define *good* and *love* in terms of conferring benefits on others.

How, then, does the city respond to these moral and social admonitions? It does so both in the range of its duties (from police services to human-resource activities) and in the methods used in fulfilling those duties.

So city managers have many satisfactions. They have the opportunity to use a wide variety of their talents. Doing the city's business gives managers chances to confer benefits upon others. Accepting the breadth and depth of his responsibilities can bring happiness and joy to a city manager.

A Career I Wouldn't Change for Anything
Elaine W. Roberts

I am the fourth town manager of Highland Beach, Florida, and the town's second woman manager. My predecessor, Eileen Mognet, and I don't look alike, but our rapport with the public was similar. Consequently, I have never encountered resistance because I am a woman.

I remember asking Eileen if I would last as long as she did (about three and a half years). She said, "Sure. Longer." Now that I'm completing my eleventh year as a town employee, most of the time as town administrator or town manager, it seems I have been here forever. On the other hand, the time has whizzed by as I have gone from being the only town employee through the positions of inspector, town-hall manager, town clerk, town administrator, and town treasurer, to town manager.

I started at age forty. At first things were strange and new and confusing. I was handling the contract post office, the bookkeeping, the collecting and payment of bills, the issuing of permits and licenses, and the formulating of a budget. Quite early I became familiar with and knowledgeable about the town charter and code of ordinances. Later, when it was my responsibility to administer the charter and the ordinances, it seemed I had done it all before.

Highland Beach has more than twenty times as many residents today as it had when I started working for the town, and it still attracts wonderful residents and a super staff. And I have become so committed to local government and all the aspects of being close and therefore responsive to the people that the excitement and interest of this job permeate almost every waking minute. It is part of my working life, my social life, my play life, and my leisure life.

At professional conferences I have encountered some interesting remarks, such as, "What would a woman know about the differences between water-storage tanks?" "How come you know what a hydropillar is?" "How can a woman talk to garbage men?" and "How do the men feel about a woman boss?" (I don't boss; I'm part of the team.)

Construction contractors have been a rather constant source of irritation. I remember one incident, when a developer sent a bulldozer to clear the dune across from the town hall. I went outside and told the driver that he could not clear any vegetation off the dune. He said, "Lady, you better get out of my way," and I told him he would have to mow me down because I wasn't moving. For about three hours I succeeded in holding him at bay—until my assistant contacted the developer, who then ordered the driver to return to his office.

I have been privileged to serve as president of the Palm Beach County City Managers Association for two years, as a member of the executive boards of the American Society for Public Administration and of the County Municipal League, and as a member of the conference committee for the 1976 annual conference of the ICMA. This is a career I wouldn't change for anything.

Editor's Commentary

The substance and range of the preceding first-hand accounts of city manager experiences prompt me to comment on some aspects of local government that do not often get the attention they must have if citizens are to be knowledgeable and effective. These aspects are: the relative importance of local government, the environment peculiar to local government, the internal impediments to better local government in America, and priorities for citizen action.

The Importance of
Local Government

Like every other member of society, each of us lives inescapably under a social organization—a system of government—that largely shapes our lives and our destiny. The particular system to which we are subject is federal in design and consists of three levels: national, state, and local (counties, cities, villages, towns and townships, schools, and other special districts).

It is safe to say that of the three levels, the local governments get the least media attention and public recognition and respect. Yet collectively our eighty thousand local units are on some counts the most important of our governments. First, they are the largest of our three governmental employers, with an aggregate payroll of 9.3 million people, compared with

2.8 million federal civilian employees and 3.5 million state government employees (1977 data). Second, in recent years their growth has been among the fastest in the nation. (Between 1967 and 1977, state and local government employment grew 49.5 percent and 41.8 percent respectively, while private, nonagricultural employment rose only 23 percent and federal civilian employment *decreased* 4.8 percent). Third, local governments touch directly, and often intimately and critically, almost every facet of our lives every hour of every day.

For example, the municipal governments considered in this book provide nearly a hundred distinct public services. With few exceptions city government is the only institution that provides us round-the-clock police protection and fire-combat service, adequate and pure water, convenient waste disposal, surfaced streets and walkways, traffic-control devices, safely constructed buildings, and maintenance of property values by enforcement of zoning regulations—to mention only a few readily apparent services. Neither the federal government, the state government, nor private enterprise provides these essentials of stable, predictable, civilized life.

With a moment's thought, then, almost anyone can apply this ultimate test of the comparative importance of local government to the everyday life of his family and himself. Think of the federal and state government activities regularly performed in your community. Now add the activities of the largest single private enterprise. Picture all these activities suddenly brought to a halt. What would be the effect? Undoubtedly the community would suffer a period of serious inconvenience and economic readjustment. Some federal and state services would be missed. There would be unemployment. Families would move elsewhere. Some businesses might close. But there still would be an orderly, recognizable community.

Now picture all municipal government activities brought to a complete halt. No police protection of life and property. No firemen to respond to alarms. No ambulance to transport the injured or desperately ill. No water in the pipes. No one to unstop the plugged sewer lines or remove garbage and trash. No one to get the traffic signals working, to turn on the street lights, to plow the snow-clogged streets. Again, only the most obvious services. But without them, in hours there would be looting, vandalism, and disorder; in days, we no longer would have a viable community.

This is hypothetical, of course. Even our smallest communities are complex, mutually dependent entities. There are important interrelationships among the three levels of government. Also local governments depend on private business to provide not only tax revenues but also supplies and services. And business and individual citizens need local government for protection and many conveniences. But if it were possible to separate and rank according to basic human needs all the interdependent elements of a modern community, it is my opinion that local government would prove to be society's single most important institution for our health, safety, and mobility and for the economic and physical protection of our property.

The Environment Peculiar to Local Government

Often men and women with successful records in private or semipublic organizations—who recognize the fundamental importance of local government and who, as citizens, strive to improve it—end up surprised, frustrated, and disappointed. Often they do so because they are unfamiliar with the environmental factors peculiar to local government.

Although there are many similarities between local government and other social institutions, there are also dissimilarities that challenge the abilities of the most able people from the nongovernmental sector. I refer to such external factors as diversity of views within a democratic society, citizen attitudes, the media, and law.

Democratic Tugs and Pulls

Despite our considerable homogeneity as a nation, local-government officials encounter a wide range of sharply differing opinions about the kind of community "the people" want. Besides having to deal with the usual divisions along economic, educational, social, ethnic, racial, and geographic lines, city councils and administrators must deal with alignments along moral and philosophical lines.

At one end of the moral spectrum may be a substantial and influential part of the population that favors an "open town"—unlimited, protected (or at least unmolested) gambling, prostitution, drug and liquor traffic, and other vices. At the other end of the spectrum may be a vocal group that demands absolute enforcement of all state laws and local ordinances respecting moral and other issues. Between will be the majority of citizens, who take no stand on either side until they are directly affected by some local government act or omission.

Philosophical alignments reflect preferences for Jacksonian democracy and the related spoils system, for a political-boss arrangement, or for a reform government. To the Jacksonian democrats politics is essentially a small-scale war, the only rules being that whatever succeeds is right and to the victor belong the spoils—control of government policies and procedures and the privilege of awarding government jobs, contracts, and other perquisites of public office exclusively to the faithful followers and supporters of the winning candidate or party.

As to the boss system, elsewhere in this volume City Manager Thomas Maxwell provides a brief first-hand sketch of the Kansas City operation under Boss Tom Pendergast. Maxwell might have added to his description the making of "eligible voter" lists from cemetery gravestones, boss-owned monopolies such as concrete and construction companies, and gangsterlike harassment and reprisals against businesses and individuals who failed to cooperate with the boss-run machine.

Reform government advocates and supporters—disparagingly called "goo-goos" (good-government types) by their detractors—prefer open, efficient government administered with equal justice under law by officers and employees who have been selected on the basis of merit and demonstrated competence.

Because most citizens have multiple interests and motivations, neither the lines that distinguish these several groups nor the individual motivations are ever crystal clear. Nor are they permanent. Individuals shift from one alignment to another according to the issue under consideration. (In so doing, they add credence to Rufus Miles' Law: "Where you stand depends on where you sit.") At one time they may be altruistic, sincere, and straightforward; at another, self-serving, fraudulent, and deceitful. The differing views and motivations respecting local government create individual and group tensions, conflicts, and inconsistencies that local-government policy-makers and managers must deal with continually. These are the struggles that make disillusioned cynics of dedicated citizens.

Citizen Attitudes Toward Local Government

During my years as a local-government insider and as a consultant to outside groups officially chartered to survey local governments, I have used both long and short questionnaires, interviews, and more than one participative-discussion session to learn what citizens know and think about local governments and services and what the same citizens think should be done to improve both. The data have been tabulated, evaluated, analyzed, summarized, put in published reports, and used as background to inform state and local officials, graduate students, civic clubs, and individual interested citizens.

Leaving improvement suggestions for later consideration, the list below summarizes the knowledge and views of hundreds of citizens. I acknowledge that the data have been gathered from so many localities and under such varied circumstances that there is a risk in drawing generalizations from them. While there are many exceptions to the following statements, there are patterns enough in the data to suggest that this composite observation may be useful to anyone seeking a better understanding of the environment in which local-government officials must function.

1. Many if not most citizens are ignorant of, or grossly misinformed about, the number of local governments they are paying for, the names and responsibilities of local officials, the structure, functions, powers, jurisdictional areas, approximate number of employees, and approximate expenditures of their local governments.

2. Except for members of a few organizations, such as the League of Women Voters, and people whose professional work requires them to know about local government, their level of information seems about the same regardless of differences in social and economic characteristics.

3. When asked what services should be reduced or discontinued, they almost never suggest reducing or dropping any service. (This citizen attitude was replicated during the tax-limitation rebellion that swept the country following California's Jarvis-Gann Proposition 13. In several surveys voters who favored Proposition 13-type voter-initiated legislation indicated they did not want fewer or lower-quality local-government services, nor were they dissatisfied with the governmental system—nor sometimes even with the people in office [who were promptly reelected]. They were rebelling against the incompetent, inefficient, wasteful, and corrupt way the system was being run.)

4. Citizens feel that local government is so far behind the times in organization, management practices, and operating technology that it is incapable of solving the problems confronting it.

5. Citizens view the larger individual governments, and the local-government system as a whole, as so irrationally arranged that these governments are incomprehensible and therefore frustrating to citizens.

6. They note that local officials are unprogressive. That is, the officials fail to look ahead and provide the leadership needed for long-range solutions to problems.

7. Also, they note that officials do not treat their employment as a public trust by keeping the public informed and being accountable for their performance and failures. Rather, many officials are self-serving.

8. As parents, many citizens would be embarrassed if a son or daughter chose to work at city hall. That is only for people who want a "soft" job.

9. They consider all payments to the local governments to be involuntary "taxes" whether they are fees for a special service or payments for general government. Although in their minds payments for privately supplied goods and services immediately become the property of the private company, to do with as it wishes, payments for public goods and services remain the citizen's property—"my" taxes.

10. Finally, citizens are convinced that local governments cost more than they need to, and that the cost burdens are inequitably distributed.

Occasionally, for help in thinking out problems and for public speaking purposes, I have looked for a short phrase that accurately summarizes the average American's attitude toward his local government. The best I have come up with is an internally contradictory two-word phrase that merges (1) the citizens' disrespect for government and the men and women who run it (people who "feed at the public trough" but "have never met a payroll") with (2) the citizens' fear of a growing government that no longer serves but has become their master with power to destroy them. Of course, the phrase does not fit all situations, but it comes pretty close to the mark. I think the general American attitude toward local government is one of *contemptuous awe.*

The Media and Local Government

Several of the foregoing city-manager episodes illustrate situations in which the media—newspapers, radio, and television—had a significant impact on the manager's performance. Probably many managers could describe how months of hard work have been nullified by a single erroneous, ill-timed, or wrongly emphasized story. Similarly, most could detail the problems of getting a "good press" on important city projects, of the continuing battle with the media about day-to-day reporting of city-hall activities, or feuds (not of their making) with news editors, and even of deliberate campaigns of vilification against them professionally and personally.

Because much well-written material is available on the whole range of local-government–media relations, I'll comment on only one aspect that seems not often to have been stressed—the other side of the story and the need for local officials to look beyond their own purposes to the media's environment and problems.

Unlike local government, the media are private, often highly competitive, businesses. Unless they produce what their readers, listeners, or viewers want, they fail. Therefore, unless the local government gives the media what will help them survive, the government cannot expect prime space and time.

Whether the media people are right or wrong, apparently they have concluded that what gets their patrons' attention is the unusual, the sensational, the bizarre—that what holds their attention is conflict. These qualities are generally the opposite of what good public managers seek to achieve, namely order, predictability, and harmony. (But there also may be differences among public officials as to what they want from the media. Unless the story is complete and correct in every detail, the professional manager may prefer that it not be released; the politically sensitive elected official, however, may subscribe to the adage, "I don't care what you say about me, just so you say something.")

Then there is the continuing debate about what really is news. Is it the unusual, the spectacular, the odd, or is it the more typical, representative, significant, and long-lasting? Two incidents suggest where some professional newsmen stand on this issue. As a university student, I was a part-time radio newscaster. One day while I was readying the material coming over the wire, a journalism professor walked in on me. "What's the news today?" he asked. I replied, "There isn't any news today." He virtually shouted at me, "Don't say that! If there were no news, that would be the biggest news in history!" More recently, I heard the noted television commentator Walter Cronkite answer a criticism that the media too often play up what does not give a true picture of America. He responded, "After all, we don't write about the cat that *isn't* in the tree."

Some of the media's operating problems suggest the need for local officials to be extra accommodating. Consider the pressure of deadlines: While it is true that local officials have deadlines, they are often of their own setting and are not matters of life or death. By contrast, the media have daily, hourly, sometimes even minute-by-minute deadlines. Almost no one is interested in yesterday's news. The media must get the news when it is fresh, or the news is dead and useless. Local government does well to keep this in mind.

Also, except in the largest jurisdictions, city hall is only one of several organizations on a reporter's beat. The reporters are often young, inexperienced, and limited in knowledge; yet they must gather newsworthy material on complex subjects from several places and translate it into unmistakable English that any twelve-year-old can understand, and do all this in time to meet an absolute deadline. Then someone else, who has not been near the reported situation, edits the story and writes the headline. Is it any wonder that occasionally a story differs from what a well-informed official would have written or said, lacks an important fact, includes a mistake, or carries a headline that doesn't fit?

Always there is the fundamental and jealously guarded matter of freedom of the press. Local-government officials need to remember that this hard-earned right was wrested, not from other private citizens, but from government. Our history of wrongdoing in local, state, and national government plus the ever-present inclination of some officials at all levels to release only favorable news about governmental affairs, to manage and manipulate other information, and to exercise censorship when possible, makes reporters justifiably suspicious. Consequently, they want to dig out their own information, draw their own conclusions, and write up both the way they see them. At times there may be abuse of this right. A certain amount of abuse is tolerable. Consider the alternative: government licensing and censoring of news.

The media are indispensable to knowledgeable citizenship and effective local government; yet the media and local government are often at swords' points. When they are, the public loses. Where necessary, it behooves local officials to initiate efforts with the media to identify mutual objectives and to cooperate toward their achievement. Exchange of information about the obstacles each faces can be a start toward achieving that cooperation.

Legal Constraints

A final external frustration for those who want to improve local government can be the legal dos and don'ts—mostly don'ts—that surround local
governments. People accustomed to managing with relative freedom find
this especially exasperating. Their dependence upon attorneys and courts
to let them know what they may do gives them the impression that the
judicial branch, not the legislative or the executive branch, is running
local government.

Long known as creatures of the state, local governments have only the
powers given them by the legislature—except in those states where the
state constitution grants them home rule. But even then the courts have
largely applied the so-called Dillon's Rule, which essentially denies local
units implied powers, leaving them with only the powers explicitly spelled
out in official action by higher authority.

Where there is home rule, the local people may by charter provisions
determine the structure and detailed procedures of the local government
and may place selected restrictions on it. But where the local charter has
granted a power, the authority may be overridden by the state if it chooses
to exercise the power for its own purposes.

Not only has the state the power of legal prohibition, but it has the
power to require certain acts by local governments. This has proved especially troublesome to local governments in states that have required them
to do or grant certain things but have not allowed the local unit the
authority to raise the funds for that purpose.

In recent years federal laws and regulations have applied increasingly
to local governments, sometimes in the form of absolute requirements or
prohibitions, at other times as a condition for receiving a federal grant.

Internal Impediments to
Better Local Government in America

If local government were only half as important to our social and economic well-being as I have stated, we still could expect it to attract men
and women who wish to make a major contribution to others, or who
thrill to the challenge of change, improvement, influence, and impact.
Why, then, is it difficult to get people who have succeeded in nongovernmental affairs to run for local-government elective office or seek
local-government management posts? Why is it so difficult to get citizens
to give more attention and time to local-government problems? Both
groups may be deterred by the external factors just described and by the

ingrained inefficiency and wrongdoing that will be discussed later. More directly and specifically, however, potential candidates for local public office may be discouraged both by the internal selection process and by the shortage of basic management tools.

The Selection Process

By definition *elective office* means an office that is filled by an individual who has been selected by the voters. This raises the question, Where do (or can) we get candidates from among whom voters can choose? If it is a partisan election, candidates are nominated by the political parties in accord with party procedure or legal requirements; otherwise, candidates get on a ballot by means of a petition circulated by a small group or by the candidate himself. In any case, because no person can be forced to accept a nomination, every candidate is either partially or totally self-nominated.

This is the first impediment to getting people of demonstrated ability to run for local-government office. Most who have achieved success outside of politics have done so through performance and results, not talk. They know from experience how difficult it is to solve complex problems, to make changes, to get results. This gives them a certain humility that stands in the way of their putting themselves forward as the one who can best solve all the community's problems. Also, having had to "put their money where their mouth is," they are reluctant to make promises that they are not reasonably sure they can fulfill.

They may manage to get over that hurdle by accepting their own judgment and others' that they really can solve some of the problems, that apparently they are the best-qualified potential candidate. The next hurdle is the campaign itself. Having developed the habit of dealing with facts and giving serious attention to problem analysis, they may have some difficulty adjusting to the circus atmosphere of political conventions, to the publicity campaigns, and to the fussing over minor, emotion-laden problems at the expense of basic and continuing issues.

Then there is the inevitable matter of cost, time, and work. Unless the candidate has an independent income or can win at little or no cost, he will have to obtain funds from other individuals or organizations. Further, the electorate is not congregated in one place at a single time. To reach the voters, the candidate must cover a lot of territory and do so at any time of day or night convenient to his potential listeners. Finally, because campaigns are won not by money alone, and because the candidate can be only one place at a time, his success will require the work of many people. Thus, the candidate accumulates obligations to those who helped him with money, work, and other kinds of support. This may lessen his ability to do what he thinks is best for the community. If his supporters are altruistic, they will think of their contribution as no more than a fair part of the burden of the cause they share. On the other hand, the candidate cannot know at what time any supporter to whom he is indebted will call in his IOUs by demanding some special, favored consideration or treatment.

Potential candidates for *appointed* local government positions are not subject to the problems just described. But they do face selection impediments, and those impediments vary, depending on whether the position is under a classified civil-service or merit system or is a high-level or confidential position that is unclassified or exempt from merit-system requirements.

If a successful nongovernment person is interested in a civil-service position, the chances of his having permanent employment—once he completes a probationary period—are substantial. But there are two major impediments before he reaches that relatively secure status: lack of confidentiality, and uncertainty and delay of appointment.

Civil-service and merit-system positions are publicly advertised. Customarily, all candidates must furnish a list of references. Moreover, they may be required to appear for a written or oral examination. Consequently, it is almost impossible to keep confidential the candidate's expressed interest in possible appointment. Any candidate who presently holds a good position and likes it would hesitate to risk losing the position, or having his employer lose interest in his further progress, by having it become known that he would probably accept the local-government job if it were offered.

Anyone who meets the advertised minimum requirements is eligible to compete. But because there may be dozens of candidates for a few openings, no candidate knows where he stands. His name goes on a register. It is referred to agencies with vacancies of the kind he is qualified to fill. They may or may not consider him for the appointment. It may be months before his name is reached on the register, and even longer before he gets an inquiry or an offer. In fact, the register may expire before he is reached, and he may have to start the process all over. Obviously, the attractions of the public job must far exceed those of the job the candidate now holds; otherwise, he will not undergo the risks, the delays, and the uncertainties. Almost no one but those with everything to gain and little to lose will submit to this process.

Appointments to unclassified jobs may be made promptly, but they are usually political appointments that last only as long as the incumbent is able to retain favor with the electorate. When he goes out, so do all his unclassified appointees. In the meantime, the appointee who accepted the job because of its seeming potential for making a major professional contribution may have found it necessary to do an increasing number of political chores to keep his superior, and himself, in office.

The Shortage of Management Tools
(An Illustrative Dialogue)

Once over the selection hurdle, the new official, elected or appointed, will likely face one or more of the following situations: rising expectations (demands) from residents for more or better service and reduced taxes, continuing racial and ethnic conflicts, increasing crime and other disorders, deteriorating physical plant, extensive petty and sometimes major corruption, a chronic money shortage, and paralyzing threats or actual litigation intended to block every local-government move to deal with its problems.

Logically, the new official will inquire of older hands–perhaps a long-time city clerk, for example–where he can find the tools with which to start doing his part to attack these situations.

The following is an imaginary dialogue that might well take place between two new officials (a new mayor and his recently appointed chief administrative officer) and a frank, knowledgeable, long-service city clerk.

Mayor. I think you know that my assistant, here, and I have never worked for a city before. I own and run some small businesses–a manufacturing plant just outside of town, a dry-cleaning business, and (my main business) the Cadillac agency I have built up during the last twenty-five years. My assistant was vice-president of Commercial Bank until I persuaded him to leave the bank and come to work for me here at the city. I thought this would be good because I hear the city has been having some financial problems. We both appreciate your taking time to help us get oriented in our new jobs.

Clerk. Glad to do it, Mayor. Congratulations to both of you. I might say that I'm in my nineteenth year on this job. I've served with six mayors. You're the seventh. Only a couple of others have done what you're doing. Usually, they start right out, without much orientation. Anyway, I'll be glad to answer any question I can.

Mayor. Good. Let me start off by asking what the objectives of the organization are. Are they written out or just understood? What are our aims? What are we trying to do?

CAO. And what are some of the major long-range plans to get where we want to go?

Clerk. Objectives? Well, Mayor, the only objective that means anything to you and the council members will be to get successfully past the next election. Oh, it'll be nice if you can get some of the things done that you'd like to, but those two years–less than that, now–will go pretty fast. As I understand, a president of the United States once said, "It's great to be a statesman, but you have to get elected first."

And long-range planning? We don't do much of that. Not much use planning past the next election, because probably we will have a new

majority on the council, maybe a new mayor. They usually come in with
their own ideas and are determined not to follow old policies. After all, in
their campaigns they told the voters the people in office were either
incompetent or crooked, so they can hardly continue what the other
bunch started.

Mayor. Well, if we don't have objectives and plans, at least we can look
at the record. Getting the facts on what we've done in the past and where
we are now will help us decide what to do next.

Clerk. I'm afraid that won't help much. You see, the comptroller (or
auditor, or finance commissioner) is elected. He's really the head book-
keeper, and each new one usually changes the bookkeeping system used by
the nincompoop he just defeated. So our financial record is not much use
for showing trends. One year the water- and sewer-system expenditures are
shown separately; the next year they're combined. One year animal control may be under the police department and be paid out of the department's patrol budget; another year animal control may be a separate item
in the public-works department budget. Anyway, we don't keep records of
work done, just how much we spent in each department for salaries and
supplies and for some of the big items we've bought.

CAO. What about unit costs of doing work?

Clerk. Unit costs? You mean how much to pick up a ton of garbage, or
cost per mile to run our police cars? No we've never kept that kind of
information. It's too much bother. Besides, nobody cares about that
because we don't need to know. If we need more money, the council can
always raise the taxes or increase the fees. Our customers can't go anyplace
else, you know.

Mayor. We may not keep a record of work done, but we must have
reports, or maps, or something that show which are high-crime areas,
where most of the fires occur, which parts of town send the most housing
and sanitation complaints, and so on. That'll help us know where to use
our resources.

Clerk. Yes, we may have that kind of information. We used to get out an
annual report showing that. Haven't done that for some time, though.
Nobody was much interested. And it was pretty boring, just a lot of
numbers. Our department heads—police, fire, public works, health—have a
pretty good gut feeling for where the problems are or are likely to be.

Mayor. I see. Well, if you'll pardon my asking, I notice that except for
the new stadium and some of the new garbage trucks, most of the city
buildings and equipment look pretty run down. Do we have money in
the budget to repair the buildings and replace equipment when it quits
running?

Clerk. Not much, really. The council is never very much interested in
putting money into the old buildings. That doesn't show very much.
They'd rather build something new when they can. A monument to their
progressive administration, you know.

Every year the council puts a little money into the budget for new equipment. And if at the end of a fiscal year we have a little left over from the department's budgets, the council may authorize them to replace some equipment. You might not know it, but the state doesn't allow us to carry over any money from one fiscal year to the next. If we don't spend it, we lose it. We usually think of something we need. I guess that isn't too bad a system. No council would want to tax the people and then leave the money in the treasury for the next administration to spend and get credit for it.

Mayor. This is all very interesting. Let me ask one more question. What do you do about emergencies—say, when a flood damages a lot of homes and tears up big sections of street, or when a fire destroys a city shop and warehouse building. How do you pay for that?

Clerk. We have situations like that now and then. In fact, we have a couple sections of town that flood pretty badly every two or three years. The engineers tell us if we'd build a retention basin up on the rise—it wouldn't cost a great deal—we could stop that. Every time we have a flood, the mayor and council members go out and inspect the damage, get their pictures in the paper, and say they're going to have to do something about those areas. But by the next budget time a lot of higher-priority things have come along, the flood problem gets forgotten, and we go through the same thing in another year or two.

If the problem were real serious—like a tornado—we could ask the governor to have the President declare this a disaster area and we might get some federal money to help out. If it's not too bad, we just have to make do for a while. Or, if we lost a building, the council might issue bonds to pay for a replacement.

Mayor. Thanks very much. This has been very helpful. I'm sure we'll be back from time to time with more questions.

Clerk. You're welcome. Any time.

Self-serving Public Employment

The mayor in this imaginary episode may be on the first rung of a ladder that will take him to a state office, a seat in the Congress, a post in the President's cabinet, even vice-president or President of the United States. Increasingly, people are using local-government elective offices as stepping-stones to "higher" (state or national) office. While this book has been in process, a former mayor of a major western city (now a federal judge), two city managers, a city councilman, and a retired League of Municipalities director have made to me unsolicited mention of this trend. What City Manager David Rowlands wrote me summarizes the observations of all of them.

When I started out in the city management profession, about thirty-five

years ago, those individuals running for the City Council were interested
in making a contribution to their community for from two to eight
years and then were satisfied to return to their role as informed citizens
of their communities. It has been my observation during the past seven
or eight years, in particular, that about half of the Council members are
using their position to aspire to higher office—County Board, State Legislature, the Congress. As a consequence, all too often the decisions they
make are strictly political in nature, decisions they hope will promote
them up the political ladder, so to speak. In brief, all too many local
officials are more interested in a career as a full-time politician than in
coming to grips with the hard choices which should be made in the
arena of the local decision-making process. I want to make it clear, however, that there are still some outstanding and dedicated public officials
on the local level. But even their task is made more arduous by the
political antics and aberrations of many of their colleagues.

If political fortune evades our fictitious mayor, or if he is unwilling to
pay the price of a political career, he can return—as a better-informed
citizen—to running his Cadillac agency, his dry-cleaning business, and his
small manufacturing plant. But what of the chief administrative officer,
who probably burned his bridges when he resigned his bank vice-
presidency to become the new mayor's principal assistant? Unlike the
mayor, he may have no business or professional practice to return to.
After a year and a half of serving as a key city official, he may be convinced of the importance of local government. If he has an opportunity to
stay on, with or without the mayor, he may become one of the thousands
of skilled and dedicated local-government employees who spend a lifetime
of meritorious, efficient, honest public service, in the smallest to the largest of our communities. They are the men and women who protect and
serve by fulfilling the police, fire, streets and sanitation, water and sewer,
health, parks, recreation, and countless other responsibilities essential to
the convenience and well-being of the rest of us. They carry on, year after
year, despite political uncertainties, unreasonable demands, little recognition, few rewards, and inadequate tools to do the job many of them
would like to do for the public.

Unfortunately, like the number of private citizens interested in
making a contribution to their community for a few years and then
returning to their private role, the number of men and women who
choose a public career out of a sincere desire to serve their fellow men
appears to be diminishing. They are being succeeded by a growing
number of militant employees—policemen, firemen, ambulance drivers,
sanitation workers, and others—who use work stoppages and occasional
violence to satisfy their growing demands, regardless of the adverse effects
on the public they are sworn to serve. Their political power is growing
rapidly.

In *Without Fear or Favor* I described the danger that I believe this development portends. I can do no better now than repeat what I wrote then.

> As for the growing electoral power of the local-government bureaucracy, I have sometimes wished that every citizen who could vote but didn't were with me in the city hall or county courthouse on election day—I mean not only the citizens who think they don't have time to learn something of the issues and the candidates or haven't time to go to the polls, but also the citizens who don't vote and complain afterward about what the local governing body and appointed officials are doing. They could see for themselves how the power over local government is slipping from their hands into the hands of their hired public employees.
> On election day local-government offices are abuzz with excitement. Informally, officials and employees encourage each other to cast their ballots. They make it a point to telephone relatives and friends to be sure to vote. They are given paid time off to go to the polls, ostensibly to set a good example for the general public but more directly to have an impact on the results. Elections are not only exciting at the centers of local government; they are serious business because public employees know how important each vote is in getting what they want.
> The danger to continued citizen control of local government rests in the citizens' own attitudes toward voting, and in a paradoxical characteristic of any government that I will explain shortly.
> In most communities there has been a steady decline in the percentage of eligible citizens who register and vote. On the other hand, voting by officials and employees of any government, and especially local government, is virtually a duty; and every convenience is provided to facilitate their voting.
> The paradox I speak of is that in government the employees are the employers of their employers. Does that sound confusing? Let's follow it through. The people who vote are the ones who choose (employ) the persons who will head the government. The people who head the government are the ones who appoint (employ) the workers. The greater the influence of the workers in elections, the greater their influence over their own employers. As the proportion of the population who work for government increases (thirty years ago one out of twelve people in the labor force worked for government; today the ratio is one out of six) and the percentage of voting by private citizens decreases, the bureaucracy's votes will become a larger and larger percentage of the total.
> ... Eventually the bureaucrats, with all their relatives and friends, will totally control elections. Already we are seeing the effect of this paradox in the frequent failure of elected officials to act in the general public's best interest when to do so is contrary to the employees' wishes. Local government is especially susceptible because it is at this level that the number of governmental employees is growing fastest and where the voting strength of the bureaucracy is most beneficial to officials who want to stay in office and who depend on the bureaucracy to elect and reelect them [pp. 334–35].

We are experiencing political application of the age-old maxim that nature abhors a vacuum. Someone must govern every society. Where the people abandon their power to govern, hired officials and their employees will fill the vacuum.

Violations of the Public Trust

Our nation was formed in the late 1700s largely in revolt against abuse of governmental power by monarchs, parliaments, and lesser officials. It was founded on the noble ideal of government of the people, by the people, and for the people. Yet our history is replete with examples of the misuse of governmental power entrusted to officials and employees at all levels—from the highest national offices to the lowest village clerkships.

From about 1820 on, the nineteenth century was marked by the spoils and patronage systems at all levels of government. The mid-1800s were a time of buying and selling state legislatures, of the rise of big-city bossism. At the federal level, following the assassination of President Garfield by a disappointed office seeker, the spoils system was slowed somewhat by the 1887 adoption of competitive (civil-service) examination for appointive offices. The opening of the twentieth century saw the beginning of a reform movement that later included the era of "muckraking" journalism (ironically so named in derogation by reform President Theodore Roosevelt), reduction of the power of the state legislatures, and the invention and spread of the council-manager plan of local government.

Currently (1980) we seem to have reverted to practices of earlier eras. Men and women who have been elected, appointed, or employed to preserve and enhance the public interest are found using their positions as places of leverage and power to achieve ends contrary to the public good and for personal benefit of themselves, other venal government officials and employees, and corrupt private citizens. Whether violations of public trust are accelerating (as some believe), are decreasing (as others claim), or are "same as always" (as noted by cynical veteran observers), we know that lack of integrity and the extent of corruption among government officials and employees have seriously eroded the confidence of the American public in their public-service personnel.

For readers unacquainted with the venality and corruption to which local governments are subject, the following litany of wrongdoing may be of interest. Because some taxpayer-readers may be helping, unknowingly, to pay the added costs of such misgovernment, and some employees and officials may be insensitive to or naive about this part of the real world of local government, both groups may benefit from being able to recognize similar activities in their communities or in the governments where they have responsibility. Most of these examples come from my direct personal exposure and my file of ethics materials. Keep in mind (1) that each of the activities listed may take different forms, (2) that all may be immoral or unethical, but not necessarily illegal in every public jurisdiction, and (3) that the classifications presented here sometimes overlap.

Election Irregularities. Local misgovernment starts with the elective process. A corrupt administration may hand-pick election officials to be sure the vote is delivered, whatever the means. The means may include fraudulent voter lists that include names of fictitious persons, of persons deceased, and of persons no longer residing within the governmental jurisdiction. Floaters may vote more than once at the same polling place or at more than one polling place. People who protest about apparent irregularities may be intimidated by threats or be physically assaulted. Ballots and voting machines may be tampered with. Voters may be paid to vote "right"—so many dollars each—or they may be promised government jobs in return for their campaign efforts and votes.

Kickbacks. Often local-government corruption is a two-way street, a kind of mutual-aid arrangement. ("You support me for office; if elected, I'll give you a government job. Then you'll kick back to me part of your salary either directly, as a straight political contribution, or to a flower fund [ostensibly to pay for cards, flowers, etc., when a fellow employee is ill or has a death in the family]. Your contribution will help pay the costs of the next campaign. This way we'll both have good jobs and a steady income.") (For female employees the kickback may be not in money but in intimate favors.)

Bribery. Once in office, elected and appointed officials and employees may be offered or solicit bribes of various kinds in return for some official but wrongful acts. The inducement may be money, gifts, trips, or other valuable considerations. The purpose of a bribe may be to buy a favorable vote or decision on a rezoning, an award of a contract or franchise, the purchase of goods or services, the granting of a license, or the certifying of an inspection that was not made.

Of course the government people don't openly solicit bribes. They only signal in various ways that they might be willing to consider a bribe. This may include: frustrating and costly delays in getting the official approvals you are required to have, for no apparent reason (and especially when others get prompt approvals); suggestions that you engage a designated party to help process your application or request; offers to "work something out" or overlook a technical violation; awards of purchases and contracts on a noncompetitive negotiated basis; a shortage of reputable bidders; and frequent rejections of low bidders for not meeting "responsible-bidder" qualifications.

Pilferage and Theft. Corruption does not always directly involve parties outside the government. Stealing is an example. Pilfering small sums from a petty-cash fund and taking small objects can be the forerunners of more significant thefts. City offices may use an excess amount of stationery about the time the school year starts. Workmen may supply themselves and friends with materials and small tools from a city shop. Parking-meter collectors have been known to skim the meter receipts, and treasurers to cover up the "uncollectibles" they have pocketed by keeping a second set of books. City employees have built private buildings, using city materials and equipment, while working on city time. Others have had their personal autos serviced, repaired, and filled with tax-exempt gasoline at the city garage. I know of one popular city-works superintendent who spent time in the state penitentiary after selling a piece of the city's earth-moving equipment and pocketing the payment.

Fraud. This kind of intentional deception takes many forms. Some of the more common might include falsifying applications for public funds, appraisal and inventory records, reports of inspections made, and certificates of work performed or goods delivered; forging signatures; misusing government credit cards; not showing at work, but having fellow employees punch their time cards; writing bogus work orders and invoices; altering receipt copies; bootlegging government revenue-producing goods; overlooking defalcations and falsifying audit reports; selling employment examination tests and altered examination results.

These kinds of fraudulent activities have long been practiced. A more recent innovation is the fraudulent use of computers by inputting false data, manipulating correct data, and producing false information. Possible indicators of fraudulent activities might be increasing numbers of citizens' complaints, unexplained changes in revenue collections, sensitivity to routine questioning, financial personnel putting in excessive overtime, and evidence of double sets of books.

Fixing. In corrupt situations, some people may make a living as fixers. They may claim to have, or actually have, connections and influence that enable them to get favorable action that is beyond the reach of the ordinary citizen. If they are part of the local political machine, they may assist confused, anxious, or frustrated citizens without charge but for the purpose of building up IOUs to be collected by the machine in the form of loyal support of the machine between elections and at the polls. Or for a fee they will get a traffic ticket "taken care of" (canceled), a license approved, a request or application expedited, or a court-imposed penalty reduced. To get results, they may have to act illegally; at the very least they will conspire with local-government officials or employees with whom they split their fee.

Favoritism. Because of the many contacts local-government people have with citizens, there are numerous opportunities to be partial in the kind, amount, and quality of service rendered. Office holders and employees may give their friends and political associates preferential treatment. There may be favoritism without a formal agreement of *quid pro quo* (one thing in return for another). However, since few people are totally altruistic, the private citizen who makes a contribution to a public official usually expects something in return, either immediately or some time in the future; similarly, the official who uses his office and governmental power

to show more consideration or indulgence to one citizen than another is likely to expect something in return. Thus, favoritism and bribery overlap.
Protection. Prostitution, gambling, pornography, drug and liquor pushing, and other vices cannot survive in a community without public patronage and tacit or outright official cooperation. Because officials run some risk of job loss or worse when they provide protection for these illegal activities, they demand at least equivalent payment. The *quid pro quo* is payment by the vice operators for partial or total protection against police harassment, raids, prosecution, and heavy fines. Of course, this means that to be effective the arrangements must involve the police, the city's legal counsel, and the courts.
Payoffs. Bribery, theft, fraud, fixing, favoritism, protection, and other activities inimicable to efficient and impartial local government involve an exchange between local-government personnel and one or more other parties. Because the arrangements usually are illegal, the parties cannot resolve in open court any differences they may have. They must rely on their own codes of conduct. This gives local officials, who have the powers and facilities of government at their command, a clear advantage. A second party who fails to pay off as agreed could suffer severe and lasting penalties. Probably the default rate of payoffs to public officials by individuals engaged in illegal activities is small.
Embezzlement. Local officials and employees often have large sums of money and materials, and costly equipment and facilities entrusted to their care and security. For various reasons, they may take personal possession of these items for their own use. They may blame their embezzlement on unsatisfactory salary, fringe benefits, and working conditions; on family problems; or on financial difficulties. Or they may simply be crooks who found an easy place to ply their criminal trade. Some early-warning signals of possible embezzlement are officials and employees living beyond their means, gambling, and drinking more than usual. Another hint may be cash-handling personnel who do not issue official receipts, saying, "Your check will be your receipt."
Payroll Padding. Compared with the sophisticated schemes sometimes devised to cover up embezzlement and fraud, payroll padding is rather straightforward. It is a matter of adding fictitious or extra names to payrolls, and getting control of paychecks. Its success is often traced to loose payroll, personnel, and accounting procedures and records, and to carelessly placing too much trust in the people who prepare the payrolls and distribute the checks. Again, living beyond one's means and gambling are possible evidence of this kind of unethical and illegal behavior.
Harassment. Because of the many contacts that local governments have with citizens, hardly any organization in the community is in a better position to torment the citizens. Harassment may be an indication that an officer or employee is open to a bribe. Sudden enforcement of little-known and relatively unimportant regulations, with no prior warning,

may indicate that inspectors, refuse collectors, police officers, and others are under pressure from higher up to increase their contributions to the political organization, and are using this means to meet their quotas.

Threats. Citizens who fail to cooperate with dishonest and unfair office holders and employees may receive verbal or anonymous written threats of injury or worse to their families and themselves. The aim is to intimidate the citizen into a state of civic paralysis, or to coerce him into complying with the officials' wishes.

Extortion. Businessmen and other private citizens who conclude that they cannot afford to defy the crooks in office, whether for economic reasons or for the physical safety of themselves and their families, and yield to the financial and other demands of these governmental leeches, only encourage bolder and expanded extortion.

Reprisals. Citizens who defy the dishonest and illegal acts of local officials and their bosses, and thus keep the latter from achieving their goals, may find themselves subjected to more than one kind of reprisal. For instance, they may get no response to their requests for service, or get careless service—garbage strewn on their property and containers unnecessarily damaged. They may be prosecuted and fined for minor violations. Or they may have their property assessment doubled or tripled, and their taxes increased accordingly.

Criminal Syndicates. Perhaps the ultimate in violation of the public trust is what has come to be known as "burglars in blue"—policemen who have organized crime rings within their own departments. Several cities have been plagued by these unconscionable situations. In Denver, for example, residents who responded to the police-department invitation to let the department know when they would be out of town so that the department would be able to provide additional surveillance, returned home to find their homes completely cleaned out. Later it was discovered that the department's own officers, from top to bottom, had organized themselves into burglary teams and, using large vans, had systematically entered the homes and carted off household goods and family belongings that they sold through illegal outlets ("fences").

So much for examples of wrongdoing by persons holding positions of public trust in local government.

When you read or hear of public officials and employees being apprehended while engaged in questionable activities and being charged with a crime, you may not recognize the nature of the wrongdoing by the terms used. Instead of being charged with "bribery," "fraud," "payroll padding," "extortion," and so on, the suspects may be charged with "nonfeasance," "misfeasance," or "malfeasance." These terms come from the root *feasance,* which a dictionary might define as "the doing of an act as an obligation or duty." Hence, "nonfeasance" is failure to perform an obligatory duty, "misfeasance" is the improper or wrongful performance of an act which is normally proper and lawful, and "malfeasance" is the commission of a wrongful or illegal act by a public official. Whether called by what they are, or by some obscure legal term, the above examples are not the only misdeeds ever committed by people occupying local-government offices. But they may be enough to suggest the nature of violations of the public trust and why they, along with the shortage of good people to run for or accept public office, the lack of effective management tools, and the number of self-serving people in the public service, are impediments to better local government.

Priorities for Citizen Action

I now present six proposals for citizen action. The first five are repeated from what I listed in the final chapter of *Without Fear or Favor.* I want to expand on three of the five and add one more to the list.

I called these five priorities *first* priorities for citizen action because "they are the fundamental steps. Without them, the improvements in organization, management, and operations so badly needed in our local governments are not likely to happen." All of them are essential, although the order in which they can be instituted will depend on local circumstances and therefore will vary from place to place. Those priority actions are as follows:

1. Establish a system for alerting citizens to pending major policy decisions and actions of special concern to them.

2. Require employment and retention of trained professional administrators to implement impartially the policies established by elected governing bodies and elected chief executives.

3. Require all local governments to use performance budgets.

4. Require an independent management audit and public report at least every four years.

5. Require prompt follow-through and positive decisions on all management audits, examinations, surveys, and studies financed with the local government's funds or through its auspices, sponsorship, or initiative.

First I intend to expand on actions 2, 4, and 5 under new headings, namely "The Policy-Administration Dichotomy, or, Separating the *What* from the *How* of Getting Things Done," and "Management Audits with Up-to-Date Emphasis." Then I will present the additional priority action.

The Policy-Administration Dichotomy, or
Separating the *What* from the *How* of Getting Things Done

Several of the city-manager episodes related in preceding sections of this book reveal the need in local governments for a more complete understanding and practice of a familiar organization principle: specialization. When practiced in the past, specialization has enabled the United States to lead the world in productivity of everything from manufactured goods to farm products. Applied to local government, the principle assures democratic control of government through the election of a representative body that specializes in determining *what* the government is to do. At the same time it assures maximum productivity from the local-government machinery by utilizing the skills of a professionally trained specialist in administration to determine *how* best to do the necessary work. The harmonious merging of the strength of democratic policy-making with the advantages of professional administration is the foundation and key to the success of the council-manager plan.

I say that specialization of this kind is a familiar principle because we are surrounded by organizations that follow this principle: The members of local labor unions elect boards of directors who in turn appoint union secretaries or business agents to serve the membership. Stockholders of private companies elect boards of directors who then select a president, general manager, or other chief-executive officer to run the business under the general direction of the board. Members of social, cultural, and charitable nonprofit organizations—civic clubs, trade associations, neighborhood-improvement groups, community chests, chambers of commerce, hospitals—elect policy-making boards of trustees who, in turn, appoint executive secretaries, executive vice-presidents, general managers, executive directors, or administrators to carry out the boards' policies. Voters elect other citizens to local boards of education. Then, by law, these school boards appoint principals and school superintendents, who apply their special and technical skills to provide continuity and high-quality administration of the educational programs. Even the national and state governments, when they have critically important and nonpartisan tasks to perform, sometimes use the policy-making board-and-professional-administrator device to serve the public. Examples are the regional authorities, quasi-independent commissions, and boards of health. But generally in government this organizational arrangement is the exception, not the rule.

In other words, with the exception of government, almost every organization that must be efficient and effective in order to achieve its objectives—or to survive—combines people who specialize in policy-making with people who specialize in policy execution (administration). The offices these people hold are arranged from top to bottom in a clear channel of authority. At the top the members or the owners whom the organization is obliged to serve elect and delegate to a governing group the authority needed to represent their interests, to establish the organization's policies, and to choose and control a qualified person or persons to carry out those policies. At the next level down, that representative board appoints a qualified administrator and gives him the authority he needs to carry out their collective policies and directives. If the organization is any but the very smallest in size, the administrator delegates some of his authority to department and division heads so that the necessary work assigned to them gets done. Thus, authority is distributed down through the organization, so that responsibility for performance and results can be identified at every level.

This principle of specialization does not mean that the parts and levels are isolated or are competitive or in conflict with one another. Nor does it mean that one is more important than the other. To use a simple analogy, these organizations are like an automobile. Each part—steering gear, carburetor, distributor, wheels, etc.—has its special and individual function. No part can perform the function of another, yet they are dependent on one another. Until the parts are assembled and coordinated ("aligned and timed," we say for the car), they are just so many parts and cannot transport people or goods. If any part is missing, the car won't run well.

The same need exists for coordinated and smooth functioning of a city government. As evidenced by some of the episodes previously described, we can have in local government the necessary parts: a citizenry that has adopted a council-manager statute or charter, an elected representative city council to make policy and appoint and control a professional manager, and a qualified professional manager to direct the executive and administrative work. But unless the citizens do their job in selecting proper representatives, and unless those representatives sitting as a council do their job, the manager does his, and the two coordinate their efforts, the governmental machine will function poorly or not at all.

What, then, are the functions of the people at these three levels? And how do they coordinate with each other in the interdependent relationships? The voters have the most important task—to recruit, even draft if necessary, council members who have a broad view of the community's needs, not single-issue tunnel vision, who work well with other people in resolving problems on the basis of facts as well as emotions, and who understand and are determined to adhere to the separate roles of policymakers and administrators. As to the council and the manager, although they are mutually dependent, the council is the higher in the channel of authority. The council sets the direction the government is to go; hence, the manager is dependent on the council for determining the focus of his administrative responsibilites. At the same time, in the continuing process of making, reviewing, and modifying political/legislative decisions about the needs of the community, and evaluating how well they are being met, the council is dependent on the manager. It is he who provides the detailed information, analysis, and professional interpretation of the data that the council needs to make original and subsequent policy decisions.

Also, the council is dependent on the manager for his professional judgment as to the administrative feasibility of options they may be considering. Thus, they may ask his help in continually identifying community needs, and in suggesting optional courses of action. They may even ask his professional judgment of the best option to choose. But the manager does not make the policy decisions. That is both the prerogative and the responsibility of the council. Then, although they hand him the policy to administer, they cannot abdicate their ultimate responsibility to the public for the policies adopted or the effective administration of those policies.

The success of council members (as measured by public approval and reelection) and the success of the manager (as measured by continued employment by the council, or professional advancement) hinge on the effectiveness of the manager's administration of the council's policies. Therefore, council members can help themselves and the manager by serving as eyes and ears of the government, ascertaining and evaluating how well their policies are working in application, and giving the manager feedback and suggestions, without taking over his job. The manager can help himself and the council by continually improving his professional skills and doing the best possible professional job for the community.

Trouble begins when (1) the manager tries to supplant the council in making policy because the council has failed to provide the policy guidance the manager needs to do his job, or (2) the council members try to take over administration because the manager has failed to administer their policies, or because they are dissatisfied with his performance. Such untenable situations are usually the result of misunderstandings or lack of acceptance of the policy-administration dichotomy I have been describing.

Here are some warning signs of impending difficulties: The manager may make repeated suggestions or requests that the council devote the necessary time and attention to one or more developing problems that are being neglected in favor of lesser, often politically motivated, matters. The administrative organization may noticeably delay acting on pressing matters while it waits for the council to "make up its mind." A third warning sign that may precede approaching difficulty is growing council-member criticism of the manager, his assistants, and their administration. Criticisms may take the form of pointed comments that the council, not the manager, represents the people, that the manager is out front and getting much politically valuable attention, or that the manager is assuming a professional, nonpartisan, noncontroversial, aloof, "I-am-above-politics" stance while leaving the really tough questions to the council.

While avoiding deep involvement in transient political issues, the manager needs to recognize that deciding the *what* of local government can be as difficult as, or more than, administering the *how* of policy implementation. Policy-making demands the best that is in our most able citizens. It requires a multitude of abilities to define and articulate the fundamental issues in the community, to draft effective alternative solutions to problems, to gain consensus in a multi-member body, to get proposals adopted in the form intended, to monitor the implementation of policy, and to protect sound long-range policy against the ravages of expediency.

In our era of participative democracy, decision making, and management, many who previously were content to accept the status quo are now determined to get into the act to advance their own causes to the neglect of broader community needs. Thus, it is particularly difficult for the local-government legislator to decide when to be merely a public-opinion conduit to the council table and when to take stands contrary to current special-interest outcries because he feels it is his duty as an elected representative of all the people. Local, part-time, amateur policy-makers need all the help they can get. It is the manager's duty to do all he can do honestly, fairly, and professionally to help the council and its individual members look good in carrying out their heavy responsibilities.

The desirability of having the specialized functions of policy-making and policy administration separate yet working harmoniously together is not a new concept in our country. On 14 November 1792, in a letter concerning the establishment of a capital city for the new nation, President George Washington wrote to Benjamin Stoddert as follows:

> It has always been my opinion, and still is so, that the Administration of the Affairs of the Federal City ought to be under the *immediate* direction of a judicious and skilful superintendent, appointed by, and subject to the orders of the Commissioners (who, in the eye of the law, are the responsible characters). One in whom is united knowledge of Men and things, industry, integrity, impartiality and firmness. And that this person should reside on the Spot.*

For several reasons President Washington's suggestion is not pertinent to the council-manager plan per se, as we are considering it here. For one thing, at that time neither the city nor the city government of Washington existed. The "commissioners" were three members of a temporary committee appointed to plan and lay out the new city. The committee members were not elected by the people but had been appointed by the President. And the committee of "commissioners" had no responsibilities as a governing body of an ongoing city. However, I mention this incident because it is another example of the application of the principle of

The Writings of George Washington from Original Manuscript Sources, 1745–1799, 39 vols., ed. James C. Fitzpatrick (Washington, D.C.: U.S. Government Printing Office, 1931–1944), 32:226.

specialization, where the policy-making group would engage a "judicious and skilful superintendent" to carry out the day-to-day execution of their policies (i.e., plans, surveys, and construction).

A more pertinent historical incident is found in the *Political Science Quarterly* of March 1887. There Woodrow Wilson (then a professor of history and political economy) noted,

> Administration lies outside the proper sphere of *politics*. Administrative questions are not political questions. Although politics sets the tasks for administration, it should not be suffered to manipulate its offices.
> . . . The distinction is between general plans and special means.
> . . . Self-government does not consist in having a hand in every-thing, any more than housekeeping consists necessarily in cooking dinner with one's own hands. The cook must be trusted with a large discretion as to the management of the fires and the ovens [pp. 210–14].

My personal experience with the day-to-day workings of a desirable policy-administration dichotomy was reported in the local newspaper when I resigned as city manager of Albert Lea, Minnesota, to accept a similar post in Fargo, North Dakota. In an editorial titled "Mr. Harlow's Resignation," the writer said in part,

> [The mayor and city councilmen] have consistently given sympathetic consideration to [Mr. Harlow's] recommendations. . . . On Mr. Harlow's side the cooperation has been no less hearty. On those rare occasions when the council has acted counter to his recommendations he has unhesitatingly accepted the final verdict and carried out the council's wishes to the letter. . . .
> His procedure has always followed the fixed pattern: This, he says, is the situation; these are the facts; here is my recommendation; what are your wishes in the matter?
> Summing it all up . . . Alberta Leans have . . . been treated to a demonstration of democracy efficiently at work, and that's as good a definition of the council-manager form of government as we know of.

I have dwelt at length on the relative positions of the council and the manager in the hierarchy of local government authority, and on the need to recognize the interdependence of the two, for this reason: The most common objection to the council-manager plan is the fallacious and mis-informed charge that the plan sets up one-man rule, and that the manager is a dictator who cannot be removed. The fact is that a city or county manager serves totally at the pleasure of the people's elected representatives. He is a specialist in administration who can help the people and their elected representatives make democracy more effective. He is a professional on tap, *not* on top.

Management Audits with Up-to-Date Emphasis

The fourth and fifth priorities for citizen action listed in *Without Fear or Favor* recommended that citizens require an outside management audit of the local government not less often than every four years, and that the results be publicly reported and promptly followed through rather than being shelved and ignored. A management audit is nothing more than what numerous successful organizations do. For any organization this audit can be likened to the annual physical examination recommended by medical doctors in order for individuals to maintain sound and vigorous health.

The recommendation for citizen action included a proviso that there be expressly authorized in each annual budget an amount for the sole purpose of financing the management audit and publication of the resulting report. There may be communities in which the citizens and officials mistrust outside management counselors or are unwilling or unable to pay for that service even as infrequently as every three or four years. For those situations, I suggest an alternative that is not as useful but may be more acceptable and would approach the aim of an objective examination of the organization, management, and operations of the local government. The alternative is an adaptation of the self-examination and self-policing device used by some professional organizations and in the field of higher education. This would be a system for accreditation of local governments by qualified local-government personnel and authorities.

Either through the auspices and assistance of a federal or state agency, an association of local governments such as a league of municipalities, or on its own initiative, the local government can have a survey team of fellow local personnel, assisted by qualified outside authorities if desired, visit, evaluate, and report their findings and recommendations. This would give the local governing body and the citizens a report on how their government looks through the eyes of others in the same field, with recommendations for possible improvements. It would provide an exchange of information among local-government people at the site of operations, in addition to meetings and publications (which are not always attended or read by those who could benefit therefrom). The development and use of measurement standards, and the wide distribution of survey reports should stimulate interested local policy-makers and administrative officials to upgrade their policies, organization, and operations and should educate the public about what their local government does, and how, and how well.

Of course, whether a management audit is conducted by an outside professional management-counseling organization or by a team of fellow local-government persons from nearby communities, no audit will be of full value without follow-through. Therefore, the steps described in *Without Fear or Favor* under item 5 should be followed. These are as follows:

After completion of any management audit, examination, survey or study agreed to, assigned by, or contracted for by a local government, its governing officials should be required to publicly review the corresponding report within ninety days. Also, the governing officials should be required to formally adopt and publicly announce a plan of action within sixty days after reviewing the report, setting forth the recommendations to be implemented, a timetable for implementation, an assignment of each approved recommendation to an official for follow-through, and a schedule of quarterly and final public reports on progress and completion of implementation.

Concurrently with the announcement of the plan of action, any recommendation in the report not assigned and scheduled for implementation should be identified and the reasons for deferral or rejection should be fully set forth and publicly announced.

I have proposed management audits that would note any lack of management practices and operating policies, methods, and procedures regularly used by effective private and public organizations, and I have proposed also the necessary follow-through on audit findings and recommendation. In so doing, I assumed that the audits would include examination of local-government methods for minimizing what have come to be called "crimes of opportunity"—opportunities for every kind of wrongdoing from election irregularities and theft, to embezzlement, fraud, and criminal syndicates composed of local-government personnel. Recent developments suggest that I add emphasis to the need for corruption-prevention in management audits. These developments are three: the continuing if not increasing frequency of corruption in local government, the attention being given to the problem and means of dealing with it (which I discuss in connection with the added priority for citizen action which follows), and the assumption by the accounting profession of larger responsibility for detection and disclosure of wrongdoing.

With respect to the last point, accountants have traditionally held that auditors do not have a major responsibility for seeking to detect and disclose wrongdoing, that their chief obligation is to verify the financial statements of the clients. This has created a major gap between what the accounting profession has seen as its responsibility, and what the public and their representatives—corporate stockholders and boards of directors, and taxpayers and their elected governing bodies—expect of that profession. In essence, the question is: If competent independent auditors do not detect wrongdoing, who will?

Recently, the American Institute of Certified Public Accountants has adopted two new audit standards dealing with corporate irregularities and illegal acts. While this action by no means holds the independent auditors wholly responsible for detection and disclosure, it does acknowledge that by training and experience the auditor should be capable of some detection and that he carries responsibility to search out irregularities and illegal acts of material importance. Although the standards have been adopted primarily in response to problems of wrongdoing in the private sector, they are equally—in many cases more significantly—applicable to the public sector.

All this is to recommend that any agreement for a management audit include a clear mandate for the audit group to examine the local government's arrangements and efforts to prevent wrongdoing; to make reasonable effort to detect wrongdoing; to disclose its findings as to preventive arrangements and, confidentially (where appropriate), evidence of wrongdoing; and to recommend ways to minimize further corrupt practices.

I turn now to the additional priority for citizen action. Together with the five priorities just presented, I believe this sixth proposal can provide the basic framework for local government that can be democratic, productive, fair, and honest.

Require a Public Servant's Oath of Honor

The 1973–74 Vice-President Agnew and President Nixon episodes may have created the most stressful period in our nation's peacetime political history. Of course, the violations of public trust exhibited on these occasions were not the first in our sometimes turbulent history. But those were the first times that the occupants of the most revered and honored public offices in our nation were so clearly and directly involved that both a vice-president and a president of the United States of America were forced to resign from their high offices.

Once the shock and trauma of Nixon's Watergate were past, many committed public servants and other concerned Americans had hopes that Watergate was the high-water mark of official wrongdoing and that the ordeal might prove to be a kind of catharsis that would enable our society to start over, with a clean, healthier body politic. Instead, almost weekly we continue to learn of new, documented exposures and convictions of brazen acts against the public interest, at all levels of government.

Is there no way to halt the stream of corruption? Some steps have been taken. Several groups have undertaken studies of corruption. And the American Society for Public Administration, the American Institute of Certified Public Accountants, the ICMA, committees of the Congress, and agencies of the U.S. Department of Justice have published findings and recommendations.

Also, it is currently popular for private and public organizations to adopt codes of conduct that apply to their members. (The ICMA has promulgated the "City Management Code of Ethics" since 1924). Recently, local and state governments have passed ethics legislation and created ethics commissions. At the federal level we now have the Ethics in Government Act of 1978, which establishes financial-disclosure requirements for legislative, executive, and judicial personnel, sets up an Office of Government Ethics and a position of Special Prosecutor, and provides for ethics training. These efforts are well intentioned, but in my judgment they are destined to fall short of their objectives because of a fundamental weakness. The weakness is in placing most of the responsibility for wrongdoing and its correction on the system instead of on the individual worker.

Employing agencies have added a euphemism to the administrative vocabulary, namely "crimes of opportunity." (These are crimes committed because the individual could not or did not resist the "opportunity" to lie, cheat, or steal.) In so doing, the agencies have accepted the blame for the wrongdoings of their officers and employees who commit corrupt acts on the excuse that their weak wills justify these acts. Thus, the employing organization gives official recognition to a moral and ethical anomaly.

This misdirected effort has a two-fold effect: One, the employing government burdens itself with the undue responsibility to identify criminal "opportunities" in its system and then to build and operate cumbersome and costly procedures to meticulously supervise and verify every officer's and employee's activities and work, to protect the government's money, materials, supplies, and equipment, and to apprehend and prosecute wrongdoers. Even more serious, this transfer of responsibility for wrongful acts from the individual to the employer enables officers and employees to justify in their own minds the irrational and irresponsible view that "It's not a crime if you don't get caught."

Although I concur with those who maintain that no single device or management technique will totally eliminate governmental corruption, I believe the solution lies more with the individual government worker than with the institutional superstructure. Therefore, I suggest that citizens and officials who are seeking ways to deal with the problem may wish to consider a move in another direction, namely requiring an oath of honor of every person who seeks and holds a position of government employment.

The wording of such an oath, and the process for administering it, should be suited to the local circumstances. A starting point for the wording may be some variation of the following, which is an adaptation to civilian public service of language long used in the military and judicial branches of our government system:

A Public Servant's Oath of Honor

I hereby swear (or affirm) that during my service with (name of agency) I will not (or I did not) lie, cheat, steal, or illegally favor one citizen or group of citizens over another (nor tolerate any public officer or employee who does).

Just as our national constitution spells out the language of the oath required of the President of the United States, so a city charter or other enabling legislation can state the oath and set forth the administering procedures. The local situation should determine the process. Some may wish to include the oath on all announcements of public job vacancies and require that the oath be signed by all candidates and applicants as a prerequisite for public office or employment. Also, the law may require a repeating of the oath-taking process at regular or irregular intervals, and may require a formal verbal declaration as well as an executed written oath. Because the purpose of the oath of honor is to reduce the amount of corruption, not necessarily to find and punish wrongdoers, a range of corrective action is possible.

Who should be required to take an oath of honor? In my opinion, all elected, appointed, or employed public servants, whether full-time or part-time. To do otherwise is to assert that only persons filling a select few positions are worthy of this recognition of the importance of personal integrity. The fact is that opportunities for lying, cheating, stealing, and committing other corrupt acts are greater in a lower-level clerk or inspector position–where applications are reviewed, laws are enforced, or large public works are under construction–than in an office of mayor, city manager, or department head.

A final comment: Some will respond to this proposal by declaring that no sworn oath is going to stop any public office holder or employee who is bent on violating the public trust; others will declare that people of integrity need no oath. I agree. But these two groups–the deliberately dishonest, and the totally honest–are at opposite ends of the human spectrum. In between are the many followers, not leaders, in the ethical area, who straddle a fence and fit the adage, "Every man has his price." These are people who lack the willpower to withstand peer pressure, who go along with the crowd because "everybody does it." The oath may be the moral crutch they need: a positive act of commitment on their part and the knowledge that their associates have made the same commitment. With an awareness of what it means to be a servant of all the people, they may be strengthened in their resolve to perform their duties regardless of personal consequence.

A universal public servant's oath of honor may achieve more than one desirable purpose. It may reestablish character in the public service; it may divert and lessen the stream of governmental corruption that has come close to inundating us all; and it may reduce present citizen frustration and cynicism about local governments and their public servants.

Learning from Others

I wrote in the preface that the idea for this book came from Professor David Booth's review of the predecessor book, *Without Fear or Favor: Odyssey of a City Manager,* for *Public Management.* I approach the conclusion with an extract from another review of the same book, this one by Mr. Michael Flannery, who recently retired as county manager of County Wicklow, Republic of Ireland, after twenty-eight years in that position. Also, I present other contributions by Mr. Flannery and by Dr. A. H. Marshall, another European authority on local government. I believe the experience and views of these perceptive observers merit our careful consideration.

In Mr. Flannery's three-page review for the Spring 1977 issue of *Administration* (the journal of the Institute of Public Administration of Ireland), he wrote,

> In some ways this is a book which can give rise to feelings of unease. Here is a record of what in great part is misgovernment rather than local government. It depicts many venal men in responsible posts. We find a great nation—at present the most powerful in the world—which can send men to the moon but cannot make reasonable provision for some of their elementary local needs. It can produce motor vehicles by the million but the streets of most cities may be a litter strewn patchwork of potholes. Water may be in short supply and sewerage unsatisfactory. Living conditions—especially housing—for quite a sizeable proportion of the population may be below standards which would be unacceptable in other countries with quite limited resources.
>   ... In the USA, in the matter of local government, they seem, according to Mr. Harlow's description, to be still where we were here in this country in the early 1920s before men of courage and foresight decided that recruitment to the Irish local service be by open competition, that the more responsible posts be filled with the aid of a specially established commission, and that mobility be ensured by carefully defined conditions of service.

About his review, Mr. Flannery later wrote me, "Now I feel that as an outsider, it is in a sense almost improper on my part to offer views on the internal administration in a friendly country—a country to which we in Ireland have been much indebted over a long period. But as I was deputed to write a critique of your book it seemed that apart from paying tribute to it, there should be some analysis of American local government."

In the same letter, which we later discussed in greater detail when my wife and I visited Mr. and Mrs. Flannery at their home in Greystones, near Dublin, Mr. Flannery wrote,

May I say that on this side of the Atlantic we find aspects of public life in the USA not easy to understand. There is evidence of idealism in the USA, which is absent elsewhere. The American people have given magnificent support to all types of humanitarian movements. They have provided food for famine-stricken countries. They have given support to public health movements everywhere. They have fought two World Wars which were not inspired by territorial aggrandisement. Marshall Aid led to a spectacular and rapid recovery in Europe in the late 1940s and early 1950s. America has assisted educational projects in many countries. The Americans have placed men on the moon. But in public life the scene can cause puzzlement to the onlooker from outside.

Right away I should say that I find it difficult to follow why in the USA there isn't a career structure in local government based on recruitment through wide-open competition, by the use of a public service commission which would ensure that all posts were filled on merit and that furthermore officials would not be liable to dismissal or being arbitrarily asked to retire through the machinations and cupidity of a party temporarily in power, or some purely self-seeking "politicos" who only seek their own personal advancement and that of their friends.

Mr. Flannery's comments did not result from reading just one book. He was aided by his knowledge and first-hand observations of the organization and workings of local government in the United States and many other places. In another letter, he referred me to a study done in the mid-1960s by Dr. A. H. Marshall, a well-known figure in English local government. Entitled "Local Government Administration Abroad," the report compared local government in the United States, Canada, (England in a limited way), Ireland, Sweden, the Netherlands, and West Germany. He dealt with several aspects of these local-government systems: historical background, political and constitutional bases, structure, powers and duties, internal administration, intergovernmental relations, citizen control, and appraisals of the various local-government arrangements by interest groups. The following observations about our local-government system are excerpted from Dr. Marshall's report. As with County Manager Flannery's comments, they suggest changes we may wish to make in our system to meet present and future needs.

Local government, not being mentioned in the American constitution, falls to be regulated by the states so that each state has its own legal code. Most of them have three or four ways of bringing local authorities into existence and may offer a wide choice of patterns of administration. Local government therefore differs not only between states but within states. There are endless variations of structure, nomenclature and scales of operations, rendering almost every generalisation subject to qualification.

Because of the rights possessed by inhabitants of an area to band together to secure incorporation—often to avoid inclusion in a larger area – thousands of almost minute local authorities have come into existence. It is not uncommon for a city of only moderate size to be surrounded by scores of such authorities. A typical example is Louisville (population about 400,000) which has 52. In the larger agglomerations there would be many more. Taken in conjunction with the numerous separate boards and commissions, the total of separate jurisdictions can rise to high figures, for example in the New York Metropolitan Region (16 million population) to 1,400 units, and constitute an almost insuperable obstacle to rationalising government in most of the 220 metropolitan areas, some straddled over more than one state. The situation, possibly without parallel elsewhere in the world, is often aggravated by unwilingness to co-operate.

The disadvantages of the existence of so many public authorities are many, and very apparent after a few weeks spent in American city halls. The fragmentation obscures the financial responsibility. It prevents the local authority from taking a bird's eye view of the services and their needs, and makes it impossible for the taxpayer to apportion the responsibility for the bill he receives. Separate jurisdictions imply at least some duplication of administration, and hamper the use of modern management techniques and equipment in which American local government is certainly not in the vanguard. But perhaps most important of all they make co-ordination in policy difficult of attainment. Now that so many services – planning, highways, transport, housing, etc. – have become interwoven, the effects of the lack of unified control are growing daily more serious. The multiplicity of authorities also presents a serious obstacle to the rationalisation of the local government structure, which has been described as 'grossly inefficient' and is in urgent need of realignment, not only in metropolitan areas but elsewhere.

All the features of central control and influence known in Europe can be found in the United States – legislation (e.g. fixing maximum tax rates), prior approval to actions, power over appointments, orders, regulations, inspections, transfer of functions, financial assistance with strings attached, reports, informal advice and assistance. But the intensity of control, though varying from state to state, is far less than in England despite a tendency for it to increase. Local authorities and also boards and commissions are comparatively free to carry on their services as they wish, except in the case of education which is subject to more stringent supervision. The police, fire, water and sewage services, for instance, are little controlled once they have been established. If a local authority is hamstrung, it is most likely to be by some legislative limitation which it is difficult to remove; its abrogation may, for example, need an alteration in the state's constitution only obtainable by an elaborate process, unlikely to be undertaken. Rural states are often a drag on local government because of their hostility to urban areas. Even those few states with active local government departments charged with the duty of fostering local government, may find their good intentions defeated from time to time by their outdated state constitutions and infrequent legislative sessions.

It would be incorrect to speak of any section of the million and a half employees of American local authorities as constituting a local government service, if by that is meant a body of persons with a professional training distinctive to local government, likely to spend most of their career in local government, accustomed to moving from one authority to another, enjoying common conditions of service, and an established level of salaries with transferable superannuation rights.

Chief officers (with the exception of city managers) are not necessarily promoted from within the service. Many thousands of them are 'elected' officials—clerks, treasurers, prosecuting attorneys, tax assessors, sheriffs, judges, constables and others—who come into office by vote of the electorate on a test of political acceptability rather than one of competence. Such officers may or may not be professionally trained. Moreover they derive an independent authority from the electors and do not fit into the normal conception of an administrative hierarchy. They are a minority. For the greater part of their employees, American local authorities draw mainly upon a general rather than a specialised local government pool of employees. Thus, with the exception of the city managers, who are dealt with later, professional employees hold the same qualifications as their counterparts in business, from which they probably came and to which they may return. American officers are likely to have a good acquaintance with professional practice generally, but a less intensive knowledge of local government than would be expected in this country, which has both advantages and disadvantages.*

Although much of American history and culture has its roots in western Europe, our governmental structure and interrelationships are significantly different from those Dr. Marshall examined in Europe. European national governments play a larger role in local-government affairs than is true in our country. And, as noted above, in most of those countries there is a tradition of professional management in local affairs by career-service public servants that goes back many generations. By contrast, in our country this concept virtually originated with the council-manager plan, which is fewer than seventy years old.

Because in Ireland the council-manager plan is universally required for all counties, county boroughs, boroughs, urban districts, and towns, and because Dr. Marshall visited fifteen or so council-manager cities in the United States over a fifteen-year period, the following descriptions and observations by Mr. Flannery and Dr. Marshall may be especially useful to us.

First are some excerpts from lectures delivered by Michael Flannery at Birmingham University, in which he described the development of the Irish local government system.

Management of Local Government, vol. 4 (London: Her Majesty's Stationery Office, 1967), pp. 64–67, 88. By permission of the Controller, HMSO.

Management in Local Government:
A Statutory System

The provision of public services at local level in the last century led not
only to an expansion in the activities of existing local authorities but to
the establishment of many new ones. The advent of a new service often
resulted in a new authority. There was much resort to the ad hoc body.
In the pattern which emerged two bodies however were predominant—
the County Council and the County Borough Council. The advent of
popularly elected bodies led to an intensification in the demand for
public services, which were ever becoming more complex and costly.
Public representatives were increasingly dealing with a mass of detail,
imposing a strain on their time, ability, and stamina. Not infrequently
this resulted in the adjourned meeting with an uncompleted agenda.

A way out of the difficulties for public representatives who combined roles of policy maker and executant was sought in the setting up
of committees to which special functions were assigned. Some of these
might be statutory but most were directionary. Some criticisms of "the
Committee System" were as follows: They tended to regard themselves
as independent entities; there was rivalry among Committees, their
Chairmen, and chief officers who advised them; they could impose a
great burden of routine work on public representatives, especially where
from choice or otherwise they were involved in a wide range of decision
making; there were inadequate links between the committees themselves, and between the committees and the parent bodies who
appointed them; for staffs, the detailed recording of a mass of decisions
and the preparation of special records for the parent body could be bur-
densomely time-consuming; committee decisions were taken behind
"closed doors" and not in public meeting.

For a number of years it was evident that there was a tendency for a
"chief officer" type to emerge in local government. This was an official
with special competence and dedication on whom a local authority
might lean heavily for advice and general guidance. But no officer had
been specially designated by law as having such functions, or carrying
such responsibilities. Views on local government also owed something
to J. S. Mill and other writers. Mill had held that "business of the elective body is not to do the work, but to see that it is properly done, and
that nothing necessary is left undone."

In the early 1920s local government came under special review in
Ireland both in relation to structure and staffing. Union and rural districts were abandoned as units as it was felt that larger units with
greater resources were required to give adequate scope for the organisa-
tion of services such as hospitals, houses, and large-scale water supplies.
In the recruitment of staff the aims were the introduction of open competition for all posts and the achievement of a high degree of mobility
through standard rates of remuneration and conditions of service,
including uniform superannuation arrangements.

In 1925 a Commission which inquired into the Poor Law System reported that elected members could not be expected to exercise the supervision which their institutions, officers, and servants required, and recommended the appointment of a paid official who would be placed in charge of services in the same way as the general manager of a company acted under a board of directors.

A special Commission set up to consider the government of the city of Dublin recommended the introduction of a city manager. In Cork an independent local group, composed of businessmen and professional people who examined local government in that city, recommended that a city manager be appointed. These bodies were influenced by the apparent speed with which decisions could be taken in large-scale business undertakings. They were also influenced by experience in the USA, where city management had been introduced some years earlier and by the 1920s had been adopted by up to one hundred municipalities. In the USA local authority was free to adopt the system if it so wished. In Ireland, when management eventually came into local governemnt, it was imposed as a statutory system.

The approach to management in local government was a tentative and cautious one. It was first introduced in the city of Cork in 1929. To Dublin it was applied in 1930. After a change of government it was applied to Limerick City in 1934. (In Limerick the elected Corporation sought it.) In 1939 it was introduced in Waterford city. In each instance special enabling legislation was passed. The management system was applied to the county councils (and to the urban councils within each county) in 1940.

Management met very little opposition in the cities, but it came in for some criticism from public representatives in the rural areas when first introduced. Members for rural areas, it seems, were more intimately concerned with the affording of individual services. Some members objected to the control of staff being reposed in management. The title *management* at the same time did not appeal to some. It was associated with "big business," cold calculated decisions, and a ruthless search for efficiency.

In the Management Acts the functions of local authorities are classified as "reserved" and "executive." The "reserved" functions which belong to the elected members include the making of the rate, borrowing money, approving of an expenditure in excess of the provision made in the rates estimates in any year, the making of bylaws, the making of a Development Plan under the Planning and Development Act, and the appointment of Committees. All functions which are not "reserved" functions come into the "executive" category and are the responsibility of the Manager. The control of staff is vested in the manager, but its exercise is subject to certain limitations. He cannot increase or decrease the number of permanent posts or vary rates of remuneration unless with the approval of the elected members. Disciplinary measures are subject to appeal, and rates of remuneration and conditions of service are the subject of negotiations with unions.

In the counties the county manager acts as manager for any

borough corporation, urban district council, or other elective body (such as joint drainage boards, joint burial boards, etc.) within the county and exercises the "executive functions" on behalf of these authorities. In this way many of the smaller authorities would have available to them the services of an officer who could be expected to have wider and more varied experience than say the town clerk of a small urban council.

Managers are appointed by county and county borough councils, but only after open competition based on standards set and examinations directed by an agency of the national government. Appointees must be well educated, possess a high standard of administrative ability, have had adequate experience in the organization and control of staff, and possess a satisfactory knowledge of local administration, finance, and social legislation. A manager may be suspended or removed by the council of which he is an official, but removal must be approved by the national minister for local government.

The manager in Ireland is a public official appointed to assist a local authority in the operation of its services. However, he holds a post defined and limited by statute.

Ever since the management system was introduced, there has been much emphasis on public accountability. In essence this means that the aim is to keep the public representatives fully acquainted and also to keep the public informed. Orders made by the manager are available to the members and to the press. The chairman and members of local authorities exercise a close surveillance over the discharge by managers of the functions specially assigned to them.

All meetings of local authorities (except in Dublin Corporation, where a committee system still operates) are held in public with the press present. Decisions at such meetings are taken by open voting. Full reports of proceedings are given in the local newspapers, and sometimes in the national daily papers.

The manager can be required to take specific action in a particular instance. The council can direct him to comply with their wishes by passing a resolution to this effect provided that the action is not one for which there is a lack of statutory authority (i.e., is *ultra vires*). An exception to this is that it does not extend to control of officers or employees.

Members continuously seek reports on proposals such as new works. The manager will then collect the necessary data, including reports from officers, and submit his views for the guidance of the local authority.

The Irish management system has survived in the cities for almost forty years and in the counties for twenty-seven. It has never been regarded as immutable. For a long period, especially in the counties, it was regarded by some as being on trial. It has been amended by statute but not in a significant way, and not in a manner which has affected the general scheme. It would probably be correct to say that it is now generally accepted as an integral part of the local-government structure.

The near future could bring some radical changes in local government. The existing units may give place to regions, and it could even happen that some existing activities might in part be transferred to new state-sponsored bodies. Such changes, however, might not materially affect the decision first made more than forty years ago to introduce a special type of management in local government.

Finally, experience of local government points to the fact that worthwhile achievements are dependent primarily on the quality of public representatives and of their staffs–this quality being expressed in their abilities and attitudes and above all in their integrity.

Following are additional excerpts from "Local Government Administration Abroad," by Dr. A. H. Marshall:

The Council-Manager Plan in the United States

According to the theory of the plan, there will be a small council of up to nine members elected at large on a non-party basis, which will appoint the mayor, determine the policies, pass the by-laws, adopt the budget, and appoint a manager to hold office at their pleasure. The manager carries out such duties as are delegated to him by the council, and in particular he appoints and dismisses the heads of departments, controls and supervises their work, advises the council, prepares, submits and administers the budget (often being allowed some powers of virement) and reports on general matters as well as on finance. He may also be required to keep the public informed of the council's activities. . . .

In the light of the diversity of conditions in the United States, it is hardly to be expected that the plan will always operate in accordance with the tenets laid down in the vast literature of the I.C.M.A., and in practice one finds bewildering variations. Hard and fast lines between policy and administration cannot be strictly adhered to any more than under alternative forms of local government. On the one hand electors invariably ensure that councillors take an interest in administration, while on the other hand managers cannot remain aloof from policy: they have a professional interest, they have the information, and their hands are upon the levers. Nothing can prevent them from advocating and often pressing major policies upon their masters, nor save them from becoming advocates and defenders of council policy. It is harder for a manager to remain in the background than for an English local government official. . . .

The tradition of allowing the manager to manage seems to be firmly established in the sense that he is allowed to carry on with all the day-to-day work. But this does not mean the exclusion of the members from a knowledge of the administrative process, nor does it save members from receiving inquiries on such matters as housing accommodation, or prevent them from taking a great interest in individual cases. Nor will a manager be exempt from members' pressures. A good manager soon gets to know what is likely to prove politically sensitive and therefore to be regarded as a minor 'policy' question by the council.

On all other administrative matters he will proceed on his own authority. . . .

The advantages of the city manager plan can be grouped under two heads; first those flowing from the introduction of professional administration, second those which are the result of integrated management. To have 45 million Americans living under a régime in which the administrator is appointed on the basis of professional skill and experience is itself of no mean value in a country which has found purity in public life difficult to establish. Without doubt the manager plan has greatly reduced undue influence and corruption, whilst it has simultaneously introduced a professional pride and a standard of ethics which are at once a driving force and a safeguard. A manager has to mind not only his local reputation but his standing in the world of managers, because upon this will depend at least in part his further progress and satisfaction. The managers are members of a profession with a growing body of expertise behind them, and ever increasing opportunities for exchange of experience.

The manager movement has given impetus to the study of local government administration in American universities and it is in managers' cities that one is most likely to find those who talk the language of local government administration. This professionalisation of management has also given an incentive to other professional employees of local government who, though overshadowed at the moment, are rapidly developing training schemes and other educational programmes. In a wider context, the growth of the manager plan has encouraged members to concentrate on policy. In short it provides at least a reasonable answer to the world's unsolved problem of securing public control with efficiency.

The internal advantages which come from integrated management are no less impressive. The whole of the administration of a well governed city manager authority is conceived as one, and not as a number of separate departments bolstered up with machinery for co-ordination. The views of all officers are brought together at an early stage, differences are ironed out in private conference, the manager is in a position to put a complete report to the council and if necessary to prepare the way with informal conversations.

Business is more rapidly executed, departmental duties are more clearly laid down and heads of departments can be readily held to account. Those dealing with the local authority from the outside, whether members of the public, commercial concerns or other governmental authorities find it invaluable to have a single point of reference on all matters of importance. Managers are in a position to check the unnecessary growth of departments, to prevent overlapping to ensure that management is streamlined, and to introduce management services, good budgetary techniques, and proper personnel policy. It is now recognised for instance that in such a city there is no longer any need for an independent civil service commission, a device introduced to defeat irregular practices in appointing staff. Commissions are now often replaced by personnel departments, supplemented by an advisory committee or appeals board, or both.

The plan has, however, some failings. Conceived in the spirit of business enterprise, it underrates the political aspects of local government. Its inventors failed to see that there are many communities in which it is difficult for an administrator to play the principal local government role. They underestimated the political gifts which a manager needs. Present day critics aver that the system has reduced the status of the real political leader, and has put in his place a somewhat politically bloodless individual, trained in dealing with things rather than people. They point out that the assumption that politics can be taken out of local government is unreal in most large mixed communities. It has been found in practice that managers have to take on many of the responsibilities of the community leader, though they are fitted by outlook and training for a different role. During the course of the investigation I heard many times the complaint that the manager system tended to leave a political vacuum. The result is that managers may go to one of two extremes. In a few instances they may be too active politically and may even indulge in the risky occupation of appealing to the electors over the heads of the council (one manager I met had stood for Congress without resigning his post). On the other hand they may be too pure and may attempt to remain too securely within the four walls of their professional code. In such instances they are likely to be wanting in social sense, and possibly out of sympathy with aspects of community development. I heard more than once the comment that when in a tough spot the manager tends to ask 'what do I do?' This is not necessarily a criticism of the individual but merely an expression of his difficult position. If he takes a firm stand, he is accused of usurping the position of the politician, if on the other hand he adopts the position of an English local government official, he is said to be responsible for creating a vacuum. This is a real dilemma, and is at the bottom of the widespread feeling that whilst the city manager system works well in small homogeneous communities, it is not suitable for the rough and tumble of large cities with mixed populations and varied ethnic groups.

Then there are some disadvantages of the concentration of administrative responsibility in a single individual. As soon as the authority gets beyond a certain size the necessity to pass everything of importance to the manager's office can create a bottleneck. In fact, the manager system can be worked in a larger authority only by means of considerable delegation, for such an authority is likely to look to its technical specialists for advice on such matters as health and planning. It is of course perfectly possible to adapt the city manager system to these circumstances, but after the adaptation has gone beyond a certain point the situation becomes very different from that visualised in the textbooks.

The merits of the manager plan are many and conspicuous. It is based on an essentially sound distinction between the nature of the contribution of the politician and that of the administrator. In many places it has spelled the death of unsavoury practices. By professionalising management in local government it has raised the status of local government administration, and by its insistence on training it has brought new men with a new code of ethics into city halls. Where the plan is in operation, local government is less likely to be at the mercy of political upheavals.

But this is not the whole story. City manager government while successful in small, middle class communities is less obviously successful in large areas and has indeed been only adopted in a few of the largest authorities. A number of reasons have been put forward for this. In such places, it is argued, the council/manager relation required by the basic premises of the plan is less likely to generate a head of steam. A vacuum can develop; the members may find themselves hampered in forming policy by their lack of knowledge of the administrative process, with a consequent waste of political experience; the power of the people is not transmitted to their local government; political conflicts can remain unresolved, and public sentiment may be sacrificed to purely adminis-trative considerations; moreover the conception of a manager standing aside from the political arena is by no means always workable. Such self-effacement is not possible in the American context, especially in a com-munity where the contribution from the politician has been thrust into the background. When managers do intervene it can become apparent that an administrator and a politician are two different animals. Obser-vers point out that a manager can be a poor substitute for a strong mayor. To these shortcomings in the rationale of the plan have to be added the practical difficulties arising in a large city from the concentra-tion of authority. There are even critics of the name "manager" which is thought to be inappropriate for a "socio-political" leader, and it is sig-nificant that so many persons during the course of the investigation spoke of the strong mayor system with an administrator as the method most in accord with the American outlook.

Notwithstanding the success of many manager cities, the progress of the plan has recently been less rapid, and the notion of combining the strong mayor with the professional, but subordinate, administrator has come to the fore in the large cities. It could be that the contribution of the city manager movement may ultimately be not so much the provi-sion of a pattern of local government administration as an injection into local government of expert administrators subscribing to the highest professional standards. The future must surely be with the ideals of the plan—impartial, integrated administration, fair personnel practices, the highest technical and ethical standards and so forth. But it would be a pity if these could be achieved only under one particular kind of gov-ernment, and one that in theory at least requires the elected authority to leave so much of vital interest in the hands of an administrator. It was thoughts such as these which prompted the comment earlier in this report that the manager plan, and indeed the role of the I.C.M.A., might well change. It is in any case now generally recognised that a manager needs to become increasingly knowledgeable about social and economic matters.*

Management of the Local Government, vol. 4 (London: Her Majesty's Stationery Office, 1967), pp. 103–10. By permission.

Conclusion

At the outset, I noted the audiences for whom this book is intended: men and women just entering public service, and others of longer service; professors and students of political science and public administration; and especially the general reader who wants a better understanding of city government and how it works, so he or she can be more effective in dealing with it and helping to improve it. The special focus on the latter is because most Americans live in cities. Moreover, they are dependent upon the governments of those cities to help them preserve and enhance many of their values—home, family, freedom, advancement, security—and the products of their labors.

But in a democracy city governments cannot perform these helpful functions alone. They, in turn, are dependent upon the participation and support of citizens who exercise their ultimate power over local government knowledgeably and reasonably. To help citizens acquire this ability, we selected one approach. We took you behind the scenes in city government with a representative group of men and women who have devoted most of their professional careers to serving local governments and their citizens.

These professional local-government administrators have shared their experiences forthrightly, the good and the bad. By describing their involvement in the political, economic, and social systems, they have provided at least one perspective of how these systems work. We have supplemented their reports with a commentary on aspects of our local governments and their operations that rarely receive the public attention they must have if those governments are to serve all our people well and honestly. In addition, we have looked to observers in other countries who see us from a different perspective. Their observations may help us come closer to realizing our ideals for public service in America.

Many of our city governments are in deep trouble financially, organizationally, operationally, and ethically. Perhaps you and your neighbors will want to "do something" to change these situations. It is the hope of every contributor to this book that the experiences and philosophy they have shared will strengthen both your resolve and your ability to help improve your city and other local governments.

Appendix

The Mayor-Council Form

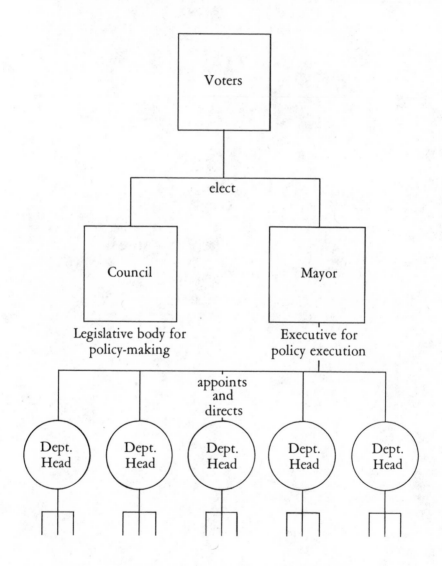

Arguments *for* the Mayor-Council Form

The mayor-council form is familiar to most Americans because it is patterned after our traditional national and state governments. The mayor is like the president of the United States or the governor of the state–the chief executive, responsible for all executive functions.

There is separation of powers among the legislative, executive, and judicial branches of the government. The council is like the Congress or the state legislature; it establishes policies and controls the purse strings. The mayor executes the policies.

Also, there are checks and balances. The council can refuse to confirm the mayor's appointments, and the mayor can veto the council's legislative acts.

Arguments *against* the Mayor-Council Form

The office of mayor gives too much authority and power to one person. It permits an incumbent so inclined to make decisions based largely on political considerations, and to use his appointment powers and administrative controls to build a political machine.

The qualities needed to win elections are not always the same qualities needed to manage the intricacies and the technical and specialized functions of a municipality.

Mayors do not belong to self-policing organizations that can censure or "disbar" dishonest or incompetent members. If the elected mayor proves incompetent or worse, he cannot be removed until the end of his term, or after an expensive and divisive recall election.

The Commission Form

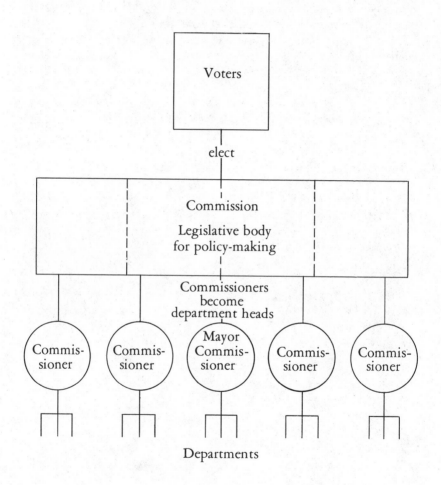

Arguments *for* the Commission Form

Under the commission form, the individually elected commissioners fill two roles. Meeting as a group, they constitute the legislative body for the municipal government. There they establish policy and pass legislation. Also as a group, they distribute responsibility for managing the departments of the government, each being responsible for one or more departments.

Once policies and legislation are available, the commissioners assume their second role as department heads responsible for executing policy and legislation. This dispersal of executive authority and power provides sufficient separation of powers, and checks and balances, so there is no need for separate legislative and executive branches.

As legislators, they can be sure their collective wishes are carried out, because they are administering policies they had a part in shaping.

The government is close to the people and highly responsive, because in their two capacities as legislators and as department heads the commissioners are directly accountable to the voters.

The commission form saves money because the legislators serve also as department heads.

Arguments *against* the Commission Form

Giving both the legislative and executive powers of any government to the same group of officials violates the fundamental American concept of separation of governmental powers.

The commission is the governing body for a single government, but the government is headless. Actually, in operation there are several smaller and virtually independent governments, each under a different commissioner.

With each commissioner in charge of his own departments, and each anxious to make a good showing to help him retain his office, appropriations are on a log-rolling basis—you vote for what I want, and I'll vote for what you want.

Employees tend to work primarily for their own departments, ignoring the needs of other parts of the government.

The commission form cannot be counted on to produce the kinds of technical and specialized leadership qualities needed by the departments.

Elected department heads are in an excellent position to use employees as a source of political contributions and as manpower in political campaigns.

The Council-Manager Form

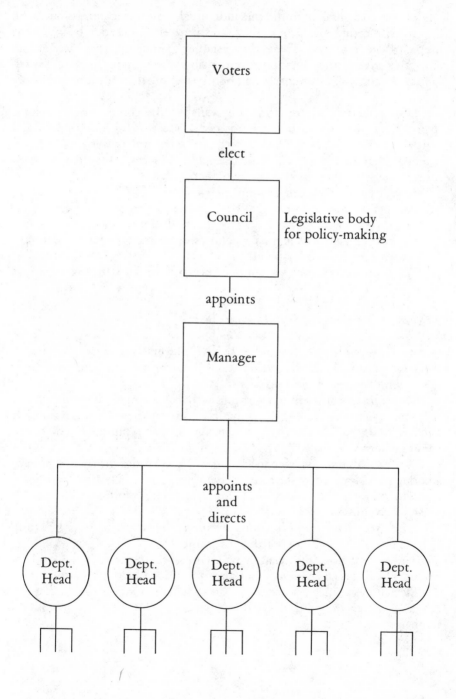

Arguments *for* the Council-Manager Form

The council-manager form is the same found in almost all organizations where performance and results count most, whether business, labor, institutional, profit, or nonprofit. That is, the "stockholders" of the municipal corporation elect a board of directors to represent their interests, and the board appoints a qualified, experienced general manager to assist and advise them and to see that board policies are carried out. The line of responsibility is simple, direct, and familiar.

The division of labor between the policy-making board (the council) and the chief administrator frees the council of administrative detail, leaving them time and opportunity to provide true community leadership and to monitor the performance of their appointed chief administrator.

Administration of city business is removed from politics by putting personnel management, including selection of the city manager, on a merit basis and limiting the manager's involvement in policy-making to recommendation, advice, and support of council-made policy decisions.

Professionally trained and experienced people are available to provide the community and its citizens with the maximum of efficient, effective, humane, and considerate municipal service.

The likelihood of obtaining and maintaining managerial competence and integrity is enhanced by the fact that the city managers' professional association requires that its members adhere to a code of ethics.

Arguments *against* the Council-Manager Form

The council-manager form gives too much power to one person, the city manager.

A professional city manager, often chosen from outside the city, does not know the community and is too far from the voters.

Councils leave too much decision-making to the manager, who becomes a dictator.

Without an elected chief executive, the community lacks the political leadership it should have.

The council-manager form is too much like a business corporation.

City managers cost too much. Local people could handle the job and be cheaper, too.

The Mayor–Chief-Administrative-Officer (CAO) Form

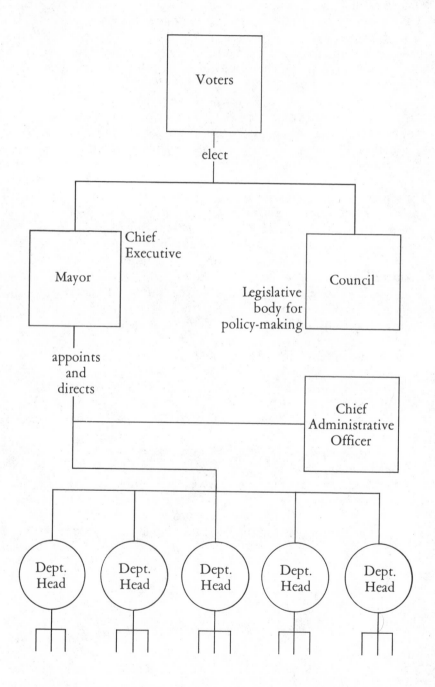

Arguments *for* the Mayor–Chief-Administrative-Officer (CAO) Form

This form assures a separation of legislative and executive powers, provides a checks-and-balance system, and gives the local government a single executive to represent the community, provide political leadership, and execute legislative policy.

The mayor has a trained and experienced administrator to assist him in his executive responsibilities. The CAO may also provide some staff assistance to the council and individual council members, from time to time.

Although the government does not have all the advantages of professional management, it avoids some of the problems such as differences over philosophy and authority.

Arguments *against* the Mayor–Chief-Administrative-Officer (CAO) Form

Separation of powers relegates the council to a policy-making role only, placing too much authority in the mayor.

The mayor may not understand and use the concept of a chief administrative officer as adviser and aide to him and, indirectly, to the council. He may be inclined to name an administratively unqualified political supporter or associate as CAO.

Department heads can be confused as to who is their superior, the mayor or the CAO.

It is wasteful duplication to have both a mayor and a chief administrative officer.

The Council–Chief-Administrative-Officer (CAO) Form

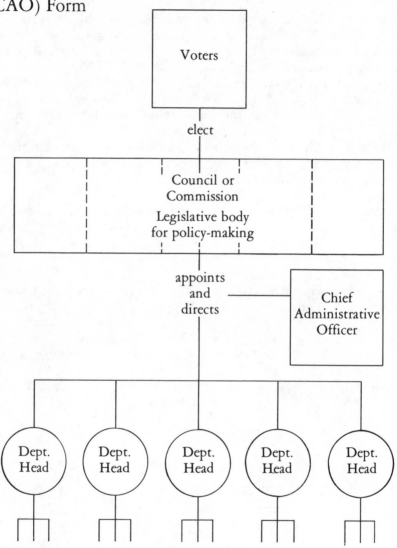

Arguments *for* the Council–Chief-Administrative-Officer (CAO) Form

This form usually does not provide a hard and fast line between policy and administration, as may be the case in charter, statutory, or ordinance provisions for a council-manager government. Total authority clearly rests with the people's elected representatives, who constitute the governing body. The governing body may delegate to the chief administrator such authority as they choose, or they may rescind it without violating the basic law establishing the form of government. Thus the administrative officer need never contest with his employer the legal limits of his authority—an untenable position for any employee.

Administrative authority may be distributed between the council and the CAO, and even among council members, if they choose.

Professionally trained and experienced administrators can be used to the extent that the council wishes.

Arguments *against* the Council–Chief-Administrative-Officer (CAO) Form

This form combines legislative and executive authority and power in one body of officials.

If council members wish to become involved in administration, they may do so. As a result, department heads may be responsible to more than one superior, and departmental policies, decisions, and operations may be politically motivated.

Professional administration is not fully utilized.

The government lacks a single, responsible administrative head.

Theme
Index

Part 1: The City Manager and the Political System

Part 2: The City Manager and the Economic System

Part 3: The City Manager and the Social System

Index

American Nazis'proposed march in
community of Jewish holocaust
survivors, Skokie, IL, 155–65; water
supply and treatment shortages:
Boulder, CO, 245–46; Colorado
Springs, CO, 188–90; North Miami
Beach, FL, 80–92; Southern Pines,
NC, 95–96
Cronkite, Walter, 299
Crowley, John C., 212
Custer, Richard H., 200, 210, 279

Dade County, FL, Metropolitan, 81–85
Dale, Bill, 261
Daley, Mayor Richard, 47, 115
Darden, Mayor Pretlow, 196
Dartmouth College case, 194
Davis, CA, 215, 221, 222
Daytona Beach, FL, 52, 108, 110–12,
192–93, 275–76
Dayton, OH, 8
Decker, Judge Bernard, 159
Delegation, 217
DeLeonardis, Tony, 83
Democracy, Jacksonian, 295
Denver, CO, 312
"Des Moines Plan," xii
Dille, Robert, 245
Dillon's Rule, 300
D'Ippolito (finance director), 260
Disaster preparedness (civil defense),
166, 178, 274
Dismissal of employees, 31–32
District of Columbia (DC), 220
Donnelly, Governor Phil M., 207
Dublin, Ireland, 329, 330
Duckworth, Mayor W. Fred, 196
Dugas, Julius, 175
Duncan, Charlie, 175
Duncraig Manor, 241–44
Dykstra, Clarence A., 206

East Ann Arbor, MI, 23–26

Eau Claire, WI, 101–2
Economic development, 278, 293–94;
community promotion, University
City, MO, 68–72; growth control,
San Jose, CA, 65–67; rejuvenation,
Norfolk, VA, 195–99; winning the
Air Force Academy, Colorado
Springs, CO, 188–91. *See also* Crisis
management
Effectiveness and efficiency: essentials
of effective democracy, 151; the
principle of specialization, 151
Election(s) in: Arlington, VA, 288;
Boulder, CO, 246; Columbia, SC,
18; Daytona Beach, FL, 275–76; in
general, 277, 301, 307; Ipswich,
MA, 19; Kansas City, MO, 22;
Kenosha, WI, 282; Lebanon, MO,
207; North Miami Beach, FL,
91–92; Winston-Salem, NC, 5, 10;
Zanesville, OH, 204
Elliott, William, 231
Elrod, Richard, 227
Emergency Employment Act, 76–77
England, 325
Environment, 249–51
Ethics, 272, 285, 308–13, 321–23
Ethics, city management code of, 321
Ethics in Government Act of 1978,
321
Ethics, Office of Government, 322
Europe, 326, 327
Evanston, IL, 33–34, 114–15, 285
Executive Office of the President,
270n

Family involvement, 101–15, 229, 264,
272
Fargo, ND, 109, 318
Favors, 18, 47, 91
FBI (Federal Bureau of Investigation),
237, 240
Federal Home Loan Bank Board, 71
Finances in: Columbia, SC, 194–95;
Daytona Beach, FL, 52; in general,

need for in, 10, 248; Winter Park, FL, 248; Zanesville, OH, 204

Public Service Company of Colorado, 244

Pueblo, CO, 188

Purchasing, 6, 256

Race relations, 7, 9, 102, 111–12, 116, 117, 119, 175

Rand Corporation, 65

Rankin, Jeanette, 173

Reclamation, U.S. Bureau of, 245

Recruiting, 33, 216, 276

Reeder, Sherwood, 196, 197, 278

Reform, 48, 283

Refuse collection and disposal, 74, 147 264–65

Rehnquist, Justice William, 161

Reich, Joe, 188

Reorganization in: Ipswich, MA, 19; North Miami Beach, FL, 85; San Diego, CA, 216–19; Suffolk, VA, 26; University City, MO, 256; West Palm Beach, FL, 259–61; Winston-Salem, NC, 7; advice on, 276–77

Resignation(s), 87; Cookingham in Kansas City, 54; Coupal in Ipswich MA, 18; when justified, 32; Perkins in Winston-Salem, NC, 10; of police chief, 89, 90, 264; of volunteer firemen, 211

Resource Recovery Council of Florida, 49–50

Reynolds Tobacco Company, 248

Richmond, VA, 197, 278

Ridley, Clarence E., 194

Rio Grande (river), 170

Roberts, Elaine W., 288

Rohrbaugh, John, 222

Roosevelt, Eleanor, 111–12

Roosevelt, President Theodore, 308

Rose, Harvey, 94

Rose, Joseph L., 33

Rousseau (philosopher), 287

Rowlands, David D., 51, 119, 128, 305

Rowlands, Jean, 102, 103

Rowlands, Peggy, 101, 103

Rowlands, Sally H., 99, 101

Rubin (councilman), 87

Saginaw, MI, 32, 48, 269

Saint Louis, MO, 8, 68, 194

Saint Louis World's Fair, 69

San Antonio, TX, 196

San Diegans, Incorporated, 63, 64

San Diego, CA, 61–64, 215–20, 221–24

San Jose, CA, 65–67, 182–87, 220, 224

San Leandro, CA, 215, 221–22

Saunders (commissioner), 75

Schwartz, Harvey, 160

Serpe, John, 280

Sewers: construction of, in Southern Pines, NC, 42–44; financing of, in Zanesville, OH, 201; need for, in East Ann Arbor, MI, 24; provided in Norfolk, VA, 197–98

Sex, 134–43, 263–64

Sharpe, Carleton, 282

Shaw, Kennedy, 23

The Siege of University City, 69

Silverculture, Professor, 249

Simmons, Richard G., 132, 283; in Haines, FL, 144; in Melbourne, FL, 50, 55, 127, 250; in West Palm Beach, FL, 251, 264; in Winter Park, FL, 49, 121, 147, 248

Singley, Dr. James, 85

Skinner, Calvin, 160

Skokie, IL: and American Nazis, 155–65; board of fire and police commissioners, 234; board of trustees (city council), 155, 235; and police strike, 226–34

Smith, Mayor Albert, 158

Smith, Harold D., 270n

Snyder, Ralph, 23

Socialist Workers of America, 156